ANTOINE CHEVRIER

THE TRUE DISCIPLE

The numbers given in the margins are those of the french edition: "Le prêtre selon l'Evangile, ou Le véritable disciple de Notre Seigneur Jésus Christ", Antoine CHEVRIER, P.E.L. 1968

Rome, September 3, 1968

Father,

The Prado owes it to itself to undertake this publication.
First of all, because your spiritual family, which is growing constantly, must have, in a better form, the instrument which its holy Founder himself prepared for it. Then also because the success of previous editions says well enough that the Christian conscience has recognized in it one of those spiritual documents that are part of its permanent heritage to which it must be able to have recourse constantly.

Thus, the Prado also had to assure to this edition all the guarantees and qualities of authenticity, fidelity and clarity that our generation may expect from a text of this type and that it demands so rigorously.

You carried this work to a good end, Father, in the manner of the Prado and, I would almost say, in the manner of Father Chevrier. He would have loved your preface, he would have loved the introductory notes. Everything is frank, direct without affectation; you wish to see clearly, tell it like it is, without high phrases or pretention, without any concern to please, confident in the truth and sincerity of your judgements so that they may be accepted and lead into the text itself. That effacement - I almost said that unwanted "poverty" - puts a striking agreement between the pages of the Father and your own. I am sure he would have recognized himself in his disciple.

For Father Chevrier's book did not wish to be easy or agreeable.

In his faith and love for Jesus Christ, Father found the strength to believe that Our Lord needed no other presentation than himself. He limited himself therefore, like Brother Charles de Foucault and hardly differently, to looking and showing rather than speaking. The True Disciple is Jesus Christ as he offers himself in the Gospel, as he expresses himself, as he acts and teaches, simply stripped of all that habit and frivolity prevent us form recognizing, hearing and accepting. It seems to me that everything else is only an echo, hardly perceptible, always almost veiled, of this discovery in the soul and the spirit of the one who knows so well how to see and hear his Master. Father Chevrier hardly hears himself cry out in admiration and joy before the One he comtemplates, in making contemplated. We feel very well that the Father is everywhere - a word, a brief remark point out this presence - but it is perceived as involuntary and it never turns the attention away.

The power of this book is in the very despoilment with which Christ presents himself to us. We feel that He is well this way, that He claims this. We knew it but we did not have the courage to say it to ourselves. Someone who has had this courage helps us to follow him in this finally sincere consent of faith. Basically, for Father, it is always this light of Christmas where everything begins for him: a grace of extraordinary power made him realize that "his God" and "this poor person" are one and the same, that "the Word of God" was really one with this "little child" lying on the straw of a stable. We understand how this light that accompanied his whole life produced such a Saint and that this Saint produced such a book. After that, everything else is simply accompaniment, preparation, development, almost secondary. No doubt, Father Chevrier would never have been Father Chevrier without the family and social milieu in which he was born and against which he often reacted; but all this only enveloped an event of an other order, an absolutely original light, the supernatural ray which, while lighting up a crib, allowed him to make an act of faith in the Incarnation.

I am sure, dear Father, that, thanks to the Prado and yourself, the benefit of this discovery of Jesus Christ will continue to spread. For the Prado to which Father destined his work; for all priests who have such need of coming back to draw at this source - and of whom Father never ceased to think. It is "the priest according to Jesus Christ" that he wished to form by this book. And finally, so many others who need to believe and find Jesus Christ the sole fountain and the end of their faith.

"How beautiful is Jesus Christ".

Your reward, dear Father, will be to have brought to sure fruition, following Father Chevrier, these same saving words on other lips. Thank you.

INTRODUCTION

THE TRUE DISCIPLE AND THE LIFE OF FATHER CHEVRIER

*Why a new edition of Father Chevrier's book The True Disciple?
To put at the disposal of all those who wish it the authentic text of this work.
On several occasions, in oral and written commentaries, the texts published so far have been accused of infidelity and it has been pointed out that the original version was sometimes more expressive and more forceful. Thus the wish for a new edition that would reproduce exactly Father Chevrier's manuscript.
In fact, there is always the danger that the one who transforms a text will also transform the thought found therein, in spite of a sincere will to be faithful. Even if we are sure of having truly grasped a man's thought in adapting his writings, we prefer at this time to have the writings in their authentic content. It is a legitimate demand of scientific exactitude.
However we must not, to praise our attempt, simply and purely depreciate the work of previous editors. That would be unjust.
Unjust, first of all, because all work on Father Chevrier's writings necessarily profits from the considerable labor of those who first gathered and sorted these writings. The volume printed in 1923 and reprinted in 1942 and 1948 is a witness to that work. It is a compilation, some would say with a touch of disdain. Yes, it is a compilation, but it was guided by the concern not to lose anything of Antoine Chevrier's writings. This accumulation of materials witnesses, in its own way, to a concern for fidelity.
It would be unjust also to depreciate the work of our predecessors on the question of accuracy. It is true that many pages of the 1923 edition are virtual mosaics whose pieces come from various sources but, in general, each piece is reproduced exactly, with very few exceptions.
Finally we must recognize yet another concern for fidelity of the first editors of The True Disciple. They knew that Father Chevrier wanted to write a book and that he died before having been able to gather in one volume the various notes, pieces and outlines prepared for that purpose. Thus the very idea of composing a book from the documents left by Father fulfilled his intentions.
He wanted to write a book to bequeath, in some way, his mission to his heirs. The latter acted legitimately in wanting to finish the work that he had begun. It is in this same direction that we wished to go, but our method is different. It seemed to us that the project of Father Chevrier's book would come out better if we gave up the compilation process.*

We thought that we should, above all, let the essential structure appear and limit ourselves to indicating the skeleton of the edifice in the parts where the architect did not have time to construct the walls [1].

To allow the reader to situate himself in the rest of this introduction, here are the essential characteristics of the life of Antoine Chevrier.

1826, April 16: *Birth in Lyons. His father is an employee of the city toll; his mother is a silk worker and the director of a small workshop. The family is still close to its rural origins, especially the mother who comes from Dauphiné.*

April 18: *Baptism in the parish church: Saint-François-de-Sales.*

1840: *Up to now, Antoine Chevrier was going to school with the Brothers of the Christian Schools. With the new term in October, he becomes a student at the clerical school of the parish.*

1843, October: *He enters as a boarder in the seminary of Argentière (diocese of Lyons).*

1846, October: *Enters the theological seminary of Lyons.*

1850, May 25: *Antoine Chevrier is ordained priest.*

May 28: *He is named assistant in the parish of Saint-Andre of la Guillotière, a populous suburb of Lyons. He gives himself tirelessly to his ministry. (In December 1955, exhausted, he must take four months of rest). From this period, he gives particular attention to the poor and he suffers that his ministry does not bear enough fruit.*

---

[1] To indicate references, we use the following abreviations:

LP=Father Chevrier's letters. We give the number and date of the letter which allows a reference to manuscript reproduction of the archives (volume XIII) as well as the photocopied edition of the Prado in 1960 and even, thanks to the date, to the old printed edition.

Ms=Manuscript reproduction of Father Chevrier's writings. This collection, made in view of the beatification process, is in thirteen volumes (I to XIII).

PB=Collection of testimonies in view of the beatification, in four volumes (1 to 4, each page covers the recto - r - and the verso - v - of a sheet).

Six=Jean-François Six: Un prêtre, Antoine Chevrier, fondateur du Prado. Paris. ed. du Seuil, 1965.

VD=Le prêtre selon l'Evangile ou le Véritable Disciple de Jésus Christ.

1856, May 31: *Catestrophic flooding on the left bank of the Rhone where Guillotière is situated. The clergy of Saint-Andre are in the front ranks of the rescuers and Father Chevrier's reputation for devotedness increases.*

June: *Antoine Chevrier has the opportunity to meet Camille Rambaud, a young bourgeois of Lyons who has converted and dedicated himself to the poor by living like them and with them. Camille Rambaud is in the process of founding the City of the Child Jesus, an undertaking that is both religious and social. It builds lodgings for workers and teaches catechism to poor children. Father Chevrier is struck by Rambaud's example.*

Christmas: *Conversion of Antoine Chevrier. Before the crib, he meditates the words of the Gospel: "The Word became flesh and dwelt among us". He understands Christ's special call to a more perfect, more evangelical life; he dedicates himself to following Jesus Christ in his infinite charity for men, his self-abasement, his humility and his love of poverty.*

1857: *Various consultations, notably with the Curé d'Ars. He is encouraged in his projects. However, his pastor and the neighboring clergy do not approve of his ideas.*

August: *He leaves the parish to become chaplain at the City of the Child Jesus. That is where he is called FATHER Chevrier. His authoritarian mother is very displeased with this orientation; she will hound her son until his death. Persons called SISTERS devote themselves to the service of the City. Maria Boisson enters that year; she is a young silk worker of 22, who will become Sr. Marie, the first superior of the Sister of the Prado. At the City, Father Chevrier also meets Pierre Louat, known as Brother Pierre, who will be the co-founder of the Prado but who did not stay.*

1859, January: *First journey to Rome. During the following months, Father Chevrier sees clearly the divergence in orientation between Rambaud and himself. They will have to part but Father Chevrier remains at the City until Camille Rambaud has received Orders and is able to assure the priestly ministry.*

1860, Dec. 10: *Father Chevrier obtains possession of a piece of property at Guillotière. It had been an infamous dance hall known as BAL DU PRADO. The name of Prado remained with the house and Father Chevrier's spiritual family. In this house, Father installed catechism classes for poor children. During the years that followed, several collaborators presented themselves. The most ardent is Father Jarico who will be ordained in 1869, but he does not have a very solid head and Father will not be able to rely on him.*

1864, Sept. *Second journey to Rome. Father Chevrier wants to present a petition to the Pope. He gives us the text in* The True Disciple ².

1865, *Birth of the clerical school of Prado. In reality, the students must be sent to the clerical school of St-Bonaventure, a parish on the right bank of the Rhone.*

1866, October: *Father Chevrier finds a professor for his students; the clerical school runs at the Prado.*

1867: *Father Chevrier is named pastor of the parish of the Moulin-à-Vent. This parish in the diocese of Grenoble was near the diocese of Lyons and its suburbs. It was understood that Father would usually live at the Prado and would have the priests who lived with him replace him in the parish. It is Father Martinet who took care of this parish. For Father Chevrier, it is a precious training ground for his principal aim,* The work of poor priests for parishes³; *but in June, 1871, without any prior notice, he learns that Father Martinet has been named pastor in his place.*

1874, end of March: *Serious illness which demands rest until the end of May.*
November: *In the countryside near Lyons, at Limonest: installation of a small community: Father Jaricot, four sisters and some twenty children from the catechism class.*

1875. May: *Third journey to Rome. At this time Father Chevrier is advised to organize his house into a religious congregation. The Archbishop of Lyons is opposed to the project and Father Chevrier does not insist.*

1876: *Father is in very ill health and the doctor prescribes a stay in Vichy (July 25-August 15).*
October: *The Archbishop has given authorization for four Prado seminarians to go to Rome. They are deacons and will form a small autonomous community to live, as much as possible, according to Father Chevrier's directives.*

1877, March 14: *Fourth journey to Rome. For two months, he will live with the four seminarians to explain* The True Disciple *to them.*
May 26: *Priestly ordination at St. John Lateran.*
June 20: *Return to Lyons. The Archbishop has promised to leave him his four new priests.*

---

² P.276.
³ Cf. p. 12.

1878, Spring: *Father Jaricot leaves for the monastery and two of the new priests also speak of going; Father Chevrier's health deteriorates* [4]. *However, Father Jaricot returns to the Prado in June.*
October 31: Father Chevrier celebrates Mass for the last time. He will be bedridden until the end.

1879, Jan.6: *Father Chevrier resigns and Father Duret, one of the four priests of 1877, becomes superior of Prado* [5].
October 2: Death of Father Chevrier at the Prado. He was burried in the chapel of the Prado on October 6.

Let us now return to The True Disciple.

Father Chevrier wanted to write a book. The testimonies, including those of Father himself, are very categorical on this point [6]. *However, the exact form of this project needs to be explained.*
When we speak of a book, we immediately see a printed work, given to the public through the book stores. The author may have some idea of the type of people who will read it but he has no direct contact with them.
In what concerns Father Chevrier, we do not know if he thought that his book would be printed some day. It is not excluded, but it is sure that he did not think of it for the immediate future. In fact, Father Chevrier wrote first of all for the priests and seminarians that lived with him. Besides, he wrote other things under the same conditions: catechisms, Gospel commentaries, etc.
He only wrote for his spiritual family and, given the small number of members and the poverty of their resources, the only process used was the handwritten manuscript [7].

---

[4] Cf. p. 17.

[5] Cf. annex IV, p. 470.

[6] "This is what I plan to do: finish my work on The True Disciple and have it examined by serious priests and go forward with their approbation. If the Bishop comes to Rome, I will shownit to him and we will follow this rule". (LP 83, April 1877).

[7] In 1889, when there was question of reproducing The True Disciple in a more practical way, they opted for the lithograph process. Miss de Marguerye paid the cost of this edition. The same lithograph process was used for other writings of Father Chevrier's. No doubt the idea was to limit the edition to the Prado Family which thus followed Father Chevrier's intention. In 1910, a new lithographed edition, with an imprimatur. The first printed edition came in 1923. In 1923, we knew that the public at large was interested in the figure of Father Chevrier. The elders at the Prado also gave another reason. They wondered how Father Chevrier's concepts of priestly life would be received among the clergy and they did not dare

Yet, behind his first companions, Father Chevrier perceives all those who will join them and he does not think that the number will necessarily be limited; but he also senses that the development will be long in coming.
He sees far and wide; that is why he undertakes to write a book. He has to erect something that is sufficiently well built to last and reach those who will come later when the Father will no longer be there. It is all the more necessary because his first disciples are young and he knows very well that he will not be long with them.
But, while seeing far and wide, he remains the modest and realistic man, full of common sense, that he has always been. He does not imagine that, in his time, his book will be of interest to anyone outside the Prado, and he is no doubt not mistaken. Thus, there is no question of a printed edition. Besides, Father Chevrier is well aware that he has no special aptitudes to write a book [8], and it is one more reason to limit himself to the readership easily counted at the Prado. Besides, his project for a book is essentially linked to another project, the one that he calls The work of poor priests for parishes [9].
Antoine Chevrier, ordained priest in 1850, spent six years in the parish of Saint-André de la Guillotière. At the time, la Guillotière was a workers' suburb.
During this period, a hidden maturation occurred in the young assistant. He has only to walk through the territory of the parish to observe the material and moral hardship of a people sociologically cut off from the core formed by those who regularly attend the parish church. The floods of May 1856 and the meeting with Camille Rambaud in June no doubt gave a new impetus to this interior evolution which culminates during Christmas night of 1856. It is what he himself called his conversion [10].
Enlightened by the example of He who "rich though he was, became poor in order to enrich by his poverty" [11], he understands the grace that is given him: to become a

---

spread them too widely. We may note on this subject that in 1939, an Italian translation had some difficulty in obtaining an imprimatur.

[8] "I have read little, I do not know the authors who have dealt with this question of religious, priestly life. You cannot imagine my ignorance in all that concerns me, but with the Holy Gospel, it seems to me that I am stronger, that I may hope, after all, it is not I, it is Jesus Christ, and with him one is not mistaken, with him one has authority, with him one is stronger and nobody can say anything. Therefore, it is on him that I will take support and in him that I will hope. Pray that I may make good use of the time that God will give me to work well.That is how I have understood the thing, for I have often asked God to force me to work for him by withdrawing me from all this bother which, after all, does not serve to the end that I propose". (LP 291, May 3, 1869).

[9] Cf. Letter of 1865, quoted p.12.

[10] We may think that this word 'conversion' is understood as an analogy with the conversion of St. Paul (cf. Gal. 1,15-16).

[11] Cf. 2 Cor.8,9.

poor priest to proclaim he Gospel to the poor." I kept saying to my-self: The Son of God came to earth to save all men and to convert sinners. And yet, what do we see? How many sinners there are in the world! Men continue to damn themselves. So I decided to follow our Lord Jesus Christ more closely, to make myself more capable of working efficaciously for the salvation of souls" [12].

Antoine Chevrier's first movement is to put himself in the school of those who have helped him to discover the poverty of Jesus Christ and of the poor. He had discovered Camille Rambaud, that young bourgeois of Lyons who, in founding the City of the Child Jesus, had made himself poor with the poor. He had perhaps hoped to find in him a leader and it is perhaps with that idea that he persuaded Rambaud to go for the priesthood. At any rate, Father Chevrier followed the Capuchins as chaplain of the City of the Child Jesus where he saw particularly to the preparation of children for First Communion.

But he discerns progressively that his personal orientation does not coincide with that of Camille Rambaud. So, after much hesitation, in December 1860, he accepts to go back to his Work of First Communion by installing himself in the Prado premises. Thus he will be able to dedicate himself to bringing the Good News to the poor and he hopes that priests, animated by the same intentions, will join him. For, from the beginning, he knows that his project will not amount to anything if he remains alone. During a retreat in May 1858, he had written: *"I promise Jesus to seek confrères of good will to associate them to me...."* [13].

1860 to 1866: new period of maturation for Antoine Chevrier. One thing becomes more and more clear: he will have companions in his work only if he forms them himself.

A number of priests have turn toward the Prado during these six years but none understood what it was all about. One or two might have understood but the diocesan authorities prevented it. But at the same time, disciples present themselves and are being formed [14].

So Father Chevrier decides to form a clerical school. It took ten years for him to accept to be a leader, ten years to resign himself to being formator of poor priests for the poor.

When it was a matter of being personnally poor with the poor, he had gone to consult the Curé of Ars, he had reflected with his confessor, with his former spiritual director of the major seminary. Such consultations were enough to make him go, with the permission of the Archbishop, to live at the City of the Child Jesus.

On the other hand, when it was a matter of founding the Prado, he hesitated a long time. On October 17, 1860, he wrote: *"What is good Brother Pierre doing! That poor young man worries me. I would like to be useful to him; he is so generous for*

---

[12] J.M. Laffay, PB 2,409 v.

[13] Ms X 20.

[14] Letter to Father Gourdon, quoted p. 15.

God. But he has too much confidence in me, he is always waiting for me, he is always waiting for me to undertake something but I do not have enough confidence in myself to dare do things that God would perhaps not approve. Yet, I must not put myself in trouble just to please him. I have very little taste for what attracts opposition or vexation from the authorities; I really do not feel my shoulders strong enough to carry such a heavy load. Besides, events do not look so good; my health is not very robust and above all, I do not have a sufficiently enlightened and ingenious spirit to take on such burdens. My vocation is rather to be in some unknown corner, ignored and doing the work that presents itself without going forward too much". [15]

After the installation at the Prado however, Father Chevrier is still anxious and the deep cause of this anxiety seems to reveal itself little by little. The project of the clerical schools seems to impose itself more and more. Here are a few manifestations of his state of mind.

"I feel my powerlessness, my incapacity so much that I often say to God: My God, did you not make a mistake in putting at the head of a great work such a poor and miserable being as me? I am so poor, so sinful, so ignorant that if God does not send somebody to do his work, it can only perish. What qualities, what virtues one needs to establish something, to do God's work well. I know that God choses those he wants and sometimes the smallest and the poorest to manifest his glory and power so that everyone may say: it is God who has done that. But that poor being must also correspond with grace; he must be a man of prayer and sacrifice and I feel that I always resist God's holy will, that I delay his work. I would need to have somebody always beside me to push me and to remind me of what I should do. How unhappy I am! How pitiful I am! If I do not do what God wants, what a responsibility, what a judgement and condemnation for me! For many years I used to say to God: My God, if you need a poor person, here I am, if you need a foolish one, here I am, and I felt that I had the grace to do everything that God would have asked of me; and now that I should act, I am lazy, I am weak. Oh! If there are no souls to pray for me, to push me, I am lost. If God were to send me a good confrère who understood God's work well, I would then feel more courageous, full of strength, but alone, always alone, I feel that I do not have the strength or I would need an extraordinary grace that I have not yet merited, for God's graces have to be bought and to buy them we cannot do too much, especially when they are to contribute to the salvation of souls and to the glory of the Church".

"Forgive me, dear child, if I speak so openly and unveil some of the sadness of my soul, but it is to find in you a soul that prays and helps me to accomplish the holy will of God, for if God has made the Prado, it is certainly not to give me a property worth a hundred thousand francs; what would I do with it? I have given everything to God and I have only asked for Holy Poverty as my heritage. There must be

---

[15] LP.n. 256, October 17, 1860.

something else. Well, help me to do what God asks, especially this work of poor priests for parishes. The priests, oh! there is only the priest who can do anything. The priest, that is all.... It is Jesus Christ on earth. I must be another Christ on earth so that those who will come here may also be other living Jesus Christs; that is the only thing that can convert souls [16]."

The witnesses report, each in his own way, what they saw in this affair. Camille de Marguerye, impulsive, apt to take her imaginations for realities, states without ambiguity:

"One day he told me that the Work of First Communion had not been his principal aim but a means to prepare and cover the principal work that he had in mind which was the formation of clerics. This work would have met with too many obstacles if he had declared it first [17]."

Father Chevrier's confessor, the Capuchin Fr. Bruno, prudently declares the opposite:

"I do not think that, at first, Father Chevrier had the idea of founding a school for clerics or a congregation of priests. His spirit of faith waited for Providence to indicate and give him the means to provide for the needs of his work; it is little by little, by a supernatural inspiration that this idea grew in him. The assistance that Providence gave him in material needs made him confident that he would not be abandoned in spiritual needs. The work did not receive canonical approbation from Rome, but he never did anything without the consent and approbation of the Ordinary [18]."

Should we not prefer the testimony of Sister Marie who lived the whole history of the Prado from the time of her entry in the City of the Child Jesus in 1857?

"Father Chevrier's first thought was always the formation of priests, only the execution came later... As I have already said, the creation of a school for the formation of priests was Father Chevrier's first thought but he could achieve it only after 1865. My part in this foundation was to take care of the lunch baskets for the little children that were sent to the choir school of Saint-Bonaventure and who took their lunch there. There were only three or four at the time. Those contacts of our children with the choir school of Saint-Bonaventure were what led Father Jacquier to retire at the Prado" [19].

Françoise Chapuis, with colorful simplicity, confirms what Sr. Marie says:

---

[16] LP n. 277, 1865. It seems to me that, to grasp fully the meaning of this letter, one would have to re-read it after having become familiar with the life and thought of Father Chevrier.

[17] Camille de Marguerye, PB 1, 73, r-v. This penitent of Father Chevrier certainly helped him a lot, especially from a financial point of view, but she was rather intrusive and Father kept her away from his work.

[18] Father Bruno, PB 1,24 r.

[19] Sister Marie, PB 1, 218, r-v.

*"Father Chevrier often spoke to me of the clerical school, long before he founded it. He was thinking of it even before he took his first associates and he prayed much for this intention. One day he told me:
- Françoise, I would like to make a nursery of priests. I would like to have priests who would be students with my children, so that they may get to understand them well.
- But Father, how will you feed them. You can hardly make ends meet with the subscriptions?* [20].
*- That is true, those subscriptions do not give very much, but I have an idea, an idea that will humiliate me, for I am proud. God wishes, I think, that I humiliate myself. My idea is to go beg at the door of the church of Charity. I will hold out my hat or my bonnet to the passers by and recite the rosary for those who will put something in it.
- Father, they will only put pennies; you will not get enough.
- No, he said, they will also put larger coins and paper.
In our conversations on this subject, he stressed the need for simple, pious priests and as I gave him the names of his collaborators, he answered: 'That is not yet it, they are not simple enough* [21].*'*

Would it be the same thing that Marie-Antoinette Laffaye, the cook at the Prado, reports?

"When Father formed the project of founding the Work of the Prado, he was greatly pushed to it by Brother Pierre. Speaking of it later he said: 'I did everything I could to get rid of this idea, but God pursued me everywhere, in spite of all my efforts, I always came back to it'. One day, pursued by his thoughts, he withdrew into the woods and remained there all day in prayer. He later told us: 'It is at that moment that, overcome by that interior voice, I said to God: if you need a poor man, here I am; if you need a foolish one, here I am'. From that day, he ceased to struggle and continued resolutely what God wanted of him, his work which was hardly beginning and was meeting so many obstacles. He himself told us several times: 'At that moment, I saw all the sorrows I would have to suffer [22].*"*

Sr. Antoinette seems to have been a rather talkative and inquisitive gossip; we cannot be too sure of her objectivity. Be that as it may, it seems probable that the decision was taken quite abruptly after a long and painful period of uncertainty. That would be totally in conformity with what we will say of Father Chevrier's character.

---

[20] Father Chevrier had seen how Camille Rambaud operated at the City of the Child Jesus. At the beginning of the Prado, it seems he had sought to get regular resources from benefactors by a system of subscriptions.

[21] Françoise Chapuis, PB 1, 105,v. She was also a penitent of Father Chevrier. She was a generous soul, a bit naive, but whose evangelical simplicity Father appreciated.

[22] Sr. Antoinette Laffaye, PB 3, 660 v.

In any case, after 1866, although Father is strongly convinced of the disproportion between his person and the work to be done, he never comes back on the decision taken. This time, to be sure of God's will, he was more demanding than ten years earlier. He wanted particular signs. He explains in a letter dated November 7, 1865, addrressed to Father Gourdon. The latter had expressed the desire to join Father Chevrier, but that never came about.

"May the will of God be done in all things, in us as in all men on earth. If the will of God permits it, come; I would be happy to be able to contribute to a work that I have cherished for many years.

Providence seems to facilitate, even demand, this meeting. At the Prado, I have place to lodge those who wish to work at this task, and I would be so pleased because I have four students that I must send to a clerical school in Lyons since I do not have a professor here; and how I would be happy to have them continually in the house to give them that spirit of simplicity and poverty which is our principal aim.

If you have students, you may bring them. I can offer you lodgings for eight or ten students.

What makes me desire it is that Mr. Magand has written me a few hours before I received yours, that he could not continue with the work of poor students because his resources did not allow him, that he had only four and that those four were paying board. I do not think that our Lord wants the death of this work that he began and is so pleasing to him. Perhaps he wants poor priests to do it. For my part, I feel ready to continue it with the help of good confrères. Here we have the beginning: the students and the premises, and resources from Providence already visible enough to give us credibility. Confidence, therefore, and the blessing from His Holiness who blessed us and you also since he gave it to all priests who would accept the holy poverty of Jesus Christ. Come, I will be very happy to receive you; get His Eminence's permission and we will begin. As for the persons that you have formed in poverty, continue to direct them in this way of Our Lord and later they will be useful to us when we get a few poor parishes to serve, IF GOD WISHES.

Oh! I was very happy when I read your letter, I saw that I was not alone either. I do have two or three confrères who have the same views but, you know, there are those toward whom the Holy Spirit seems to send us more. Let us pray God during these days, let us ask that his holy will be done and that the obstacles may be leveled. I promise you that I will carry this intention in the Holy Sacrifice during these days 23*."*

The signs that convinced Father Chevrier can be reduced to four: the Pope's blessing, the authorization of the Archbishop, the protection of Providence on the Prado, the meeting with priests with the same orientations.

---

23 LP n. 51, November 7, 1865. Father Gourdon was then assistant at Millery, a village in the neighborhood of Lyons.

As early as 1864, Father sought a pontifical approbation. He had to be satisfied with a blessing. However, it was a blessing in the true sense of the word. The Pope had 'spoken well' of the project and he 'hoped good would come from it'. "The work is good", he had said [24].
The Pope sent the question back to the Bishops. They will have to testify to the timeliness and success of the undertaking. Father Chevrier followed these orders, interpreting them in his own way [25].
Of course, he asked his Archbishop for the necessary permissions and when he thought the stakes were serious, he knew how to insist to obtain what had been first refused.
That is how he obtained the authorization to organize himself the last year of formation of the seminarians Broche, Delorme, Duret and Farissier. From the major seminary of Lyons, they were deacons in June 1876. It is to them, in Rome during the spring of 1877, that Father Chevrier consecrated all his time and his last strengths to explain The True Disciple.
But for another matter, with heavy consequences, where he does not see God's will clearly, opposition from the Archbishop is sufficient sign. It is the matter of the organization of the Prado as a religious congregation. In 1875, advised no doubt by a missionary bishop, Msgr. Dubuis, and by the Capuchins, Father Chevrier had undertaken a number of consultation but the Archbishop of Lyons was not favorable to this project. Without disobeying, Father could have insisted and renewed certain steps, but he chose not to listen to the advice of those who would push him to found a religious congrevation and decided to remain secular. Finally, at the time of his death, he bequeathed to his spiritual family a very clear and precise order: "We look upon the Archbishop as our immediate superior [26]."

The reference to the third sign comes to us from the pen of Father Chevrier himself. It is the "resources from Providence already visible enough to give us credibility." That is not a simple notation. Besides, we know what importance he attached to it [27].
For the fourth sign, we can say that Father Chevrier was not very demanding. He had to be satisfied with the strict minimum in this area. He wrote to Father Gourdon: "I saw that I was not alone", but all his life he could only look upon the Promised Land from afar, because it is to the same priest that he must write shortly after that:
"If we are obliged to remain apart in body, let us remain united in spirit and let us practice the holy poverty of Our Lord according to our abilities. This decision of the council, though it must not surprise us, we must respect it and submit humbly. These

---

[24] Pp. 276.
[25] Ms X 253.
[26] Ms X 253.
[27] See P. 11, testimony of Father Bruno.

gentlemen cannot guess the motive that makes us act, neither do they see the necessity of a new priest at the Prado [28].*
If we now wanted to sketch Antoine Chevrier's spiritual journey, we would see him as fully conscious of his personal vocation in 1856, after six years of ordinary parish ministry. He has decided to follow Jesus Christ more closely.
In 1860, with the foundation of the Prado, he is firmly established in this way discovered four years earlier but, at the same time, he senses anxiously a new dimension of his mission. God wants to give rise, through him, to similar vocations and,after 1866,he no longer doubts the breadth of this mission. Hence- forth he walks humbly but firmly. He knows,in particular, that he cannot and must not leave the instruction of his disciples in the way of the Gospel to others.
But to accomplish his destiny, Antoine Chevrier must cross another threshold. He must consent to the destruction of the work to which he has given himself completely. Yet, he had greatly dreaded this work and had only undertaken it on divine orders, so he thought.
In this instance, we are surprised to see how he accepts failure in all humility, without losing any of the certainties acquired in 1856 and 1866. The work is from God. It is in 1878 that the trial comes, when Father Jarico left for the Trappist monastery of Aiguebelle.
"Your example produces admirable effects! For several days Father Duret has been telling me that he is unable to teach catechism, that one must work at one's salvation above all, that a man is not necessary to such a beautiful task, that God will see to replacing him, that God will not abandon me; that he feels the need to retire and work, that he has to go to the Grande Chartreuse;that it would have been better if he had remained a Brother and devoted himself to the Work without taking on the responsibilities of a priest, that this responsibility scares him and that he fears God's judgement; that after he has spent a few years at the Grande Chartreuse, he will come back more sure of his vocation; that the vocation to the Prado is very beautiful and he would choose no other, but that he has to go... I do not know if he will go after this series [29].
Father Farissier still has a desire for the missions and occasionally lets his desire to go to China surface.
Father Broche prefers Limonest to the Prado and I think he will stay with M. Jaillet. Father Delorme's health is not good and he will not be able to manage alone, in spite of his courage. He would need to spend a few months in the country and the departure of his companions is hardly encouraging for him.

---

[28] LP n.54, June 3, 1866.

[29] At the Prado, there was a First Communion ceremony every six months. The preparatory catechism classes lasted five to six months and this period of preparation was called "series". At the time of Father Chevrier this did not evoke the idea of assembly line, as it might today.

If things continue as they are, I will ask the Latinists to go to the seminary and I will not be able to take the children for First Communion. I do not feel that I have the health or the courage to do as before. God had given me help, good collaborators; now he is taking them away: may his holy name be blessed. God is showing me very clearly that he does not need anybody to do his work. You all say that God does not need anybody, that he can manage without us, that is evident; I think that after us God will send others who will do better than us; that is my only consolation and my only hope for I would nevertheless experience a certain sorrow if I saw the Prado deserted and without children when, for eighteen years, it has been the place of so much sweat and work for conversions.

Go, everyone of you, to pray and do penance in the cloister. I am only sorry that I cannot go myself for I need it much more than you because I am older and consequently I have many more sins than you. But if I do not go, I might go to Saint-Fons, and I will have the consolation of having made Trappists and Carthusians and missionaries, if I have not succeeded in making catechists; although, it seems to me that this is the need of the Church of our time.

Good-bye, dear friend, pray for us and especially for me who thought I had done something, a work, and I see that I have done nothing. May this humiliation instruct me and expiate all my sins of pride and other sins of my life.

Your brother in Jesus Christ abandoned on his cross [30].

Note Father Chevrier's exact thought. He is hurt if the work of the Prado is interrupted but he sees clearly that the failure has to do with the work of apostolic formation begun with the clerical school. "I thought I had made catechists and I see that I have done nothing." And this occurs at the moment when it is no longer possible for him to begin anew. In fact, the letter to Father Jaricot is dated April 9, 1879; Father Chevrier has already been sick a long time. He will not assist at the destruction of his work but he will have to leave on October 2, 1878, leaving to God the care of consolidating what he had only begun.

It is impossible to evaluate the bearing of Father Chevrier's ultimate trial. God alone knows its effects. But in the light of Divine Wisdom, isn't this trial a sign for us, is it not the seal fixed by God on the life of Antoine Chevrier who was drawn to evangelize the poor and especially to form others for this mission?

This trial is also a seal fixed on The True Disciple. This book comes from the experience of Christ that Antoine Chevrier had at Christmas 1856. It comes out of his experience of poor priest for the poor of the City of the Child Jesus, of the

---

[30] LP. n.88, April 5, 1878. Fathers Farissier and Delorme left the Prado after the death of Father Chevrier. Father Broche succeeded Father Duret and thus became the third superior of the Prado.

Prado, of the parish of Moulin-à-Vent. It comes ou of his consent to the task that God asks of him: to form catechists [31].
And it has remained unfinished. Those who would want a work of spiritual literature or a treatise on pastoral theology will only be disappointed. To the one who feels called to the same way that Antoine Chevrier was, suffice it to say: "Take and read". If the work, from the very first pages, seems to you to be unfinished, it is providential. In reading it, you will not be able to forget how God asked the author to put the last stroke on his work, not by fihishing a book, but by uniting himself to Jesus Christ abandoned on the Cross.

PORTRAIT OF FATHER CHEVRIER

We must now attempt to draw Father Chevrier's portrait. It is necessary to understand him while reading him. It is necessary but very difficult to do.
We can never succeed in telling a man perfectly, no matter who he is, and we always remain very far from expressing the profound mystery of his being. But in living with someone we acquire, through familiarity, a certain perception of his mystery and we can invite others to enter also into this familiarity.
Only a knowledge of this kind may allow a correct interpretation of the author's thought in a book. I do not say that it suffices to have read these introductory pages to read Father Chevrier correctly; I only wish to indicate toe road to take.
It takes time to become familiar with Father Chevrier. This is true of everybody; it is especially true of Father. Vigorous personality, we will see, but hidden under a self-effacing manner - it has been called insignificant [32] *- it takes time to unveil itself. He is not brilliant and detests what is only brilliance. He prefers the true, the solid, the great, even if they do not appear to be, and he noted that ostentation is very often a temptation to dissimulate to others and to oneself a poverty in the area of the essential. "Poor, simple and clean; nothing showy, flashy, elegant, that excites curiosity; everything must be grave, modest, solid. The beautiful and the great can be very simple: thus a gold chalice can be very simple, yet it will be beautiful and great* [33].*"*
Father Chevrier wrote this concerning the objects of worship. Without thinking he drew his own portrait. Should we see in this the Lyons character of Antoine Chevrier and a mark of the Dauphiné influence? Would he have transposed to the spiritual level a well known tendency to reduce exterior signs of wealth to better preserve them. It is possible.

---

[31] That is why Sister Marie can say in all honesty: "Father Chevrier painted his own portrait in The True Disciple of Jesus Christ" PB 1, 220 v.
[32] Six, p, 12.
[33] P. 262.

Antoine Chevrier is certainly from Lyons, very much so; but how is he exactly? Those kinds of things are strongly felt but always hard to define. Those who are not from Lyons seem to recognize infallibly the "Lyons mannerisms" of Antoine Chevrier; his friends from Lyons are more circumspect.
Father Chevrier's Lyons poverty, for example. His economic concepts are poles apart from those of his compatriots; he does not want to have any revenues and he does not have the work ethic. In his room he wants everything to speak of the poverty of Bethlehem while his compatriots would prefer, in houses of modest exterior, to find a comfortable and esthetic interior. He does not want to launch into the building of large and rich churches while his confrères, with their parishoners do not hesitate to demonstrate wealth to manifest their piety. Yet it is true, Father Chevrier's life bears the mark of the world where he was born and which formed him.
He is the only son of modest, hardworking people, anxious to climb the social ladder. A milieu apt to be on the side of authority which maintains the order favorable to ambitions rather than to sympathize with revolutionaries, a populous milieu; and Antoine Chevrier will maintain the populous mentality all his life. Then, at the age of 14 he enters into a clerical milieu.

At the time, more so than in our day, this milieu wants to form future priests, not only in the spiritual life, the greco-latin humanist culture, theological science, the practice of the ministry, but also in a style of human relationships called "ecclesiastical conveniences".
Antoine Chevrier accepted simply the priestly ideal presented to him and he never denied it. That is something that we must never forget. Father Chevrier received much from all those who contributed to his formation and the influence of the superior of the major seminary on his future has no doubt been noted [34]. At the same time, he lets himself be instructed docilely in the ecclesiastical conveniences and, upon leaving the seminary, he is able to speak of the Mass by calling it the "august sacrifice" [35].
His passion for the Gospel and his love for the poor will crack the veneer coating and Father Chevrier will regain his original populous senses. That is seen in his speech.
After 1856, when he regains daily contact with the people, his style evolves rapidly and henceforth his letters have a simplicity that contrasts with those of the preceding period.
"By Father Broche who has so graciously accepted to do so, I am sending a jar of calf's liver paste and marshmallow candies for the good friend Delorme. Take good care of him and do not neglect anything to cure him. Buy what is necessary from the Sisters. If it were possible to make him swallow every morning two fresh eggs with a

---

[34] Six, p. 63-71.
[35] LP n. 2, May 22, 1850.

little wine, it might do some good to his weak chest. Speak of it to the Director, I have already said a word to him.
Our holidays are happily over.
We always pray for you. Always be very good.
I will write a longer letter soon. It is late in the night. Greetings [36]."
How Antoine Chevrier is at ease with this popular therapy of the good people of la Guillotière!
However, the veneer of ecclesiastical conveniences endures and, even in severe trials, traces always remain. Father Chevrier does not hesitate to address his priest correspondents as "Dear and venerated confrère" and when he castigates slippers as a sign of ease and comfort, he writes without thinking of being humorous that "these shoes stink of daintiness" [37].
Nor must we be too surprised to find in him traces of a romantic pomposity that was the spirit of the time. That spirit had its share of influence on ecclesiastical language. We must not be alarmed by expressions that gain their true meaning when they are placed in the romantic context of the time.
Father Chevrier speaks of the body as a quagmire, an infected swamp, or of the nourishmont necessary for the body as putting us on the level with animals. Instead of seeing in these expressions a persistent influence of Jansenism,[38] we need only make a transposition to recognize simply that we do not always easily master our body and that the nutritive functions in us are totally analagous to those of animals. The value of the whole is too well affirmed to be called into question by details.
It is good that the Gospel has returned Antoine Chevrier to his popular origin. But that is not the most remarkable. Rather, we must admire how the Gospel allowed him to give his full measure. The seeds of grandeur planted in every child of the people took root and blossomed in Antoine Ch vrier, under the effects of the Gospel. Neither servile nor agressive with regard to other social milieux, without ceasing to be himself, he could impose himself on those who thought themselves to be great ladies. Camille de Marguerye had remarked that he was not impressed with the rich, while being very polite with them, as he was with everyone [39].
It seems to me that his sense of dignity is a very characteristic aspect of what I would like to make understood here. He has the dignity of a man of the people who does not have a sense of inferiority before other social clases; he is not dazzled by the fortunes, power or even learning that others may possess: "Reason for reason, I am just as pleased with mine as with yours [40]." We notice this particularly in the

---

[36] LP n. 90, May 1872.
[37] P. 259.
[38] Pp. 153 and 160. cf. Introduction to renunciation of self, p. 141.
[39] PB 1, 75 v.
[40] Ms VIII 34.

independence of judgement of Father Chevrier; he does not let himself be boxed into a mentality.

And this popular sense of human dignity was sharpened by the awarenes that he had of the grandeur of the priestly mission. His independence of judgement is dictated by his evangelical fidelity, and he sees well that, to be truly priest, he must submit his mission to Christ, to Christ's representatives, and to no other.

This human development under the influence of the Gospel is noted also in his manner of writing. More than once, in his conviction and impregnated with the texts of the Gospel and St. Paul, he expresses himself with a true eloquence which bears the mark of his profound personality. We hope that the typographical method adopted for this edition of The True Disciple will allow the reader to see more easily the passages where Father Chevrier's own style appears. Here is a particularly striking example drawn from his letters.

"*Courage, therefore, dear children, do not be disturbed by the small annoyances that may arise, you have to get used to them. It is sufferings and humiliations that make real men; a man who has suffered nothing and endured nothing knows nothing and is good for nothing. Those who are always flattered, caressed and honored are only wet rags* ⁴¹."

He begins with a rather banal phrase with "*dear children*" and the "*small annoyances*". Then he gets stronger with the mention of "*real men*" to end with the real thrust to which nothing can be added: "*A man who has suffered nothing and endured nothing knows nothing and is good for nothing.*" After that, who would dare groan or complain or who would dare contradict? That would be to put oneself among the good for nothing. And for our joy, Father Chevrier returns to his popular language of Lyons with the "*wet rags*". In contrast with the real man, we see the poor man limp as a rag.

Father Chevrier does not always write with his personal style, he does like most of us. But we must highlight that style because it is in the moments of personal eloquence that the mouth reveals the treasure hidden at the bottom of the heart ⁴².

Two aspects of Father Chevrier's character are revealed by his writings, his letters in particular, and it is useful to know them to read him: a basic passionate temperament and a realistic intelligence.

He has a basically passionate temperament. I do not think that we can think of him as a vehement, authoritarian man, obstinate to arrive at his ends. He is not carried away by sentimental passion. He is rather naturally meek and humble and a realist who does not like sentimentality. But that only makes him more deeply passionate. This passionate character is revealed by absolute expressions that he uses often enough to express his spiritual experience. Like all those whose life is unified by a

---

⁴¹ LP n.143, April 25, 1877. The expression "patte mouillée", in the popular language, meant a flabby person, like a wet rag.

⁴² Cf. Lk, 6, 46.

passion, he has recourse to ALL and NOTHING *to express himself, like John of the Cross* [43].

Be that as it may, we can say that an assiduous meditation of the Gospel and St. Paul gave Father Chevrier means of expression well adapted to his temperament.

He has a realistic intelligence. This does not mean a mundane person but a penetrating spirit who can reflect on what he has lived. As J.F. Six has shown so well, in other words, an experimental [44].

It seems that he has little imagination, which explains why his expression usually lacks brilliance. This explains also why he cannot find attractive titles. His manner is at opposite poles from that of journalists. The latter, wishing to attract the public's attention, run the risk of doing so to the detriment of truth and of the respect of the readers. The newspaper headlines are too often misleading. Father Chevrier also manages to have misleading headlines but by opposite excess. Under a drab appearance there lie great riches. For example, he announces: 'Renouncement of one's spirit' and he does speak of that, but he also tells us how 'the Spirit blows where He will' and makes the saints do admirable things and makes them draw all their inspirations and their thoughts from God's infinite love [45].

On this topic, we may note also that he rarely uses imagined or invented comparisons. For example, in The True Disciple we find the comparison of the artificial tree. If Father Chevrier manages to make himself understood in this passage, from the literary point of view, it is not the best vintage [46].

On the contrary, he knows very well how to exploit all that he has observed and, by using his experience, he manages to express briefly and strikingly what he wishes to say. For example, if we have noticed the eloquence with which a worker who loves his work speaks about it, we understand the significance of this simple remark: "May the mysteries of Our Lord be so familiar to you that you may be able to speak of them as of a thing that is dear, familiar to you, as people are able to speak of their state, their dress, their affairs [47]."

This natural gift, transformed by grace, was exercised especially in the intelligence of God's work, an intelligence that was all the more penetrating as his spiritual [48] and apostolic experience became wider and richer.

---

[43] We know that on March 20, 1868, Father Chevrier was with the Carmelite Fathers to pray God a little and to study the poverty of Our Lord (LP n. 67, March 20, 1868). He may have learned of the works of John of the Cross with the Carmelites. (Translation by Father Cyprien of the Nativity in the XVII century or by Father Gilly in 1865).

[44] Six, p. 86, for example.

[45] P. 200.

[46] Pp. 193.

[47] LP n.67, March 20, 1868.

[48] Spiritual experience. We find this expression often. We should explain what we mean by this.

25 *This personal trait of Father Chevrier helps us to understand several things. First, his slowness in making decisions and his firmness in keeping them once taken and the persevering strength to carry them out. Slowness in deciding: that may be the clearest gap in his temperament. He weighs at length the pros and cons and seems not to dare to launch out.*
This prudence may be a trace of the Dauphiné rural ancestry. Without any doubt, it also manifests a desire to do only what God wants. But unlike others who were just as much men of God, he is not the man to imagine the future and, drawn by his interior vision, try to achieve them. Let us repeat, he needs to base himself on experience, on the real. That is why he needs signs in matters that cannot be perceived directly.
But once taken, decisions based on human and spiritual experience are not called into question by daily difficulties; these are not on the same level and cannot contradict the certainty gained.
Thus Father Chevrier is perplexed for a long time, especially if it is a matter where he has to grope. But he is not hesitant and, without being opinionated, he carries out perseveringly what he experiences as being the will of God. These lines written about Paul du Bourg, Camille Rambaud's companion, reveal his own personality: "He does not have enough trust in God's Providence that has always led you, he

---

We speak of 'experience' to signify that it is some sort of direct knowledge, a person to person meeting. We say that this meeting is spiritual, that is, the work of the Holy Spirit in us and that he thus manifests his presence.

Consequently, 'spiritual' in this case does not mean something that would remain purely and simply on the level of ideas. 'Spiritual' means real, more real than anything. But it is a matter of the mysterious majesty of God that can only be met in faith.

By the very fact of believing, every believer has a spiritual experience. But to go to the end of this experience, it does not suffice to declare: God exists, there is one God in three persons. I must be conscious that in saying Father or in addressing Christ, I am really on a first name basis with the Father, with the Son, in the grace of the Holy Spirit.

This spiritual experience makes us take Scripture to the letter: "May Christ dwell in your hearts through faith" (Eph. 3,17). "And the proof that you are sons, is that God sent into your heart the Spirit of his Son crying Abba, Father" (Gal. 4,7).

It is also the spiritual experience which makes us attribute to God all the good that we do, without denying that it is at the same time the work of our freedom. Here again we must take Scripture to the letter. "Without me you can do nothing". (Jn. 15,5). "Not that we are sufficient of ourselves to claim anything as coming from us; our sufficiency is from God, who has qualified us to be ministers of the new acovenant." (2 Cor.5-6).

Father Chevrier comments: "To know that all good sentiments, all good thoughts come from God himself and thank him for it" (p.103).

does not dare, he does not believe enough, he does not have that faith in the work that is the strength of a man who begins, undertakes and pursues with vigor [49].*

A little further we will see Father Chevrier's laborious search for a plan of composition for his book. We can say that his lack of imagination and his spontaneous desire to follow experience did not make the task easier for him. It is the exact opposite of a novelist.

This realistic intelligence also explains his manner of loving truth. He is not a speculator and, if he loves truth, it is as a man of action. What there may be of a little timorousness in his character it is compensated for by the realistic sense that he has of truth. For him, truth is something to do because one has tasted its strength. He does it patiently like a laborious worker.

With Father Chevrier, this sense of truth to be done is well marked by the use that he makes of the word TRUE (that he uses more often that the word REAL). The true is recognized from a certain efficaciousness that comes from love: the TRUE disciple *follows his Master*, TRUE *men are not good for nothing* [50], the spiritual family is TRUE when it gives the services that its members need [51], the TRUE poor really live poverty, etc...

Even if this corresponds to natural dispositions, we see also how it is inspired by the Gospel of St. John where it is so often a question of truth.

Father Chevrier's realism leads him to a kind of evangelical humanism. His sense of poverty, for example, makes him understand that there is only one reality in this world and that is man. That is totally along the lines of the Gospel: life, the body, that is to say man, are more than food and clothing [52], and also along the line of St. Paul [53].

For him what counts is the God-Man and the transformation of the image of the God-Man, it is the use of the means that God wished to take for that, and above all, it is finding the men that God wants to send for this work of the restoration of man.

And he is attentive to what is most human in man. That is why he has the spontaneous sense of the incomparable grandeur of everyone, particularly the little ones that one is tempted to scorn. In fact, what makes a great man is very little compared to the worth of every human person. And again, this manner of rendering homage to man is very evangelical [54].

Father Chevrier, an experimental? It is not exaggerated to say that behind every indication, orientation, commentary given by Father Chevrier there is an

---

[49] LP. n. 19, April 15, 1859. Another well turned phrase.
[50] Cf. letters quoted p. 22.
[51] Cf. p. 132.
[52] Cf. Mt. 6, 25.
[53] Cf. Eph. 4,24.
[54] Cf. Mt. 18,10.

experience. He gives us the reflection of his own life. It is this life, this experience that we must grasp behind the phrases of his book:
"The knowledge of Jesus Christ necessarily produces love" [55].
"Devout women especially invite many priests to come and see, especially the ones who have nothing to do [56]*."*

27 *"Unfortunately, there are those who think that, because they have a task, have a particular charge, everybody must help them, receive them, give to them* [57]*."*
Sometimes Father Chevrier simply gives the observations that he has made but these observations often provoke ironic reflections, a kind of tendency to social satire of which we find many examples in The True Disciple. At other times it is a lucid and penetrating psychological intuition. Finally there is also his personal spiritual experience and his apostolic experience, especially the experience of apostolic collaboration.
This openness of Father Chevrier's to experience was also facilitated by his openness to others. He was not sentimental but he was certainly very sensitive. This sensitivity made him commune to the joys and sufferings of others. We find this sensitivity in the importance that he gives to the kindness and compassion of the apostolic man [58], the importance given to the family spirit, affection in the spiritual family [59].
To end this portrait of Father Chevrier, we must say that his was a personality profoundly unitied and pacified in faith in Christ. For him, this faith was really the proof the realities that we do not see [60] and these realities were, for him, the most fundamental, the most attractive. When he speaks of them he likes to use the adjective 'beautiful'.
How beautiful is Jesus Christ! How beautiful is faith! Christ words, how beautiful they are! The poor priest, how beautiful is that man! *Such expressions were found frequently in the mouth and under the pen of Father Chevrier. Such is the testimony of Father Duret, his first successor, in reporting his words:*
"...O my children, Jesus Christ, the Word made flesh, is the living letter that God has sent to the world and the world does not know him. Oh! we should read it on our knees, with great respect. You must study Jesus Christ and love him, attach yourself to him and follow him." *And Father Duret continues:*
In the catechism classes, he wanted us to insist on the divinity of Jesus Christ. He often urged us: "It is the basis of Christian life, we do not know Jesus Christ enough, we do not believe or we believe very superficially, very vaguely, in his divinity. We

---

[55] P. 100.
[56] P. 155.
[57] P. 273.
[58] pp. 325; 386.
[59] P. 132-133.
[60] Cf. Heb. 11, 1.

must absolutely bring the world to believe in Jesus Christ-God; that is the fundamental truth that we must put into the souls of the children. Jesus is our Master, Jesus Christ is our Model, Jesus Christ is our way, our life. "These words were constantly on his lips, the study of Jesus Christ delighted his soul and when he spoke to us of Our Lord, I heard him more than once cry out with enthusiasm and the accent of a strong conviction: "How beautiful is Jesus Christ, my children, how beautiful he is! 61"

As we have noted, this portrait of Father Chevrier did not pretend to deferentiate what is of nature and what is of grace. Besides, such an undertaking would be pointless.

One may perhaps think that the portrait is too flattering. Did he not have any faults? He certainly had deficiencies. I noted his lack of imagination, his slowness in making decisions. I noted also how he felt the limitations of his milieu and time. There is no doubt that, like the rest of us, he had to struggle against pride and egoism.

But it is difficult to have an exact idea of the limitations of striking men. On the one hand, those who bring their testimony, especially if a reputation of holiness is at stake, are apt not to embellish but to say conventional things. We need only listen to funeral eulogies or others, in all milieux, whether religious, rationalist or academic! Therefore it is very difficult to get information.

On the other hand, when a type of man is a success, we cannot reproach him for having limitations. We only wish that many men had so few deficiencies.

It is my conviction that Antoine Chevrier was very successful in his humanity. After having been repelled by certain aspects of his personality, I must admit that the more I have known him, the more I have become attached to him and I understood better what human values developed the evangelical grace in him. It has been said that he was an ordinary man. I would say instead that he had everything to remain a very ordinary man but that his attachment to Christ and his will to follow him have revealed the true virtue of his nature.

On the contrary, more brilliant men, apparently more humanist from among his contemporaries were not able to rid themselves of their times and build a durable work for the future.

This destiny is a lesson: the value of a man is drawn only under the eye of God [62].

---

[61] PB 4, 1065 v-1066 r.
[62] Cf. 1 Sam, 16,7; Jer. 17, 10; 20,12.

ELABORATION OF THE TRUE DISCIPLE

After having traced the history within which The True Disciple *was born, we might attempt to give the history of the book itself, from Father Chevrier' various essays* [63]. *We know with certainty that we must begin with a rule of life written in December 1857. The continuity in the orientation of the rule of 1857 and the text on which Father Chevrier works twenty years later, in Rome, is striking. It is no less striking to note that the first writings approach immediately the theme of* the imitation of Jesus Christ our model. *"To study Jesus in his mortal life, in his Eucharistic life will be my whole study.*

To imitate Jesus will be my sole desire, the sole end of all my thoughts, the end of all my actions. I want to resemble you, O my Divine Savior; what surer model could I take. Grant that I may resemble you, be so conform to you that I may be one with you, that I may truly and worthily be your representative on earth in your powers and virtues. I take you for my master and model, I will be your disciple and your image; enlighten me and strengthen me.

The priest is Jesus' most perfect image on earth; he is the priest of the God of the crib, the God who humiliates himself even to taking what is weakest, what is most abject and becomes one with his creatures degraded by sin. He is the priest of the God of the crib, the God of the Cross, the God who gave his blood for his executioners, who was patient in suffering and contempt. The priest is established to revive all the virtues, the examples of Jesus Christ. He must be Jesus' most perfect image on earth [64].*"*

"To imitate Jesus is, then, my sole end, the sole end of my thoughts and action, the object of all my wishes and desires. Without that, I shall never be a good priest and will never work effectively for the salvation of souls. To study Jesus, that is my study. To imitate Jesus, O my God, how much meaning in that simple word! [65]*"*

What follows stresses the following of Jesus Christ: *an imitation which is the fruit of knowledge and union.* Father Chevrier has become more consciously mystical in the apostolate and that is the way that he wants to teach.

In what order should we place the various essays? That is not our aim. We sought rather to designate the most elaborated text, but throughout the whole ensemble we perceive very well Father Chevrier's method of development.

Father Chevrier always begins with his essential intuition which he explains more and more by going over his work several times. *This manner of proceeding is the same that he uses in his instructions. Whether it be preaching to the faithful, teaching catechism to the children or the formation of priests, he uses what could be*

---

[63] Father's Chevrier's manuscripts present a succession of outlines that are more developed as they progress. (cf. P. 35).

[64] Ms X 8-9.

[65] Ms X 24.

called a global method. To justify this method Father Chevrier can place himself on several levels.
When it concerns catechism, thinking of the often uneducated children for which the Prado was made, he writes: "We must always go from the coarse to the refined. We always want to go to the refined. We must be content with the coarse and go to the refined only as much as the people are capable of it [66]*."*
But in so doing, it is not only a matter of adapting to the difficient mental aptitudes of an audience. It is a matter of finding a fundamental law of religious knowledge (and of all knowlege, we might add). In its essence, faith is a unified, global knowledge because it is adherence to someone. Before answering the question: WHAT *should we preach? Father Chevrier answered:* WHOM *should we preach?*
He proceeds along the same principles with the seminarians. He composed many notebooks for the use of the young students of the clerical school and these notebooks very naturally served as prelude to what he wanted to do with the older ones, those who made profession at the time that they were going into philosophy at the diocesan major seminary.
In Father Chevrier's many writings, we seemed to be able to perceive the following progress in the development of his thought.
The essential intuition is first expressed in this form: to know Jesus Christ, that is all. Then the word to know *is developed:* to know, to love, to imitate or to follow. *To know and to follow will concur to express in one word the whole content, like what is found in Scripture, in Saint John for example. "Eternal life is to* know *you, the only true God and he whom you have sent, Jesus Christ* [67]*." "He who follows me will not walk in darkness but will have the light of life* [68]*."*
Then it is the name of Jesus Christ *which evokes not only his person but also his life and is developed in the "Tableau of Saint-Fons", the Crib, Calvary, the Tabernacle* [69]*. Thus to follow Jesus Christ is to become like him: poor, crucified, eaten. Each of these three aspects will be explained.*
Finally, the everything *will also be developed ipso facto throughout the book as a result of the preceding developments. We will know that to* have *the spirit of God is everything, everything for oneself, everything for the community. To have what is necessary and know how to be happy with it is everything. To love God and instruct the poor is everything. And in a thousand other less literal forms, we find this everything, the inestimable price of each aspect of life whenever it is a matter of conformity to Christ.*

---

[66] Ms VII 553.

[67] Jn. 17, 3.

[68] Jn. 8, 12.

[69] At the Prado, this three-part tableau is called "The tableau of Saint-Fons" (cf. Annex V, p. 477).

To express his thought, Father Chevrier willingly borrows the schemas of others. We are practically sure that the three parts of the tableau of Saint-Fons are not his invention. The manner of approaching the mystery of our conformity with Christ is more than classic and spiritual reflection tends to it more or less spontaneously.

With the notebook entitled "The Priesthood" Father Chevrier really begins a book. He tried to followva plan that seems inspired in part by that of a theological treatise for the first chapters give an abstract division of the subject: Aim, excellence, nature of this union (to Jesus Christ), its necessity, its effects.

Finally, Father Chevrier adopts a plan that he found in the Gospel. "If somebody wishes to follow me, let his renounce himself, take up his cross and follow me [70]." The wanting to come after him is the fruit of the knowledge of Jesus Christ, that knowldege which necessarily produces love and gives a thrust to respond to the call of the one who says: "come". This response is achieved by renouncing oneself, carrying one's cross and following the Master.

By dint of studying the Gospels and Saint Paul, Father Chevrier, having amassed material and gathered observations, must complete his plan. Other words of Jesus invite him to it. To the renunciation of oneself one must add the renunciation of the family and the world [71], and renunciation of the goods of the world [72].

To deal with each part, Father Chevrier follows various methods. For example, he borrows from psychological analysis when he divides renunciation of self according to four areas: body, heart, spirit, will.

He is always seeking a certain logic which is not easy to discover, for himself or for the readers. It happens that we may find a kind of spiritual progression through the plan. In that case, we can observe hesitations on the order to follow which is not exactly the same in the various manuscripts.

It also happens that the order is simply dictated by the succession of things in the Gospel. For example, in the last part of The True Disciple, there is question of following Jesus Christ first of all in fasting.That is because the Gospel shows us Jesus fasting for forty days in the desert before inaugurating his preaching. Then comes prayer which is associated to prayer in the Scriptures.

Finally, the order of development is also marked by Father Chevrier's apostolic experience. That is no doubt he case of the last chapters of the book, as will be shown later [73].

At any rate, in the detail of the historical exactitude of the progress that we have just traced, we may hold that no line of The True Disciple has any meaning except in the

---

[70] Mt. 16,24.
[71] Cf. Mt, 10,37; Jn. 15, 19.
[72] Cf. Lk, 14,33.
[73] Cf. pp. 41, 293.

light of the initial intuition: "Everything is enclosed in the knowledge of Jesus Christ [74]." *Outside of that light we can only end up with false interpretations.*
There is also no doubt that the movement that runs throughout The True Disciple is also that which is found throughout the Tableau of Saint-Fons.
The first part of The True Disciple *is turned toward the mystery of the Incarnation and what produces the knowledge of this mystery, a communion with Christ, source of impoverishment, of abasement. It is the Crib. By the same movement, the one who has been able to become poor is willing to take up the Cross already present in his life of poverty. Then, having become good bread, he is ready to work in perfect union with the living Bread who came down from heaven, by following him everywhere and in everything, to give life to the world.*
What kind of book does Father Chevrier end up with? We have already noted that he is in constant contact with his public when he writes. The text is tested as it is written for it is composed in dialogue with the users.
In Rome, during the spring of 1877, Father is living with his first disciples. It is during that period that Father writes to Joseph Jaricot: "I am working on my True Disciple. I explain it every day. We are going to begin to see the practical; that is where there will probably be a few difficulties [75]."
The conditions in which this book was written are still the conditions for which it is done today. Without hesitation we must apply to this case what Father Chevrier says about catechism: "It is not the book that instructs, it is the priest [76]."
Father's book is totally at the right place when it is in the hands of a priest charged with priestly formation and who comments on it by provoking dialogue with the seminarians.
It is a manual, if you wish, in the sense that it is normally to be put in the hands of the student and especially held in hand by a priest who wants to establish a conversation with the students [77].
This is supported by the concept of formation that Father Chevrier had. He explains it himself in The True Disciple. *The great method is to take the people with himself, to instruct, correct, put into action, as Jesus did with the twelve [78].*
Thus this manual for priestly formation is made to maintain the formator on the level of the hidden mystery of this task. Christ takes with him those he has called to follow him in order to form them. A mystery which is achieved through the person of those whose mission it is to form to the evangelical life.

---

[74] P. 99.

[75] LP n.83, April 1877.

[76] P. 401.

[77] This does not mean that the manual in question cannot be used in other conditions and by others besides seminarians. Long experience shows that people have found what they sought in this book without necessarialy having a master to comment on it.

[78] P. 195.

The True Disciple *is a book of priestly formation because it does not limit itself to describing the exterior behavior of the priest, but it is especially attentive to the spirit that produces that behavior and the source from which this spirit is drawn. To draw from the source and to become familiar with this spirit is the essential thing in priestly formation. And this explains how a priest can use this book until the end of his life; one must draw ceaselessly from the same spirit and the same source as of yore to be, as we say today, in a state of on-going formation.*

A manual for priestly formation and a description of a type of priest: these two aspects of the book are present even in the title given to the work by Father Chevrier: The priest according to the Gospel or the True Disciple of our Lord Jesus Christ.

Must supremacy be given to one or the other? Some, for reason of historical fidelity, others for reasons of adaptation to present mentality, would opt for the first part of the title [79]. *At the Prado, we have the habit of saying* The True Disciple. *At the time of the canonization process, the usage was already well established and there is no question that Father Chevrier himself used that title* [80].

A very practical reason argues in favor of this usage: the words The True Disciple *are quicker and more easily pronounced than the other. Perhaps that is why Father used this title more often. Yet, we must make another suggestion because, in my opinion, Father Chevrier may have had very precise reasons for prefering the second title.*

On the one hand, he wants to characterize the esential attitude of the priest or the future priest as being that of the disciple who acquires the knowledge of Jesus Christ; opening the book is a manifest proof of that [81]. *On the other hand, the expression True Disciple is used equally by Jesus in St John and applies to the apostles* [82].

34 *Finally, Father Chevrier's spiritual family does not include only priests. The Brothers and Sisters were by his side before the priests. It is with full rights that they can consider* The True Disciple *as written for them also. And, with all these,*

---

[79] Cf. Six, p.379. The Spanish edition of VD (Desclée de Brouwer, 1961 and 1963) translates only the first part of the title.

[80] Cf. letter quoted page 31. In fact, only one manuscript, the principal one, has the double title; everywhere else we find only *The True Disciple*.

[81] P.43.

[82] Cf. Jn, 8,31; 15,8. We know that Saint Ignatius of Antioch also used equivalent expressions: "I am God's wheat and I am ground by the teeth of beasts to become Christ's immaculate bread... It is when the world will no longer even see my body that I will be the true disciple of Jesus Christ." (Ignatius of Antioch, epistle to the Romans IV,1 and 2). We see that this martyr, condemned to the beasts around 110, had discovered well before Father Chevrier, that we must be good bread, well baked by death to oneself. (LP n.53, January 22, 1866).

lay people also have discovered in The True Disciple *a help which continues that which Father Chevrier gave to the lay people of his surroundings.*

It is also evident that, if priests accept to live as true disciples of Jesus Christ, they will be, by the very fact, priests according to the Gospel. Each one is free to prefer one title or the other.

What book did Father Chevrier refer to in writing The True Disciple? *Besides the Latin Bible, he may have had various translations at his disposal but we must remember that the editions of the Bible were not then what they are today. For the Gospels, he readily used the Mastaï-Ferretti volume: Les Evangiles unis. This manner of weaving together the texts of the four Gospels goes back to ancient times and, in the history of the Church, there have been several attempts to thus popularize the evangelical text. Father Chevrier used Mastaï-Ferretti assiduously because it gave him an integrated text of the Gospels. He recommended this work to those around him. Today, with the progress in Biblical studies, this type of method is no longer admissible. We have at our disposal a synopsis of the four Gospels. In his preference for the Mastaï-Ferretti work, we must note Father Chevrier's desire not to omit any evangelical text.*

When it is a matter of the Old Testament, Father Chevrier quotes most often in Latin and he does the same for the New Testament when he seems to be quoting from memory. Most of the time they are passages that are familiar to him because of their frequent use in the liturgy and the breviary.

Father Chevrier had the intention of using all of Scripture [83] *but he gives an eminent place to the Gospel and we can say that he had recourse to scriptural texts continuously. Yet, at the same time he gives an important place to all the New Testament and especially Saint Paul's epistles.*

Let us not be surprised to find certain awkward or even inaccurate interpretations. For example, page 170, concerning Romans 6,13: "your members as instruments of righteousness", Father Chevrier comments: "instruments of righteousness to punish you". This application to corporal mortification considerably restricts the meaning of the word righteous *for Saint Paul.*

Another example, page 130, concerning the words of Jesus to Mary at the wedding feast of Cana. In this translation and commentary, Father Chevrier simply echoes Mastaï-Ferretti in whom he trusts. At the time there were no special courses in Sacred Scripture in the seminaries.

However, all things considered, the blunders are rare for Father Chevrier does not seek a new interpretation of the Gospel but the practical consequences of the Gospel in his life, by an assiduous reading, meditation, prayer. Thus the evangelical immersion which ensued assured an essentially correct interpretation.

---

[83] In a notebook that includes a study on prayer, he had researched all the biblical references. He also studies all the prophetic announcements of Jesus Christ.

Outside scripture references, we find in The True Disciple *a number of other references but they cannot give sure indication on Father Chevrier's reading. They are scholastic adages or Latin maxims that ecclesiastics used to like. One of them is a deformed phrase from Saint Augustin* [84].
There are a few allusions to different people. To the Curé of Ars; that should not surprise us since Father Chevrier knew the holy Curé. References to Saint Anthony the hermit, Saint Benedict, Saint Francis of Assisi and others that he got to know, no doubt through "The Lives of the Saints", a classic of the time and through the readings in the breviary. Father Chevrier recommends the reading of "The Lives of the Saints". We know that the Curé of Ars had attached some importance to this work.

But, in the final analysis, all this weighs very little in comparison to the mass of Scripture quotation. Father Chevrier was very aware of the situation. He saw the inconvenience but he had no choice. To fulfill his mission he had to proceed in this manner [85].

Practically, at least for the parts of The True Disciple *entitled "follow me", Father Chevrier seems to have used the following method.*

1. He personally researches, in the Gospel and Saint Paul, the passages that deal with the subject studied. He takes a sheet of paper, usually rather long because he likes vertical lists. He notes the passages of Scripture as he goes along by a phrase which summarizes each passage and follows that with a number that refers either to the "Evangiles Unis" of Mastaï-Ferretti or to a translation of Saint Paul. Here, for example, is the beginning of a study of this kind:

36 Follow me in my sufferings.
   He was born in a stable *(27) (that is, Luke, 2,7).*
   The angels give his poverty to the shepherds as the sign by which they will recognize him *(28) (that is Luke, 2,12).*
   etc... [86]

2. He goes over this list, seeking to put it in some logical order, for example, by distinguishing between the actions and teachings of Jesus Christ.
Among the manuscripts we find sketches of plans and also pages where Father has noted again the same passages, but not in the same order; he is following the sketched plan.

3. Father Chevrier then asks somebody else to intervene. He entrusts the preparation of a notebook to a seminarian, a sister or one of his penitents.

---

[84] P. 289.
[85] cf. Letter quoted page 10, note 8.
[86] Ms XII 665. This manuscript contains some fifty evangelical passages.

On the pages of the notebook (school size: 17 x 23) he draws two margins of 40 to 50 mm, one on the right and the other on the left. In the central part are copied the integral quotation from Scripture indicated by Father Chevrier. Father's phrases summarizing the corresponding text are put in the left margin. They form a series of subtitles. The right margins remains empty; in principle, it is kept for Father Chevrier's commentaries. These will sometimes be written on the left or in the center of the page; they thus modify the subtitles.

4. *It seems that another work usually followed. In collating all the commentaries in the right margin, Father Chevrier has the sketch of the text of* The True Disciple. *But, for the last chapters, this last phase of the work was only outlined and, in some cases, not broached at all. Consequently, we can consider the texts of the last chapters as preparatory studies, especially beginning with* "Follow me in my charity [87]."
After minute examination of the manuscripts, it seems to me that this view really corresponds to reality; but let us not forget that Father Chevrier did not box himself into a system. Whether it was a matter of composing a book or governing his house, he always obeyed two imperatives: he felt strongly the need for a certain organization in order to be efficacious and he always learned from experience to modify the organization.

OUR EDITION

Since Father Chevrier started many times to write his book, we had to make a choice among the great number of manuscripts that he left. A considerable part of the work was done by Father Emile Desroche and Sister Renée de Limairac.
For a good part of it, from the beginning to the end of "Renunciation of self", *he choice was made, for a big notebook composed of various bound fasciles, certainly represent the most completed state of Father Chevrier's work. Much of the notebook remains blank. Father Chevrier meant to copy on these blank pages the texts prepared in other fasciles [88].*
Fortunately, we also have the plan of his work. Modified several times, this plan might have undergone more changes in a definitive edition but we do not see what could have caused important changes. In the introductions to the different parts, we will indicate the hesitations that we may have on the subject.
For the parts that were not reproduced on the principal manuscript, we had to choose. But here again, the choice was not too complicated for the most elaborated texts were easily apparent.

---

[87] P. 369.
[88] Cf.p. 239.

We will see, however, that the last chapters are not so well developed as in the first part. Father Chevrier did not have the time.

Therefore, if we do not pay attention to the general structure of the work, we may arrive at an inaccurate interpretation. Thus, in particular, the part concerning the renunciations appears inordinately long compared to the last part entitled "To follow Jesus Christ", contrary to the importance that the latter had in the mind of Father Chevrier [89].

Next to the texts held as fundamental, we present parallel texts. We did not want to quote all the parallels. On the one hand, this luxury of erudition would have been of no interest for the presumed readers of this book and, on the other hand, if someone needed to do a scientific work by having recourse to the comparison of Father Chevrier's various manuscripts, he could easily consult them in the archives of the Prado.

The parallel texts that have been reproduced were judge interesting because they sometime express themselves more forthrightly than the fundamental text.

In the annexes we give some texts of Father Chevrier's which were not immediately destined for The True Disciple. The are useful for a good understanding of his thought.

We wished to maintain the typographical disposition of Father Chevrier in order to follow his thought as much as possible. In fact, when we look at the manuscripts, we see that the disposition of the text is of great importance.

Things reproduced in series, in a compact typography, do not permit one to grasp the meditative attitude with which Father Chevrier wrote the same words but disposing them differently, in columns for example. Then we see that it is not an enumeration to be read rapidly but a series of ideas that have to be meditated. Thus we respected all the alignments, and they are very numerous.

Father Chevrier's text is in straight characters; what we have added is in [ ]. Those are a number of conjunctures necessary for the flow of ideas, where words are apparently missing or were illegible. We put the punctuations which were most often omitted in the manuscript. The parallels are reproduced in the same manner but in smaller characters.

As for the titles, we respected what was foreseen in Father Chevrier's plan and we reproduced them in their logical place even if, here and there, Father Chevrier had forgotten to transpose a title to a notebook.

The Latin quotations are left as such with a translation in the notes. When there is no note it is because the accompanying text itself gives the translation.

We wanted the reader to have Father Chevrier's exact text and yet that it be directly usable. That is why we had recourse to all these procedures.

---

[89] Cf. p. 293.

ADVICE TO STUDY FATHER CHEVRIER AND THE TRUE DISCIPLE

All the readers will easily understand that this last part of the introduction is specially for Father Chevrier's spiritual family, so that this volume may respond as much as possible to Father's intentions.
We have seen that this book is an instrument to be put in the hands of an apostle whose mission it is to form other priests: It is not the book that instructs, it is the priest. *But this condition cannot always be fulfilled and there is need for a supplement of personal work. Besides, for those who are charged with formation, a few practical indications might be useful.*
This study is neither a historical research nor a work of scientific theology. Such works are needed but they are at the service of another indispensable work for the members of Prado: a personal study to familiarize oneself with the person and thought of Father Chevrier and to live of the grace of which he lived, which is granted today to all his heirs. The following indications are directly related to a work of spiritual assimilation.
It is not rare for people to present themselves at the Prado without having any particular interest for the person of Father Chevrier. Others have sought to read a "life" of the Father or a part of his writings and have been disappointed: "Nothing to grasp on to".
Father may thus appear almost useless or even, for some, he would be an obstacle in the measure that they would want to refer to him for their lives of today.
If we believe Father Chevrier himself, these difficulties are not new. As early as 1866 he wrote: "I wrote to Father Merle and I don't know what has become of him, I have not seen Mr. Lainé again; those fruits are not yet ripe. I think that the Prado frightened them a little. In fact, one does not know on whom to rely in this poor shack; God is really the only one who is keeping it together and they do not see him. They only see a poor miserable person who holds God's place badly and they are tempted to keep away rather than to come [90]*."*
How are these difficulties expressed? I see three principal ways.
1. *Instead of speaking to us of Father Chevrier, some might say, speak to us of the Gospel.*
2. *Father Chevrier is a man in the Church among many others who are greater. Return him to his proper place.*
3. *If you wish to be faithful to Father Chevrier, seek not what he said and did in his time but what you should say and do today.*

Let us take each one of these points.

---

[90] LP n. 54, June 3, 1866.

1. Speak to us of the Gospel and not of Father Chevrier.

An illusion often seems to underly this difficulty: there should be somebody who could give us the pure and simple Gospel. Jesus alone could do that and he did. He gave the Gospel in deposit to the Church; but in the Church there is no-one who, by himself, can totally penetrate the Gospel in perfect purity, for himself or to present it to others.

The treasure is at our disposal; we can and must draw from it; but the treasure infinitely surpasses our possibilities of investigation and, as long as we are not in the full light of heaven, we can only see the Gospel as restricted by our own judgement and that of those who teach us. In thinking that I am going to the pure and simple, I run the risk of trailing behind a man or enclosing myself into my own spirit.

Fortunately the Holy Spirit is there to raise up the spiritual guides that we need, "scribes trained for the kingdom of heaven, like a householder who brings out of his treasure what is new and what is old [91]". *Father Chevrier is one of those; that is why the Church has recognized him as founder of the Prado.*

From this we can draw two consequences. First, when I have difficulty in entering into one of Father Chevrier's expressions, in a recommendation, I should see if, perhaps, Father Chevrier is not trying to open me up to a more profound, broader meaning of the Gospel.

Next, if one has really taken Father Chevrier as spiritual guide, he must be careful to have recourse with him to the Gospel, to grasp how what he says is inspired by the knowledge of Jesus. He must attach himself personally to Christ, as Father himself did.

2. Father Chevrier is only one man among others in the Church.

Nothing is more true, but as with all others, what is important is to know the role that God assigned him. One must not deny the Holy Spirit the power to raise up founders, men who receive a grace big enough to become spiritual guides of the family that comes out of them.

However it is true that we cannot have the spirit of God - Father Chevrier himself says so - if we do not have recourse to the Church and the Saints. Moreover, it is to be in the school of Father Chevrier to have frequent recourse to an important spirtual author who seems to be particularly suitable. Besides, a wide knowledge on this point is necessary for a priest. It may also happen that another spiritual master who has impressed one more be the one to introduce us to the knowledge of Father Chevrier and a comparative work could be useful in that case.

---

[91] Mt. 13,52.

The fact remains that we must not be surprised if, in a period of more specialized formation, one has recourse mainly to Father Chevrier: it is fidelity to the Spirit of God for those whom God calls to the same way.

3. Let us seek what we have to do and say today.

It is evident that this is what we must do, but there are several ways to do it. We may be impelled to invent something entirely new, without wanting to be inspired by anyone. To think that we could do so would be an illusion because, in all the most personal initiatives, we remain marked by the mentality of our milieu, by our past, by our own temperament. All this marks us in a providential way but we must be aware of it and not resign ourselves to remaining in a narrow circle which, spontaneously, we think is vast enough because we feel at ease in it.

If, on the contrary, we have the certainty that a man has enjoyed an exceptional spiritual and apostolic experience to inspire a whole line of people who will continue it, we must conclude that the Holy Spirit can use that privileged experience to render our lives of today fruitful.

Perhaps the man in question does not easily unleash enthusiasm. Should we not say: So much the better, for then his true place may be given him. And then, what is this man going to say to us? Not: "This is what I would do, if I were in your place", but "Here is how you can find what Jesus would do in your place", or better still, "what Jesus wants to do through you and with you, today".

Finally, this call to seek what we must do today must wake us up to another very important thing: to be true, recourse to Father Chevrier must be accompanied by recourse to his family as it lives today for, thank God! we are not alone; we have brothers and sisters who have understood something of this life following Jesus that we desire.

Let us not be afraid to look at them, without voluntarily excluding anyone. They all help us to understand Father Chevrier and especially to know Jesus Christ better, to work better in the Church, with the whole Church, at God's work, by proclaiming the Gospel to the poor.

With the doctrinal orientation that comes from Vatican II, we regain the habit of giving more attention to charisms in the Church and we see better that spiritual families exist to perpetuate, as long as God wishes, the special mission and the particular gifts given to the one who is recognized as founder.

The term of founder does not incline us to see things under this essentially spiritual aspect. It has a rather juridical resonance in present language and those who want to be faithful to the founder are suspected of wanting to perpetuate a society for itself. We must see the founder especially as an initiator, a man who received a particular gift for the service of the People of God, what is called a charism, and that man is also a privileged witness for those to whom God has given a similar grace. In is in reference to him that they can follow the personal grace that is in them and it is also in reference to him that they form a same spiritual family. "True unity is in the union of the same spirit, thought and love and it is Jesus Christ who is its center, through the Holy Spirit [92]."

42   Two things are necessary to accompany the study of The True Disciple: to know the life *of Father Chevrier and to read* his letters.
We have quoted many times the book of J.F. Six: Un Prêtre Antoine Chevrier. *This is the most recent that we must read if we do not want to be satisfied with a short biography. Among other things, it places Father Chevrier in the history of his time.
Father Chevrier's letters are interesting, particularly because they show how he applies in every day life the orientations drawn out in* The True Disciple. *They have been reproduced in two forms. One printed volume gathers a choice of letters. The choice wa well made; unfortunately, to make the text more presentable, corrections, sometimes very important ones, have been introduced by the editor [93].
All of Father Chevrier's letters that have reached us have been photocopied; this series is out of print.
For a progressive work, one may follow the plan given here:*

a) *For a first contact with* The True Disciple, *it is usually better to begin by reading the following passages in the order indicated.*
Attachment to Jesus Christ, P. 95
Renunciation of the goods of the world, P. 241
Renunciation of one's spirit, P. 179
Carry one's cross, p. 285
To follow Jesus Christ, P. 293

b) *A very profitable work is to search in Father Chevrier's letters all that relates to the various chapters of* The True Disciple, *for example, the study of Jesus Christ, poverty, the Cross, catechism, etc...*

c) *For a sustained work throughout the book, one may read in following with the help of fundamental themes which serve as unifying thread. Here are a few examples.*
   1) Love
   - the mystery of the Incarnation, manifestation of God's love in the world,
   - the knowledge of Jesus Christ which necessarily produces love,
   - the renunciations, expression of the love that wants to rid itself of all that is not agreeable to Jesus Christ,
   - the Cross, expression of love, distinctive sign of Christ and his disciples,

---

[92] P. 203.
[93] Lettres du Vénérable Antoine Chevrier, Ed. Vitte, Lyon-Paris, 1927.

- *to follow Christ, a life in love, on the personal level as well as in the accomplishment of the mission.*

2) The Mission
- *Christ, the Incarnate Word, God's envoy,*
- *the knowledge of Jesus Christ: opens us to the totality of Jesus Christ's mission in our regard,*
- *attachment to Jesus Christ: to hear the call to mission "Come follow me",*
- *the renunciations, especially poverty, freedom of the missionary,*
- *the Cross and to follow Jesus Christ: As the Father has sent me, so also I send you. One and the same mission accomplished in the same spirit, in the same manner.*

3) Man in God's plan
- *knowledge of Jesus Christ, sent by God because Son of God made man,*
- *attachment to Jesus Christ: God calls other men through his Son,*
- *renunciations: for God's work it suffices that one man be sent from God to men. The whole mission, all the strength of the envoy comes from his being sent. To be free with regard to all the rest.*
- *the Cross: the proven apostle is the man who knows how to suffer, he has the strength, the intelligence, the know-how for it.*
- *to follow Jesus Christ: the action of the man sent by God to men to be saved; an action always for man and not for works.*

4) The Word. *This theme is no doubt the most essential of* The True Disciple.
- *In God there is the Word through whom all things were made,*
- *The Word became flesh, he took time to speak to us, he enters into and remains in conversation with men.*
- *We must attach ourselves to this Master by receiving his word with the simplicity of* the true disciple.
- *The word of God, the Gospel of Jesus Christ, produces in us an effect of purification, of transformation, with the interior action of the Holy Spirit, so that we may be able to think and act according to God.*
- *The word of the Lord gives us the interior strength to carry the cross with joy.*
- *We must follow Jesus Christ in the proclamation of the Gospel, beginning where he began, in prayer, fasting, presenting himself to men with his meekness, his humility, his goodness.*
- *We must proclaim the Word with authority, fidelity, simplicity, to everyone, always and everywhere.*
- *We must go to the end of this mission accepting the unavoidable consequences of preaching the Gospel: struggles and persecutions.*

44   *- We must accomplish God's work in the sacrifice of one's life like Jesus Christ himself did: it is through his ministry that God's envoy journeys toward the Passover that will introduce him into glory.*

d) To study a particular chapter, *a passage of* The True Disciple, *one must try to find two references, to Holy Scripture and Father Chevrier's experience, that is, what he saw, heard, lived.*

For example, let us take simply the opening page. [94]

"In the Gospel, Our Lord often speaks of his disciples". Let us go to the Gospel and note, if possible, all the passages where the word Disciple is used and the characteristics that accompany it. We will soon have an eloquent tableau.

"Our first work is therefore to know Jesus Christ in order to belong totally to him". Where does Father Chevrier get this certainty from? His personal experience and his apostolic life showed him that the fruits that last flow from the knowledge of Jesus Christ. Any other way produces nothing or only passing results.

In some passages, it is the reference to Scripture that comes immediately to the surface. In others, it is the reference to experience. But it is worth seeking both ceaselessly. Thanks to this research, one will more easily find the transpositions to be made and more easily overcome the things that cause difficulties.

In conclusion, is it necessary to add that it is absolutely useless to read this book as a novel. If it is not received as a meditation, it will not yield its secret.

---

[94] P. 43.

OPENING [1]

In the Gospel, Our Lord Jesus Christ often spoke of his disciples. He chooses his disciples, he speaks to his disciples, he takes them apart to instruct them, he gives them particular laws. In a word, it is a special choice of men who are his and who go with him.

What is a disciple in general? A disciple in general is a man who has taken another for his master, who follows him, listens to his word, trusts him, accepts his doctrine and puts it into practice.

What is a disciple of Jesus Christ? Thus, a disciple of Jesus Christ will be a man who takes Jesus Christ for his Master; who follows him, puts all his trust in him, listens to his doctrine and puts it into practice and has no other desire but to serve him, loves him and does everything that he teaches[2].

What must one do to become a true disciple of Jesus Christ? To become a true disciple of Jesus Christ one must first know him, know who he is.

The knowledge that we have of him will help us to give ourselves to him and, the more we will know him, the more we will attach our selves to him, the more we will love his doctrine, the more we will desire to follow him and practice everything that he will teach us. Our first work, therefore, is to know Jesus Christ to belong entirely to him.

---

[1] Reference to the principal manuscript in the copies: vol. XI, P. 269-482 and in this volume, up to 239, except 207-214.

[2] Ms XI 6; XI 39. A disciple is a friend who follows another, who takes someone for his master and in whom he places all his trust, his heart and his will (Ms XI 6). A disciple is a man who follows another: who has taken somebody for his master, listens to him, follows him, gives him all his trust and is ready to sacrifice himself for him. He admits his doctrine and puts it into practice. (Ms XI 39).

FIRST PART

KNOWDLEGDE OF JESUS CHRIST

I - THE TRINITY

FIRST PART

KNOWLEDGE OF JESUS CHRIST

I - THE TRINITY

From the very first words, Father Chevrier surprises us by immediately approaching the mystery of the Blessed Trinity.
He does so by having recourse to the classical theology of the West, that which, following St. Augustine and St. Thomas Aquinas, has recognized in the exercise of our intellectual faculties, resemblance to the intimate life of God. It is Scripture itself that puts him on this road by designating Jesus Christ as the Word.
Father Chevrier does not appear very skillful in presenting this theology. His professor may have proceeded with the same awkwardness in the theology lessons in the seminary.
But that is not the most important. We must note the expression IN GOD, *which recurs several times and the final phrase: We can now say what is Jesus Christ. Father Chevrier is well aware that the knowledge of Jesus Christ, the Father's envoy, is inseparable from the knowledge of the only true God.*

Preliminary notions on the existence of the three divine persons.	We must know that in God, as in ourselves since we have been created in the image of God, there are the being, the thought and love;

that these three things are absolutely necessary to constitute an intelligent and complete being.

As in God everything exists in the perfect state because if there were something imperfect in God he would no longer be infinite or perfect, the thought which comes from God, that comes out of God as principle is perfect as God himself and forms a person distinct from the principle that engendered it.

So also in me I feel that my thought is from me, that it comes out of me, that it comes from me, that it is something of me and yet it is distinct from the being that produces it in me, and also distinct from the love that ensues.

In God, this thought is called Word and interior Word as long as it is not produced outside and is something of God, which emanates from God, which is the second person in God, which engenders his thought or his Divine Word.

This second person in God is his divine thought, eternal and divine, it is the interior expression of his eternal and immutable thought and it is as old as God because God has been thinking from all eternity and he cannot exist without his thought which is as essential to God as God himself.

In God, therefore, there is God and his Word which is nothing else that his thought itself in the state of a person.

This thought or person cannot exist without intimate relationships with the principle that produces it.

God sees his thought engendered by himself, coming from him, coming out of him, perfect as himself; he contemplates it as another himself because it encloses all his light, intelligence, wisdom; nothing is more beautiful, more perfect than this infinite thought which is one, perfect and infinite; he loves it absolutely.

For his part, the Word or the thought of God sees his author and his principle from which he comes in a perfect state, he sees this principle that engendered him and he admires all his infinite and eternal perfections and he loves this principle with an infinite love; and from the love of these perfect and infinite substances is born a third person that is called Love or Holy Spirit because it emanates from the first two principles and it possesses the one and the other.

And since this love proceeds from the two persons and that the first two persons were not able to exist without knowing and loving each other, and that the first two persons are eternal, necessary to their own existence, it follows that the third person who is Love or the Holy Spirit exists at the same time as the other two persons. And since this love proceeds from the two perfect, infinite principles, it follows that the Holy Spirit is eternal, infinite like the Father and the Son and that the infinite love that the first two persons have cannot produce a person inferior to them; and that in God himself there cannot be anything imperfect or finite, otherwise he would not be God.

That is what there is in God and it cannot be otherwise, even to the eyes of reason.

Need of these three persons for a perfect God.

Coexistence of these three persons who cannot exist one without the other.

Equality of these three persons.

Distinction of these three persons.

Inseparability of these three persons.

Comparison with our soul and with the flame which necessarily produces light and heat.

That is what there is in God and it cannot be otherwise and these three persons in God are but one and the same thing.

God, principle of everything, thinks and loves; his infinite thought like God himself becomes an infinite and eternal person like its principle.

And his love becomes an infinite and eternal person like the principle from which it emanates.

And everything in God is perfect and infinite.

And these two persons are eternal like the principle from which they emanate because the Father or principle of these two persons cannot exist without his thought and his love.

These two divine persons receive everything from the first principle by an infinite generation; infinite principle which communicates to the other two persons everything he has without destroying himself, without lessening himself because he is an infinite principle and having an infinite life, he communicates everything that he has of himself without losing anything of himself.

Having understood these first ideas, we can now say what is Jesus Christ.

II

WHAT IS JESUS CHRIST   55

We may compare the pages that follow with the preceding ones. If Father Chevrier was awkward in speculative theology, in a direct commentary of Scripture, he is very much at ease and does not hesitate with rather bold formulas (for example page 57 concerning God's need to communicate himself).

Behind these pages, especially behind the last vibrant lines there is the spiritual experience of Christmas 1856 which lives continuously in the contact of the soul with this phrase from Scripture: "The Word became flesh and dwelt among us."

St. John answers this question very clearly in the first chapter of his Gospel when he says:

In the beginning was the Word. That is, at the same time that God was, *the Word was also,* because God cannot exist without his thought or his Word, an inteligent being without thinking and God who is wisdom itself, intelligence itself, cannot exist without thinking, without his thought.
In the beginning was; he does not say: was created, but was.
There is a difference between this beginning of the Gospel of St. John and the beginning of Genesis where Moses says: "*In principio Deus creavit*[1].

And the Word was in God. That is, he had not yet come out of God as later on.
He was in God as my thought is in me, part of myself; I feel it, I feel its existence. Thus the Word was in God as interior Word, he was in God like my thought is in me, and since I cannot exist without my thought, so also God possesses his interior word, not yet manifested to the world, from all eternity.

And the Word was God. This Word engendered by the Father who is God, being God's perfect thought, his thought, his knowledge, his wisdom; this Word who has received everything from the Father through an infinite and divine filiation, without any abstention, forms one Divine person who is God, as the principle from which he proceeds, as the child who comes out of his father is like his father and consequently becomes a man like his father.
Thus, the Word who is engendered by the Father in an infinite manner, receives everything from him and is like him, perfect like him, God like him.

He was in the beginning in God. From the beginning, before anything, he was in God, one in being with him, God himself, of one nature with him. He was in God as my thought is in me, and this from the beginning, that is, from all eternity. Thus, in these words we see the unity of his nature and the eternity of the Son of God and yet his distinct existence, because he was and the preceding word says that he was God.
In the beginning, that is before manifesting himself to the world, as he does later, he already existed, he was in God.

All things were made through him and without him nothing was made. It is through his Word that God the Father created all things.

---

[1] In the beginning, God created.

Is it not by our word that we command, that we have things done? When we have something to do, something to produce outside of ourselves, we say, we speak and we do by our word. The general of an army commands and he is obeyed. Thus God does everything through his Word: *ipse dixit et facta sunt*[2].

Everything that was done outside of God was done by his powerful and infinite Word: the angels, the heavens, the earth, men, everything was made by his Divine Word who is the divine expression of the will of the Father and who, being his Word, has the same power as the Father and can only want and do what is in him and with him.

In him was life.   The life of the Father as well as the life of men.

Is it not in his thought that life is found? Take away the thought from an intelligent being and what does he become? A dead person. And just as he draws life from the Father who is life in essence, so also he communicates this life of thought, of intelligence to all the beings to whom he gives being, and in giving them being, he gives them life, intelligence and the Holy Spirit gives them love.

Thus each person communicates something:
> the Father gives being to his Son
> the Son gives life and intelligence
> and the Holy Spirit communicates love

61 and these three benefits are absolutely necessary to make of us good beings capable of doing good.

In him is the principle of life that he communicates to us in creating us: intelligence, thought, reason, faith.
> natural life
> spiritual life.

In him was life and life was the light   In this life that the Word communica-
of men.   tes to men in creating them, there is found light,

true light that enlightens all men coming into this world. In fact, is it not in the Word who is God's thought that is found the true light that makes us know God and heavenly things? Is it not in this Word that is found all the wisdom of the Father, science, the knowledge of God and all the divine and human sciences?

It is from this divine Word that emanate the rays of that divine sun which shines on all intelligent and christian creatures to raise them, enlighten them and make them know the spiritual and divine things without which man remains in the ignorance and darnkess of his own reason.

Light of the angels, of men, of Adam, of Moses, the prophets, the saints.

---

[2] He spoke and it was made (Ps 32,9).

The Word became flesh and dwelt among us. This interior word which is God's eternal thought, who is in God from all eternity, took on an exterior form to manifest himself to men. The thought is essentially internal and to become external, to manifest itself outside, it has to take on an exterior form. Thus, as long as we do not speak or write, our thought is interior, hidden and not known by anybody and to manifest it we must give it an exterior form.

So also, in God his Word remained hidden within and unknown as long as it did not take on a form, and to manifest itself he had toe an exterior form.

It is to be noted that the manifestation of our thought is necessity for us, that we cannot live without manifesting our thoughts. It is a need for us; even the mute find ways of manifesting their interior thoughts.

The thought cannot remain captive and chained, otherwise our thoughts would be useless to us and others.

This need that we have to manifest our thoughts, desires, wishes and feelings to others: who gives it to us if not God?

If God gives us this need, which is good, why would God not have this need to communicate himself to us who are his creatures, his intelligent creatures, his creatures that he formed in his image and likeness? Why would he have created us in his image and likeness and given us a supernatural end if he had had nothing to tell us and to teach us? God could not create us intelligent and form us in his image and likeness without saying anything to his creature and giving it a sign of his will for it. What would we say of a father who brings children into the world and leaves them alone without in any way manifesting his will and their duties? This would be unworthy of a father and nothingness would be better than such a situation.

God had to speak to men and he certainly did. He spoke to them through his Word because the Word is his thought, his wisdom. And just as to reveal our thought we dress it in an exterior form of word or writing, a letter or a messenger who carries our will to others, so also the divine Word took on a form to manifest himself to angels and to me .

He manifested himself to all intelligent creatures: first to the angels by taking a spiritual form; since he was spirit like them he did not have to take a material form.

He manifested himself to Adam by taking a visible and material form. How? Scripture does not say, and when we read that God spoke to Adam, it was already the Word who was beginning his mission on earth of speaking to men and manifesting to them the will of his Father.

Nobody has every seen God, but it is the Son who makes him known to us (Jn,1,18). He spoke to Abraham in the form of angels. He spoke to Moses and the prophets in more or less palpable forms. Finally, after many centuries, when the moment decreed by Providence had arrived, he spoke to all men, he himself personally, by taking a human form.

It is Saint Paul himself who tells us: multifariam multisque³.
And the Word became flesh and dwelt among us.
O ineffable mystery! God is with us, God came to speak to us, he came to dwell with us to speak to us and instruct us.

63 What he had done before in passing, so to speak, in a hurry, he now does it in these last times in a more palpable, durable manner.

He himself took the form of man in order to dwell with us and have the time to speak to us and to tell us all that the Father wanted to teach us through him.

We are not beings abandoned by God.

We have a God who is truly a Father, who loves his children and wants to instruct and save them.

---

³ In many and various way God spoke of old to our fathers by the prophets. (He.1,1).

III

DIVINITY OF JESUS CHRIST

Everything in him proves that he is the Eternal Word who comes to earth....
After that affirmation there comes an accumulation of evangelical references. Ocassionally a commentary crops up. Titles show the desire to put some order in the quotations from the Gospel.
The whole shows well that it is not a matter of proving the divinity of Jesus Christ nor of expounding a biblical theology on Christ. In the prolongation of the preceding commentary on St. John's prologue, we are invited to have a contemplative look on every page of the Gospel, sure that we will find there the Son of God.
This is confirmed explicitly in the important final remark[1]. *This attention to the divinity of Jesus Christ as manifested in the Gospel, tests the faith that thus becomes more alive and more capable of guiding the believer in all things, capable also of meeting unbelief for a truly apostolic labor.*
Finally, it is intersting to note the mention of the Church as sign of the divinity of Jesus Christ. In 1870, the first Vatican Council proclaimed: "The Church.... is in itself a great and perpetual motive of credibility and an irrefutable testimony of its divine mission[2].*"*
Today we are more clearly invited to go further in looking at the Church, not only as a sign that confirms the divinity of Christ and sends us to its past life as the Gospel shows it. The Church is still more a present manifestation of the presence of Jesus to his own and we can look at it with the same contemplative look that we have for the Gospel, recognize "Jesus Christ, yesterday, today and the same for all eternity"[3]. *Besides, the Church never presents itself without the Gospel.*

67

---

[1] P. 74.
[2] La Foi Catholique, Paris Ed. de l'Orante, 1961, p.275, n.452.
[3] Heb. 13,8.

This Word made flesh is Jesus Christ on earth to manifest God's thoughts and will. Everything shows that he comes from heaven and that there is nothing terrestrial in him, except his body which he took from a Virgin's womb[4], with which he clothed himself to speak to us and show us the way to heaven.

Everything in him proves that he is that eternal Word who comes 69

First he is named and declared as such by the angel Gabriel on the day of his conception (Lk.1,26).

The Angel Gabriel, having greeted the Virgin Mary, who had been chosen by God to give physical birth to God's Word, tells her: "Do not fear Mary, for you have found favor with God; you will conceive in your womb and you will bear a son and you will name him Jesus. He will be great; he will be called the *Son of the Most High* and the Lord will give him the throne of David his father.

Mary, fearing for her virginity, asks the angel how this will come about since she is consecrated to God in virginity. The angel reassures her by telling her: The Holy Spirit will overshadow you and the virtue of the Most High will cover you with his shadow; that is why the one who will be born of you, being holy, will be called the *Son of God*. Nothing is impossible with God.

Behold the handmaid of the Lord, be it done to me according to your word.
- his mother is a virgin
- he is conceived by the Holy Spirit
- he is holy 70
- he is called Son of the Most High
- he is called Son of God.

Therefore, it is the eternal Word who takes on a birth, a life in the womb of a virgin, and that is as it should be because a man cannot engender God. Only God can engender his Son. He who thinks is the only one who has the right and the possibility to engender his thought, to express it exteriorly; a stranger cannot express the thought of another. Therefore, it is the Father only who has the right to engender his Word exteriorly, through his Spirit who is love and who produces exterior acts of love. He alone has the right to engender him in time because he alone engendered him from all eternity.

A man cannot say: I gave life to a God, I engendered a God.

It is an angel who announces it to Joseph.

While St. Joseph, Mary's spouse, surprised at Mary's condition,

---

[4] In becoming the Son of God, he wished to insert himself biologically into the human race. On the word terrestrial, see the explanation on page 124.

was thinking of letting her go, an angel appeared to Joseph and told him: do not fear to keep Mary as your spouse for what is born in her is from the Holy Spirit. She will give birth to a son and you will give him the name of Jesus because he is the one who will save his people from their sins. And all this was done to accomplish what the Lord had said through his prophet: behold a Virgin will conceive and bear a son and he will be called Emmanuel, which means God with us. And Joseph kept Mary as his spouse.

The angels proclaimed it at his birth.   At his birth, the angels came down from heaven
and proclaimed that this child brings peace to the world and all glory to God. They tell the shepherds of Bethlehem and proclaim that a Savior is born to them, that this child lying in a manger in Bethlehem is *Christ, the Lord.*
A star announces it to the inhabitants of the East and wise men follow this sign and come to adore him, recognizing him as their king and God.

It is God the Father who proclaims him as His Son on the day of his baptism.   After having received baptism from John, while Jesus was at prayer,
behold the heavens open and the Holy Spirit descends on him in the form of a dove and rests on him. And a voice was heard from heaven saying: You are my beloved Son, with you I am well pleased.

7 1 **And at the transfiguration.**   When Jesus was transfigured on Mount Tabor,
in the presence of three of his apostles who were witnesses to all the great things that were happening among Jesus, Moses and Elijah, a voice came out of the cloud that enveloped them and said: This is my beloved son in whom I am well pleased; listen to him. It is St. John the Baptist who proclaims him the Christ, the true Lamb of God and attests that he is the Son of God (Jn. 1,15). Raising his voice before his disciples and the crowd, St. John said: This is the one of whom I said: he who is to come after me was before me, and it is of his fullness that we have all received, grace for grace, for faith was given through Moses, grace and truth came through Jesus Christ. Nobody has ever seen God, but the only Son who is in the Father is the one who has made him known to us.
(Jn. 1,19): When the Pharisees ask John who he is, he answers that he is not the Christ, nor Elijah, nor the prophet; that he is the voice of one crying in the desert. I baptize in water, but there is oni among you that you do not know, who will come after me, who was before me. He is the one who will baptize in the Holy Spirit and I am not worthy to untie the thong of his sandal (Jn. 1,29). Seeing Jesus come toward him, John said to his disciples:
    Behold the Lamb of God,

behold the one who bears the sins of the world,
behold the one of whom I said: after me comes a man who is over me because he was before me,
and it is so that he may be recognized in Israel that I have come to baptize in water.
John saw the Holy Spirit descend like a dove from heaven and rest on Him. And he who has sent me to baptize told me: The one on whom you see the Holy Spirit descend is the one who will baptize in the Holy Spirit. I saw and I attest that he is the Son of God.

Saint John (Jn. 3,28): Elsewhere, in speaking to the Jews, he says:
You know that I have told you that I am not the Christ but that I have been sent before him. He must increase and I must decrease.
He who comes from above is above everything.   72
He who comes from the earth is earthly.
He who came from heaven is above everything: He attests to what he has seen and heard, yet no one accepts his testimony.
He who has accepted his testimony affirmed that God is truth, for he whom God has sent speaks the language of God, because God does not measure out his spirit[5].
The Father loves the Son and has put everything into his hands.
He who believes in the Son has eternal life.
But he who does not believe in the Son will not see life[6].
But God's anger remains on him.

It is the crowd that follows him that proclaims his divinity.

It is the crowd of sick people that comes from all parts to ask their cure. (Mk, 1,32)

There are the devils themselves who cannot help calling him the Christ and the Son of God. (Mk.3,11)

It is all of nature that obeys his word and bows before him as before its creator. (Mk. 4,31)

---

[5] God gives him the Spirit without measure (Jn. 3,34).
[6] He who refuses to believe in the Son...(Jn. 3,36).

There are the apostles who confess that he is the Christ and go to preach him everywhere after his death. (Mt. 16, 16)

The most striking testimony is that which he gives of himself by his words and actions.

| He speaks as a God, as the Word of God. | He is the divine Word, he is the very Word of God, therefore he must speak as a God himself |

7 3 or rather as the very thought of God, expressed exteriorly in human form, or better, the form is nothing, it is the thought, the intelligence that is everything.
As eternal Word or thought of God, he really comes out of God. It is God who engendered it from all eternity and it became visible, sensitive since the time that he took a body to manifest himself to men, but it is always the same Word, the same thought; it is not the tone of his voice that I examine, that is essential but his thought that those signs express; that is everything, the essential.
And the Word, expressed exteriorly to the world, is always this true interior Word of the Father who truly calls him his Son, because in this exterior human form, there is his eternal Word which he engendered from all eternity.
That is why also, Jesus Christ can always truly call God his Father, because it is God who has truly engendered him from all eternity although he took an exterior form in time. Thus he always calls God his Father and never gives him any other name because he really came out of him and he is the interior Word although he is expressed exteriorly in a visible form.   Just as my thought is always my thought although it may be expressed exteriorly by exterior signs.

He always calls God his Father.

| And God calls him his Son. | This is my beloved son in whom I am well pleased. |

| He calls God his Father in the strict and true sense. | It is not by adoption, like us, that he calls God his Father, but in the strict and true sense. |

Just as the child comes from his father, comes out of his father, has the same nature, the same life, the same power, the same life because he truly comes out of his father. As my thought comes out of me, so Jesus Christ comes out of his Father. That is what he expresses by his divine words.

He came out of God. Before leaving this world, he said to his apostles: I came out of God and I came into the world. I am leaving the world and returning to my Father. To the Jews who called God their Father, he said: If God were your father, you would love me. For it is from God that I proceed and that I come, for I do not come from myself, but it is he who has sent me. And St. John expresses this idea by saying: Nobody has ever seen God. The only Son who is in God is the one who makes him known.

74

He has the same nature as the Father. And Our Lord tells the Jews: my Father and I are one, we are one, that is, the samething. Don't you believe that I am in my Father and my Father is in me? At least, believe it because of my works. Believe in my works so that you may know and believe that my Father is in me and that I am in my Father.

He has the same life as the Father. As the Father has life in himself, he has also given to the Son to have life in himself, eternal life. Before Abraham was, I am. He is called Principle, in him was life and the life was the light of men. He was in the beginning in God, in the beginning was the Word.

He is in the likeness of the Father. He who sees me sees the Father. He who sees me sees the one who has sent me. I am in my Father and my Father is in me.

He is equal to the Father in power and greatness. All power has been given to me in heaven and on earth. My Father is always at work and I work with him. All that the Father does, the Son does as well. All things were made through him and without him nothing was made.
Equal in riches. All things were given to me by my Father. All that is my Father's is mine.

He is worthy of the same honors as the Father. The Father has given all judgement to the Son in order that all honor the Son as they honor the Father. He who does not honor the Son does not honor the Father.

75 **He deserves the same confidence as the Father.**

The will of my Father who sent me is that whoever sees the Son and believes in him have eternal life.

He who believes in me does not believe in me but in the one who sent me. You believe in God, believe also in me.

He may thus justly call himself Son of God.

To Caiaphas who asks him if he is the Son of God, the Christ, he answers: *I am, you have said so.*

To the Jews he says: To me whom the Father has sanctified and sent into the world you say: you blaspheme, because I have said that *I am the Son of God*. If I do not do the work of my Father, do not believe me, but if I do, even if you do not want to believe me, believe in my works, so that you may know and believe that I am in my Father and my Father is in me.

He really speaks as a God.

In fact, what man can speak like that? What man can truly say: God is my real father? I came out of God. I come from God. It is from God that I proceed. God and I, we are one and the same. God is in me and I am in God. I am the life, the principle of all things and just as God has life in Himself, I also have life in myself and no one can take it away from me if I do not wish him to do so. He who sees me sees God himself in me. For I am in God and God is in me. I have all the power of God in heaven and on earth. Everything that God does, I do myself. Everything that God has, I have myself. He who believes in me believes in God and I give eternal life to him who believes in me; such is the will of God. I am the Son of the living God. He who believes in me shall never die and I will raise him up on the last day and he will have eternal life.

Who is the man who has ever dared to speak thus?

What is strongest and most convincing is that he calls his works to witness to his own words.

Indeed, a man could say: I am so and so, I am the son of so and so... count, worker, tailor architect, if he does not prove who he is with his papers or his works, his words are looked upon as void and he is only a liar.

76

But if his works correspond to his words, then he is credible and we are obliged to believe what he says and admit his testimony, his title and identity. That is what Jesus himself does when he brings his works as second witness to his divinity as Word of God. And he is not afraid to say so himself: believe in my works. If I do not do the works of God my Father, do not believe me, but if I do them, *you are obliged to believe in me.* Believe in my works so that you may know and believe that my Father is in me and I am in my Father and that we are one and the same.

Not only does he speak as a God, but he also acts as a God.	He puts into action that word which he speaks to the world: all power has been given to me in heaven and on earth.

Everything that the Father does, the Son does likewise. My Father acts ceaselessly and I act with him. The Jews could have challenged Jesus and said: you say, but you do not do as you say. But to answer everything, Jesus says: Believe in my works and my works are not hidden. I do them before the world, it is the crowd, the people and you yourselves who are witnesses to them every day.

He orders nature and nature obeys him as to a God, its creator; he calms the storm.	When he is on the sea with his disciples and the storm threatens to sink them, the frightened apostles cry out: Lord save us, we perish.

Jesus wakes from his *sleep, for he was asleep,* and tells them: What are you afraid of, men of little faith. And rising, he threatened the wind and said to the sea: be still; and immediately the wind *died* out and there was a great *calm;* and they all were in admiration and a great fear seized them and they said to each other: who is this man? He commands the wind and the sea and they obey him. Ah! It was the creator of the world. *Ipse dixit et facta sunt. Omnia per ipsum facta sunt et sine ipso factum est nihil*[7].

He walks on the waters and makes Peter do the same.	Another time, the apostles were crossing the sea alone and Jesus had remained

on the other shore with the people to send them away after the multiplication of the loaves, and the apostles were wearing themselves out in rowing because the wind was against them. After having rowed for a few hundred yards in the night, they saw Jesus coming toward them, walking on the waters and he made like he was going to pass them by. They thought they were seeing a ghost and they let out a great cry. But Jesus said to them: have faith, it is I, fear not. Peter, having heard the voice of his master, said to the Lord: if it is you, bid me come to you over the waters. And Jesus said: come. And Peter, getting out of the boat, walked on the water to go to Jesus. But for one moment he was afraid because of the violence of the wind and he began to sink, and he cried out: Lord save me, and Jesus, stretching out his hand, grabbed him and said to him: man of little faith, why did you doubt? They

---

[7] He speaks and it is done (Ps. 32,9)
Everything was made through him and without him nothing was made (Jn. 1,2).

took him with them and, when he was in the boat, the wind died down and they reach land in an instant. Those who were in the boat came to adore him saying: In truth, you are the *Son of God*, and their astonishment grew more and more. Because, in fact, they found them-selves before the Master of the world, the eternal Word who is able to command the winds and the seas, and make the waters firm under his feet and under those of his disciples when he wishes. Indeed, who would not have been taken with fear on finding themselves in such company, that of the Son of God?

He commands the fishes of the sea who come into Peter's net.	Jesus had gone into Peter's boat to teach the people whowwere on the shore.

When he was finished he told Peter to put out to sea and throw out the nets to fish. Master, says Peter, we have worked all night and have taken nothing, but at your word, I will cast the net. And they took so many fishes that their nets were breaking and they filled two boats to the point of sinking. On seeing this Peter fell at the feet of Jesus and said: depart from me for I am a sinful man. For they were struck with astonishment at the great catch that they had made.

He multiplied bread in the desert.
(Jn. 6,1)

He changed water into wine at Cana. (Jn. 2,1)

7 8 **He caused a fig tree that had not born fruit to dry up. (Mt. 21.18)**

He is the master of life and death; He commands the sick and the dead and the sick and the dead obey him.	It is the accomplishment of that word which he said: I am the resurrection and the life. He confirms this word by his works the gives health to the sick he gives back life to the dead and he gives it back to himself.

He cured Peter's mother-in-law. (Mk. 1,29)

He cured the man born blind. (Jn. 9,1)

He cured two blind men (Mt. 9,27)

He cured a leper. (Mk. 1,40)

He cured a deaf-mute. (Mk. 7,31)

He cured all the sick who presented themselves. (Mt. 15,29)

He cured a withered hand. (Lk. 6,6)

He cured the paralytic. (Mk. 2,1; Jn. 5,1)

He cured the hemorrhaging woman. (Mk. 5,25)

He cured all those who touched his garments. (Lk. 6,19)
He cured the centurion's servant. (Mt. 8,5)

He cured the son of an officer. (Jn. 4,46)

He cured ten lepers. (Lk. 17,12)

He cured the daughter of the Canaanite woman. (Mt. 15,21)

Summary of all his miracles where we note the infinite power of the one who does them. God is the only one who can act like that. Master of life. He is also Master of death.

He raised the son of the widow of Naim. (Lk. 7, 11)

He raised the daughter of Jairus. (Mk. 5,22)

He raised Lazarus. (Jn. 11,1)

Not only is he Master of the life of others, he is also Master of life for himself.	He himself said: As the Father has life in himself, he has given the Son life in himself.

I lay down my life to take it up again, nobody can take it away from me, but I lay it down myself. I have the power to lay it down and to take it again (Jn.10,18). He remained 40 days and 40 nights without taking any food. In Nazareth, when his enemies chased him out of the Synagogue and brought him to the brink of a high mountain to throw him down, when they arrived at the top of the mountain, he turned around and, passing in the middle of them, he went his way and nobody dared say anything to him. He made himself master of all those rebellious and enemy wills; they have no power on his life, his hour has not yet come.

80 Several times, his enemies come to take him but they cannot lay hands on him; an invisible force prevents them from getting near him: it was not yet the hour to let himself be taken. When they come to take him in the garden, he says only one word to those who question him to take him: It is I, and at these word, they fall back. To show them that he is more powerful than they, and that if they can take him, it is because he allows it, and when he allows them to take him he makes them understand that it is now their hour and the power of darkness.

If he dies on the Cross he gives such a great cry that the soldiers are surprised and cry out: surely, this was the Son of God, truly he was the Son of God. And the most dazzling miracle of all is that he took up his life himself after men had taken it away from him; as he had predicted long before to his apostles.

Reflection on this power that he has over himself[8].

In his infinite wisdom, he knows all things; the future and what is most secret in the hearts of men.

He read in the heart of the Samaritan woman. (Jn. 4,17)

He knew Nathanael without having seen him. (Jn. 1,48)

---

[8] This sentence may announce explanations that never came, or it may be a simple note to prepare explanations to be given orally, or again an invitation to personal meditation.

He knows those who really believe in him and those who do not. (Jn. 6,64)

He knows his disciples interior grumblings on the Eucharist. (Jn. 6,61)

He predicts to Peter his triple denial. (Mt. 26,34)

He announced to Peter his death. (Jn. 21,18)

He announced his own passion to his apostles and how he himself was to die. (Mk. 10,33)

He predicted Judas' betrayal. (Mk. 14,18)
He knew those who were pure and those who were not. (Jn. 13,10)

Not only is he Master of time, he is also Master of eternity:

He forgave the sins of the paralytic. (Mk. 2,5)

Of the sinful woman. (Jn. 7,11)

He promised salvation to the hemorrhaging woman. (Mt. 9, 22)

He promised heaven to the grateful leper. (Lk. 17, 19)

He gave heaven to the good thief. (Lk. 23, 43)

He promised heaven to the one who believes in him. (Jn. 11,25)

He promised it to his apostles who have left all for him. (Mt. 19,27)

What is most astonishing is that he communicates his power to his apostles. (Lk. 9,1)

And the apostles accomplish the same miracles that Jesus Christ himself did. (Lk. 10,17; Acts 3)

The existence of the Church is the greatest miracle there is and the confirmation of all the preceding ones.

Let us not forget the great act of faith in Jesus Christ, Word and Son of God[9].

---

[9] Cf. Introduction, p. 61.

IV

TITLES OF JESUS CHRIST 83

This manner of approaching the person of Christ is traditional[1]. *Here it refers to the bonds that the Son of God contracts with us in his Incarnation: God gives us his Word who becomes everything for us*[2].
These titles of Jesus Christ show him in his work of Savior. We must never neglect this essential aspect of the bonds that exist between Christ and us.
Father Chevrier found these titles in Scripture. Some are only found implicitly, as for example, the title of center. An important place is given to the title of Master that Father often studied, as his manuscripts attest.
Here, for example, is what he had written on a sheet of paper which was stuck to a wall or a board, according to a common practice of his. That is how an idea matured and developed from an outline that he could have always before him as soon as he had a free moment in the midst of a life full of preoccupations from all sides.

85

Necessity of a Master
- necessity - what a divergence of ideas!
- need for a master - one cannot carry on by oneself alone - occupation, apprentice, science, study.
- reason - the world - men - philosophers.

It is to leave the self-styled masters to attach oneself to Jesus Christ: reason, men, one's imagination, oneself. Need for a master.
What do we do without a master? Nothing or badly; in spite of ourselves we seek a master, we are happy to have found one. We feel our incapacity, our smallness - limited, error[3].

In some of Father Chevrier's writings we find other lists of titles, for example:

86

- Sent by God or Messiah
- Son of God
- Son of Man
- Savior-Jesus
- Redeemer
- Priest)
- King) Christ
- Master
- Judge [4]

---

[1] We find this in the Fathers of the Church and we can say that the New Testament itself, in speaking of Christ, borrows titles from the Old Testament: Son of Man, Christ, Prophet, Elected of God, Lamb, etc.
[2] P. 79.
[3] Ms XI 511.
[4] Ms. VIII 133.

Why did Father Chevrier not take such important titles in writing The True Disciple? Here is one explanation.
Some lists of titles were prepared in view of a catechism. The children who come to the Prado to prepare for their First Communion do not always have the faith; at least not an explicit faith. Father Chevrier searched the Gospel to find ways to make them discover progressively the person of Jesus:
With what wisdom and humility and prudence Jesus Christ presents himself to the world; how he goes slowly, prudence, charity! He is called Sent by God, the most simple, most intelligible title; he says that he has nothing to say of himself, he does not impose himself but he comes from God, he does not command, he does not say: I am the Son of God, you must believe... but he opens minds to this great act of faith in him: God his Father. That is how Moses and the prophets acted: It is from God that I speak to you; it is God who orders you: always the same step, the same spirit[5].
It would not be surprising if the same process was proposed to the students of the clerical school. Various manuscripts suggest it.
These various titles are implied in The True Disciple. Suffice it to note that the commentary on the prologue of St. John presents Jesus as the envoy of the Father and that this chapter details the traits of Jesus Christ Savior. St. Paul's exclamation comes to mind: "Before your eyes Jesus Christ was publicly portryed as crucified"[6].
The spiritual experience of 1856 is always present in this meditation of the titles of Jesus Christ. It appears particularly when it is a question of the beauty of Christ, his light.

87 *To have us commune in this experience, Father Chevrier invites us to prayer. He composed the prayer: O Word! O Christ![7] The exercise of faith of which we have spoken[8], blossoms in prayer. In the same sense, other prayers are proposed in various passages[9].*

---

[5] Ms. VIII 152.
[6] Gal., 3,1; cf. the title of King, p. 82.
[7] P.93.
[8] P.61.
[9] Pp. 238, 284, 363.

He was given to us by God to be our Light our Wisdom our Justice our Sanctification and our Redemption. (1 Cor. 1,30)	God could not give us a greater gift, give us a greater treasure than to give us his Word, his adorable Son, because he is everything for us.

89

1. Our Wisdom	He is our wisdom by spreading around us that divine light that enlightens us and shows us the truth and the true value of things.

Since sin, man has lost wisdom because he is no longer enlightened by God but has followed his own lights: he has fallen in all sorts of vices, misfortunes and crimes.

By giving us the true light that is to guide us on the road of life and instruct us.	Jesus Christ was given to us to repare this misfortune and he becomes our Wisdom by enlightening us with his divine lights,

to teach us to distinguish the true and the false, the good and the evil, the just and the unjust, and to judge everything in its proper light, value, to put in their proper place the terrestrial, the spiritual, time and eternity. For that, he is the true light that enlightens every man in this world. He is the Divine Word; in him we find life and life is the light of men. He comes from above, with all the beauty, glory and splendor of the heavens.
Thus he is called

> *Oriens ex alto*
> *sol justitiae*
> *candor lucis aeternae*
> *splendor patris* (Heb. 1)[10]

90

It is not simply a ray of light that comes to us from above, as in the saints and prophets, but the whole divine light which comes to enlighten us in its splendor. Thus Scripture says that a people that walked in darkness saw a great light (Mt. 4,16). The light shone in the darkness (Jn. 1,5).

Nunc lux in domino[11].
So that we may walk as children of light, to be able to distinguish and know the true, the just, the good and the well.

---

[10] Light from on high (Lk.1,78), Sun of justice (Mt. 3,20), brilliance of the eternal light (Wis. 7,26), Splendor of the Father.

[11] Now you are light in the Lord (Eph. 5,9).

In lumine tuo videbimus lumen[12].
So that you may be children of light and of the day (1 Thes. 5,5).
Our Lord does not fear to tell us himself that he is the light of the world: *Ego sum lux mundi*.
When God creates the world, he gives the sun to enlighten the eyes of our body. But when God creates our souls, he gives Jesus Christ, his Word, to enlighten our souls and our intelligences, because he was life and life was the light of men. It is through Jesus Christ that we receive life and light, and the true light, Lux vera, to distinguish this light from above from all those other little human and terrestrial lights that often come to enlighten our darkened souls with their false light.
Jesus Christ is the light of our souls like the sun is the light of our bodies. Just like the sun delights our eyes, enlightens us, shows us objects, makes us know and appreciate each thing and shows us the way to take, shows us the value and color of things, and the use that we must make of them. What immense benefits the sun has for our bodies!
Thus Jesus Christ is the Sun of our intelligences and our souls. It is in his light that we must learn to know each thing, to know the truth, the spiritual value of every terrestrial thing, to know the true from the false, the just from the unjust, the good from the bad.
How much greater is this spiritual knowledge of things than the material knowldege that the sun gives us of visible and created things! Therefore, when we want to know something, judge it, give it its value, we need only seek the light of Christ and he will enlighten us and teach us what it is worth and how we must estimate it, know what he thinks about it, what he does with it... and we will have the true light... the true judgement of things. By the very fact that he is our true light, he is our wisdom, because if we act according to this light we will not be mistaken; if we act according to this light we will not get lost. If we appreciate things in this light, we will judge justly, because he is the true light that comes from heaven and which came out of God himself to enlighten us.
For the light from heaven is divine wisdom. In him are all the treasures of knowledge and wisdom (Col. 2,3). He grew in age and in wisdom before God and men, and grace was in him. Full of grace and truth[13].

---

[12] In your light, we see light (Ps. 36,10).

[13] Ms. XI 147 -
He is knowledge and truth, He teaches us truth, makes us know the true from the false, the real good, what the world is; the wisdom of the world is folly for Jesus Christ and the wisdom of Jesus Christ is folly for the world. This wisdom permeates his whole life; his actions, his words, are so many traits of wisdom and light that enlighten us and show us howtwe are to act to be truly wise.

2. Our Justice.

It is he who makes us just. He is called the sun of justice. *Sol justitiae* and Saint Paul tells us: may you be filled with the fruits of righteousness which come through Jesus Christ, to the glory and praise of God. We become just through him by accomplishing the law which he gave us. It is he who has given us the divine law that we must follow, the precepts and counsels that we must observe and that will make us just in the eyes of God by making us walk in the way that God himself has marked for us by his Son. For love of us, God treated his Son, who did not know sin, as if he had been sin itself, making his own Son die on the cross so that in him we should become just of the justice that comes from God (2 Cor. 5, 21).

3. Our Sanctification.

Again, it is he who makes us saints by giving us the grace that purifies and sanctifies souls. It is of his fullness that we have received grace for grace, says Saint John. Grace and truth have come to us through Jesus Christ (Jn. 1,17). He himself is full of grace and truth (Jn. 1,14). He sanctifies us, makes us holy by the sacraments that he established. Since sin had entered into the world, sin reigned in us. But Jesus Christ expelled it by his grace. We become holy in God's eyes by Jesus Christ. From impious and evil that we were, we become holy through Jesus Christ. He is our sanctifier.

He is our rule of conduct, our model and we must constantly look at this light to see how we ourselves must act.

In great men we sometimes find a grain of wisdom, a small ray of that light that enlightens us, but Jesus Christ is the whole Wisdom. Man cannot reach the whole Wisdom but Jesus Christ posesses it entirely because the Holy Spirit was not measured out t him

We need not go far to find wisdom; it is in Jesus Christ. It suffices to know, to study Jesus Christ.

Some seek him in great books, in philosophies, in voyages, in study, it is in Jesus Christ.
I only know Jesus Christ, says Saint Paul, and Jesus Christ crucified.

      We are only wise in Jesus Christ

      ....

      We will only be just in Jesus Christ

      ....

      We will only be holy in Jesus Christ.

We simplify this finale to highlight the three affirmations that conclude each paragraph.

4. **Our Redemption.** It is he who redeemed us by giving himself up for us, by paying out debt to his Father,
by accomplishing the penance that we had merited by our sins, by dying for us on a cross, like a guilty person, like the worst criminal in the world, because he wished to bear our sins.
Behold the lamb of God who bears the sins of the world. Jesus redeemed us from the curse of the law, making himself cursed for us (Gal. 3, 13).

9 3 For love of us, God treated his Son who did not know sin, as if he were sin itself, making his own Son die on the cross so that we might become just of the justice that comes from God (II Cor. 5,21). Jesus was given over to death to atone for our sins (Rom. 6,25). He abolished the decree of our condemnation by nailing it to the cross (Col. 11,14).

Jesus King notebook[14].

5. **He is our King.** He comes to govern us, to command us.

Our only King. God, the great and only king of the world, established him king of men, as we see in the psalms and the prophets.

I will give you all the nations in heritage. He will rule from sea to sea. On the day of his conception, the angel proclaimed his future greatness and royalty. He will be great and will be called the Son of God and the Lord will give him the throne of David his Father and he will reign over the house of Jacob and his kingdom will have no end (Lk. 1,32). Saint John the Baptist prepared his kingdom. At his birth the kings themselves came to adore him asking in Jerusalem where the king of the Jews was born. During his life he is proclaimed king by the people who bless his name and his kingdom. Some acclaim him, others deny him. We have no other king but Caesar. *Nolumus hunc regnare super nos*[15].

When Pilate asked him if he was a king, he answered: Yes, I am. For this I was born, and for this I have come into the world, to bear witness to the truth. Every one who is of the truth hears my voice (Jn. 18,37).

He explains in what his kingship consists: he is king of truth. My kingdom is not of this world; if my kingdom were of this world, my supporters would certainly fight for me, but my kingdom is not of this world. This kingship of Jesus Christ does not depend on soldiers, fortresses, houses, boundries.
It is a spiritual kingship.

---

[14] Here Father Chevrier uses a separate study, which explains the greater development.
[15] We do not want him for king (Lk. 19,14).

It is the kingship of truth.
He is the king of truth. *Ego sum veritas.*
I came to give witness to the truth.
This kingdom is not limited, truth has no limits, no frontiers, it is everywhere, it is the inheritance of souls. Whoever loves truth takes Jesus Christ for his king.
This kingdom is not defended by arms, fortresses or soldiers. It is the kingdom of souls, it is in the whole universe, everyone is called to it, everyone can enter in it.
It is the only true kingship, it is the only true kingdom; the others are only terrestrial kingdoms who quarrel over a piece of land, who seek only land and men. Jesus' kingdom is very different, far superior. The head of this spiritual kingdom is very different from other kings. The kings of the earth have magnificent castles, he has only a stable as shelter and during his life he will have nowhere to lay his head. The other kings have a crown of gold on their heads, he has a crown of thorns; (his) throne? a cross. The others have purple and gold cloaks, he has only rags to cover himself. The others have a gold scepter, he has only a reed as sign of his royalty. And yet, in spite of this attire, so poor, so dispicable, Pilate shows him to the people saying: behold your king. The true meaning of these royal insignia: they are true and just for this king of truth.
How does this kingdom exist in the world?
This kingdom of truth really exists. It was established 1870 years ago and nobody has been able to destroy it, it works. It has its head, its officers, its soldiers, its subjects, its enemies and it is spread throughout the world. What a beautiful kingdom is that of Jesus Christ! What a great king is Jesus Christ! How small are the kings of the earth before Jesus Christ, the only true king of the universe and of men! Let us bow before Jesus Christ our king and let us hail him as our true and only king.
Rex regum, Dominus dominantium; sedenti in throno et agno benedictio honor et gloria in saecula saeculorum[16].
And it is at the end of the world that he will appear under the beautiful title of king, when he comes to judge the world, reward those who have served him and punish those who would have disobeyed him. Then he will give paradis to the good and condemn the evil to hell. Then will begin the eternal reign of Jesus Christ in heaven. How great that kingdom will be! How beautiful that kingdom will be! How numerous will be this kingdom! since Jesus Christ until the end of time and before him all those who hoped in him. A kingdom holy, pure. Where there will no longer be the reign of Satan, where everything will be in justice and charity, where we will bow before the 24 elders to sing, the virgins, the martyrs, the saints..... Oh! the beautiful kingdom of Jesus Christ!

---

[16] King of kings and Lord of lords (1 Tim. 6,15). To the one who sits on the throne and to the Lamb, praise honor, glory and power forever (Apoc. 5,13).

6. He is our sole master[17].

We give the title of Master to the one who teaches and instructs us. Jesus Christ is our sole and unique master. He is the Word of God in whom are all the treasures of knowledge and wisdom. As Word, he is the very thought of God, he possesses all knowledge of God, the the Father's knowledge. He is the word of the Father, adorned with an exterior form to speak to us; he comes from heaven to speak to us and make us know the will of God his Father. He himself is the living letter that the Father has sent us so that we may read it and accomplish it.

It is God himself who teaches it to us: Behold my servant that I have chosen, my beloved in whom I am well pleased, I will let my spirit rest on him and he will proclaim justice to the nations (Is. 42,1).

On the day of his transfiguration, it is the Father who proclaims him saying: behold my beloved Son in whom I am well pleased: hear him (Mt. 17,5). God so loved the world that he gave his only Son so that all who believe in him may not perish but have eternal life (Jn. 3,16).

---

[17] Ms. XI 26.

Necessity of a master - We cannot lead ourselves alone. Our ignorance is so great, our reason so little enlightened, we are so apt to make a mis-take, have illusions, take the evil for the good, the false for the true.

Qualities of this Master. If we need a master for material things, to learn to read, to write, the profane sciences, to learn a trade, a state...how much more do we need a Master to lead us in spiritual things... In him we want to find a superiority of authority and intelligence... In him we want to find truth, holiness, justice, sound doctrine that does not mislead us...; examples in conformity to his words, something from heaven on which we can lean without fear, a sure and solid foundation, something infallible in the one to whom we can give ourselves with confidence. That is so important for the faith and the conduct that we are toihold.

Where to find such a master? We will not find him among men, nor in our-selves. I feel that I can go wrong and I feel that all men can also go wrong. Therefore, that master will not be among men; he will have to come from God, that he come from heaven, that God send him to instruct us; otherwise there is nothing solid, nothing sure, nothing certain.

Was God able to refuse us this Master? No. God who created us in his image, who created us with intelligence, who gave us the knowledge of the good, the beautiful, the true, evil, could not leave us to go haphazardly without instructing us, without being concerned with us, and without making us arrive at the end for which he created us: he had to give us a master. God so loved the world that he gave it his only Son so that whoever believes in him may have eternal life. That is my well-beloved Son in whom I am well pleased: hear him.

Who is this Master? It is Jesus Christ. He alone fullfils all the conditions that we ask of a true master, as we wish him and as we have a right to ask for.

His great role is to instruct the world. That is what he explained to the people of Nazareth when he explained the words of the prophet Isaiah.
The Spirit of God is upon me. That is why he has consecrated me by his divine unction and he has sent me to evangelize the poor (Lk. 4,18). He would say to his disciples: Let us go preach; that is why I came. *Ad hoc veni.*
I must evangelize the kingdom of God; that is why I came (Lk. 4,43). I was born and came into the world to give witness to the truth, to teach in truth (Jn. 18,37). I am the light of the world; as long as I am in the world, I am the light of the world (Jn. 9,5). I am the way, the truth and the life (Jn. 14,6).

It is his title. And to his disciples he said: You call me Master and Lord, and you do well, for I am (Jn. 13,13). One only is your Master; the Christ (Mt. 23, 8). The Samarita woman said to him: when the Messiah will come, he will teach us all things. Jesus answered: I who speak to you am he (Jn. 4,25).

What he teaches he does so only according to his Father who sent him. My doctrine is not of myself but of the one who sent me (Jn. 7,16).
The one who sent me is true and what I have heard from him I speak in the world. The words that I have spoken to you I do not say of myself but my Father who is in me himself does these works (Jn. 14,10). I speak of what I have seen in my Father; I, a man, who have told you the truth that I have heard from my Father (Jn. 8,38). The word that I have spoken to you is not from me but from my Father who sent me (Jn. 14,24). I have not spoken of myself but my Father who sent me has told me what to say and what I must speak and I know that his commandment is eternal life; thus, what I say, I say as my Father has commanded me to do (Jn. 12,49).

He knows God the Father. He knows God the Father, he is his Word, therefore, he is always with him and in him (Jn. 8,35).
Nobody has ever seen God, but the only Son who is in the Father is the one who makes him known to us (Jn. 1,18). No one has ever gone up to heaven except the one who has come down, the Son of God who is in heaven (Jn. 3,13). The one who sent me is with me and he does not leave me alone because I always do what pleases him (Jn. 8,29). You are from below, I am from above. I am not of this world (Jn. 8.23). Thus, he can speak the truth: You believe in God, believe also in me (Jn. 14,1). He who believes in me believes not in me but in the one who sent me (Jn. 12,44). In truth, I tell you, the one who listens to my words and believes in the one who sent me has eternal life; he has gone from death to life (Jn. 5,24). Thus, he is truly our Master. He alone has the right to teach us the eternal truths. He has received from God the great role of teaching men, that is why he has been sent; he

alone can instruct us because he alone knows God and has received orders to do so. In listening to him we listen to God himself and in believing in him we have eternal life. He is our Master.

The apostles do not call him anything but Master.

When they are on the sea and the storm is threatening to submerge them, they cry out: Master save us, we perish (Lk. 8,24).

When Jesus asks the crowd who has touched him, Peter says, Master, the crowd is pressing you for all sides, and you ask who touched you? (Lk. 8, 45). John, speaking to our Lord says: Master, we saw a man casting demons in your name and we forbade him because he does not follow with us (Lk. 9,49). Seeing a man born blind, the apostles asked Jesus: Master, who has sinned, himself or his parents, for him to be blind? (Jn.9,2). When Jesus says to his apostles: let us return to Judea, they answer: Master, the Jews want to stone you and you want to return to Judea? (Jn. 11, 8). James and John want to obtain a favor from Jesus and they say: Master, we want you to do for us whatever we ask of you (mk. 10,35). Passing by the dried up fig tree, Peter says to Jesus: Master, the fig tree that you cursed is dried up (Mk. 11,21). Not having understood the meaning of a parable, the apostles say to Jesus: Master, explain this parable to us (Mt. 15,15). In seeing the beautiful stones of the temple, the apostles exclaim: Master, see what beauful stones and what a beautiful building! (Mk. 13,1). Wanting to know when the end of the world was to occur, the apostles ask: Master, when will all those things happen? (Lk. 21,7). Judas himself, when he greets Jesus to betray him, says: Hail, Master (Mt. 26,49). Finally, it is always this title that they give because they had recognized in him that divine right to instruct them and teach them, which was the great role of the Savior Messiah.

Others also give that title and do not call him otherwise; that was the authority of his word, so penetrated were they all by this great role of the savior with regard to them.

99 Martha

When Martha called her sister to tell her that Jesus was there she said: Mary, the Master is s calling you (Jn. 11,28).

Magdalene

Recognizing Jesus after the Resurrection, Magdalene has no other name for him than Rabboni, Master (Jn. 20,16).

Scribes and Pharisees

The scribes and pharisees themselves do not give any other name when they speak of him.

A scribe wants to become his disciple and he says: Master, I will follow you wherever you go (Mt. 8,19). The pharisees said to the disciples: Why does your Master eat with sinners (Mk. 2,16). The pharisees and the scribes said to Jesus: Master, we would like to see a sign (Mt. 12,38). After the multiplication of the loaves, the crowd found Jesus who had taken refuge in Capharnaum and said to him: Master, how did you get here? (Jn. 6,26). The father of the possessed boy, having brought his son to Jesus for a cure, falling on his knees, says: Master, I have brought you my son (Mk. 9,16). The lepers, raising their voice, say to Jesus: Master, have mercy on us (Lk. 17,13). Bringing the woman caught in adultery to Jesus to have her condemned, the pharisees say: Master, this woman has just been caught (Jn.7,4). A young man, wishing to know from Jesus what he must do to go to heaven says: Good Master, what must I do to have eternal life? (Lk. 18,18). The blind man of Jericho cries out: Master, that I may see! (Mk. 10,51). The pharisees, indignant at all the praise that Jesus was receiving said: Master, rebuke your disciples (Lk. 19,39). A doctor of the law questions Jesus and says: Master, which is the greatest commandment? (Mt. 22,35). Thus, it was the ordinary title that was given to Jesus. It must also be the one that we give him. For us, his word must be that of the Master, a true word, an infallible word, the word of God. The Master has spoken, it suffices. To whom shall we go? You alone have the words of eternal life. Verba mea spiritus et vita sunt[18]. He who believes in me has eternal life.

7. He is our head.

To guide us, he is our head. Our first. Our leader and we must follow him.

And you, land of Judah, you are not the least among the cities of Judah, for it from you that will come forth the leader who will lead his people (Mt. 2,6). In him dwells the fullness of divinity and he is the head (Col. 2,10). In these last times, God has spoken to us through his Son and since he is the splendor of the Father, the glory, the perfect image of his substance, he has raised him above the angels because his name is greater than theirs (Heb. 1,2-4). He is before everything (Col. 1,17). God has raised him above everything and given him a name that is above every name (Phil. 1,2). God has put everything under his feet (Heb. 1,22), and given him as head to the Church (Eph. 5,23). Jesus is the head of his body, the Church (Eph. 5,23). I want you to know that Christ is the head of every man (1 Cor. 11,3). We grow in all things in Jesus Christ as in our head (Eph. 4,15). He is the head of the body, the Church, the first-born from the dead that in everything he might be pre-eminent,for in him all the fullness of God was pleased to dwell (Col. 1,18). I want you to know that Jesus Christ is the head of every man (1 Cor. 11,3). He is the head of the Church (Eph. 5,23). It is in the head that is found intelligence, the eye that sees, the ear that hears, the word that commands. We are the members. He leads us. Ego sum via[19].

---

[18] My words are spirit and life (Jn. 6,64).
[19] I am the way (Jn. 14,6).

Follow me. He who follows me does not walk in darkness. Let us have no other head but him.

8. He is our model.

He is perfection itself. He is the image of the invisible God (Col. 1,15). The image of God (2 Cor. 4,4). The stamp of his nature (Heb. 1,3). Splendor partis[20]. Speculum[21], he who sees me sees the Father. Thus, in seeing him we see the invisible God with all his perfections. In imitating him we are sure to act wisely. This is my beloved Son in whom I am well pleased (Mt. 17,5). On earth, he took the form of a man in order to give us an example. I have given you an example so that you also may do as I have done (Jn. 13,15). Sicut et ipse ambulavit et nos debemus ambulare[22]. Imitatores mei estote secut et ego Christi[23]. He is perfection itself. Ego sum via, voie[24].

---

[20] Splendor of the Father.
[21] Mirror.
[22] As he (Christ) acted, so too must we act (1 Jn. 2,6).
[23] Be imitators of me as I am of Christ (1 Cor. 4,16).
[24] Ms X 738 - Ms X 642

Sacerdos alter Christus

That is our motto. Jesus is the priest par excellence, he is the true priest, he is the wellbeloved of the Father. He is our model. Our duty is to imitate him.

There are two ways of being another Jesus Christ: by the powers and by the virtues. The one who only resembles Jesus Christ by the powers is only a mechanical man, useless, without fruit, who indicates the way without going himself, who saves others without saving himself. A sign post that indicates the road, whose writing is often erased, a clanging cymbal, a canal that lets the water flow without keeping anything.

To be truly another Jesus Christ, we must resemble Jesus Christ in his virtues. That is what the true resemblance between the priest and Jesus Christ consists of. Therefore, it is very important that we study the life and virtue of Jesus Christ to conform our lives, our doctrine, our words and our works to it. Everything that Jesus Christ did on earth in terms of virtue, the priest must seek to do also; everything that he said of himself, the priest must seek to be able to say it also and have others say it. To resemble Jesus Christ, then, is our continuous work, the constant attention of our spirit and the sincere desire of our heart (Ms. X 738).

Everything that Jesus Christ said of himself, the priest should be able to say of himself. Our union to Jesus Christ must be so intimate, so visible, so perfect that, on seeing us, men must be able to say: behold another Jesus Christ. We must reproduce, exteriorly and interiorly, Jesgs Christ's virtues, his poverty, his sufferings, his prayer, his charity. We must represent the poor Jesus Christ in the crib, Jesus Christ suffering his passion, Jesus Christ allowing himself to be eaten in the Holy Eucharist (Ms X 642).

9. The Principle and Creator of all things.

When the Jews ask him who he is, he answers: The principle, I who speak to you (Jn.8,25).

It is through him that all things in heaven and on earth were made, all things visible and invisible, thrones and dominations, principalities and powers, all were created through him and for him (Col. 1,26). In the beginning was the Word and the Word was in God. Everything was made by him and nothing was made without him (Jn. 1,1). He is the principle, the first born, because it pleased the Father that all fullness dwell in him (Col. 1,18-19). There is only one God who is Father from whom all things have their being and who has made us for himself; and there is only one Lord who is Jesus Christ, through whom all things were made and through whom we are all what we are (1 Cor. 8,6).

10. He is the foundation of all things.

That is to say that all things must rest on him.

Noone can place other foundations than those that have been placed, and this foundation is Jesus Christ (1 Cor. 3,11). Omnia in ipso constant (Col. 1,17). Everything rests in him. Everything is supported by him. Nothing solid can subsist without him. You are built on the foundation of the apostles, united to Jesus Christ who is himself the cornerstone on which the whole building rests and rises to form a temple (Eph. 2,19). Walk in the ways of our Lord Jesus Christ, rooted and built on him as on your foundation (Col. 2,6). Take Jesus Christ away from the earth and what solid foundation is left? None. All that is left is men; but men cannot be solid foundations if they themselves are not supported by God. Nisi Dominus aedificaverit Domum in vanum laboraverunt qui aedificant eam. Nisi Dominus costodierit civitatem frustra vigilat qui costodit eam[25]. Therefore, those who wish to build and construct anything without Jesus Christ are mistaken and build only ruins. He is the stone that has become the cornerstone of God's building, in heaven and on earth. Whoever falls on this stone will be broken and whomever it falls upon will be crushed (Mt. 21,44). The comparison that Jesus Christ uses at the end of his sermon on the mount: the one who hears the word of God and puts it into practice is like a man who builds on a rock; nothing will shake that house. But he who hears and does not practice builds on sand: his house will fall. Thus we must build on Jesus Christ, on his word and put it into practice, and our house will be built on rock[26].

---

[25] If the Lord does not build the house, in vain do the workers labor. If the Lord does not guard the city, in vain do the guards keep vigil (Ps. 126,1).

[26] Ms. X 21 - X 635

Jesus Christ spiritual foundation. (Fundamental article in the first prepratory drafts of TD).

It is vain to try to build if God is not with us, if he is not the architect, if he does not direct the work, give the plan, choose the workers and direct everything himself. One bad stone or

104 **11. He is the root from which we must draw the sap that will give us life.**

In a tree, it is the root that we do not see that is the most important part. It gives life to the whole tree; it sends the sap to all the leaves and makes them live.

So too for Our Lord. He is for us that root, that vivifying sap that communicates spiritual and divine life. I am the vine, you are the branches. He who remains in me and I in him bears much fruit, because without me you can do nothing (Jn. 15,5). I am the living bread come down from heaven. If someone eats of this bread, he will live forever (Jn. 6,51). He who receives me will live through me. In him was life and the life was the light of men (Jn. 1,4). The living bread is the one who came down from heaven and who gives life to the world. I am the bread of life. He who comes to me shall not hunger. He who believes in me shall not thirst (Jn. 6,35). Walk in the ways of Jesus Christ, rooted in him and built on him as on your foundation (Col. 2,). Speaking truth in love, we are to grow up in every way into him who is the head, into Christ, from whom the whole body, joined and knit together by every joint with

---

one that is badly placed and the whole structure will be shaken. Omnia per ipsum et cum ipso et in ipso (*Everything through him, with him and in him*) .

Thus, it is Jesus Christ that we must seek, it is on him that we must build, it is for him that we must build, it is his spirit that we must seek, it is him that we must seek and place as the foundation of everything...

The knowledge, study of Jesus Christ, prayer; that is the first thing to do to become a stone in God's spiritual building. Only what is founded on Jesus Christ can last; what is founded on another cannot last nor be solid. Thus all exterior acts of obedience, humility, charity, exterior mortification are nothing if they do not issue from the knowledge of Jesus Christ, the love of Jesus Christ and if Jesus Christ is not the principle. Those exterior things come naturally when the life of Jesus Christ is in them; on the contrary, they are only illusory, forced or hypocritical actions when they doenot come from the principle which is Jesus Christ. Thus, it is up to him to do every-thing; to choose, call, build, reject, call whom he pleases.

All that we can do is to show the way, to make known what Our Lord himself said, the way that he followed, then it is up to each one to see if he wants to follow Our Lord in this way and take his plahe in God's House.

It does not suffice to begin with God, we must act and finish with God. All that I see my Father do, I do with him. Enter yourselves intoethe structure of this building as living stones, to become part of a spiritual house and an order of holy priests in order to offer to God spiritual sacrifices that are agreeable to him (1 Pt.2,5).

Jesus Christ must be the one to choose the stones of his house (X 21). One bad stone or one that is badly placed can shake the house, make it fall. Who would dare meddle in the construction of a building? dare be the architect, do the work, be God's architect or God himself? Let God do it (X 635).

which it is supplied, when each part is working properly, makes bodily growth and upbuilds itself in love (Eph. 4,15).

12. He is the center on which everything must converge.

In a circumference, there is a center from which all the rays emerge and to which all the rays converge.

It is the center where everything meets and from which everythings goes out. Jesus Christ is also the center where everything must meet and from which everything must go out. To go to heaven, one must pass through this center. The crib, Calvary, the tabernacle: are they not the centers where all men must go to receive life, peace and go forth from there to go to God? That is what St. Paul explains: God has abundantly poured the wealth of his grace upon us, filling us with intelligence and wisdom, to make us know the mystery of his will, according to his good pleasure, according to which he proposes himself, after the accomplishment of the alloted time, to reunite all things in Jesus Christ, everything that is in heaven and on earth. 105 And it is in him that we have been called (Eph. 1,1). He is our peace, who of the two peoples makes only one, breaking in his flesh the wall of separation, that enmity that divided them and forming in himself, one man of the two peoples by making peace between them, to reconcile them to God by his cross, having united them in one body. It is through him that we all have access to the Father in the same spirit. You are no longer strangers or sojourners but fellow citizens (Eph. 2,14). There is no longer Greek or Gentile or Barbarian. We are all one in Jesus Christ. In ipso. Per ipsum et cum ipso[27]. Omnia vestra sunt. Vos autem Christi. Christus autem Dei[28].

There are no longer Jews or Gentiles, slaves or freemen, men or women: you are all one in Jesus Christ (Gal. 3,28). Admirable fusion which unites us in Jesus Christ, sole center in which we must all fuse entirely.

13. He is the end toward which everything must tend.

He is our end, he must be the end of our thoughts, desires, actions and our life and he must be the one toward whom we must tend with all the strength of our soul.

It is in Jesus Christ that all God's promises have their truth and it is also through him that they are all accomplished for the honor of God and our glory (2 Cor. 1,20). It is before him that we will appear one day to render an account of all our actions; he will then be our reward if we have loved and served him. He who believes in me has eternal life. To see Jesus Christ, to possess him will be our eternal happiness. Whether we live or die, we belong to Jesus Christ (Rom. 14,8). He who does not go

---

[27] In him, through him and with him (conclusion of the Eucharistic prayer of the Roman Missal).

[28] Everything is yours. But your are Christ's and Christ is Gods (1 Cor. 3,23).

to Jesus Christ goes to death. He must therefore be the end of our works, our actions, the end of our whole life; we belong to him in every way.

106 **14. He is resurrection and life.** First of all, resurrection in this world by making us pass from the death of sin to the life of grace.
Resurrection by calling us one day from the grave to give us eternal life. Resurrection of souls, resurrection of bodies, spiritual life, eternal life. I am the resurrection and the life. He who believes in me, even if he were dead, will live and whoever lives and believes in me will never die (Jn. 11,25). In truth, I tell you, whoever listens to my word and believes in the one who sent me has eternal life and will not be judged, but he has passed from death to life (Jn. 5,24). The Father raises the dead and gives them life, thus the Son gives life to whom he wants (Jn. 5,21). As the Father has life in himself, thus he gives it to the Son to have life in himself. The hour has come when the dead will hear the voice of the Son of God and those who will hear it shall live (Jn. 5,25). As all died in Adam, all have life in Jesus Christ (1 Cor. 15,22; Eph. 2,1). I will raise him up on the last day (Jn. 6,40). I am the life. I am the living bread come down from heaven. He who eats of this bread has eternal life and I will raise him up on the last day.

Summary of the titles and of grandeurs of Our Lord Jesus Christ.

Jesus Christ is the Eternal Word. This Word God who was in God from the beginning and who as engendered by the Father, is eternal like the Father and also God like him.

It is through him that all things were made and nothing was made without him. In him was life and that life was the light of men. He came on earth to enlighten the world with his divine light, he is the true light.
Because he himself is the sun from above, the brilliance of the eternal light,
    the splendor of the Father,
    the figure of his infinite substance,
    the image of the invisible God,
107   the eternal wisdom,
    the infinite beauty of heaven become visible on earth.
It is the mirror in which God contemplates and reproduces himself.
It is that divine light that opens our eyes to the true light, to make us know God and make us love him.
He was given to us to be
    our wisdom,
    our justice,
    our sanctification,
    our redemption.

He is the way, the truth and the life.
He is our king, our master, our head and our model.
He is the principle of all things, he is the foundation on which everything must rest, the root from which we must draw the sap that is to give us life, the center toward which everything must converge, the end to which everything must tend. Finally he is the resurrection and the life.

Behold Jesus Christ!

O Word! O Christ! 108

How beautiful you are! How great you are!
Who can know you? Who can understand you?
Grant, O Christ, that I may know you and love you. Since you are light, let one ray of that divine light come to my poor soul so that I may see you and understand you. Give me a great faith in you so that all you words may be for me so many lights that enlighten me and make me go to you and follow you in all the ways of justice and truth.

O Christ! O Word!

You are my Lord and my one an only Master.
Speak, I want to listen to you and put your word into practice. I want to listen to your divine word, because I know that it comes from heaven. I want to listen to it, meditate it, put it into practice because in your word there is life, joy, peace and happiness. Speak Lord, you are my Lord and my Master and I want to listen to none but you[29].

---

[29] Ms XI 162.

O Word! O Christ! How great you are! How beautiful you are! Who can know you? Who can understand you?n Grant, O Christ, that I may know and love you. Let me look at you, O infinite beauty! Take away a little of your great light so that my eyes may contemplate you a little and see your divine perfections. Open my ears to your divine word so that I may hear your voice and meditate your divine teachings. Open my mind and my intelligence so that your word may penetrate to my heart and that I may be able to taste and understand.

O Word! O my Master! O my Head and my King! Speak. I wish to listen to that divine word because I know that it comes from heaven; I want to listen to it, to meditate it, to put in into practice because in that word there is life, joy and happiness.

Speak Lord, I want to listen to you.

Speak Lord, you are my Master and I want to have no other Master but you.

V

ATTACHMENT TO JESUS CHRIST 109

This part presents the effects of knowing Jesus Christ. For the one who gives himself to this knowledge, it necessarily produces love[1]. 111
We can compare the first pages[2] *to the degrees of love in St. John of the Cross*[3] *or to the degrees of humility in St. Ignatius of Loyola*[4].
This chapter obliges us to give a spiritual meaning to the whole book. That is to say that all the demands of evangelical life put forth afterwards can only be understood as visible fruits of a grace that is invisible in itself. It is not a matter only of a love that is logical in itself; it is a grace that makes grace fruitful[5].
The primary result of this knowledge of Jesus Christ is an attitude of simplicity. This evangelical simplicity is the required disposition for a spiritual accomplishment of the priestly ministry[6].
Father Chevrier outlines this spiritual concept - charismatic, we might say - of the ministry through partly contestable explanations on good priests, the bad ones and the perfect ones. In a footnote, we put an older text where he approaches the question by the classical distinction between the two ways: the one of the precepts and the other of the counsels.
Here again he has to make an effort in speculative theology where he is not at ease. He tries to dispel the objections that he has heard and which we have to discern behind his text: if you wish to remain in the ranks of the secular clergy, do like everybody else, if not, address yourself to a religious congregation[7]. *A certain impatience with these objections make him say inaccurate things about religious who would not find recognize themselves in them*[8]. *Vatican II renewed the manner of* 112
approaching this question.
We must not stop at the more or less apt and polemical refutation but at the conviction that he wants to communicate: the situation of the priest who is to live among men is in itself an invitation to evangelical perfection.

---

[1] P. 100.
[2] PP. 99-102.
[3] Saint Jean de la Croix, Oeuvres spirituelles, Paris, Ed du Seuil, 1947, pp. 635-645.
[4] Saint Ignace de Loyola, Exercises spirituels, Paris Ed. de l'Orante, 1956, pp. 83-84.
[5] PP. 102-104.
[6] PP. 105-110.
[7] P. 235, note 10.
[8] See also p. 118.

To know Jesus Christ is everything

Everything is enclosed in the knowledge of God and of our Lord Jesus Christ. 1 1 3

Haec est vita aeterna ut cognoscant te solum Deum verum et quem misisti Jesum Christum[9].

Jesus Christ is the eternal Word
    the living word of the Father on earth
    his knowldege and his wisdom.

In him are all the treasures of knowledge and wisdom. Thus Saint Paul wished for his faithful nothing else but to know Jesus Christ. I bend my knees before the Father of Our Lord Jesus Christ, from whom every family in heaven and on earth is named, that according to the riches of his glory he may grant you to be strengthened with might through his Spirit in the inner man, and that Christ may dwell in your hearts through faith; that you, being rooted and grounded in love, may have power to comprehend with all the saints what is the breadth and length and height and depth, and to know the love of Christ which surpasses knowledge, that you may be filled with all the fulness of God. Now to him who by the power at work within us is able to do far more abundantly than all that we ask or think, to him be glory in the Church and in Christ Jesus to all generations, for ever and ever (Eph. 3,14). No study, no science must be prefered over this one. It is the most necessary, the most useful, the most important, especially for the one who wants to be a priest, his disciple, because only this knowledge can make priests. The other sciences are but secondary and circumstancial.

He who has found Jesus Christ has found the greatest treasure.

Everything else is nothing. Heaven and earth will pass away, but my words will not pass away. 1 1 4

He has found wisdom, light, life, peace, joy, happiness on earth and in heaven, the solid foundation on which he can build, forgiveness, grace, he has found everything. Super aurum et topazion[10].

(qui me invenerit inveniet vitam)[11].

He who believes in me has eternal life. He will never hunger, he will never thirst. He will never die and even if he dies, he shall live. I am the way, the truth and the life. Come to me all you who labor and I will give you rest. You do not want tor-

---

[9] Eternal life is to know you, the only true God and him whom you have sent, Jesus Christ (Jn. 17,3).

[10] More than gold or topaz (Ps. 118).

[11] He who finds me finds life (Pr., 8,35).

come to me to have life? he said to the Jews. Ut vitam habeant et abundantium habeant[12].

He esteems nothing above Jesus Christ.   Because Jesus Christ is all for him. St. Paul expresses it very well. Whatever gain I had (*before my conversion*), I counted as loss for the sake of Christ. Indeed I count everything as loss because of the surpassing worth of knowing Christ Jesus my Lord. For his sake I have suffered the loss of all things and count them as refuse, in order that I may gain Christ and be found in him, not having a righteousness of my own, based on law, but that which is through faith in Christ, the righteousness from God that depends on faith; that I may know him and the power of his resurrection, and may share his sufferings, becoming like him in his death. (Phil. 3,7). I wish to know nothing but Jesus Christ and him crucified (1 Cor. 2,2).

He gives up everything to possess Jesus Christ.   Because Jesus Christ is everything for him and he esteems nothing above Jesus Christ.
The Kingdom of heaven is like a treasure hidden in a field; he who finds it hides it again and goes and sells all he has to buy the field in order to own the treasure (Mt. 13,44). The kingdom of heaven is like a merchant who looks for good pearls; when he has found one of great price, he sells all he has to buy it (Mt. 13,45). That is what the apostles did when they had found Jesus Christ: they abandoned their nets and their parents and followed him (Mk. 1,38). And having left all, they followed him (Lk. 5,11). The apostles said to Jesus: We have left everything and have followed you (Lk. 18,28).

He wants to please only Jesus Christ.   Because Jesus is his joy, his happiness, his Master, his God. Am I now seeking the favor of men or of God? Or am I trying to please men?
If I were still pleasing men, I should not be a Servant of Christ (Gal.1,10). The knowledge of Jesus Christ necessarily produces love and the more we know Jesus Christ, his beauty, his grandeur, his riches, the more our love for him grows and the more we seek to please him and the more we reject far from us all that does not lead to Jesus Christ. That is what made Saint Paul say: if any one has no love for the Lord, let him be accursed (1 Cor. 16,22), and look upon everything that turned away for Jesus Christ as refuse and dross. The love of Jesus Christ turns us away from everything that does not lead to him, from everything that does not go to him, even our parents, friends, those who are close to us; we cannot endure anything that does

---

[12] I came so that the sheep may have life and have it in abundance (Jn. 10, 10).

not turn to the glory and love of Jesus Christ, and we say like Jesus Christ himself said to Peter who did not think as God did: Get behind me, Satan; you are a scandal for me. He does not fear to displease men and the world to please Jesus Christ. Like the Saints: *Saint Francis of Assisi.*

He does not even fear to appear foolish for the love of Jesus Christ.	Let no one deceive himself, says St. Paul to the faithful. If any one among you appears wise according to the world, let him become foolish to be wise.

For the wisdom of this world is foolishness before God, according to what is written: I will surprise the wise in their own wisdom; and elsewhere: the Lord knows the thoughts of the wise and he knows that they are vain. Let no one put his glory in men (1 Cor. 3,18). We are foolish because of Jesus Christ. You are wise in Jesus Christ. We are weak but you are strong, you are honored; we are despised (1 Cor. 4,10). In this part, St. Paul distinguishes two types of people or of priests who belong to Jesus Christ: those who act a little according to the world and those who are totally to Jesus Christ. The world cannot receive Jesus Christ, his spirit (Jn. 8,23). But far be it from me to glory except in the cross of our Lord Jesus Christ, by which the world hs been crucified to me and I to the world (Gal. 6,14). The one who belongs to Jesus Christ must totally set aside the existence of the world, of the glory of the world. Let the world think what it will, I do not care; let it think I am foolish, I do not care; I belong to Jesus Christ. I follow him. I walk in his footsteps, *qui pie volunt vivere in Christo persecutionem patientur*[13].

Nothing can separate him from Jesus Christ.	After having spoken about what Jesus Christ has done for the elect, St. Paul says:

Who shall separate us from the love of Christ? Shall tribulation, or distress, or persecution, or famine, or nakedness, or peril, or the sword? As it is written, 'For thy sake we are being killed all the day long; we are regarded as sheep to be slaughtered.' No, in all these things we are more than conquerors through him who loved us. For I am sure that neither death nor life, nor angels, nor principalities, nor things present, nor things to come, nor powers, nor height, nor depth, nor anything else in all creation will be able to separate us from the love of God in Christ Jesus our Lord (Rom. 8,35).

---

[13] All those who wish to live righteously in Christ are persecuted (2 Tim. 3,12).

All his happiness is to follow Jesus Christ.

He has heard and understood this word of the Master: follow me. He has understood that other word: You have no other Master but Jesus Christ.

Ego magister, the Master says. He who loves me keeps my word and my Father will love him and we will come and dwell in him. He has understood these other words: *exemplum dedi vobis ut quemadmodum ego feci ita et vos faciatis*[14]. And he wants to become like Jesus, his Master and model (Rom. 8,29). And he says with generosity and sacrifice: Lord, I will follow you wherever you go. Lord, I am ready to give my life for you. Let us go and die with him. When we sincerely love somebody, we are happy to follow him, to walk in his footsteps. We like to see him, to hear him and we do everything to imitate him.

He lives only for Jesus Christ.

For the love of Christ controls us, because we are convinced that one has died for all; therefore all have died. And he died for all, that those who live might live no longer for themselves but for him who for their sake died and was raised (2 Cor. 5,14). You are not your own, you are Jesus Christ's who redeemed you (1 Cor. 6,19). None of us lives to himself, and none of us dies to himself. If we live, we live to the Lord, and if we die, we die to the Lord; so then, whether we live or whether we die, we are the Lord's. For to this end Christ died and lived again, that he might be Lord both of the dead and of the living (Rom. 14,7).

Jesus Christ is his life.

Mihi vivere Christus est[15]. I no longer live, it is Christ who lives in me (Gal. 2,20).

Jesus Christ must be our life, that is, Jesus Christ must be our habitual and constant thought, towards whom all our desires, affections are directed night and day.
The mother lives for her child,
The bridegroom for his bride
The bride for her spouse,
The friend for his friend,
The miser for his money,
The egoist for himself,
The merchant for his business.
That is the life of each of those persons; he puts his life in what he seeks, in what he loves and when he is separated from that object, he weeps, he moans, he groans until he is reunited with the object of his love. For us, our life is Jesus Christ. In a clock,

---

[14] I have given you an example so that you may act as I have acted with you (Jn. 13,15).
[15] For me, to live is Christ (Phil. 1,21).

there is a spring that moves the whole mechanism and shows the time. Jesus Christ must be this hidden, invisible spring that makes us always show Jesus Christ himself. Where our treasure is, there will our heart be also. If Jesus Christ is our treasure, our heart and thoughts will always be with him. Mihi vivere Christus est. Cupio dissolvi et esse cum Christo[16]. He has no other thought, no other occupation but Jesus Christ. Jesus Christ occupies, takes up all his thoughts.

118

All this is very beautiful, but all do not understand it. Non omnes capiunt verbum illud sed quibus datum est[17]. Quis potest capere capiat[18]. Let him who has ears to hear, hear (Mk.4,23).

Verbum velatum[19]. When Jesus Christ spoke of his passion to his apostles, the words that he was saying were: verbum velatum for them. The Blessed Virgin and St. Joseph did not even understand what the Child Jesus was telling them when he to spoke them: et ipsi non intellexerunt verbum quod locutus est ad eos (Lk.2,50).

One needs a special grace from God to understand it. No one can come to me unless the Father draws him (Jn.6,44).

It takes God himself to make us understand his word and what he says of himself. For nobody knows what is in God but the spirit of God. The animal and carnal man does not conceive of the things that are in the spirit of God; they seem to him to be foolishness and he cannot understand because they must be judged in a supernatural light (1 Cor. 2,11). By ourselves, we are not able to have a good thought, but God makes us able (2 Cor. 3,5). The Holy Spirit is the one to give us the sense of spiritual and divine things and shows us Jesus Christ; who gives us eyes to see, ears to hear and especially a heart to feel and draws us to himself. And if we feel or understand something, know that all good feelings, all good thoughts of faith and love come from God himself and thank him for them. That is what Jesus made Peter understand when he had made his profession of faith in Jesus Christ saying: I believe that you are the Christ, the Son of the living God. Then Jesus said to him: Blessed are you, Peter, for flesh and blood have not revealed this to you, but my Father in heaven (Mt. 16,17). St. Paul says: Ego plantavi, Apollo rigavit sed Deus incrementum dat. Neque qui plantat est aliquid, neque qui rigat, sed qui incrementum dat Deus[20]. Thus, we can do or say what we will, if God does not give

119

---

[16] I have the desire to go and be with Christ (Ph. 1,23).

[17] All do not understand this language, but only those to whom it has been given to understand (Mt. 19,11).

[18] Let him who can, understand (Mt. 19,12).

[19] This word remained hidden from them (Lk. 18,34).

[20] I planted, Apollos watered, but God gave the growth. So neither he who plants nor he who waters is anything, but only God who gives the growth (1 Cor. 3,6).

the growth to what we say and do, everything is worth-less. However, if there are a few plants that are lost, usually not all are lost and the gardener does not always see all his work perish. We must hope that it will be the same for us. We must do violence to ourselves, pray, plead, do penance. The kingdom of God is proclaimed and everyone enters it violently (Lk. 1,16). The kingdom of God suffers violence and only the violent will enter (Mt. 11,12).

Do you feel this grace being born in you? That is, do you feel an interior attraction that draws you to Jesus Christ?

An interior feeling that is full of admiration for Jesus Christ, for his beauty, grandeur, infinite goodness, which impels him to come to us; a feeling that touches us and impels us to give ourselves to him. A little divine breath that impels us and comes from above, *ex alto*, a little supernatural light which enlightens us and makes us see a little of Jesus Christ and his infinite goodness. If we feel this divine breath in us, if we perceive a little light, if we feel drawn, even the least bit drawn to Jesus Christ, ah! let us cultivate this attraction, let us make it grow in prayer, meditation, study, in order that it may grow and produce fruit. And let us say with the spouse of the Song of Songs: trahe me post te, curremus in odorem unguentorum tuorum[21] [22].

120 **If we have this grace, we must also feel the call of Jesus Christ in us.** Come. Follow me. I am Wisdom. I am your master. Ego magister. I am the way, the truth, the life. Follow me. I am the light of the world. He who follows me does not walk in darkness.

I am the way, the truth, the life. I have come to bring fire upon the earth and how I wish it were already burning. It is my Father's glory that you should become my disciples and that you bear much fruit. The disciple is not above the Master; it suffices to be like the Master. I have given yo the example so that, as I have done, so also you should do. Nolite timere, ego sum[23]. Venite ad me omnes, jugum meum suave est et onus meum leve[24].

---

[21] Draw me after you, let us run in the odor of your fragrance (Ct.1,3).
[22] Ms XI 2.
Do you wish to belong to Jesus Christ?
Do you feel the desire to belong to Jesus Christ?
To whom to you want to belong, if you do not belong to Jesus Christ?
Listen to the call of Jesus Christ.
Listen to his promises.
[23] Fear not, it is I (Mt. 14,27).
[24] Come to me, all you...my yoke is easy and my burden is light (Mt. 11,28-29).

To what does he call us?   To perfection. There are three kinds of Christians in the world: the good, the bad and the perfect.
There are also three kinds of priests in the Church: the good, the bad and the perfect. The good ones are those who accomplish their duty of priests, who follow the laws o the Church, say their Mass, their Breviary, preach when it is time, avoid mortal sin, scandal, do the good that presents itself; in a word, there is nothing to say against their behavior, they are even edifying. The bad ones are those who live in sin and indifference to their duty, neglect the sacred duties of their ministry and all too often give scandal to the Church. There are the bad scandalous priest who shame the Church. There are also the hidden bad ones who live in sin without being known and are no less harmful to souls by their negligence and omission of prayer and all spiritual life. The perfect ones, or rather those who tend to perfection, who seek to follow Our Lord more closely, who have the desire to work for the glory of Jesus Christ, who feel his love in them and wish to imitate him in his poverty, his meekness, his charity, his zeal for souls, in his sufferings, in his cross. There is a great difference between the good priests and those who strive to be perfect. The good remain in that state but do not seek to follow Our Lord closely,to imitate him seriously; they even reject poverty, devotedness and sacrifice; they still care for their person and do not wish to be too opposed to the world or the tastes of their brothers. The one who strives for perfection sees only Jesus Christ, he loves Jesus Christ and puts Jesus Christ before everything else. He loves and seeks to imitate the one he loves as faithfully as possible.It is to that perfection that Jesus Christ calls us and not to a merely good state which is that of a great number. Perfection is the state of the small number. There are few who follow him like that. Yet, a holy prsest does more good than a hundred who are only good. A holy priest gives more glory to God than a hundred and he converts more souls to God than a hundred others convert to themselves[25]. Thus, it is to perfection that Jesus Christ calls us, to become his true

---

[25] Ms X 739-740.

For the priest as for the faithful, there are two ways to go to heaven, to God and fulfill the mission that has been entrusted to him: the way of the precepts and that of the counsels.

The first suffices to go to heaven. It is the way of many number, that is all one is held to; it suffices for salvation.

But those to whom God gives light and grace must follow the second one.

The way of the counsels is that of true love, it glorifies God more on the earth, it contributes to the salvation of souls, it draws many graces to the earth and to the Church, it assures our salvation.

It is this way that brings us closer to Jesus Christ by conforming us to him, to his life, seeking to reproduce his life in ours and having no other desire than to seek to imitate him as perfectly as possible.

....

disciples. The particular graces of which we have been the object prove it clearly. Grace of choice. Particular vocation. Very particular care from Providence, spiritual and temporal, all commit us to following Jesus Christ in his perfect life. Besides, that is our aim and I ask nothing except that you respond to the call of Our Lord and to ours.

If you hear his voice,	Do not harden your hearts, do not close your ear to his voice.
We must respond with joy	Ecce adsum[26]. Ego tuus sum[27]. Ecce ego[28]. Speak, Lord, your servant is listening.

Lord, where would I go? you have the words of eternal life. You are my light, my way, my life, my wisdom and my love. I will follow you, Lord, wherever you go. I am ready to die with you, I will give my life for you, I will go to prison, to death. You are my king, my head, my master. Lord, if you need a poor one, here I am! If you need a foolish one, here I am! Here I am, O Jesus, to do your will, I am yours! Ego tuus sum.

Let us listen to the first warning that Jesus Christ gives us about listening to his word and becoming true disciple.	Truly, I say to you, if you do not become like little children, you will not enter the kingdom of heaven (Mt. 18,3). Whoever does not receive the kingdom like a little child, will not enter (Mk. 10,25).

Religious observe the evangelical counsels; why would secular priests not observe them also? Is perfection not for them as well as for the others? In the ministry, should not the priests draw near to Jesus Christ as well as the others? And should they not do so even more, they who are in the midst of the world and who must carry the good odor of Jesus Christ everywhere and be a living light that must shine among men? Religious are in their cloister but the priest is made to live among men and he, more than the others, must be more holy and more perfect than the others, he is called to do more good because he has the necessary relationships with the faithful; and we must surpass the religious by this light, this halo of glory and holiness that must shine in the priests in ministry.

Nevertheless, those to whom God gives the grace to follow Jesus Christ in his counsels must not despise those who only observe the precepts. Each one will give an account to God of the graces he has received. We must glory in nothing and be very careful not to say any word against love of neighbor; we must make God's grace fructify and judge no one.

[26] Here I am (1 Sam.3,4).
[27] I am yours (Ps. 118,94).
[28] It is I (Jn.6,20).

I give you thanks, O Father! Lord of heaven and earth, that you have hidden these things from the wise and prudent of this world have revealed them to the little and humble (Mt.11,25). Let the little children come to me, for the kingdom of heaven is theirs (Mk. 10,14). Blessed are the poor in spirit for the kingdom of heaven is theirs (Mt. 5,3). Whoever humbles himself and becomes like a little child, he will be great in the kingdom of heaven (Mt. 18,3).

Explanation of the preceding words. One must receive the kingdom of God, that is, the word of Jesus Christ which will establish the kingdom of God in us, like a child receives the word of his master, with attention, submission, respect and love. Attention to understand what he tells us, understand it and grasp it. Submission, without discussion, as it is. We are not to argue with our masters; it is 1 2 3 up to them to teach us and to us to listen and accept. The submission of a child. That is what Our Lord recommends especially in listening to his word. What is there to discuss with Jesus Christ, the divine Master? Either you want to be perfect or you don't. If you don't, say simply: I do not wish to follow this way but I wish to remain in the inferior way, and that is the end of it. But if you wish to be perfect, accept his divine word as he has given it and seek to put it into practice with God's grace and do not act as that rich young man in the Gospel to whom Jesus Christ says: if you wish to be perfect, go sell what you have and give it to the poor. He reasoned within himself and did not accept the word. This submission of spirit to the word of Jesus Christ is absolutely necessary to enter in the kingdom of heaven where only the good Master's privileged souls enter. Listen like a child[29]. A child goes to school to learn and not to discuss, he strives to understand what is said; he does not go to reason but to accept. If he does not understand, he questions, not to discuss but to learn and accept. What would we say of a child, an ignorant person, who would discuss with an astronomer or a geographer on the position of the stars or an area on the earth, when the learned person says: it is thus? It is the same with us and Jesus Christ; we cannot discuss with him about what he teaches us. The child receives, accepts the master's word; it enters into his heart like the finger in melted wax, he receives the word. While those who are not children want to discuss, reason, listen to the word but do not receive it. It becomes like a stone that bounces and returns to

---

[29] Ms. XI 42; 81-82.
It is the Word of God who speaks to us through his Son (42).
We must accept God's words with simplicity, with that divine authority that is his and set aside all human reasoning that comes only from pride or our interior passions that do not want to accept such a pure, heavenly doctrine. We must not come with the intention of reasoning, discussing, nothing of that: God says, we must do (81-82).

where it came from[30]. There are subtle, narrow, quibbling, fussy spirits who find difficulties everywhere and reason on everything, accept only what agrees with them, is convenient to them and enters into their spirit[31]. Nothing is more opposed to the spirit of God and thus to the title of child that Our Lord demands for entry in his kingdom. He who is of God listens to my word. If you do not listen to my word, it is because you are not of God, said Our Lord to the Jews. They did not listen to the word of God, they did not receive it, they only listened to it to discuss and reason on this word and even to surprise him and to accuse and condemn him. Children do not yet have passions, they do not yet find oppositions to the word of God in their young souls, they accept it simply, without opposition. Nothing is more opposed to this submission of spirit than our petty passions[32]. The word of God is so elevated, so pure, so heavenly, so much above us that when we hear it our thousand petty passions rise and revolt against it, because they find themselves in direct opposition to that word that condemns them and destroys them. Our heart and our spirit cry out. Our laziness, our greed, our negligence, the love of well being, of ease, pride, self-seeking, satisfactions: all that rises together against that divine word and calls it exaggerated, impossible; it says that the Gospel is folly and that it is not possible to live it. Then we say that we do not want to exaggerate, that there is a prudence to be followed, that the Gospel is for a very small number, only for the saints, that it is too difficult to reach[33]. So we listen with caution and reservations and, with the pretext of being prudent, we leave aside the Gospel to follow our petty reasoning. We see this every day in what concerns poverty, penance, sacrifice, devotedness, the really evangelical virtues. The Holy Spirit says somewhere that he stands at the door and knocks; he says more: he says that he pushes the door to enter: *ecce sto ad ostium et pulso*. Thus, our heart is like a door on which the Master knocks and through which he seeks to enter. And a door can be in several positions. And when someone knocks

---

[30] Ms XI 172.
We must receive the word like a child receives the word of his master. Knowing well that the master knows more than he does and that what he says is true and that we must accept it as it is. The child who does not understand, asks questions to understand, to be able to grasp the meaning but not to discuss, to reason. We must respect the authority of the word, the authority of the master.

[31] Ms XI 81.
A little detail, a fly, a cobweb, a little spot will worry them more than the whole; they will leave aside the beautiful, the great, the useful, to reflect and think only of a little fault, of a little detail that will worry them and make them lose the fruit of an instruction or of some good example.

[32] Ms XI 82.
Oh! how we must silence our passions to understand Jesus Christ! He is so beautiful, so elevated, so pure, that his words cannot enter into a heart where there is any passion.

[33] Ms XI 173. What is impossible to men is possible to God.

on this door and one comes to open, it can be left shut and not opened at all, it can be opened a crack and leave those who knock outside, or it can be opened wide to let those who knock come in. That is how we can do with Jesus Christ, our Master, with regard to the door of our heart, when he seeks to enter. The one who does not open his door is the one who refuses entry to the Master and totally refuses to receive his Master, to follow him, who prefers to follow his own ideas, his passions, the world. The one who only opens halfway is the one who listens without allowing the Master to enter his house; he remains the master of the door of his house and of his heart. He listens but only takes what he wishes and does what he wants with it, he takes what is conven-ient and leaves what does not please him. He receives the Master with reserve and prudence and listens more to his reasonings, his petty passions who are his masters than to the true Master who wishes to enter; he is wary, he is afraid, he opens his heart only halfway. And the Master cannot enter to govern as he should[34]. The last one opens his door wide and allows the Master who knocks to enter his house. He is happy to receive him and gives him a place of honor, he listens willingly and has only one desire: to understand what he says and put it into practice. He does not discuss but seeks means of practicing what he hears. Like Mary, he remains in spirit at the feet of his Master and does not allow himself to be caught up in reasonings nor by the passions that revolt. The Master speaks, he has no other thought, no other desire but to understand what he hears and to put it into practice, to nourish his soul on it. It is love that guides him and nothing else. He wants to enter into the kingdom of heaven; that is his sole desire. He tramples underfoot all that reason and passions may say to him. Jesus Christ is his sole Master and he wishes to follow only him. A submissive and generous soul, he does not say: that is difficult, that is impossible, that is opposed to prudence, to the way of doing things, nothing of that; the Master has spoken, the Master has said it, it suffices.

126

Examples of simplicity.

Zachaeus who climbs a tree to see Jesus Christ his Master: a rich man, he could well have said: what am I doing?
I am acting like a child, climbing a tree to see a man pass by! Nothing of that. He wants to see Jesus Christ, his Master; he is not concerned about men. The shepherds who go to the manger on the word of the angels. The wise men who leave their countries to undertake a long and unknown journey to go see a new born. Saint Magdelene who goes to Simon the pharisee's house where Jesus was dining, to ask forgiveness for her sins. Saint Anthony does not reason when he hears in a church

---

[34] Ms XI 173.

We can never do too much. What are you afraid of? Are you afraid of being hungry? of being persecuted, despised, rejected? What is all that? Can the one who loves Jesus Christ be afraid of anything?

this word of the Gospel: if you wish to be perfect, go sell what you have and give it to the poor, and you will have great treasure in heaven. He goes, sells what he has, gives it to the poor and retires in solitude. St.Francis of Assisi also heard this word in a church: have no gold or silver, no shoes or spare tunic. He took that for himself and left everything to become the real poor of Jesus Christ in the world. That is the simplicity of a child that Our Lord de-mands of his true disciples. What reasonings the saints who followed the evangelical way could have done to prevent them from entering in such an elevated, perfect way, difficult to nature, and if they had allowed themselves to be caught up in all these reasonings they would never have become saints. Our Lord was so right in saying: unless you become like little children, you will not enter into the kingdom of heaven. That means, if you are led by human reasonings, if you consult your reasonings, the world, your ideas, your passions, you will never listen to my word and you will never put it into practice, because my word comes from above and your reasonings come from below. He said, I am from above, you are from below. If he is from above, let yourselves be led simply and do not seek to put yourselves on the same level as him, since he is above us and do not lower his doctrine to our petty reasonings. It is reasoning that kills the Gospel and takes away from the soul that thrust that would impel us to follow Jesus Christ and to imitate him in his evangelical beauty. The saints did not reason so much. Is it because there are so many reasoners that there are so few saints! Let us not be afraid, nolite timere, it is I. And even if we should walk on the water, like Peter, should we not go to Jesus, if he said to us as he did to Peter: COME! Let us then remain in spirit at the feet of Jesus Christ, like little children at the feet of their master, with a sincere desire to listen to his word and put it into practice.

This requires great strength of will.	Regnum Dei vim patitur et violenti rapiunt illud[35]. We must not have soft, effeminate people.

---

[35] The kingdom of heaven suffers violence and the violent take it by force (Mt. 11,12).

SECOND PART

FIVE CONDITIONS TO BE FULFILLED

IN ORDER TO BECOME

A TRUE DISCIPLE OF JESUS

SECOND PART

FIVE CONDITIONS TO FULFILL IN ORDER TO BECOME A TRUE DISCIPLE OF JESUS

In the general introduction, we saw how Father Chevrier had elaborated his plan progressively[1]. The editing of the following passage shows the rather laborious efforts to find this plan.
The orientation is totally apostolic: it is a matter of fulfilling the apostolic duties[2] *by giving the signs that should accompany the proclamation of the Gospel.*
The reference to the three parts of the Tableau of Saint-Fons is explicit. It does not come in passing but as the summary of these pages, at the end. This confirms what we have already said on this subject[3].

131

---

[1] Pp. 29.
[2] P. 117.
[3] P.29; cf. Appendix V, p.477.

Seeing a great crowd following him, Jesus took the opportunity to teach them how to really fol low him in spirit and in heart.	As a great crowd of people was following him, Jesus turned around and told them: if anyone wishes to follow me and does not hate his father, mother, wife, children, brothers and sisters, and even his own life, he cannot be my disciple. And the one who does not want to carry his cross after me cannot be my disciple.
Before really following him we must consider seriously if we are able.	Who among you, wanting to build a tower, does not sit down to figure out the necessary ex penses and if he will be able to finish it.
It is a matter of building a very high tower, that of perfection.	For fear that after having placed the foundation and not being able to finish, those who will see it will begin to laugh at him saying: this man started to build but was unable to finish.
The fight is against powerful enemies. And to build this tower, to fight these powerful enemies, it is as necessary to renounce family, oneself, the goods of the earth as it is necessary for a man to have the money to build a house, as it is necessary for a king to have the soldiers to wage a war.	Or what king, before waging war against another king, does not consider before hand if, with ten thousand men, he can face the one coming against him with twenty thousand? Otherwise he sends a delegation, while the other is still far off, with proposals for peace.
And the one who would undertake this war or that building without having the means would be like a man who would build without money or wage war without soldiers.	

133 appears at the first right-column paragraph; 134 appears at the last right-column paragraph.

Thus, whoever among you does not renounce all that he possesses, cannot be my disciple. Salt is good, but if it becomes insipid, with what shall it be flavored? It is not good for the earth or for the dung heap, but only to be thrown out. Let he who has ears to hear, hear!(Lk. 14,25). Besides, Our Lord tells us: If anyone wishes to follow me, let him renounce himself and follow me (Mt. 16,24).

The five conditions demanded by Our Lord Jesus Christ to become his true disciple.

According to these words of our divine Master, we see clearly that, to become his true disciple, one must, first of all: renounce one's family and the world,
renounce oneself,
renounce the goods of the earth.
Then, when one has renounced all those things, one must take up one's cross and follow him in the practice of all the evangelical virtues[4].

---

[4] Ms XI 84 - XI 583.

If we do not fulfill these conditions, we are good for nothing.

There is nothing more logical or natural than to fulfill these conditions to be the true disciple of Jesus Christ.

It is very easy to understand that the one who is occupied with things of the earth, with business affairs, cannot be concerned with the things of God; that the one whose heart is divided between God and creatures, who has a wife and children or who loves creatures, cannot give himself totally to God.

It is easy to understand that the one who is preoccupied with himself, who constantly seeks himself, who does not renounce himself, will be stopped constantly; he will have to take care of himself, of his father and mother, of his crying children... and that before following Jesus Christ, one must have renounced all that, without these conditions, one can do nothing.

How true are these words of Jesus Christ! (Ms XI 84).

Complete renunciation of every thing that one possesses. He wants us to renounce everything to belong to him. He does not want half of us; he wants us entirely. (Ms. XI 583).

Need for studying these five conditions to become a true disciple of Jesus Christ.	Such are the conditions imposed by the divine Master on whoever wants to become his disciple Without fulfilling these conditions, we fulfill only half, or not at all, our apostolic duty which is to be,
	    salt of the earth,
	    light of the world. (Mt.5,13).
	We are only an insipid salt, an unlit torch, and we are only good to be thrown out, according to the word of the Master. So we must know how to practice this renunciation,
	of creatures and the world,
	of oneself,
	of the goods of the earth.
	What is this cross that we have to carry? What is this road that we must take to really follow Jesus Christ and become his disciple? That is what Jesus Christ himself teaches in his holy Gospel and that we will study in the following pages?
		135

Explanation of these words: You are the salt of the earth.	Salt of souls. The property of salt is to preserve from corruption, to conserve and to give taste to foods. That is what we must be for Christian souls: to preserve them from the corruption of sin, conserve them in the grace of God and give them the spiritual taste by putting faith and the love of God in them. If you are he salt of the earth, if the salt loses its virtue, with what will it be salted? It is only good to be thrown out and be trampled underfoot by men.	136

You are the light of the world.

137

You are the light of the world.

A city on a mountain top cannot be hidden and a light is not to be placed under a bushel but on a lamp stand, in order that it may enlighten all those who are in the house. Thus, may your light shine before men, in order that they may see your good works and glorify your father in heaven (Mt. 5, 13). Therefore, we must shine in the world through our light, that is, by our good examples and our virtues.

We must practice the virtues opposed to the vices of the world, and the more the world is corrupt, spoiled, the more we must shine in its eyes by the opposite virtues, and draw it, astonish it by our words and especially by our examples. The more the world loves luxury and wealth, the more we must love and practice poverty. The more the world loves well-being and softness, the more we must shine by our mortification and penance. Charity, devotedness, sacrifice: the world must see our works. The difference with a cloistered religious: he lives for himself, and the priest in the world: he lives for others and owes himself to everybody by his devotedness, sacrifice and good example [5]. There are different lights: the sun, the moon, gas, the lamp, the vigil light and the extinguished torch without oil, without wick. If you do not believe in my word, believe in my works, Our Lord said to the Jews. Would that we were able to say the same and show our works to men to make them believe and be converted.

---

[5] Cf. p. 97.

See how am poor,
See how I am nailed to the cross,
See how I allow myself to be eaten by
you, without saying anything, for your
good[6].

---

[6] Ms. XI 565.
Promises of our Lord Jesus Christ: If you can understand these things and put them into practice, you will be happy (Jn. 13,17).
The love of Jesus Christ, Our Master!

FIRST CONDITION

ONE MUST RENOUNCE
ONE'S FAMILY AND THE WORLD

After Christmas 1856, Antoine Chevrier wanted to put into practice immediately the type of priestly life that he had just conceived. He met with two oppositions: that of his mother and that of his fellow priests. He had already experienced the maternal opposition when, as a seminarian, he had thought of going to the foreign missions. Those two types of opposition are not obstacles but more or less painful trials, on condition that one seeks spiritual freedom with regard to one's family and every sociological milieu, including the ecclesiastical milieu. In fact, when priests tend to conform collectively to a particular sociological milieu,. there is created among them a collective mentality which unconsiously enslaves them to the prejudices of that milieu: the world is found even in the assemblies of our fellow priests[1].
A particularly hard struggle waged against a domineering mother explains in part the importance that Father Chevrier gives to the renunciation of family. But no one can elude this question and most of those who have been set aside for the Gospel[2], *have found themselves, at one time or another, in the painful necessity of imposing suffering on those who are dear to them by freely deciding to answer God's call.*
Besides, we must know that, after the death of his father, Antoine Chevrier took his mother with him at the Prado, keeping in mind what he knew of her and organizing things in such a way that she could not intervene in the running of the house but felt useful anyway.
Here, Father Chevrier's two major concerns are to highlight in all its strength the spiritual family and to maintain freedom. Freedom to proclaim the Gospel and to live close to the poor.
That is why renunciation of the world is especially the refusal of an allegiance to a world that put its sociological empire on the clergy of the time and perhaps, more or less of all times. According to the different cases, it will be the world of grandeurs, the beautiful world, the cultivated world, the worldly, etc. There is always the danger of seeking social promotion with the priesthood. But, Father Chevrier notes, Jesus did not elevate his family according to the flesh[3].
For Father Chevrier, this renunciation of the world is also a quest for freedom with regard to political systems and groups. That is what he wants to affirm when he refuses to spend an evening in a parlor talking politics[4]. *In fact he knows what obstacles are created among the poor of his time by the collusion of the clergy with the political options of certain social classes. However, let us not ask him to deal with the relationships of the Church and the world in the manner of Vatican II. He has no personal idea on the matter.*

---

[1] Ms XI 599.
[2] Rom. 1.
[3] Ms VIII 431.
[4] P. 135.

He has understood well that the different meanings of the word "world" have to be clarified, but he announces an explanation without giving it[5]. *The Gospel is in part responsible for this lack of clarity. In St. John, "the world" designates either the universe or the human race or those who refuse Christ. Let us say that in* The True Disciple, *the world is all the human influence that could prevent us from taking the Gospel seriously. When we have met Christ, like St. John or Saint Paul, we can only find such pretentions intolerable.*

Other terms are also ambiguous: celestial and terrestrial[6]. *To understand Father Chevrier, we must refer, like him, to Saint Paul*[7], *who opposes the terrestrial man to the celestial man. The latter is the new man, recreated in the grace of Christ, vivified, led by the Spirit and who is certainly not dispensed from having his feet on the ground. The terrestrial man, the old man, is the one who is still given to his caprices and the descendant of sinful Adam.*

If Father Chevrier's reference to Scripture is indisputable when he uses the terms "world", "celestial", "terrestrial", we can nevertheless admit that his language is influenced by the rhetoric of his time[8].

However, he asks us a question that no one can avoid: are we free spiritually with regard to the world and particularly our family?

---

[5] P. 135.
[6] Cf. p. 133 and elsewhere.
[7] Cf. 1 Cor. 15,47 (quoted p. 171 and 235).
[8] Cf. p. 21.

It is the first act of renunciation that our Lord Jesus Christ 143
asks of the one who would come after him. In fact, it means that we cannot belong to God and the world and that we must necessarily leave one to give ourselves to the other. And, as Jesus says, we cannot serve two masters. Either we will love one and hate the other; or we will adhere to one and despise the other. We cannot adhere to God and the world because of the opposition that there is between God and the world. And if, in Holy Scripture, God says that the bride will leave her father and mother to adhere to her husband, how much more should the one who wishes to adhere to God leave all creatures. It is the first act that God asked of Abraham when he called him to himself.

Our Lord Jesus Christ's doctrine on the renunciation of family and the world.

Do you think I have come to bring peace on earth? No, I tell you, but separation. For I tell you, henceforth in a house, five will be divided, three against two and two against three.

They will devided:
- the father against the son,
- the mother against the daughter,
- the daughter against the mother,
- the mother-in-law against the daughter-in-law,
- the daughter-in-law against the mother-in-law (Lk. 12,51).

Do not think that I have come to bring peace on earth. I have not come to bring peace but the sword.

I have come to separate:
- a man against his father,
- a son against his mot er,
- a daughter-in-law against her mother-in-law,

and the enemies of a man will be those of his own house (Mt. 10,35). He who loves his father or his mother more than me is not worthy of me and he who loves his son or daughter above me is not worthy of me (Mt. 10,37). If any one comes to me and does not hate
- his father and mother,
- his wife and children,
- his brothers and sisters,
- and even his own life,

he cannot be my disciple (Lk. 14,26).

To renounce the world.

Woe to the world because of scandals! (Mt. 18,7). Do not love the world nor what is in the world.

If any one loves the world, the love of God is not in him (1 Jn. 2,15). Love of the world s an enmity against God. Whoever wishes to be a friend of the world becomes an enemy of God (Jas.4,4). Do not be conform to the present age (Rom. 12,2). You are not of the world, said Jesus Christ to his apostles. You cannot serve two masters.

Why one must renounce one's family and the world.

We know that the whole world is under the domination of the evil one (1 Jn. 5,19). The world cannot receive the Holy Spirit because it does not know it and does not see it (Jn. 14,17).

If someone loves the world, the love of God is not in him. For everything that is in the world is either concupiscence of the flesh or concupiscence of the eyes or pride of life. What does not come from God, but the world.... and the world passes and the concupiscence of the world passes with it. But the one who does the will of God remains forever (1 Jn. 2,15). There is the wisdom that comes from below; that wisdom is terrestrial, animal, diabolical. Where there is jealousy and contention, there is also trouble and all sorts of evil. But the wisdom that comes from above is, first of all chaste, then friend of peace, moderated, equitable, docile, susceptible of all good, full of mercy and the fruits of good works. It does not judge. It is not devious, nor does it dissimulate (Jas. 3,15). The animal man does not conceive of these things that are of the spirit of God; they appear as folly to him and he cannot understand them because they must be judged in a supernatural light (1 Cor. 2,14). The wisdom of this world is folly before God, according to what is written: I will confound the wise in their own craftiness. The Lord knows the thoughts of the wise and he knows that they are futile (1 Cor. 3, 19-20).

I come from above,
> you are from below,
> you are of the world,
> I am not of the world (Jn. 8,24).

They are of the world. That is why they speak according to the world.

As for us, we are from God and the one who knows God listens to us; but the one who is not from God does not listen to us and that is how we know those who are animated by the spirit of God, of truth, and those who are moved by the spirit of error (1 Jn. 4,5). The world places all its happiness in exterior and sensual things. Jesus places it in spiritual things. Mary chose the best part.

Examples that confirm this truth: opposition between Jesus Christ and the world.

And when his relatives heard of it, they went out to seize him, for they said: he is besides himself, *in furorem versus est* (Mk. 3,21).

His brothers did not believe in him (Jn. 7,5). No prophet is accepted in his own country; there is no prophet without honor except in his own country, his own house, among his relatives (Mk. 6,4). (Here it is a matter of the good prophets, the good priests, the good servants of God who do not live like the world, and not those who follow the ideas of the world and their family.) Jesus' brothers told him: go away from here, go to Judea so that your disciples may see the works that you do, for no one acts for his work to be hidden, but he himself seeks to show it. If you do such things, show them to the world (Jn. 7,3). It is in Nazareth, his native country, that Jesus is expelled from the synagogue, led to the brink of the mountain by the people who wanted to throw him down. But Jesus, passing through their midst, *went his way* (Lk. 4,30). The more we are God's, the more we are opposed to the ideas and follies of the world and the more the world hates and persecutes us. The mother of the sons of Zebedee comes to Jesus asking that her two sons be seated on his right and on his left in the kingdom; the two sons make the same request and Jesus tells them: you do not know what you are asking, can you drink of the chalice that I drink and be baptized of the baptism that I will be baptized?(Mt. 11,38).Peter himself, before having received the spirit of God, is strongly reprimanded by Jesus Christ. Jesus speaks of his passion and announces what is to happen. Taking him apart, Peter begins to reprove him saying: Please God, Lord, this will not happen! And Jesus, turning around and looking at his disciples reproved Peter saying: Get behind me, Satan, you are a scandal for me because you do not hear what is from God but what is from men (Mk. 8,31).

How Jesus Christ himself practiced this renunciation of family.

At the age of twelve, the child Jesus remains in Jerusalem to begin the mission with which his father had entrusted him in the world.

He remains in the temple, unknown to this parents. And when the Blessed Virgin comes to him and asks him why he has acted this way with them, they who had been looking for him for three days, in sorrow and sadness, he answers: Why were you looking for me? Did you not know that I have to be about my father's business? (Lk. 2,49.

148

The wedding at Cana.

At the wedding at Cana, Jesus answers his mother who had told him that they had no more wine:

What is that to you and to me? My hour is not yet come (Jn. 2,4).

Jesus on the cross.

And on the cross, Jesus seeing his mother at his feet, says to her: Woman, here is your son (Jn. 19,26).

The woman who calls Mary blessed.

A woman raising her voice in the crowd, cried out: Blessed is the womb that bore you and the

breasts that nursed you! And Jesus replied: Rather blessed are those who hear the word of God and put it into practice (Lk. 11,27). Somebody said to Jesus: your mother and brothers are outside and wish to see you, and Jesus answers them: Who is my mother; who are my brothers? And looking around him and pointing to his disciples, he says: My mother and my brothers are those who listen to the word of God and put it into practice. Whoever does the will of my Father who is in heaven is my brother, my sister and my mother (Mk. 3,21).

What Our Lord Jesus Christ requires of those who would follow him, regarding their family.	Whoever comes to me and does not hate his father and mother, his wife and children, his brothers and sisters, cannot be my disciple (Lk. 14,26). He who loves his mother and father more than me is not worthy of me (Mt. 10,37).

Jesus said to a young man: follow me. But this young man said to Jesus: allow me first to go bury my father. Jesus told him: follow me. Let the dead bury the dead, as for you, go and proclaim the kingdom of God (Lk. 9,60). Another young man said to Jesus: I will follow you, Lord; but allow me first to take leave of the people in my house. Jesus said: Any man who, having put his hand to the plow looks back, is not fit for the kingdom of heaven (Lk. 9,61).

Rules to follow with regard to one's family and the world.	According to the words and example of our Lord Jesus, we see that a true disciple of Jesus Christ must first of all:
Leave his father and mother.	To leave one's father and mother, in the example of the child Jesus, at the age of 12,

to consecrate oneself to God's work; and he does not even need their consent. When God calls us, we must obey. He is our first Father. He who loves his father and mother more than me is not worthy of me (Mt. 10,37). And when they come looking for us, we must say as the child Jesus said: why are looking for me? Do you not know that I must be in the service of my Father? Our first duty is to concern ourselves with the things of God who is our first Father. We have a father who is in heaven, who is above all fathers of the earth and to whom we must obey first of all. This Father is above you. He is your Father and mine. I come to separate the son from his father.

To no longer have anything in common with the family, except the relationships of charity and necessity[9].	And once this first separation has been made and we have consecrated ourselves to God and his service, we must have nothing in common with the family. That is what Our Lord Jesus Christ teaches us when he answered Mary,

---

[9] This commentary on John 2,4, is no doubt Father Chevrier's greatest blunder in his interpretation of Scripture. It is not his personally. He follows the orientation given by the notes

his mother, at the wedding in Cana: what is there in common between you and me? Woman, my hour has not yet come. We must study each word because each word contains a lesson.

Study of this word from Our Lord: What is there in common between you and me? Woman, my hour has not yet come.

What is there in common between you and me? That is, there is no longer anything in common between you and me. Since I have left you to consecrate myself to the service of God and neighbor. 150

I have left my natural family to enter into a spiritual family. I have broken carnal bonds to take up spiritual bonds. God is my Father, the Church is my mother. God's children are my brothers and sisters.

That is my family.

There is no longer anything in common between you and me, you no longer have any right over me and I have nothing to do with you. I have no other bond but those of charity and gratitude that cannot be broken. That is very simple since we come out of a natural way to enter into God's spiritual family.

Woman.

This word that Our Lord uses to speak to his mother makes us understand that, since he has begun his divine mission on earth, he has become the eternal Priest, Mary has lost her maternal rights over him and that he no longer recognizes in her the right to command him in what concerns the kingdom of God and his divine mission. He recognizes no other master, father, superior but God, his Father. His mother is no longer anybody else but a woman.

My hour has not yet come.

I know what I must do and when I must do it. I have my Father to whom I must obey and who fixes the moment when I must act and how I must do it. It is no longer up to you to tell me what to do, nor to determine the moment of my actions. I have no orders to receive from you in what regards my divine mission. It is to God alone that I owe obedience and it is he who determines the moment of my actions. When I act, I must obey neither flesh and blood nor any natural sentiment; I must consult only God's will. What a great lesson Our Lord gives us in these words, and it is to instruct us that he pronounced them in these circumstances; these apparently harsh words show us the separation that must occur between the priest and his family.

---

in Mastaï-Ferretti: "Jesus wishes to teach his disciple that, in the apostolic function and ministry, they must no longer let themselves be led by flesh and blood, but uniquely by the will of God." (Mastaï- Ferretti, p. 80).

151 We must form among us a true spiritual family.

Somebody came to tell Jesus: your mother and brothers are outside and wish to see you. Jesus answers: Who is my mother and who are my brothers? And looking around him and pointing to his disciples he says: behold my mother and my brothers, they are those who listen to the word of God and put it into practice. For whoever does the will of my Father who is in heaven is my brother, my sister and my mother (Mk.3,31). How well Our Lord makes us understand by his words that the natural family disappears to give way to the spiritual family whose bonds are not flesh and blood but God, his word and the practice of this word. That is the great bond between souls. And the bonds of this spiritual family are more intimate and stronger than those that exist in the families of the earth, that are only terrestrial and carnal bonds[10].

When two souls, enlightened by the Holy Spirit, listen to the word of God and understand it, a very intimate union of spirit is formed in those two souls, whose principle and knot is God. It is the true bond of religion, the true bond of soul and heart. This knowledge of God produces first of all love of God and also love of the one who thinks like us and according to God; and this bond of the spirit, founded on God, is infinitely more intimate and stronger than all other natural bonds. And when the practice of this same word is joined to this spiritual bond, a truly spiritual family is formed, a Christian community having God as foundation, his divine word for bond and the same practices as an end.

And there can be no Christian family or community without this union of spirit founded on the knowledge of Jesus Christ, his divine word and the practice of the same works. The love of Jesus Christ, the desire to keep his word is the foundation of all Christian family, and we will only be truly united in spirit and in heart in the measure that this precious foundation is established among us. Then is this word of Jesus Christ accomplished for us: Those who listen to the word of God and put it into practice are my brothers.

152 We become his brothers because we are united in faith and in thought and his blood flows in our veins. We become his mother by producing him on the altar and by giving spiritual birth to other children by teaching the faith and in the sacraments. Happy family! Happy bonds that unite all the members of this family in the same charity and the same desire to make Jesus Christ known and loved!

And when this family really exists, we must find in it everything that is found in a true family: love, unity, support, charity, all the spiritual and temporal cares that are necessary for each one of its members, without there being the need to go look el-

---

[10] Father Chevrier insists on the contrast and in so doing he exaggerates for the natural family is well founded on the word of God (Mt. 19,5), and the Christian family is founded on the sacramental word. Yet we find this presentation by contrasts in St. Paul (compare 1 Cor. 7,32-34 and Eph. 5,25-32). See renunciation of one's heart, pp. 209-210.

sewhere for what is necessary for the needs of the soul or the body; otherwise the family is not whole or true. That is what is expressed by those titles of brother, sister, father that we give to each other. Those titles should express only what exists interiorly, otherwise they are only pathetic and illusiory.

According to the words of Our Lord, we see clearly that a true disciple of Jesus Christ must leave his father and mother to devote himself to the service of God, no longer have anything in common with them and enter in the spiritual family of God's children and recognize as father and mother only God and one's superiors and as brothers and sisters only those who belong to Jesus Christ.

False ideas that parents continue to have about their children when they are priests.

Parents think they still have rights over their children when these are priests. And because they are not cloistered, that they are priests in the world, the parents think that they may still advise them, lead them, have the priests with them, give them advice, and since their advice is terrestrial, it is always not to tire themselves out too much, to take care of themselves, not to exert so much effort, this advice is always harmful to the good of souls and their own children because they inspire negligence. They do not consider the good of souls[11] but the good of their children. It is then that we must have in mind and on our lips these words of Jesus Christ, our Master: *What is there in common between you and me*? And that other word of Our Lord to St. Peter: get behind me Satan, you are a scandal for me because you do not understand what is from God but only what is from men. Woe to the one who lets himself be led by this harmful and pernicious advice! He only leads a very natural life, he no longer serves God but only himself and his parents.

In what sense we must hate our father and mother.

The one who comes to me and does not hate his father and mother, his wife and children..(Mt. 10,37). That word does not mean that one must despise one's parents, wish them ill, not look at them, not be attentive to them, not render them any service. No. But this word means that our parents, being in the natural and terrestrial way, and we being in a spiritual and celestial way, our thoughts, ideas, aspirations, affections, must be as high above them as the sky is above the earth. The thoughts and affections of our parents are usually very terrestrial; our thoughts, desires, aspirations must be very celestial. *Nostra conversatio in caelis est* (Phil. 3,20). We must draw our thoughts and affections in heaven and not on earth,

---

[11] In the language of the time, souls meant the human person. We will see later on that Father Chevrier does not make a distinction between soul and body but distinguishes between body, heart, spirit and will.

in creatures. We must hate and despise what is terrestrial and seek and love only what is celestial and imitate Our Lord's behavior with St. Peter, whom he greatly loved, yet he did not hesitate to call him Satan, when Peter expressed thoughts so different and opposed to those of the Master. Get behind me, Satan! You are a scandal for me.

That is the way that we must answer anybody who would turn us away from our duty and from the true way that we must follow. We must hate our father and mother, that is, not be afraid to hurt them in certain circumstances, by going directly against their ideas, when it is a question of the glory of God and the salvation of souls.

What often holds us back in our determination is the fear of hurting them, the sorrow that our behavior will cause them: if I do such and such a thing, what sorrow that will cause them! They will say: he no longer loves me, he no longer cares for me, he abandons me, he is ungrateful. That is precisely the moment to accomplish the word of the divine Master and to act towards them as if we did not love them, as if we were abandoning them, even though deep down we love them sincerely. He who loves his mother or father more than me is not worthy of me. It is in those circumstances that we must appear cruel and fight against the feelings of nature and put into practice the Master's words: hate one's father and mother. We must always remain in great freedom of action in what concerns the service of God and the salvation of souls.

We must have greater love and esteem for our spiritual brothers than for our brothers according to the flesh.

That is what Our Lord Jesus Christ makes us understand in his answer to the woman in the crowd who raised her voice and cried: blessed is the womb that bore you and the breasts that nursed you.

At these words in praise of Mary, Jesus answers: rather blessed are those who hear the word of God and put it into practice (Lk. 11,27). Thus the title of mother disappears before that of servant of God and he prefers a true servant of God to the one who would have only a futile title of father or mother. We can also draw the same conclusions from those other words addressed to the one who told him that his mother and brothers were waiting for him outside, when he pointed to his disciples and said: my mother and brothers are those who listen to the word of God and put it into practice. The true family, the true brothers who deserve all the affection of our heart and the first place in our affections, are those who love God and put his word into practice.

| In what concerns our ministry, we have no advice to ask of our parents or of the people of the world. | This follows from the preceding article: our parents' thoughts, those of the people of the world, are terrrestrial; ours must be celestial |

We must not complain to the people of the world, tell them our business, sorrows, concerns. Unless they are in a more elevated sphere than the people of the world, those people are usually unable to give us good advice. That is what Judas did when he complained to the people, the Jews, the pharisees and he received only words of discouragement, he lost his vocation, sold his Master and went and hanged himself. He received advice from this one and the other, advice opposed to the spirit of God and he lost himself.

| With the people of the world we should have only relations of necessity and for the good of their souls. | Your are not of the world. I have chosen you and separated you from the world, said Our Lord to his apostles (Jn.15,19). Since we are not of the world, that we have been chosen and separated from the world by Jesus Christ, |

we must not love the world, nor follow the world, nor act like the world. We must feel repugnance and opposition, even hatred for all the futility, vanity of the world, its conversation, feasts, dinners, pleasures, enjoyments; otherwise we do not have the love of God in us because St. John says: if someone loves the world, the love of God is not in him (1 Jn. 11,25). And St. James also says: the love of the world is enmity with God (Jas. 4,4). By going often in the world, we necessarily acquire the tastes and ideas of the world. We are so bent to natural things, we have such a hard time to remain at the height of our vocation that contact with the world can only be disastrous for us. In frequenting worldly people, we quickly become worldly. *Tell me who you associate with and I will tell you who you are.* It is also a great loss of time to go often into the world: what useless things! what inane conversations that mean nothing! How sad it is to see a priest spend his evening in a parlor, speaking of the rain and nice weather, of politics and other useless things, losing his time, when there are so many souls to be converted![12] A priest should never sit down to chat and say useless things. When a priest goes into the world often he soon loses his authority, his ascendency over souls. One must be a great saint to go into the world and conserve one's authority of priest over others, especially when he is young. The people of the world are quick to see our faults, our misery; they examine them and make them the topic of their conversation and we quickly become the subject of their criticism and blame, and instead of having edified them we have scandalized them. It is very difficult to remain at the height of one's ministry and not

---

[12] Cf. 123.

weaken at times; it is better for people to come to see us than for us to go out to them. People invite us, urge us to come to them, are very polite and make a thousands flattering advances. Let us not believe them. In this case, it is better to appear uncouth than to appear as a socializer. It seems to me that the priest should only be seen in the pulpit, the confessional and at the altar; with the poor and the sick. Everywhere else the priest exposes himself to criticism and to becoming worldly by taking the tastes and ideas of the world. It seems that the priest should also flee public places where people ordinarily take their leisure. The priest must flee all that smells of the world and, when he needs to relax a little, he must go to some place apart. Prudence and discretion are needed with everybody, but especially with people of the world. When Our Lord Jesus Christ invites his apostles to take some rest, he does not bring them in the world and to the feasts; he leads them apart: *venite seorsum in desertum locum requiescite pusillum*[13].

What we must understand by "the world".

Not to go out without necessity and when we go into the world, to remember that we are the salt of the earth and the light of the world.

We are the salt of the earth. We are the light of the world, according to the word of Jesus Christ. Therefore, when we go out into the world, to is not to do as the world does and say *AMEN* to everything that is said and done, as we so often do, unfortunately,

but to be an example to the world. The priest must be in the midst of the world as a lamp that shines in all its splendor. We must show that we are not of the world, that we are the masters of the world and not its servants In this, imitate Jesus Christ who shows himself Master everywhere: he is Master among the pharisees, at their table as well as in the synagogue; he speaks, he rebukes, he instructs, he gives a lesson to the people, to the head of the house, to the doctors, the scribes. After his example we must not lose - never - our authority of priests and we must have it respected every- where.But how difficult it is to do so and one needs great wisdom, great prudence and often we can do more harm than good by our imprudence and clumsiness.

It is better to stay home than to go out to others and give them a lesson; for that one needs great authority, prudence, wisdom.

---

[13] Come away by yourselves in a lonely place amd rest a while.

Accept the hatred and contempt of the world which feels the just consequences of our behavior toward it.

In acting thus with the world, our parents and friends, in behaving in a manner so opposed to the world, we could do less than attract its scorn, hatred and sacrarsm. But that is precisely our glory and what makes our happiness and gives us the assurance of belonging truly to Jesus Christ. Since Jesus Christ himself says:If the world hates you, know that it has hated me before you. If you were of the world, the world would love what belongs to it; but because you are not of the world and that I have chosen you and separated you from the world,that is why the world hates you. But remember what I have told you: the servant is not above the Master (Jn. 15,18).I have given them your word and the world hates them because they are not of the world, like I myself am not of the world (Jn. 17,14). I am crucified to the world and the world is crucified to me (Gal.6,14). The world hates me freely. The world hates me because I give testimony that its works are evil (Jn. 7,7). Since you scorn the world and its maxims, the world can only scorn you as well.

How can we know that we love the world?

When we take pleasure in going out, when we prefer the company of the world or our family to that of our brothers.

When we find it difficult to refuse the invitations and society of the world. When we take pleasure in talking of our family, the world, of the greatness, their titles, their happiness and especially their wealth; of their property, their revenues and their manners. All this indicates an attraction for the world and luxury.

Promises of Jesus Christ to the one who has left his family and the world for him.

Whoever does the will of my Father in heaven is my brother and sister and mother (Mt.12,50). There is no one who has left house or brothers or sisters or mother or father or children or lands for my sake and for the gospel, who will not receive a hundredfold now in this time, houses and brothers and sisters and mothers and children and lands, with persecutions, and in the age to come eternal life (mk. 10,29).

Practical conclusion to this chapter on renunciation of family and the world.

We must leave our father and mother to devote ourselves to the service of God. We must hate our father and mother in the Christian sense. No longer to have anything in common with our family except what is necessary to accomplish the duty that charity imposes. To go in one's family or to one's parents only through motives of true charity and not simply to satisfy the affectionate feelings of nature, of the ones as well as of the others. To form a spiritual family among ourselves. To have more love and esteem for our spiritual brothers than for our brothers according to the flesh. Never ask advice of people of the world[14], to complain or gossip. Have no relationships with people of the world except through necessity and for the good of their souls... direction, prudence. Not to go out without permission and, when we go into the world, always remember that we are the salt of the earth and the light of the world. Accept the hatred and scorn of the world and one's family, which is the just consequence of our conduct with the world. *He is crazy.* Rely on Our Lord's words who promises the hundredfold to the one who will have left all for his sake.

vacations

(We may permit vacations with one's parents up to the philosophy or rhetoric class, because the knowledge of Jesus Christ is not yet sufficiently great in these young souls to totally sacrifice the family. By the time of rhetoric or philosophy, one must begin to understand the great maxims of Jesus Christ and to put them into practice, and then it is no longer affection that must lead souls, but duty, Jesus Christ who must begin to become the Master of these souls. Or if they are not able to follow these precepts, they cannot go forward[15].)

---

[14] Ms XI 192: For what concerns the duties of the priest.
Ms XI 590: For what concerns the kingdom of God.
[15] Renunciation must flow from the knowledge of Jesus Christ. (cf. p. 141).

SECOND CONDITION 159

ONE MUST RENOUNCE ONESELF

The preceding part already dealt with abandonment and renunciation. To speak of renunciation of oneself helps us to understand that it concerns a freedom to be acquired and not of acting as if things did not exist. Renunciation of the world does not consist in living as if the world did not exist but in taking the liberty of following Jesus Christ, Savior of the world; just like renunciation of oneself does not mean running to suicide but it means having understood practically that to follow the Master one must be entirely free of everything including oneself[1].
Could we not find another expression, perhaps more exact, than that of renunciation; for example surpassing oneself?
Father Chevrier found the translation in Mastaï-Ferretti which he reproduced in TD: If anyone would come after me, let him renounce himself[2]. *He felt that it was difficult to give a good explanation of this word of Jesus; that is why he gives the Latin text and even tries to explain himself by coining a word - which he does nowhere else: to abnegate oneself*[3].
Besides, to speak of surpassing or any other expression would not correspond to Father Chevrier's thought. Neither would it correspond to any commentaries that the spiritual masters have given on Jesus' word. They all refusea to water down Christ's teaching because they had experienced that, in taking the Gospel seriously, one had to achieve such a dispossession of oneself and everything else that we can only speak of it in terms of abnegation.
The renunciation that does not flow from the knowledge of Jesus Christ is worth nothing[4], *and the knowledge of Jesus Christ necessarily produces love, but this is only produced through a spiritual experience that only terms such as renunciation, nothing, death can evoke. It would be such a pity not to be able to arrive at EVERYTHING because we had refused to admit that we have to pass through NOTHING.*
On this, Father Chevrier's teaching is indisputable.
On the other hand, there is room for discussion on the motives given to explain the need for renunciation. On this point Catholic tradition conveys two currents, one that we can call pessimistic and the other optimistic. Both affirm the corruption of human nature inherited from Adam, but one current makes this corruption deeper, with wider consequences, than does the other. Both recognize that there remains something good in corrupt man, that the grace of Christ restores human nature more magnificiently than the first creation had established it in its initial grace and that this restoration occurs through the cross.
We give these summary explanations to try to situate Father Chevrier properly. Sometimes we hear on this topic: Is he not still marked by Jansenism? That is not

---

[1] Ms XI 98.
[2] Mastaï-Ferretti, 344-345.
[3] P. 145.
[4] Cf. p. 138, note 15.

the question at all. Jansenism as such is not primarily an exaggeratedly pessimistic concept of man's corruption but rather a narrow concept of the power of God's salvation. Father Chevrier is at the opposite extreme of this doctrine. The question is this: is he in the pessimistic current?

If The True Disciple *were a theological work, I think that we would have to answer yes. Everything that we have from this birth from Adam is spoiled, corrupt, says Father Chevrier[5]. But, on this theological level, he does not have a personal opinion and is not concerned with having one. Yet, in his expressions, he is influenced by the dominant pessimistic theological current of his time and his expressions are somewhat harsh for us, for it is the optimistic current that dominates our time. (That is no reason to label the pessimistic current as heretical when it remains within reasonable limits.)*

But The True Disciple *is not a speculative theological work. We repeat, Father Chevrier takes the point of view of spiritual experience and from that point of view, who would hesitate to say that a congenital impurity, caused by pride and selfishness, is mixed in with our best actions? It is only in hope that we are saved[6]. This does not mean that human nature is not essentially corruption; it is not a pronouncement on its corruption; we merely affirm, from experience that, at every moment, the effects of a certain corruption are present and the spiritual man, enlightened by the pure light of Christ, sees that in all his actions there is found a certain impurity, a mixture, says Father Chevrier, and this* mixture *is unacceptable before God[7].*

163 *Moreover, apostolic experience only confirms this inextricable co-existence of good and evil in every man and we wonder what apostle would be able to contradict from experience such phrases as:*

> It is very difficult to keep perfect chastity[8].
> It is very difficult to totally abandon one's reason, one's knowledge, one's natural life, one's faults of spirit, to be filled with the spirit of God and act only according to the spirit of God[9].
> At times it is difficult to sacrifice one's will[10].
> The one who has not renounced himself is always troubled, agitated, restless[11].

Besides, everybody is quickly convinced of all that. But there are those who continue to hope, in spite of their weakness and their infidelity, in the Word of God and those who find it more convenient to conclude: God does not ask so much.

---

[5] P. 145.
[6] Rom. 8,24.
[7] P. 153.
[8] P. 158.
[9] P. 200.
[10] P. 220.
[11] P. 236.

*So, is Father Chevrier pessimistic? I don't know.
On the level on which he places himself, that of the true apostles of Christ, let us ask of him an imperturbable optimism in the world of salvation achieved by Christ and he has this optimism:*

The more we are dead, the more we have life, the more we give life[12].
It is an echo of St.Paul: So death is at work in us, but life is in you[13].
Let us ask him to be realistic. What good is it to a man to believe himself healthy if he is sick? But the one who has not found the doctor prefers not to look too closely at his health for fear of falling into despair. It is the same for the true knowledge of sin in us, which is an integral part of the renunciation of self, flows from the knowledge of Jesus Christ.

It is in his light that we must learn to know each thing, to know truth, the spiritual value of each terrestrial thing, to know the true from the false, the just from the unjust, the good from the bad[14].

*Father Chevrier announces a four part division, considering that we are body, heart, spirit, will. In catechism, he certainly learned that man is made up of body and soul. Later, in philosophy, this definition was explained. But here the division shows that it is not a similar distinction. It defines four areas of human activity, an activity which absorbs us entirely, body and soul.
The body is the whole area of activity which is at the service of our biological subsistence as, for example, the fact of eating and everything that goes into the preparation of food. The heart is the whole affective area, the spirit includes all the activity that we deploy at the service of thought and will, it is the area of action, that is, all our undertakings.
Seen in this practical light, this division seems satisfactory. It is simple and corresponds to common sense. In this it is certainly convenient to Father Chevrier.
How did he elaborate it? His personal common sense, his gift of reflection based on experience could have sufficed. The various manuscripts of the TD bear the marks of a certain research, of hesitation, either on the number of parts to adopt (for example, the heart is not always mentioned) or on the order of the four parts.
However, it would not be surprising if Father Chevrier had borrowed this division from somebody else. In fact, many works of spirituality can point us in this direction; but we cannot tell with any certainty, nor even with any probability, which one he would have used.*

---

[12] Appendix V, p. 477.
[13] 2 Cor. 4,12.
[14] P. 80.

One must renounce oneself. It is the second act that Our Lord Jsus Christ demands of those who would come after him. After having renounced one's family and the world, one must also renounce oneself in order to be able to follow Jesus Christ. It is easy to understand that, to follow Jesus Christ, we must not be encumbered with our family nor belong to the world. Nor must we be encumbered with ourselves and all the miseries that accompany us, otherwise we would be obliged to stop at every moment[15].

Our Lord Jesus Christ's doctrine on renunciation of oneself. If anyone wishes to come after me, let him renounce himself, take up his cross and follow me (Mt.16,24).
That is Our Lord's word. *Abneget semetipsum.* To "abnegate" oneself, to renounce oneself, to consider oneself as n nothing. One must consider as nothing all that is of oneself, all that composes our being, all that we are, all that constitutes our person.

What can we claim as ours? We can claim as ours, as forming *OUR SELF*, our person, our individuality, our body, our spirit our heart, our will.
That is what really constitutes our being, our person. Well! Jesus Christ wants us to renounce all that to follow him.

Why does Jesus Christ want us to renounce ourselves? Because, he tells us, all that is born of the flesh is flesh, what is born of the spirit is spirit (Jn. 3,6).
That is, all that we bring from this birth from Adam is spoiled, corrupt; we must be reborn to take up a new life. *If a man is not born again, he cannot enter the kingdom of heaven* (Jn. 3,2). We were conceived in iniquity and *we were* born in sin, so that there can be nothing good in us. An impure well cannot give clear and limpid water. The first man is terrestrial, being from the earth and his children terrestrial (1 Cor. 15,47). Since Adam's sin, we have been sold to sin by concupiscence, as St. Paul explains in strong terms when he says: I am carnal, sold to be subject to sin. In fact, I do not approve of what I do, for the good that I want I do not do but, on the contrary, the I do the evil that I detest (Rom. 7,14). I am subject to the law of God by the spirit and to the law of sin by the flesh (Rom. 7,25). And Jesus says: If the grain of wheat, falling in the earth does not die, it remains alone, but if it dies, it bears

---

[15] Ms XI 91 - XI 624.
Why this renunciation of oneself? To live in Jesus Christ (Ms XI 91).
The more we die to ourselves, to our spirit, the more we live in Jesus Christ (Ms XI 624).

much fruit (Jn. 12,24). The picture of what we are. If we do not kill this carnal and vulgar nature in us, we will bear no fruit, but if it dies, we will bear much fruit[16].

Trees do not naturally bear good fruit; the fruits that come naturally are usually sour and wild. What does the gardener do? He chops off the head of the tree, slits it and places a good branch in the slit. This good branch grows, becomes strong and bears good fruit and the tree becomes good, but if a twig grows outside this branch, it is no good.

A picture of what we are. That good branch is Jesus Christ. Those branches that must be chopped off are us, our natural works that are worthless. It is Jesus Christ that we must put in us to make us good; without him we will produce only wild fruit worthless for heaven. Thus we must renounce all that comes from that first nature, all that we have brought from that first vitiated and corrupt birth. We must renounce ourselves.

What is renouncing oneself?

Renouncing oneself is renouncing all that we are composed of, that is, renouncing
> one's body,
> one's spirit,
> one's heart,
> one's will.

---

[16] This is not an immediate application of the phrase that precedes this one in St. John, for that phrase speaks of Christ's death on the cross and not of death to self.

Renouncing oneself is [169]
1. Renouncing one's body.

This is a hard chapter to present. These pages are often shocking in our times. Were they less shocking for his contemporaries? Certainly, for the mentality, still imbued in romanticism, admitted manners of speaking which lack sobriety for us. But we must not think that all this was easy to accept. When Father Chevrier speaks of gluttony and idleness, he denounces abuses that he saw in the clergy of his time. And, in the things that shock us, might he not be denouncing abuses of our time? Nevertheless, to have a good understanding of his thought, we must place these pages in their time.

The living conditions were different. There was no question of baths or showers for the poor, and in populous areas one shaved only once a week. The mentality was different, especially in relations between men and women. It was unthinkable to have women doctors, lawyers, representatives, for there were no girls in the universities, not even in the secondary schools[1].

Finally, in spiritual matters, it was considered normal to have minute examinations of a multiplicity of faults. This did not alter the good humor of people who listened to all this like to a well known refrain whose words we know by heart but to which we pay little attention.

We must also place these pages in the life of Father Chevrier. People found it good to live with him. He was not the suspicious man, smelling evil everywhere, severe and somber like a living reproach.

He was careful to give more than necessary to everyone so that they could all eat their full and on first Communion days at the Prado, the table was laden as for a country wedding. He was concerned with giving the necessary time of rest to his collaborators. With the Sisters of the Prado and other female members of his surroundings he had a simplicity of relationship that was perhaps not current at the time.

After this, what is left of all that he tells us on renunciation of one's body? There remains, first of all, the general design of a progressive spiritualization of the body, that is, an ever deeper ascendancy of the Holy Spirit. Nothing in us should remain outside the influence of God's Spirit and all our visible behavior should give witness to Christ whose members we are.

The fact also remains that, by his whole life, Antoine Chevrier showed how a priest consecrates himself physically to the mission he received.

First of all, concerning chastity, he wanted to live in truth the celibacy that he had accepted, without flirting with the little compensations that all too often degenerate into serious lapses, as experience proves. If we are more optimistic on the subject of human nature than in Father Chevrier's time, we are also more naive at times; and that is no progress.

One needs great esteem for chastity[2] *and understand well what it is.*

---

[1] Cf. Six, P. 205, note 76.
[2] P. 158.

As for work and food, suffice it to say that Father Chevrier "died of hunger"[3] at the age of 53, accomplishing what he had written:

It is better to live ten years less in working for God than to live ten years more doing nothing[4].

Keeping in mind the necessary adaptation to the changes in living conditions, let us listen in these pages on the renunciation of the body, to a call to take seriously the words of He who strongly denounced the rich who dined well while Lazarus went hungry[5], the lazy servant who did not do the work expected by the master[6], the man who looks at another man's wife with desire[7].

---

[3] Six, P. 359-376.
[4] Ms X 252.
[5] Lk. 16,19-31.
[6] Mt. 25, 24-30.
[7] Mt. 5,27-28.

In studying the doctrine of Our Lord and his apostle St. Paul, we find that renouncing one's body consists first of all in:
   not allowing oneself to be governed by the body,
   not pampering the body too much,
   renouncing sins of the body,
   making an instrument of peanance of the body,
   making one's body a living host through the practice of justice and virtue,
   correcting the exterior faults of one's body
   willingly accepting the sufferings and death of one's body.

1. Not allowing oneself to be governed by the body.

God said to Cain: you will master your evil instincts (Gen. 4,3). Walk by the Spirit and do not gratify the desires of the flesh (Gal. 5,16).

Make no provisions for the flesh, to gratify its desires (Rom. 13, 14). And elsewhere: do you not know that if you become slaves of someone to obey him, you remain the slaves of the one whom you obey, either of sin to find death or of obedience to find life (Rom. 6,16). According to all these words of Sacred Scripture, we see that it is not up to the body to command, but to obey; that we must not satisfy its desires, make provisions for the flesh, obey our caprices, become slaves. It is not up to the body to command, but to obey. We must consider our body as a servant and not as a master. It must be subject to the spirit; the body is only an instrument that we make use of to work and for all exterior things that can contribute to the glory of God and the good of others. It is a servant who must obey; we must lead and direct it as we lead an animal, as we command a servant. If we give too much freedom to a servant, he abuses it, becomes insufferable and does what he should not do.

Practical conclusion.

Consider one's body as a servant who must obey the soul and not as a master to whom we must submit.

Command one's body with authority and firmness.

2. It is renouncing the worship of one's body.

St. Paul tells us that we should dress our bodies modestly and soberly and not with braided hair and costly attire (1 Tim. 2,9).

St. Peter also recommends it in his epistles: Let not yours be the outward adorning with braiding of hair, decoration of gold, and wearing of robes, but let it be the hidden person of the heart with the imperishable jewel of a gentle and quiet spirit, which in God's sight is very precious (1 Pt. 3,3). Therefore we must strip from our exterior all useless ornament and be much more concerned with adorning the interior man that is not visible than the exterior man that is visible. We must remove all exterior ornaments such as rings, flowers, earrings, gold or silver chains, bows, gold watches, jewelry, even if those things come from the family. We should not have any exterior ornament, not even devotional, except the crucifix.

We must remove from our clothes everything that smacks of luxury, elegance, stylishness, the refined, excessive cleanliness, such as fine well presssed linens, collars, cuffs, polished shoes, laces, etc..., everything that pleases, is beautiful, graceful, lovely, that flatters the look.

We must avoid taking too great a care of our body, of our shoes, of our face, hands, finger nails, skin. Never use lotions, perfumes, perfumed soaps, looking glass; a mirror suffices for shaving, washing our face and combing our hair once; never admire or contemplate ourselves, seek good manners, bearing, tone, etc.. Never use those delicate and silky things that people of the world use; that makes of the body a little idol that we adorn to have it admired in the world or at home. How this worship of the body is opposed to the evangelical spirit! Loss of time, preoccupation with oneself, forgetfulness of God and one's duties; the more we think of ourselves, the less we think of God and others.

175 The true ornament of the the body is purity and modesty. In the world, one takes much to much care of the body. The saints took very little care of it: Benedict, Hilarion, Francis, Benedict Labre.

When one seeks God and neighbor, one does not have time to concern oneself with the body.

Practices.   To all this we can add:
    Wear short hair,
    a serge cassock without pronounced cut,
    simple and poor shoes, and the same with the rest.
    Shave twice a week.
    Take a bath only when it is necessary.
    Take the tonsure on our knees to remind ourselves of this renunciation of our body and also our spiritual royalty over the world and all its vanities.

3. To renounce one's body is to renounce the sins of the body.   St. Paul tells us: do let sin abide in your mortal bodies, to make you obey their passions.

Do not yield your members to sin as instruments of wickedness (Rom. 6,12). Act according to the spirit and you will not accomplish the desires of the flesh, for the flesh has desires contrary to those of the spirit, and the spirit's are contrary to those of the flesh; they are opposed to each other. And the works of the flesh are easy to recognize. They are: immorality, impurity, licentiousness, idolatry, sorcery, enmity, strife, jealousy, anger, selfishness, dissension, party spirit, envy, drunkenness, ca-

rousing and the like. I warn you that those who do such things shall not inherit the kingdom of God (Gal. 5,19).
In all these pronouncements, we see that we must renounce the sin that is in us, not give in to the desires of the flesh and not yield our members to sin. We see that the principal sins of the body are impurity, gluttony and laziness and, consequently, we must renounce those three types of sin.

We must renounce impurity. St. Paul tells us: put to death what is earthly in you: immorality, impurity, covetousness, evil desires, for it is those things that attract the wrath of God (Col. 3,5). The body is not made for impurity but for the Lord, and the Lord is for the body (1 Cor. 6,13). For this is the will of God, your sanctification: that you abstain from immorality, that each one of you know how to control his own body in holiness and honor, not in the passion of lust like heathens who do not know God, for God has not called us for uncleanness but in holiness (Thes. 4,3). According to these words, we must renounce all impurity, all sensuality, all unclean desire and know how to hold the vase of our body in holiness and cleanliness.

The body is naturally bent to impurity and to all sensual and unclean pleasures. Our body is like a quagmire, an infected swamp. On the surface, the water appears clear and pure, but at the bottom is infected mud. Let a foreign body be thrown into the water or a gentle wind brush the surface of the water and immediately the water becomes troubled and the mud of the bottom comes to the top and makes all this water impure. So it is with our body; as long as nothing troubles it, it remains calm and pure on the surface. But as soon as a foreign body penetrates it or the light wind of a thought or an affection passes over it, it becomes troubled. The impure mud comes to the surface and gives birth to trouble, agitation, impurity, shameful desires which are found in this mixture of a foreign body which has penetrated in our spirit, our heart or our body.

All that is opposed to purity, for purity does not suffer any mixture, any contact; nothing must penetrate in us except God who is purity itself, the body belongs to the Lord, he owns it, he alone has the right to enjoy it[8].

Thus, it is to all foreign mixture, all contact that we must renounce to remain totally pure and be able, as St. Paul says, to possess the vase of our body in holiness and cleanliness.

---

[8] Ms XI 648 - That is, that we belong to God and he is the only one who has a right to penetrate in us, because he alone is our master, he alone does not soil, like the rays of the sun do not soil the water into which the sun penetrates, on the contrary, they only make it more beautiful, more radiant; it is the same with the Lord. While when a foreign object plunges into it, it troubles and obscures it; so also when foreign creatures penetrate our hearts.

Pp. 21 and 143-144.

St. Paul compares our body to a vase: just as when we carry a precious ointment in a fragile vase we are careful, we walk cautiously, we do not tilt it to the right or the left for fear of spilling a few drops, so also must we carry the vase of our body cautiously to maintain it always within the bounds of chastity and cleanliness.

177 **Rules of purity.**

Renounce all acts contrary to purity. To remain pure, one must renounce all forbidden pleasures of the body, all agitation, emotions that trouble the flesh and give it sensual sensations, all guilty or agreeable actions such as caresses, useless touchings that can move the flesh and be agreeable. We must renounce not only what concerns us personally, what concerns our body, but also what may come from creatures and not allow anybody but God to enter into our heart[9].

Avoid all that might make us fall into sin. Our Lord speaks forcefully when, speaking of the need to avoid all occasion of sins of this kind, he says: If you eye is a source of scandal, pluck it out, if you hand... (Mt. 5,29).

Renounce all too natural affection. We must renounce all too natural affection for whomever it may be. We see that an affection is too natural when we think often of a person, that we like to think of that person, that this thought softens our heart, awakens our senses, that we seek the company of those persons. It may even happen that the desire to do good to those persons, to be useful to them spiritually, is only a specious pretext that hides the evil that is in us.

Practice modesty of the eyes. Avoid affectionate or prolonged looks for whoever it may be and especially on persons of the opposite sex.
It is through the eyes that love enters the heart and throughout the body to move it. One must never look a person directly in the face, especially in the eyes; besides not being decent and polite, it is totally contrary to chastity and Christian modesty.
There are people who have the habit of looking straight at those to whom they are speaking; that always indicates a tendency to affection and the desire to be loved.

178 David fell into sin because he began to look. Eve looked at the forbidden fruit and her prolonged look fanned the flames of concupiscence in her and made her fall into evil. Job had made a pact with his eyes.

---

[9] In ecclesiastical language of the time, creature meant the human person and often enough, women in particular. It is not created beings in general.

Whoever looks at a woman with lust to desire her has already commited adultery in his heart. If your eye is a source of scandal, pluck it out....

Avoid unnecessary relations with women.

In the Gospel, we see the apostles very surprised to find Jesus speaking to the Samaritan women, yet it was on the road, in a public place. This surprise reveals all the behavior of our Lord Jesus Christ with women, with what reserve he speaks to them and what examples of prudence he gives in this respect.

For us, to follow these examples of our Lord:
we do not receive women alone in our room, we receive women in a public parlor, the doors of the parlor must be glassed, we may receive women in our room when they are accompanied by their husband or their children, but never alone, and this may be necessary in certain cases.

Never visit women needlessly.

We must deny ourselves unnecessary and frequent visits to women and devout persons, visits that are often done to pass the time, for pleasure or through frivolous affection. Those visits only maintain a too often natural affection, they usually concern only useless and frivolous things; women question, want to know what is happening in the rectories, houses, works; we yield to gossip, indiscretion, imprudence, which later on, have unfortunate consequences.

Devout women especially, invite priest to come and see them, especially those who have nothing to do. Those visits always end up by scandalizing the neighbors who are always more apt to see evil than good and one oftens ends up being the topic of conversation of the neighborhood or the parish.

One cannot say enough how important this article is and how many priest have lost themselves through useless visits.

Act with prudence and reserve in encounters, excursions, trips where we may find ourselves with women.

Through prudence, we must avoid 179 prolonged conversations with women in the street; if we meet someone that we know and we have something important to say, we must be brief in these meetings.

And, without being impolite or rude, disengage ourselves from their company by saying that we cannot tarry any longer. Neither is it appropriate to walk up and down the streets with women. We must also avoid excursions with women, on foot or in a carriage; that is not appropriate at all. We can never take too many precautions in this matter, in the evil and corrupted times in which we live. We must not give others the opportunity to speak ill of us; they have enough to say without our giving them cause. We must consult the rules of prudence and wisdom before undertaking trips with women; these are always disagreeable for ourselves and often scandalous for others, especially when we go to a hotel. What we say about women goes also for religious women; they are no less subject to criticism than the others.

Avoid all familiarity with women.

We must avoid all familiarity or exterior marks of affection with women, such as hugs, closeness, holding hands or other similar gestures which, without always being mortal sins, are too often venial sins, show a too natural affection, awaken the senses and scandalize others when they notice it.

After his resurrection, when Our Lord said to Magdalene, Noli me tangere, he wanted to show us that, if before he had allowed her to embrace his feet, when she was a sinner, it was to show her that he accepted her tears and sorrow, but now she no longer needed those exterior signs to love him and that she had to wean herself from all those exterior signs if she seriously belonged to God, to live a truly spiritual life.

There are people who try to kiss your hand (it is the custom in many countries to kiss the priest's hand), we may let men do so without inconvenience. As for women, we must distinguish between the ones who do it through a real respect for the priest and those who do so merely for the pleasure of kissing your hand and through a feeling of natural affection; the latter must be prevented from doing so.

Once one has become a priest, or even when one has taken the cassock, one must no longer embrace one's sisters, cousins, relatives in public, nor even address them familiarly, especially the young ones. As for elderly relatives such as mothers, aunts, elderly women, one should do it only when it seems appropriate and necessary in certain circumstances: feast days, on return from journeys.

However, we cannot refuse an embraee to those persons, especially when we see that they do it with such simplicity. Yet we must avoid doing it in public because there are always evil eyes who see evil where there is none. Affectionate embraces among persons of the same sex.

Reciprocal attraction inter virum et mulierum.

God has put a natural attraction between men and women because they were created for one another and it is only through a very supernatural grace and a special help that they can live apart from each other and do without each other. This being the case, one needs a great grace from God to guard against a certain natural pleasure in being together, living together and being mutually helpful, which Providence has provided one for the other.

Thus we must be careful in our relationships with women because, even if we have renounced having a woman as a wife, we have not destroyed the natural feeling that

carries us toward them, and when we notice that we experience some affection, however light, for a woman, we must immediately be on our guard to turn away; and when we notice that a woman loves us, however little, we must also separate her from us in order not to give her the opportunity to love us more.
It must be very difficult for a man to live with a woman without experiencing some temptation for her, and conversely, it must be very difficult fer a woman to live with a man and serve him without experiencing some temptation of love for him; there is only a special grace that they must both draw from constant prayer, communion and the rules of great prudence and great reserve one toward the other. To make chastity easier for us, to better practice the spirit of mortification and penance, after the example of Saint Paul, we will not take women in our personal service, but we will take men, a boy or two, for the service of the church and the house. In case of sickness, if there are no men able to do so, we may take a nurse among the religious or elderly women.

Do not receive gifts from women. Gifts maintain affection and mutual relationships. We may receive nothing for ourselves, but we may receive things for the church, the community, the poor, things that may be useful for everybody.

Do not visit religious women without necessity. Religious women are not more exempt from criticism than the others and they may be more so when they seek the company of priests too often and they receive visits too often. We must visit them only through necessity, and when we do go, we do not sit down, unless it is to teach catechism, preside a meeting, fulfill a duty, but never remain to chat, spend time in useless conversation.

Avoid too affectionate caresses with children. We are so carried to evil that we find, even in children sometimes, an occasion to awake concupiscence in us, especially when they have some natural quality, some exterior grace; affection is often born of these qualities and they impel us to embraces, unseemly caresses that awaken the senses and lead to sin. We must guard are relationships, even with children; not that we should avoid evidence of affection and tenderness, since we see Our Lord himself embracing the little children; but we must do it with honest motives, to lead them to God and not for personal satisfaction.

Avoid all coarse, equivocal or rude words. (Eph. 4,29).

It is difficult to maintain total chastity.

Means to keep chastity.
Vigilance.
Prayer.
Work.
Penance.
Have great esteem for chastity.
Renew one's vow of chastity from time to time.

182 **Summary and practical conclusions.**
Renounce all acts contrary to purity.
Renounce all too natural affection.
Keep modesty of the eyes.
Avoid all unnecessary relations with women.
Do not receive women alone in your room.
Do not visit women unnecessarily.
Act with prudence and reserve during meetings, excursions, trips.
Avoid all familiarity with them, even those of one's family
Do not take women in personal service
Do not receive personal gifts from them.
Do not visit religious women unnecessarily.
Avoid affectionate caresses, even with children.
Avoid coarse, equivocal and rude words.
Watch, pray, and work to keep chastity.
Have a great esteem for chastity.
Renew your vow of chastity every year.

One must renounce gluttony, the second sin of the body.
(there are many things in this chapter that should be in the chapter on poverty).

Gluttony is the second sin of the body that we must renounce. Here it is not a question of those excesses that make us lose our mind. It would be an abomination to see privileged souls, called by God to such a holy vocation as that of the priesthood, let themselves go to such excesses and dishonor their habit and their brothers by making *a god of their bellies*, as Saint Paul says. It is merely a question of what wounds modesty, mortification, poverty and of knowing how the true disciple of Jesus Christ must take his food.

The body naturally seeks nourishment; it was given to it by God to maintain its life. But if we do not moderate this action, this natural ardor to take food, if faith does not moderate this all too animal action, we indulge avidly and greedily, we seek what is good, we savor the food and take more than necessary. We consider it with pleasure, eat greedily; we drink and eat more through satisfaction and pleasure than to satisfy the necessities of life, or we are never satisfied with anything: it is too hot, too cold, too salty, too ill prepared, too clear, too thick.

Our Lord's words and example on this subject.

From the words and examples of Our Lord Jesus Christ, we can draw lesson to regulate our conduct in this matter.

During the temptation in the desert, when the devil tells him to perform a miracle to satisfy his hunger, Jesus answers: *Man does not live by bread alone, but by every word that comes from the mouth of God.*

Another time, Jesus was thirsty and was standing by Jacob's well, waiting patiently for a drink. A Samaritan woman comes along to draw water; Jesus finds an occasion to instruct her and give her the living water of faith. When his apostles returned they said: Lord, eat; and he answered with these admirable words: I have a food that you do not know; my food is to do the will of my Father.

And elsewhere he says that he himself is our nourishment: I am the living bread come down from heaven; he who eats of this bread will live eternally. Your fathers ate of the manna in the desert and they died; he who eats of the bread that I will give you will never die.

By his words, Jesus shows us that our first nourishment is the word of God, that we should be more concerned with nourishing our soul than our body, that our true nourishment is Jesus Christ himself, since he is the living bread that gives life. While the bread of the earth is a bread of death: Your fathers ate the manna in the desert and they died. He who eats of this bread will never die. That we must have as much ardor for the works of God and his divine word as the people of the world have for the nourishment of their body. My food is to do the will of my Father.

We must not give more attention or importance to this nourishment of the body than Jesus himself did when, being thirsty, he waited patiently by Jacob's well for somebody to come and give him to drink, being hungry, he crushed grain in his hand, along with his apostles; being hungry, he sought figs on a fig tree in Jerusalem or refused to perform a miracle for the devil to satisfy his hunger.

According to these words of the divine Master, we must conclude that the disciple, after the example of the Master, must take his nourishment with faith, humility, gratitude and sobriety.

Take ones nourishment with faith.

While taking our material nourishment, we must think of that spiritual and divine nourishment

184 which is the only true one since it is that one alone that can lead us to eternal life and that corporal nourishment cannot make us escape death, that the only true nourishment is Jesus Christ, his divine word, his sacred flesh, his adorable blood, that one day we will be called to that eternal banquet of heaven where we will be nourished with the eternal light that will be our life.

With humility. This animal nourishment puts us on a level with beasts.
Like them, we eat the grass of the fields, the fruit of the trees and the animals of the earth. We must eat only as much as we have earned by our work, since we have been told, after the first sin: *you will eat your bread by the sweat of your brow.*
We are unworthy of living since the sinner who offends God does not deserve to live, since he uses his life to outrage God and the one who does not serve his master is unworthy of life.

With gratitude. Because everything comes from God and it is he who sends us the food necessary for our life every day.
It is he who, each year, covers the earth with flowers and fruits to nourish men and puts at our disposal the animals of the earth, the sea and the sky to nourish us, that he nourishes us in a more particular and providential manner than the others and that we must never forget the prayers that precede and follow the meals, after the example of the divine master who always gave thanks to his Father in those moments. Those prayers are:

before breakfast:
>   the simple Benedicite
>   and the same for the graces after.

before the noon meal we will say a short form of that of the breviary:
>   Kyrie eleison
>   Christe eleison
>   Kyrie eleison
>   Pater
>   Benedicite, Dominus; nos et ea quae sumus sumpturi benedicat dextera Christi[10].

after the meal:
>   Agimus tibi gratias
>   Pater
>   Benedicamus Domino

---

[10] May the right hand of Christ bless us and what we are about to take.

Fidelium animae
at the evening meal: the same prayers as for the noon meal.

With sobriety. We must eat to maintain the life of the body, we must be satisfied with what is necessary and not go beyond; a surplus is more harmful than useful, no matter how we look at it. Saint Paul notes it often in his epistles:

Sobrius esto[11].
Sobriety is the guardian of chastity; those who eat and drink beyond what is necessary have great difficulty in being chaste.

Vinum res luxuriosa[12].
Sobriety leaves the body free and available, while intemperance, however light, takes away our willingness to work, numbs us or agitates us and carries us to many interior and exterior faults.
In the desert, St. John the Baptist *vinum et siceram non bibet*[13]. All the saints were very sober in their food.
  Not to serve oneself too copiously,.
  avid, delicate, glutton, eat too much.

Sobriety and mortification. There is sobriety during meals. There is also sobriety and mortification outside of meal times.
It is totally contrary to mortification to be constantly eating, to have something to nibble on in one's room or in one's pocket and to take them at every moment without necessity. When we go to the kitchen or elsewhere, to take fruit or other food, if there is any, for the sole pleasure of eating. If we go to the garden, we take fruits, grapes, apples, without nocessity, for the pleasure of tasting and eating. Those habits indicate a man without control, without mortification and who lets himself go to the desires of the flesh without surpressing them.
In everything we must act with reserve and moderation. Gluttony impels us to theft, and that without our being aware of it, for those acts of gluttony are often petty thefts from the neighbor. And the scandal that ensues for the neighbor, especially for the children who have a tendency to take; in acting like this we authorize faults in others.

---

[11] Be sober (2 Tim. 4,5).
[12] Wine carries to excess (Pr. 20,1).
[13] He will drink no wine or fermented drink (Lk. 1,15).

sugar, beer, syrup, liquors, fruit, a drop[14], tea, candy.

186 Mortification during meals, one must not lack sobriety and mortification in oneself or have others lack it by pressing them to drink and eat, which is contrary to politeness, to good manners and to mortification. To achieve the ends of divine Providence, food must fulfill several conditions. They are: cleanliness, quantity and simplicity.

Cleanliness. Cleanliness is the first quality because it is the most useful for life; uncleanliness is harmful to the body and to health and indicate laziness, negligence and lack of charity in those who prepare it. Thus, it is a great duty for the cooks to prepare the food cleanly, to wash and peel the vegetables, to keep the food clean, not to leave it hanging around. Sickness and discomforts that occur often come from the uncleanliness or negligence that went in the preparation of food. Those things must be done with charity and help must be sought if one cannot cope alone.

Exactitude. In a community, the meals have to be ready at the time indicated on the schedule, otherwise it could cause a lot of problems. And also, everybody should take their meals together at the same time, unless there are serious reasons to be dispensed. Order and edification depend on the fulfillment of this article. If each one comes to take his meals at the hour that pleases him, that is a great burden for the cooks and a lack of charity because it makes their job, already so arduous, harder still.

Quantity. The function of food is to maintain the life of the body, therefore one must give the body the food that it needs. The quantity varies according to age, temperament and state of health. We must never look at what others eat. But we must see to it that they have what is necessary and not expose them to not having enough, without looking to see if one takes more and another less; that is up to the conscience of each one. Those who eat more sometimes make more acts of mortification that those who eat less.

    breakfast: a soup, two desserts
    noon: soup, two dishes, two desserts;
               or three dishes and two desserts
    night: soup, a dish, two desserts.

---

[14] In popular language, to take a drop is to have a glass of alcoholic beverage.

Quality. This condition concerns the sick and those whom we must take care of in charity.
Charity imposes the duty of caring for the sick and the weak, and it would be a fault to let them lack what they should have, when we can give it to them.

Simplicity Simplicity consists of taking away from food all thats smack of luxury, vanity, refinement, satisfaction of tastes and gluttony. It is not the foods that are the most refined, tasteful, well seasoned, well prepared, that look good that are the most beneficial to health. On the contrary, they are harmful to the body because they excite it, irritate it, attack the nervous system and blood stream and give rise to many sicknesses. The Holy Spirit says that intemperance has killed more men than the sword; one shortens one's life by the use of refined and well prepared foods. On the contrary, simple and frugal food maintains the strength and vigor of the body and preserves us from any illnesses[15].

Eat quickly without ceremony. It seems to me that it is an activity that should be done in passing without attaching to it the importance that we usually do. Do we not give to much importance to this animal function? Those preparations of tables, rooms, place settings, linens, dishes, elegant and precious utensils that are multiplied for the various kinds of foods and wines. How opposed this is to simplicity and mortification; how much more simply the poor live! They do not put so much importance and preparation in their meals. Often their only table is their knees, their chair is a bench or a stone, their utensils are earthen or wooden bowls and a wall to support their back tired by work. And what do we find on their table? A potato soup, some cheese, vegetables, sometimes a piece of meat. If only we could do like them and eat as poor people! Did not our Lord often eat as a poor person, when he sat by the side of Jacob's well and his apostles told him to eat? Did he not eat as a poor person when his apostles, forced by hunger, crushed the grain and ate it? Did he not eat as a poor person when he sought a few figs on a fig tree when he was hungry? This corporal food was of little importance to him, he had another food with which he fed his soul: I have a food that you do not know. Let us leave to the people of the world, to the bourgeois, this care of tables, this importance, this work, these decorations and ce-

---

[15] Ms XI 707 - The more one draws near to simplicity in everything, the more one is in the true way. This goes for food as well as for styles: the farther one goes from simplicity in dress, the more one is ridiculous; the farther one goes from simplicity in food, the more one harms one's health. One must draw as close to simplicity as possible to have good health. The more we take things in their natural state, the better they are; the more people add their influence, the more they spoil them.

remonies that they attach to the nourishment of this poor body. Let us be happy with little, let us take what is necesary but avoid those apparels, those ceremonies in use among the rich and the bourgeois, let us eat as sojourners and poor people[16].

How simple and poor it would be to do like the soldiers and cook everything in the same pot: meat, vegetables, put the pot or a big dish that contains everything on the table and take what is necessary from the pot and eat our share standing or seated on a bench against the wall, as do the poor and the travelers.

How much more simple it would be, more in conformity with poverty and mortification. Is that not what the soldiers do, and they are not the worse for it. Are we not God's soldiers?

It is in thus despising this terrestrial and material nourishment that we can arrive at saying with the divine Master: I have a food that you do not know: my food is to do the will of my Father. What good example would come out of it for the faithful and the children! Do not the faithful and the children always have their eyes on what we eat? If we have something more refined, more delicate, more appetizing, does that not excite their envy and jealousy? and they say or think: he is much better than we.

If we want to have ascendency over them, we must be poor with them, we must be small. We must not separate ourselves from the poor, even in the matter of food, and not give them cause to say: he is treated better than we are. What is the use of becoming poor if we do not live like the poor? And this is an important point because it is in part from the mouth that comes good or bad example, edification or scandal. Should we not be ashamed to be treated better, better fed than the others? of having good and nice pieces on our table? well seasoned, well prepared, beautifully roasted dishes? while others barely have the necessities. Should we not share everything that we eat with the poor, our children? Does a father not share with his children? All the saints were little concerned with food and looked upon this function as the most humiliating of all, so to speak. How beautiful and edifying was the poor curé of Ars, crossing the public square with his pot of soup in his hand, eating his soup while going to visit the sick! He did not have time to eat, as the Gospel says of the apostles themselves: they ate as they worked, walked, as do the poor, and they converted more sinners by living like this than by eating at a well laden tables, because this type of example is more striking than the others, given that people are more apt to satisfy themselves that way.

The good curé of Ars usually cooked a pot of potatoes that he ate with bread as long as the supply lasted; he had even tried to eat grass in the field. He bought the bread of the poor, begged from door to door and gave them his, tohhave the happiness of eating like the poor. How poorly the saints treat themselves in this regard! And how

---

[16] XI 672. In the food there must be cleanliness, quantity and simplicity; the rest is nothing. Does it not often happen that, when we eat at the table of the rich, we are less nourished than at the table of the poor? that the ceremonies and apparels are not nourishment?

he loved the poverty and simplicity and pushed away from their table all that smelled of luxury, refinement, ceremony, pomp, well-being!

Little corollary concerning tobacco. It is forbidden to smoke and one should take snuff only through necessity.

Summary and practical conclusions. To renounce gluttony is to renounce all excesses that can trouble the spirit, reason or soften the body, it is to renounce all that is not necessary and serves only to flatter the taste, the palate, such as delicate foods, *fine wines, liqueurs, coffee, sweets*, rare and exotic things. We must use these things only in true necessity and with great moderation; at home, we must only use them with permission, we must not expose ourselves to temptation by keeping liqueurs, wines and other similar things, but these comestibles must be kept apart to be given when there is a real need. It is to renounce all that smacks of luxury, refinement, well-being, pomp and ceremony in meals. It is to be happy with the ordinary in what concerns bread, meat, fruits, vegetables, etc... unless one is sick. It is not to eat outside meal times without necessity, it is avoiding dining outside, because gluttony is too often satisfied there; avoid going to other people's houses for coffee and snacks, take nothing at other people's houses, this to avoid gluttony and many little scandals and useless expense for others; necessity alone can dispense us from this point.

Avoid wasting time at table; eat with haste and without ceremony.

One must renounce laziness. Laziness is the third sin of the body. In the Gospel, Our Lord Jesus Christ often speaks of the sad consequences of this unhappy fault.

When he speaks of the barren fig tree that will be thrown into the fire because it bears no fruit, of the servant to whom the master has entrusted a talent and who was put in prison because he did not make it profit, of the servants who fell asleep and let weeds be sown in their master's field.

All those examples are parables that show how much God hates laziness and how he punishes it, even in this world and expecially in the next. Laziness is a great apathy to which we let ourselves go and which makes us totally neglect our religious and temporal duties.

Laziness leads us to idleness, sleep and softness that are the three daughters of laziness, so to speak.

Idleness. *Idleness* consists in spending one's time doing nothing.

We were condemned to work by God and we were born to work. You will eat your bread by the sweat of your brow. Jesus Christ worked like a poor person until the age of 30. Saint Paul work with his hands, night and day sometimes, to see to his needs and not to be a burden to anybody and he himself said: if anyone does not work, he should not eat. There are different types of work; there is manual work and work of the mind. Each one should do the work to which he was called with zeal, activity, submission and charity.

To lose one's time is an irreparable thing; it is to disobey God, an injustice to the neighbor and to render oneself unhappy and insufferable. Idleness is the mother of all evils. The idle man is exposed to all temptations. On the contrary, the one who works is sheltered from many bad thoughts; when the mind is occupied with work, it does not have time to think of evil.

If anybody on earth should work, it is the priest since his work is so elevated, so important for him and for others; since his mission comes from God and the glory of God and the salvation of souls, the happiness or unhappiness of men in time and eternity depend on his work. Before such a mission, such a great duty, can the priest cease his work for one instant, since in ceasing his work, he may be the cause of many souls being lost. O priest! how great is your responsibility and how you must consume yourself in work for the glory of God and the salvation of souls! And yet, if there is a man who spends a lot of time doing nothing, it is the priest![17]

It is true that his work is all of the mind and is not always seen, but it is also true that we often see the priest unoccupied and spending his time uselessly. That is so true that, if we go out for a serious reason, we find people who come to breath in our face and say: Good morning, Father, you are going for a walk, you are returning from a walk. As if all we did all day was go for a walk. That is the reputation that we have in the world, of going for walks, of wasting our time. Sad reputation! Alas, if we were seen less often in the streets and public square, less often dining with other people, less often on useless visits, more occupied with the poor, the sick, in good works, more often preaching and attracting people by our faith and our charity, we would not be asked so often if we are going for a walk.

The priest, more than anyone else, must work all day. Masons work all day, so do carpenters, cabinet makers, farmers, tailors, etc. All those people work all day and sometimes at night, to earn their living and that of their children, and the priest would have a softer lot, he whose job is so far above these. Is it not because the priest did not work, or worked badly, that the field of the head of the household is in such bad shape? that ignorance has invaded our poor workers and that they rise up against us today? If we had worked well and done a good job, we would not be so

---

[17] It is a hard blow. Typical attitude of Antoine Chevrier. He knows that people accuse the priest of idleness. He does not seek to justify himself but seeks means of giving no one the opportunity for scandal so that his ministry may not be decried (cf. 2 Cor. 6,13).

unhappy and persecuted. If the field is fallow and produces only weeds it is because we did not till it or plant it.
We must work at preaching and catechizing, night and day. That is our work! The faithful and the people of the world must not see an idle priest; that is the greatest scandal that we can give because, from our idleness, they conclude many other things. We must not seem to be going for a walk, of having nothing to do.
When we need some fresh air or a bit of recreation, we should try to do so in a solitary place, in order not to be seen by people.
To chat in the street, to stop and say useless things......
We see our Lord inviting his apostles to rest after the arduous work of their mission, but they do not go into the world to seek rest in the feasts of the world; he leads them apart *seorsum in desertum locum requiescite pusillum*[18].
    recreations
    excursions
    vacations
    parlors
Dispose one's time with order.
If we do not put order in our work, we do nothing, or if we work we do not achieve anything because the work is not sustained. There are some who arrive at the end of their day, week, year, life without having done anything because they did not do a sustained work; they began many things but finished nothing, many undertakings but nothing finished: unfruitful work.
Work must be constant, persevering and regular every day, every week, and then we may achieve something, finish something.
Otherwise, nothing. And how many, unfortunately, fall in this fault of irregularity and inconstancy in their work. On seeing them, one would think that they work a lot; they move around, they come and go, they have spoken a lot, they have moved about a lot to do nothing and to end up with nothing. That is the great misfortune.
In speaking of those people, and of himself through humility, the curé of Ars would say: much labor, very little work.
One must establish the time of one's work and, once we have begun a task, some work, not to abandon it before it is finished, to undertake something else.
Nor must we waste our time in little visits to each other among brothers. Take the habit of being brief. It happens that we lose a lot [of time] in visits to each other's room: we sit down, we chat, we waste time. We must say what is necessary and, when that is finished, leave in order not to our waste time and make others waste theirs.
In the language of the street, that is called *"loafing" "loafer"*, who does nothing, who spends his time in chatting, stretched out or sitting, going here and there to kill time. That is what we are, more or less

---

[18] Come apart, in a desert place, and rest a while (Mk. 6,31).

It is good to have serious work to do and a firm will to finish it, to have one's attention and mind constantly fixed on it and to allow few distractions from this work that we can do and finish. Then our mind is occupied.

Summary.   The priest must be a man of work par excellence.
We must never see him idle or unoccupied. We must put order in our work and be constant in what we do. We must be occupied in serious work and not waste time in useless and frivolous things. We must not waste our time in useless conversations or visits with our brothers; not be among those who are called *"loafers"*. Always be occupied in order not to give the faithful the opportunity to look on us as lazy, people who have nothing to do.

Sleep.   Sleep is a rest that God has given us to repair the strength lost during the day's work.
We must only take the rest necessary to return our body's ability to work. To remain in bed without any necessity, for the sole pleasure of it, is a sin of laziness. And when we remain in bed without sleeping and without necessity, we expose ourselves to many temptations and faults.

Remember that it was while the workers were asleep that the enemy came and sowed tare in the householder's field. And that reproach that Jesus Christ addressed to Peter when he said: Peter, are you asleep? Could you not watch one hour with me? We must go to bed early and rise early. Know that night work is painful and harmful to the health and that it is a great fault to delay our work, breviary, prayers until the evening; we do them badly, to get rid of them, rather than to fulfill our duty and we draw no fruit from them.

On rising in the morning, the day is always better filled if the meditation is made, the breviary said at the proper hour; we are happy, everything goes better during the day, we are not late. If we begin the day badly, we cannot expect it to finish any better.

Practice.   For those who are in good health, the necessary time for rest is usually seven or seven and a half hours.
We must go to bed at nine or half past nine and rise at half past four; that is the rule of the house. If we have reasons for doing otherwise, we must not do so, never, without permission. Health is often altered because we do not take the necessary rest and go to bed too late. If we do not waste time during the day, we will have time to do everything. Let us establish the hours of work and various occupations and everything will go better for rising and retiring. Rising and retiring are very impor-

tant articles to spend the day well. We must not sleep during the day without necessity or permission; if we do, we accuse ourselves of it.

Indolence Indolence is a soft, effeminate or careless attitude of the body that one takes which comes from laziness. We must renounce indolence. Indolence denotes a soul that seeks its comfort, that wants to suffer nothing, endure nothing, a soul without strength, without energy, that does not know how to endure anything, not even the little discomforts.

One can be indolent, careless in many circumstances. We must avoid bad postures in bed, in our room, on a chair when we are seated, in church when we are kneeling or seated.

Avoid slouching when standing or seated, taking indolent positions by leaning the back or the elbows.

Avoid stretching the arms and legs, yawning, crossing the legs, especially in the presence of others, or even when alone.

Avoid stretching on chairs, armchairs, sofas; tilting back in a chair, taking any indolent or effeminate posture.

Wherever we go, but especially in church, not to chose the most convenient place; it is better to do without a prie-Dieu and take the first available place, leaving the good places for others. A Christian, and especially a priest or religious should have a decent, Christian, good, mortified bearing.

We must glorify God in our body.

The body impels us naturally to sin, its terrestrial and sensual inclinations constantly lead us toward laziness, gluttony, impurity.

It is up to us to struggle constantly against this poor body and the struggle is continuous and tiring.

That is what made St. Paul say: O unhappy man that I am! Who will deliver me from this body of death? (Rom. 7,24).

4. To renounce one's body is to make of one's body an instrument of justice and penance.

After having renounced the sins of the body, we must still do penance to obey our Lord who recommends it so much in the Gospel.

Do penance, says Jesus Christ. If you do not do penance, you shall all perish (Lk. 13,3). And John the Baptist said to those who came to see him in the desert: Bear fruits that befit repentance, and do not begin to say to yourselves, We have Abraham as our father; for I tell you, God is able from these stones to raise up children to Abraham (Lk. 3,8). That is what the apostles preached when Our Lord sent them to announce the word to the people:Repent, for the kingdom of God is near (Mt. 3,2). In his writings, St. Paul does not cease speaking of repentance. Do not yield your members to sin as instruments of wickedness, but yield yourselves to God as men

who have been brought forth from death to life, and your members to God as instruments of righteousness (Rom. 6,13).
Arms of justice, to punish you[19]. He tells us further that those who belong to Jesus Christ have crucified their flesh with its passions and immoderate desires (Gal. 5, 24). Mortify the members of your body that are on earth (Col. 3,5). And speaking of himself, he said: I chastise my body and reduce it to subjection, for fear that, after having preached to other, I myself be condemned (1 Cor. 9,27). The obligation to do penance is thus clearly shown by all those word of Our Lord and St. Paul.

>We must do penance,
>bear fruits of repentance,
>make of our members instruments of righteouness, after they have been instruments of sin.
>We must chastise our body,
>we must crucify the flesh.

We crucify the flesh by refusing it what it demands. We crucify our feet by not going where they would like to go, by condemning them to rest; our hands by not doing evil, by holding them extended in the form of a cross. We chastise our body by taking the discipline, by wearing some instrument of penance, by marking it with the signs of the passion, as St. Paul: I bear on my body the marks of Christ (Gal. 6,17), by stretching it on the cross, on the wood.

The body is reduced to subjection by not letting it command, by keeping it subject to the spirit and faith, like a slave must be submitted to his master. It has enough time to be demanding and be master when it suffers and is sick.

Penance atones for past sins, preserves from future failings, gives strength to the soul for the practice of virtue, prevents us from falling into tepidity and indolence and makes us earn many graces for ourselves and others.

Penance makes us conform to Jesus Christ and gives us a share in his merits.

St. Paul said that he completed in himself what was lacking in the passion of the Savior. To conform to the passion of Jesus Christ in order to have a share in his resurrection.

All the saints did penance; we cannot read the life of a saint without being astonished at the penances that he did.

Practice.

>Take the discipline at least once a week wear some instrument of penance occasionally, with the superior's permission.
>Sleep on a board occasionally, with the superior's permission.
>Rise during the night to pray, for example, say 5 Our Fathers and Hail Marys, with the arms in the form of a cross.

---

[19] Cf. Introduction, p. 33.

Bear the discomforts of life without complaining.
Accomplish one's duty, despite the repugnance of nature.
We can find occasions to do penance from morning till night, if we want to take the daily opportunities that present themselves.
There is a penance that comes from God, that is found in work, suffering and death.
There is a penance that comes from the neighbor, in bearing all that comes from him, without complaining and without making him aware of it.
There is a penance that comes from ourselves, by inflicting voluntary penances upon ourselves.

5. To renounce one's body is to make of one's body a living host through the practice of justice and virtue.

The body belongs to the Lord, St. Paul tells us (1 Cor. 6,15). If our bodies belong to the Lord, they must be for his use; we cannot do what we want with them, and we must act in such a way that they serve the best possible way.

And that is why St. Paul adds: Glorify God in your mortal bodies (1 Cor. 6,20). Christ will be glorified in my body (Phil., 1,20). And he says more: our bodies are the members of Jesus Christ (1 Cor. 6,15). That is why he draws this conclusion: I urge you therfore, brethren, by the mercies of God, to present your bodies as a living sacrifice, holy and acceptable to God, which is your spiritual worship (Rom. 12,1). According to these words we see that we are to glorify Jesus Christ in our bodies. If our bodies are the members of Jesus Christ, we must render them worthy of that glory. That we must live as celestial men, as St. Paul tells the Corinthians[20].
Since the first man is terrestrial, his children are also terrestrial, and as the second man is celestial, so also his children are celestial; since we have borne the image of the terrestrial man, let us also bear the image of the celestial man (1 Cor. 15,47).
If we must live as a celestial man, we must die to the terrestrial man that is in us, make him disappear as much as we can. We must make of our bodies living hosts, carry the death of Jesus Christ in our bodies so that the life of Jesus Christ may shine through. We become living hosts by consuming ourselves for God like a victim that immolates itself each day for him, like a candle is consumed by fire, like the incense that is consumed by burning and is destroyed by spreading a good odor before God.
Everything in us must spread this good odor of Jesus Christ, must transpire in our exterior this divine life that we must have interiorly. We must offer to God the sacrifice of ourselves and Jesus Christ must come out of us.

---

[20] On the terms "celestial" and "terrestrial", see explanation p. 124.

198. We are the members of Jesus Christ. Jesus Christ must be seen in our members, in our whole exterior and we must eradicate from our exterior everything that would dishonor this title of member of Jesus Christ.

Jesus Christ must be seen in our exterior, in our bearing, our attitude, our word, our action, our hands, feet, eyes, head, in our whole being, because our whole being must reveal Jesus Christ and spread the good odor of his virtues. The body is the expression of the soul. It is through the body that we edify. It is also through the body that we scandalize. The faithful do not see the soul, they see only the body. Thus, it is through the body that we must edify our neighbor and reproduce Jesus Christ who is in us. It is not I who live, it is Jesus Christ who lives in me. Therefore, we must eradicate from our exterior all that is coarse, carnal, terrestrial, all that smacks of the flesh, indolence, sensuality, laziness, and become celestial men; take from the earth only what is necessary to maintain the life of the body and make of it the members of Jesus Christ. Just like when we open a bottle of perfume the good odor escapes from the bottle, so too with ourselves, when we speak or act, the good odor of Jesus Christ should come out of us, that is to say, his faith, love, kindness, humility, charity.

6. We must undo and correct all the exterior faults of the body that are an obstacle to the glory of Jesus Christ in us and do not edify the neighbor.

We all have exterior faults which, without being faults, are obstacles to the manifestation of Jesus Christ in us and separates the neighbor from us by giving him cause to criticize or ridicule us.

199. Therefore, we should seek to know these exterior faults and work at correcting them for the glory of God and the salvation of souls. If anybody should work at correcting those kinds of faults, it is surely the priests, religious men and women who, by their vocation, are held to glorifying Jesus Christ in themselves and to carry him in their whole exterior. One does not pay much attention if a man of the world appears coarse, simple, rude, brusque, abrupt, but if a priest or religious has those same exterior faults he does great harm to himself, religion, God and his brothers in religion. Thus it is very important to work at correcting one's exterior faults. Moreover, are not priests and religious God's favorites, his privileged children, his chosen children, the courtiers who form his court on earth, who represent God among men and who should give men a great idea of God, since they are with him, his chosen men. Then, is it not to dishonor God to be full of exterior faults and to represent him so badly in the eyes of the world, and in seeing us with all our faults, our miseries, won't they be tempted to ridicule us and despise God whom we represent so badly. Thus we must conclude how important it is for each one of us to correct our exterior faults. Besides, our exterior faults are always the expression of our interior faults and in working to correct the former we will also correct the latter.

Different exterior faults of the body. We may have exterior faults in our
manner,
bearing,
appearance,
deportment,
tone,
way of walking,
voice or words,
look,
actions,
gestures,
carriage,
overall appearance of the body,
exterior.

Exterior faults of the body[21]

manner:	bearing:	tone:
proud	disconcerted	arrogant
haughty	awkward	high
disdainful	borrowed	brusque
	aggitated	imperious
		of anger
		or irritation
		irritated

manner:	posture:	tone:
angry	cowardly	affected
anger	improper	cuddly
irritated	rude	suave

manner:	appearance:	tone:
arrogant	dirty	weepy
bold	neglected	complaining
insolent	disordered	inane

manner:	appearance:	tone:
light	too tidy	grumbling
dissipated	refined	moaning
dizzy	snug	
	stylish	

---

[21] Father Chevrier drew up this chart on a separate sheet of paper which was later inserted in the manuscript note book. By whom? Since this sheet was stuck with sealing wax, we may believe that it is an old insertion. If it were of more recent insertion, glue would have been used. Besides, it seems that the place in the manuscript notebook was kept for this insertion. Further on, this list of faults is repeated and blank spaces were left for commentaries which were never made, at least not in writing. We only find rare notations of little interest such as these: "The faults of manner are painted on the face". We will not reproduce all this to avoid useless repetition. (Ms XI 420-422).

manner:	deportment:	the
shy	affected	haughty tone
self-conscious	wordly	good tone
simpleton	fussy	bad tone
wishy-washy	excentric	
	contorted	
	showy	

manner:	deportment:	way of walking
sad	brusque	brusque
wild	coarse	cavalier
pouty	rude	noisy
bored		hurried

manner:		way of walking
indifferent		slow
distractred		heavy
		sluggish

manner:	awkward	words:
smug		sharp
self-satisfied		soft
at ease		flattering
		racy
		biting
		mocking
		halting
		insolent

look:	exterior:	
hypocritical	soft	
deceitful	agreable	
cunning	polished	
bad	honest	
	pleasing	
	devious	

look:	exterior:
tender	hard
staring	severe
loving	stiff
	repelling

201

look:	exterior:	
scrutinizing	elegance	
curious	refined	
jealous	showy	
envious		

carriage:	action:	gesture:
straight	slow	tiresome
stiff	precipitous	misplaced
curved	impetuous	nervous
lop-sided		affected
balanced		

202 Such are the principal exterior faults of the body; if we recognize some of those faults in us, it is our duty to correct them and practice the virtues opposed to those exterior faults. We must glorify Jesus Christ in our body. We must carry him within ourselves and for that work at the disappearance of these exterior faults. The principal exterior virtue is that modesty which St. Paul recommends and which molds our whole being: modestia vestra nota sit omnibus hominibus, to be modest in everything (Ph. 4,5).

Summary and conclusion.
   We must have a grave and serious manner,
   a worthy bearing,
   clean and proper appearance,
   polished and decent deportment,
   a tone full of kindness and charity,
   a calm and silent way of walking,
   a humble and modest look,
   words full of reserve and prudence,
   Our whole body should edify the neighbor and remind him that we carry God in us and that we represent him to the world.

7. To renounce one's body is to accept suffering and the death of one's body.

To suffer and to die, that is the condition of our body on earth. Remember that you are dust and to dust you shall return.

It is written that every man must die once. Suffering announces death every day and warns us that we are not immortal, but that our body will have an end. That is why St.Paul said: I die daily *Quotidie morior*. To suffer and to die, that is our destiny. The submissive prayer of our Lord Jesus Christ in the garden of olives shows us with what submission we must accept suffering and death when God sends it to us. Your will, not mine be done. I must be baptized with a baptism and I wish it were accomplished. Do not fear those who kill the body but fear those who kill the soul. The one who has truly renounced his body must have that attitude of spirit toward death. He accepts the daily hardships of his body with humility and submission to the will of God. He avoids constant complaining over insignificant things or little aches that are not worth it. He avoids those little services, those self-seekings, those exaggerated cares of his body, his health.

Exaggerated cares.
He does not have that apprehension of death that those who have loved their bodies too much have. He only takes care of his body when it is necessary or when he cannot go any longer. The body goes every day.

Quotidie morior.
One must assist at the demise of one's body every day and make the sacrifice of it at every moment. We must lose something of ourself every day: hair, teeth, one day it is a member that does not work, tomorrow it will be another. All those are warnings that death is approaching and that we will not live forever.

Tempus resolutionis meae instat[22].
Happy the one who hears those warnings properly and on time, by not having illusions on his coming death. Charity demands that we take care of the suffering. And renunciation of our body commands us to forget ourselves and not pay too much attention to our body. Exaggerated care of our body would be, for example, listening to ourselves in sickness, going to great expense to find a cure, going to foreign countries for treatment, call in foreign doctors.

Exaggerated care of the body
There are many little exaggerated cares that in no way become the generous and Christian soul. The one who has renounced his body always has too much, he is embarrassed to have others take care of him, he refuses rather than accept and, if he accepts, it is with much gratitude and humility.
On the contrary, the one who loves his body, never has enough, he always requires particular services, he is never happy, he demands, he needs 36 servants, every one around him is busy serving him, they must go here and there to bring him all sorts of things: cushions, armchairs, footstools, he complains continually [...][23] Nothing is more opposed to the spirit of humility and gratitude and poverty than all those demands, and it also scandalizes the people outside as well as those inside.

---

[22] The moment of my departure has arrived (2 Tim. 4,6).
[23] Illegible word.

Practice.
To remain in these sentiments, we endure with submission and humility the little indispositions of the body; we will avoid complaining at every moment, being demanding in our sufferings and illnesses, repeating often these words of Our Lord's: Your will, not mine be done. Once a month we will make a monthly retreat to prepare ourselves for death and reimmerse ourselves in fervor and death to ourselves. It can be done while begging; it must be done in such a way that our duties do not suffer.

How to behave in the sickness of the brothers.
How to assist the dying.
Sacraments, agony, burial.

To renounce oneself, one must   205
2. Renounce one's spirit

What do we mean when we speak of our spirit? This can be understood in two ways. It may mean our ability to understand, judge, our intelligence. In this sense, there is no question of renunciation, it means nothing.

The second meaning is our own and spontaneous manner of thinking, judging, we could say our personal mentality and in this sense we can speak on renunciation of one's spirit.

The renunciation of our spirit does not consist in suppressing the exercise of our intelligence. It does not mean: I renounce my capacity to understand, to judge. Nobody can achieve this result and those who think that they have are fooling themselves. To renounce one's spirit is to wish to set aside one's own and spontaneous manner of thinking to adopt another because one knows that the other is better.

Consequently, to renounce one's spirit means: I want to think, judge as much as possible in the most intelligent manner and to do so I do not want to hold on to my ideas but to adopt the ideas of those who know better than me. Therefore, the very act of renouncing an exercise of the intelligence is at the purely natural level, it is what we call common sense. But unfortunately, we are apt to think that those who do not have our ideas reason against common sense. That is a false idea of common sense. The true common sense consists in asking ourselves first of all who is better placed to know the truth of the matter.

It often happens that we cannot admit the supernatural demands of renouncing our spirit because we have not accepted the natural demands of common sense.

Without forgetting these natural demands[1], Father Chevrier speaks of renouncing one's spirit on the supernatural level. That it to say, it is a matter of yielding one's own mentality to adopt that of Christ; submitting the exercise of one's intelligence to the action of the Holy Spirit.

This is the principal article and the most important of all, says *Father Chevrier, and to convince us of this importance, he draws up a impressive list of faults of the spirit. That those faults exist, and many more besides, is unquestionable. It does not follow that each one of us has them all but the one who would beleive himself exempt from all faults of the spirit would be very stupid. We need only look around us to see that one is a charming companion but inconstant; another is full of good will but not very practical; another is a man of duty but very authoritarian, etc.*

How important it would be to arrive at a certian lucidity to recognize our own difficiencies. Yet we must go beyond that lucidity. Father Chevrier does not stop at the psychological analysis. He speaks as a spiritual. He knows that, to be totally open to the light and impulse of the Spirit of God, we must unite ourselves, in the obscurity of faith, to the judgement of God on our spirit. The one who would hold only to the lucidity that he can acquire, would remain in the flesh and could only do the works of the flesh, as St. Paul says[2].

---

[1] P. 107, note 29.
[2] Cf. Gal. 5,16-25.

Principal article and the most important because it lets us perceive Father Chevrier's essential idea on the priest and the spiritual experience that Father had of this state.
That essential idea is expressed with simplicity in the following lines:
> Jesus Christ is sent by the Father
> The priest is sent by Jesus Christ.
> All that Jesus Christ says of himself on this point, the priest must apply to himself.
> Like Jesus Christ, he is robed with the characteristics of an envoy and must fulfill those obligations[3].

That is only a logical explanation of Jesus' words to his apostles: As the Father has sent me, I also send you[4].
The priest is sent like Jesus Christ, that is, according to Father Chevrier:
> Jesus knows his Father, he speaks according to him, he acts according to him and everything that he does and says, he does and [says] in union with his Father.
> So also, the priest must act and speak according to Jesus Christ and be united to him, and in so doing he will be united to the Father and do everything according to God[5].

How can this be done? By renouncing one's spirit for, according to Father Chevrier:
> It may be the most important article and all the rest flows from it. To renounce one's spirit to take that of God, that of Jesus Christ. And it is only in the measure that the spirit of God is in us that we will understand the things of God, that we will become spiritual and accomplish what the spirit teaches us[6].

Here again, we have a commentary on the Gospel: As the Father has sent me, I also send you. Having said this he breathed on them and said: Receive the Holy Spirit[7].
This article is important also because of the practical consequences that Father Chevrier draws from it. These consequences concern mainly apostolic formation. At first sight, they seem to be a contradiction of what he says on the need for renunciation.
> Our misfortune is to have been conceived in iniquity, we are entirely carnal and bad, unable even to have a good thought[8].

---

[3] Ms X 715.
[4] Jn. 20,21.
[5] Ms X 715.
[6] Ms. XI 224.
[7] Jn. 20,21-22.
[8] P. 182.

Having taken off on that track, we might expect very rigid conclusions on the need to dictate a line of conduct to people, otherwise they will follow their nature and go astray. But quite to the contrary:

Neither is the spirit of God in this exterior regularity or discipline. When you have established this whole system of order, arrangement, mechanical regularity in your men, if you believe that the spirit of God is in that you are mistaken; it can very well not be there at all[9].

Father Chevrier preaches at length on a method of formation that is full of flexibility and liberality. That is because, in fact, God alone can produce in us an authentic renunciation of our spirit that is an act of supernatural intelligence. We need the Spirit's grace of wisdom and intelligence and that cannot be the work of man but of Jesus Christ[10].

A liberal method of formation, but a demanding one, first of all for the formator who must give himself totally:

The true rule that we must impose on others is this: follow me, do as I do...[11]

This liberality and demand are found in what concerns the life of an apostolic community[12]. *Here more than ever, Father Chevrier speaks from experience.*

The Spirit of God, the expression comes up often in the following pages. Should it be written with an "S", that is, is it the Holy Spirit, the third person of the Blessed Trinity? or should it be written with an "s", that is, is it the mentality produced in us when we let ourselves be led by the Holy Spirit? Father Chevrier wrote without paying attention to those details.

We cannot always say for sure. At any rate, one is not found without the other. This difficulty of distinction between the two meanings is also found in the Bible.

When there is question of buying, of acquiring the spirit of God[13], *there is no doubt that it is that transformation of mentality produced in us by the influence of the Holy Spirit. It could not be a question of buying, acquiring the Holy Spirit who communicates himself freely in sovereign liberty*[14]; *but it is he who makes us accomplish the costly actions necessary for our spiritual renewal.*

---

[9] P.192.
[10] Cf. Is. 11,2.
[11] P. 194.
[12] P. 203.
[13] Pp. 191, 199.
[14] Cf. appendix I, p.455.

After having renounced one's body which is the exterior part of our being, one must renounce one's spirit which is the principal part of ourselves since it is the inteligent part, and it is the one that governs us, that thinks and gives impetus to our whole being.

We can truly say that it is the principal and most important article of all since it is with the spirit that we think, conduct ourselves and that, if the spirit is good, all the rest will be good, but if it is evil, all the rest will be evil.

The eye is the lamp of the body, if our eye is simple, our whole body will be in light, if our eye is evil, the whole body will be in darkness (Mt. 6,22; Lk, 11, 34)[15].

Doctrine of Our Lord Jesus Christ on renunciation of one's spirit.

If anyone wishes to come after me, let him renounce himself, take up his cross and follow me (Mt. 16,24). What is more of ourselves than our spirit, since it is by it that we are what we are?

Speaking to Nicodemus, Jesus said: Truly, I tell you, if a man is not born again, he cannot see the kingdom of God. And when Nicodemus did not understand, Jesus explained: If a man is not reborn of water and the spirit, he cannot see the kingdom of God (Jn. 3,5). To be reborn of water and the Holy Spirit, what is it if not to reform one's spirit, leave the first spirit to take the spirit of God? And elsewhere Jesus tells us: If you do not become like little children, you will not enter the kingdom of God (Mt. 18,3). Whoever does not receive the kingdom of God like a little child, will not enter it (Mt., 10,15).

Explanation and confirmation of this doctrine.

Our Lord could not explain more clearly to show us the need to renounce our own spirit, because he wants us to be reborn in a new spirit,

that of the Holy Spirit, that we become like little children. It is not through the body that we can become little and be reborn, but by the spirit.

Why we must renounce our spirit.

Our Lord himself tells us when he explains this second birth to Nicodemus:

---

[15] Ms XI 224 - Ms XII 37.

It may be the most important article of all and all the rest flows from it. To renounce one's spirit to take that of God, of Jesus Christ. And it is only in the measure that we have the Spirit of God that we will understand the things of God, that we gill become spiritual and accomplish what the spirit teaches us. (Ms. XI 224).

The spirit of God and the spirit of man are very different: the spirit of God is wisdom, the spirit of man is folly (Ms. XII 37).

What is born of the flesh is flesh; what is born of the spirit is spirit (Jn. 3,6). Even though our spirit is not born of the flesh, it nevertheless participates in the faults of the flesh and, coming from us, it loses its beauty, justice, first qualities it holds from God from its origin, it participates in our misfortune..... in the vice of our birth from Adam, in the vices of our flesh. We were conceived in iniquity. St. Paul tells us that the Lord knows men's thoughts and that they are futile (1 Cor. 3,20). By ourselves we are not able to have even one good thought (2 Cor. 3,5). Our misfortune is to have been conceived in iniquity, we are totally carnal and bad, unable to have even one good thought; on the contrary, without the grace of God, we can only produce bad thoughts[16].

What is renouncing one's spirit? First of all, it is being convinced that, by ourselves, we are but misery and have only faults that we must be serious about renouncing and work wholeheartedly to reform our spirit. It is to renounce all the faults of our spirit. We do not know ourselves, we are full of faults without knowing it and it happens that we take our faults for qualities.

213 **What are the faults of our spirit?** Speaking to the Jews and wanting to make us understand the evil that is in us, the evil foundation that is in us, Our Lord says: It is from the heart of men that come *evil thoughts, adultery, fornication, homicide, theft, greed, wickedness, fraud, immodesty, the evil eye, false witness, blasphemy, pride, folly.* All those evil things come from within and pervert man (Mt. 15,19; Mk. 7,21).

In listing the carnal things, that is, the works that do not come from God but from us, from deep within us, from our spirit, from within us, St. Paul says: the works of the flesh are *immorality, impurity, licentiousness, idolatry, sorcery, enmity, strife, jealousy, anger, selfishness, dissension, party spirit, envey, drunkenness, carousing and the like.* I warn you that those who do such things shall not inherit the kingdom of God (Gal. 5,19). It is important to list the various faults of the spirit so that we may find ourselves and work to correct them.

---

[16] On the pessimistic impression that this paragraph gives, see introduction to Renunciation of oneself, p. 141.

Faults of the spirit[17]

spirit	spirit	spirit
of pride	of criticism	all-knowing
of arrogance	of mockery	presumptuous
of independence	of wickedness	connoisseur
of ostentation		undertaking
of hautiness		breaking
of domination		peremtory
spirit	**spirit**	**spirit**
reasoning	of opposition	sick
stubborn	quarrelsome	full of imaginings
disobedient	of discord	worries
	of revolt	illusions
	of division	fancies
		follies
spirit	**spirit**	**spirit**
susceptible	teasing	pleasing
demanding[18]	quibbling	caustic
	belligerent	farcical
spirit	**spirit**	**spirit**
light	subtle	airy
superficial	narrow	capricious
poetic	scrupulous	brusque
roaming	pharisaic	changing
distracted	defiant	careless
not practical	stiff	
incostant	tenacious	
	no sociable	
spirit	**spirit**	**spirit**
grabbing	gay	sad
selfish	jocular	savage
vengenful	laughing	touchy
scornful	childish	closed
of domination		

---

[17] A chart drawn up separately and inserted in a notebook like that concerning the faults of the body. Here also we omit Ms XI 420 which would only be a repetition of the chart. (Cf. p. 174, note 21).

[18] The only good is what they do, evil is what others do. (remark drawn from the omitted chart).

spirit	spirit	spirit
hypocritical	exaggerated	chatty
lying	false	loquacious
of finesse	crooked	dawdler
of ruse		lazy
treacherous		
	spirit	witty
	curious	great talker
	talkative	flattery, witty[19]

215

In the enumeration of all these faults, we see the importance of this article.	To how many faults of the spirit we are subjected, and yet it is according to them that

we conduct ourselves, that we judge, that we are led. How much false progress flows from that! How many chasms we fall into! As our Lord says: the eye is the lamp of your body, if your eye is evil, your whole body will be in darkness. If we are blind in spirit, how will we be able to lead ourselves and others? A blind man cannot lead another blind man, they will both fall into the pit.

Faults are like clouds, veils that are in front of us and that prevent us from seeing and leading ourselves. Therefore, it is of prime importance that we correct our faults of the spirit and ask for the good spirit each day. How important it is to seek the good spirit, it is everything!

There are three lights in us to enlighten us:
        reason,
        the devil,
        God.

It is very difficult to distinguish by what light we are led, if we do not have supernatural light to enlighten us on our own light which all too often is only darkness.

How to work at this renunciation of the spirit.

First one must struggle against one's spiritual faults.	We must know that all that comes from the flesh is flesh and that we must struggle against the flesh,

that is, what comes from

---

[19] The good is what they do; the bad is what others do. (Remark drawn from the omitted chart.)

this vitiated and corrupt nature, as St. Paul says. Walk according to the spirit of God and you will not do the work of the flesh for the spirit struggles against the flesh; they are opposed to each other (Gal. 5,16).

I pray you in the Lord, says St. Paul, not to live as the Gentiles do, in the futility of their minds, whose spirit is full of darkness, they are alienated from the life of God, because of the ignorance that is in them due to the hardness of their heart (Eph. 4,17).

I am carnal, sold under sin, in fact, I do not approve of what I do, I do not do the good that I want, but on the contrary, I do the evil that I hate (Rom. 7,14).

First we must fight against ourselves, it is the great battle that we have to wage; a terrible, incessant battle that we cannot wage without a great grace from God. Once we know a few of the faults of our spirit, or even only one, we must declare war against it and fight against it until we have conquered it with the grace of God.

We must strip off the old man. It is only in fighting continually against our faults that we will arrive, little by little, at stripping off the old man.

We must arrive at stripping ourselves. Cast off the old man and his works and put on the new man who, by knowledge of God, is renewed according to the image of the one who created him (Col. 3,9). And elsewhere he says: rid yourselves of the old leaven in order to be a new dough, as you really are unleavened. For Christ, our paschal lamb has been sacrificed. Let us therefore celebrate the festival, not with the old leaven of malice and evil, but with the unleavened bread of sincerity and truth (1 Cor. 5,7)

To be renewed in the interior of the soul. To be renewed, that is, to destroy what is old to take something new.

St. Paul tells the Ephesians that they have been instructed in the school of Jesus Christ to cast off the old man according to whom you lived in your first life so corrupt, by following the illusions of his passions, and to be renewed in the interior of your soul, to put on the new man who is created according to God, in true justice and holiness (Eph. 4,22).

And become a new man by a new birth in the Holy Spirit. We must put on the man who was created according to God, in true justice and holiness (Eph. 4,22).

Nova creatura. We must become new men by becoming little children, leaving behind gradually everything that we have received from our first evil birth and taking on gradually everything that is good in the new man that is proposed to us. If a man is not reborn of water and the Holy Spirit, he will not enter in the kingdom of God. If you do not become like little children, you will not enter in the kingdom of heaven. Therefore, this new birth is necessary to enter the kingdom of the children of God who form the kingdom of God. The good communities on earth that begin the kingdom of heaven.

217 **This second birth is achieved by filling ourselves with the good spirit, the HOLY SPIRIT.**
Be filled with the Holy Spirit (Eph. 5,18). It is the Holy Spirit who, in communicating him self to us gradually, forms new men in us.

As the apostles were transformed by the Holy Spirit when they had received him. For us, it must be our daily work that achieves this change, the grace of God, study, prayer.

Where to find the good Spirit?

He is not in the world.
The world cannot receive the spirit of God, it does not know him and does not see him.

There is too much opposition between God and the world for the spirit to be found there. The wisdom of the world is folly before God, says St. Paul, according to what is written: I will catch the wise in their craftiness (1 Cor. 3,19). Animal man does not conceive of the things that are of the spirit of God; they appear as folly and he cannot understand them because they must be judged in a supernatural light (1 Cor. 2,4)[20].

Neither is the good spirit in science and genius.
Science inflates, says St. Paul, and does not always give the Holy Spirit.

It is the Holy Spirit who gives the true science, but the science that does not come from the Holy Spirit does not communicate the spirit of God. How many scientists unfortunately do not have the spirit of God! He is not in genius, reasoning, because the thoughts of men are futile and we are not capable, by ourselves, to have good thoughts.

One may be learned, have beautiful reasonings, be a great philosopher, a great mathematician, know all the sciences, and not have the spirit of God.

It is St. Paul who teaches us: If I speak in the tongues of men and of angels, but have not love, I am a noisy gong or a clanging cymbal. And if I have prophetic powers 218 and understand all mysteries and all knowledge, and if I have all the faith possible, if I do not have love, I am nothing (1 Cor. 13,1).

---

[20] Ms XI 545 - If we are of the world, if we think like the world, [with the] ideas of the world, we cannot receive [the Spirit of God]; we must strip ourselves of ourselves to receive him and understand him.

One may thus have science, all possible knowledge, a transcendent genius, without having the spirit of God. Alas! how many examples of that kind, even in [the Church]![21]; do we not often see beautiful geniuses, the greatest minds, stumble and fall into error and evil? They were learned but did not have the spirit of God or lost it after having received it. The proof that the Holy Spirit is not necessarily in science [nor] in the scientists is that Jesus Christ chose his apostles from among the poor and the humble, to do his great work.
Infirma mundi elegit Deus ut confundat fortia[22].

Our Lord gave thanks to his Father for having communicated himself to the little ones and the humble and hidden himself from the great and powerful. What does that mean, if not that the great and powerful, however learned they may be, however great geniuses they may be, are often unworthy and incapable of receiving the spirit of God[23].

Our Lord tells us that the ways of the Holy Spirit re unknown to us; we do not know where he comes from nor where he goes; if he came from science we would understand his ways. We often see science with wickedness and impiety[24]. He is not even in the learned philosopher, the learned theologian, though these sciences come from the Holy Spirit. One may have these sciences without having the spirit of God. Do we not often see the greatest theologians fall in error and abandon truth? Science and reasoning often kill and destroy simplicity and common sense that come directly from God and the Holy Spirit.

There are souls who sense truth naturally and accept it joyfully and happily as soon as they see it; these souls have more of the spirit of God than the great learned theologians who can only arrive at it through endless reasonings and deductions.

God has put in certain souls a spiritual and practical sense which encloses more common sense and spirit of God than there is in the head of the great learned men. Witness certain peasants, several good workers, women who understand immediately the things of God and can explain them better than many others.

He is not in exterior things.   He is neither in lodgings nor in dress, 219
neither in wealth nor in titles, neither
is he in low or elevated positions.

---

[21] The manuscript gives the word EXAMPLE; we do not know how to interpret Father Chevrier's thought other than suggesting the word CHURCH.

[22] God chose what was weak in the world to confound the strong (1 Cor.1,27).

[23] In Ms XII 12, Father Chevrier quotes 1 Cor. 8,2: If any one imagines that he knows something, he does not yet know as he ought to know.

[24] "Often": Here as in the following paragraph, the tone is a bit rhetorical. It is a diatribe in the manner of St. Paul in 1 Cor. 17-31. At any rate, "often" does not mean "most often".

He is not even in exterior practices of piety; the pharisees fasted, prayed, gave alms, and our Lord condemned all their justice, however great and rigorous they may appear in the eyes of men.

St. Paul himself says: Even if I distributed my goods to the poor and gave my body to be burnt, if I do not have love, all that is worthless.

He is not in titles, nor in high places, fame and honors. Exterior things suppose the spirit of God but do not give him. One may be priest, canon, bishop, superior, religious and not have the spirit of God, because the spirit of God is not attached to titles, honors, fame; those things suppose but do not give him[25].

What a gross error is committed by those who think they have the spirit of God because they are decked out in a costume, a cassock, or some dignity or other and that, in this exterior appearance they can govern, command with impunity as they see fit, as the whim takes them, to highlight their title, their position, as if that made them wiser, more experienced, more enlightened and especially incapable of making a mistake. We see especially young priests acting without reserve and without prudence, without wisdom and yet believing that they are infallible and demand that everybody bow before them and submit to their authority, their government.

What error! What folly! And how must this kind of people attract scorn upon themselves and especially upon the habit that they wear.

With how much prudence and reserve, fear and trembling we must act, especially when we are young and inexperienced, because we are exposed to many blunders, and not to think that our cassock gives us wisdom and virtue.

God is the only one who can give us his spirit and we cannot have it without having bought it, even at great price and at our own expense[26].

We must think charitably that all those who have some dignity, a holy habit or an elevated position, have the spirit of God; but those who have the habit and the dignity must fear not having it and take all the means to acquire it more and more and ask God for it.

Neither is the spirit of God in that exterior regularity or discipline that we admire every day; in those pedagogical exercises that turn men into veritable machines that we move around by signs.

When you have put this exterior system of order, arrangement, mechanical regularity in your men, if you think that the spirit of God is there, you are mistaken; he may very well not be there at all, for the spirit of God is not in the exterior, he is in the interior: *regnum dei intra vos est*[27]. Where is there more order, discipline, regula-

---

[25] Father Chevrier is outspoken. One thinks of the sculptors of the Middle Ages who did not hesitate to put a bishop among the damned.

[26] Cf. 183.

[27] The kingdom of God is within you (Lk. 17,21).

rity than in the barracks, in prisons, in a communal school? and yet, where is there less the spirit of God?[28]
The exterior supposes the spirit of God but does not give it[29].
Here is a comparison that may illustrate the point. There are two trees, one is artificial, the other natural. They look absolutely the same. The artificial was hand made: the trunk, branches, leaves, flowers, fruit are beautiful, nice colors, form; they look exactly as the natural tree, it is charming in its order, arrangement, form, color and resemblance. But this tree has neither *roots* nor *sap*; it has no life, it is dead, has only an artificial life, a life of likeness. Man has made all this, God has done nothing. It is beautiful to see but it has no interior life and has no real fruits; its fruits are not good to eat and the birds of the air do not come to rest in it and find nourishment.
On the contrary, in the natural tree, man has done very little. He planted, pruned, watered, but it is God who gave growth. There is a mysterious interior sap that we do not see, that comes from God and gives life. It is this mysterious sap that produced the trunk, flowers, leaves, fruits; and those fruits are good to eat. In this tree there is an interior life that comes from God and it does not exist in the other; no matter how beautiful the artificial tree may be, it will never be anything but a dead tree while the other is a living tree.
It is the same with all this exterior work in which we put so much energy, especially today, and to which we give so much importance in our houses, lay and even Christian schools; we are much more concerned with the exterior than the interior. We do not put the living sap, we create artificial trees, we make dead trees. That is because it is much easier to make an artificial tree than a living one.
The artifical tree only requires very little care, work, firmness, exactidude, regularity. While to make a living tree we have to find the vivifying sap, communicate it to the souls that we instruct, and to communicate it we must have it, we must give grace, life, faith, vivivying love and we cannot give this if we do not have it and we do not acquire it without effort and without God.
It is a spiritual work that is much more difficult than any material work. In us, it is the Holy Spirit who must produce the whole exterior. We must begin by putting the spirit of God in us, and once he is there, he acts as the sap of the tree, he produces the whole exterior in us[30].

---

[28] We may deplore this enumeration and especially the mention of communal schools after the prisons. It was the climate of the time.

[29] Ms. XII 16 - What often happens? As soon as you come out of your exterior, of that habitual regularity, you are no longer the same, the robot no longer works; then you no longer pray, study.

[30] Ms XII 15... without him, we are like artificial plants.

We must be more concerned with the interior than the exterior, give more importance to the interior than the exterior. Put the interior in souls and the exterior will follow; put the exterior and you have done nothing.

We may say that the exterior is the indication of the interior but that is not always the case. There are people who are better able to contain themselves exteriorly than others and who are less agreeable to God than others who have less exterior and more interior, who have more good will, who make more efforts. Do not judge according to appearances, at face value, says our Lord. To put the exterior without the spirit of God is to have a body without a soul. To begin with the exterior is to build in the air, without foundations, it is to build machines, weather vanes.

First of all we must put faith, the love of God, the interior sap. *Spiritus est qui vivificat caro non prodest quidquam*[31].

The exterior is like a habit with which we clothe ourselves; it may be nice, well made, give an air of elegance, gracious, noble, but it does not give health. When the doctor wants to know if you are well, he does not look at your habit, but he takes your pulse, looks at your tongue, takes your blood presure; that is where your health is, your strength, your life. The exterior is nothing and cannot give an indication of our life, our health[32].

That is not to say that we must neglect the exterior and not demand anything in that area. No, we need order and regularity. But the principal foundation must be the interior, the spiritual sap that must give life to the exterior, otherwise we do nothing solid, nothing real, durable. *Haec oportuit facere et illa non omittere*[33], said the Lord to the Pharisees, in speaking of the two interior and exterior precepts. Is it not also what we notice in the behavior of Jesus Christ with regard to his apostles? First, he chose them.

> (At the same time that he gave the the great evangelical and perfect principles, he made them practice it by putting them into action.
>
> He gave them no other rule than this one: *Follow me*, I am your rule, your life, the exterior form that you must imitate. There are some who begin with exterior regulations, make many rules; all that is nothing. The true regulation to be imposed on others is this: *follow me, do as I do*, I do not ask anything more difficult that what I myself do. *Follow me*: that is the great regulation.)

During the three years that he spent with them to form them to the evangelical and apostolic life, we see that he does not strive at all to give them exterior and regular

---

[31] It is the spirit that vivifies; the flesh is worthless (Jn. 6,63).

[32] Ms XI 120 - The rule, regularity, is like a beautiful habit that covers us, but within, underneath, there are sores, ulcers, illnesses; the habit covers, hides the sores and does not cure them; the spirit heals and, for ornament and dress, gives grace, charity.

[33] That is what we had to do, without omitting the other (Lk. 11,42).

forms of discipline; they lived according to the times, as best they could. But we see that he is constantly occupied with the interior transformation of his apostles. He instructed them ceaselessly, he rebuked them at every moment, he initiated them in everything, formed them in everything.

To instruct, rebuke and put into action, to make them act, that was the great method to form people and give them an interior life.

To *instruct, rebuke, put into action, make them do*, that is the life, the sap and the means of communicating; but to place people in a niche, pour them in a mold, is to force people, repress faults and not to correct them.

> (In the foundation rf the Church, the greatest work of the All Mighty, the most beautiful work on earth, Our Lord does not use any exterior means. He takes a man to whom he communicates his life, his spirit, he chose twelve whom he formed in the evangelical life; but it is not in stuffing them into a mold or making them march in step that he formed them; he did not beat, nor does he beat any drum or music or concert or theatre; on the contrary, he forbids them from using any exterior means, without money or outward appearance; I send you like lambs among wolves, ite docete[34]; preach, instruct, heal; virtus de illo exibat[35]; exterior means do not end up in anything, the cross, suffering, grace, patience).

We must let faults surface to be able to reprove and correct them. If we force them to hide themselves, we cannot know them and, consequently, correct them.

You are my disciples, if you love one another. That is the principle of all our actions: charity, love, the life of God; the spirit of Jesus Christ is in charity: that is the principle of life that comes from the Holy Spirit and who is love by its essence. We must give ourselves as models for the world, by living in a stable, living on a cross, allowing ourselves to be eaten every day, like Jesus Christ; then we will convert the world.

> (Everybody ran to Jesus to hear him, be healed and delivered from demons; people must come to us to hear us, be healed and delivered from the evil spirit. This is what must draw people, how we must draw them to us, and not by exterior means that must come only long afterwards. There were more solid Christians in the catacombs than there are in our beautiful churches. There are those who are frenetic in using exterior means to attract and they think that they convert people. How mistaken they are and they are in contradiction with the Gospel! A warning then, for the spiritual works that we might undertake.)

---

[34] Go, teach (Mt. 28, 19).
[35] A strength went out of him (Lk. 6,19).

Love of God and neighbor, that is the principle and the vivifying sap of everything, that must produce everything in us; when that is in a soul, there is all that is needed. It is better to have charity without an exterior than to have an exterior without charity. It is better to have disorder in love than order without love.

That is what the Curé of Ars expressed in a rather funny way when, speaking of the little girls of his Providence who were led according to principle since his girl Catherine did not know the disciplinary methods, and speaking of that type of life and comparing it to the new method that was being introduced in his Providence, when he was obliged to leave the direction to someone more capable according to the world, he said that he loved his little free for all of old. That is to say that, in his time, the children acted from their heart and not on signal, they came to him, loved him and led a family life and not a regimental life.

Texts that support this doctrine.

> Regnum Dei intra vos est.
> Caro non prodest quidquam, spiritus est qui vivificat.
> Martha, Martha, sollicita es et turbaris erga plurima, porro unum est necessarium. Maria optimam partem elegit quae non auferetur ab ea.
> Exercitatio corporalis ad modicum utilis est, pietas autem ad omnia utilis est.
> Quinimo beati qui audiunt verbum Dei et custodiunt illud[36].

224 Not be too attached to the bark; many think only of the bark, see only the bark, judge only by the bark. The bark is necessary to let the sap flow, but what iss the bark without the sap? a dead tree. The bark of the tree must be protected, but the tree must be watered, fertilized so that it may have a strong and vivifying sap; then it will be beautiful and magnificient. Take care of the roots.

The spirit of God or the good spirit is in Jesus Christ.

Jesus came to Nazareth and entered the synagogue, as was his custom, and he stood up to read and there was given to him the book of the prophet Isaiah. He opened the book and found the place where it was written: The Spirit of the Lord is upon me, because he has anointed me to preach the good news to the poor. He has sent me to proclaim release to the captives and recovering of sight to the blind, to set at liberty those who are oppressed, to proclaim the acceptable year of the Lord. And he closed the book,

---

[36] The Kingdom of God is within you. (Lk. 17,21).
The flesh is of no avail, it is the Spirit who vivifies (Jn.6,63)
Martha, Martha, you are anxious and troubled about many things; one thing is needful. Mary has chosen the good portion, which shall not be taken away from her (Lk. 10,41)
Bodily training is of some value, godliness is of value in every way. (1 Tim. 4,8)
Rather, blessed are those who hear the word of God and keep it (Lk. 11,28).

and sat down; and the eyes of all in the synagogue were fixed on him. And he began to say to them: Today this scripture has been fulfilled in your hearing (Lk. 4,16).
Speaking of the Holy Spirit who had descended,on Jesus Christ while he was at prayer after his baptism, St. John says: The heavens were open and he saw the spirit of God in the form of a dove descend and rest on him, and a voice from heaven was heard saying: You are my beloved Son, in you I am well pleased (Mt. 3,16 and parallel).
And elsewhere John says: I saw the spirit descend as a dove from heaven, and it remained on him. I myself did not know him; but he who sent me to baptize with water said to me, He on whom you see the Spirit descend and remain, this is he who baptizes with the Holy Spirit (Jn. 1,32). And again: For he whom God has sent utters the words of God, for it is not by measure that he gives the Spirit (Jn. 3,34).
Thus the Holy Spirit has come *upon him*, he has received it *without measure* and it remains *totally* in him. Such are the testimonies of St. John and of Jesus Christ himself. It is because the Spirit of God is in him that he says nothing of himself, that he does nothing of himself and that all his words and actions conform to the thought and will of the Father, being dictated by the Holy Spirit who is the union of those two persons. Therefore, he does not fear to say: My doctrine is not my own, but that of the one who sent me (Jn. 7,16). The one who sent me is true and what I have heard from him, I say in the world (Jn. 8,26). The words that I have spoken to you, I do not speak them of myself, but the Father who is in me does those works himself (Jn. 14,10). I speak of what I have seen in my Father, I who have told you the truth that I have heard from my Father (Jn.8,38). The word that I have spoken to you is not from me but from my Father who sent me (Jn. 14,24). I have not spoken on my own authority; the Father who sent me has himself given me commandment what to say and what to speak. And I know that his commandment is eternal life. What I say, therefore, I say as the Father has bidden me (Jn. 12,49). As I hear, I judge and my judgement is just because I seek not my own will but the will of him who sent me (Jn.5,30). I can do nothing of myself (Jn.5,30). The Son can do nothing of his own accord, but only what he sees the Father doing; for whatsoever he does, that the Son does likewise (Jn. 5,19).
That is how, in Jesus Christ and his Father there is but one Spirit, but one manner of thinking and acting; it is the same spirit that thinks and judges; the same spirit that acts always in union with the Father and the Son. So that in hearing Jesus Christ, it is the Father that we hear; *he speaks the language of the Father*, says St. John. In seeing Jesus act we see the very actions of the Father because the Son does nothing of his own authority and it is the Father himself who does his works. What a beautiful harmony! What an accord between the Father, the Son and the Holy Spirit in Jesus Christ!
What, then, must we do?
    study our Lord Jesus,
    listen to his words,

examine his actions, in order to be conformed to his and filled with the Holy Spirit.

Since everything that Jesus Christ said, everything that he did is done and dictated by the Holy Spirit, we must study his words and his actions, and conform our life and our words to what he said, to what he did; then we will act and speak according to the Holy Spirit.

This, then, is a sure and certain rule to be filled with the Holy Spirit and act and think according to him. The Gospel contains the words and actions of Jesus Christ[37]. The spirit of God is poured in his whole life, in all his actions. His words, his actions are as so many lights that the Holy Spirit gives us, from the crib to Calvary. Each word of Jesus Christ, each example is like a beam of light coming from heaven to enlighten us and give us life.

226 He who wants to be filled with the spirit of God must study Our Lord every day: his words, his examples, his life; that is the source where we will find life, the spirit of God.

In the little treatise on prayer, we speak of this study of Our Lord to receive, acquire his spirit[38].

The spirit of God is in the Church.

The spirit of God is in our Holy Father, the Pope.

The spirit of God is in the Saints[39].

The spirit of God is in a good rule drawn from the Gospel and approved by the Church.

The spirit of God is in our superiors[40].

---

[37] Cf. appendix II, p. 461.

[38] Ms XI 118 - Ms XI 545.

Therefore, the spirit of God is in the holy Gospel, the word of God, behold where the spirit of God, truth is found.

In the little details of Our Lord's life, his words, his actions; that is mainly where we find the spirit of God. It encloses the whole of the spiritual life, God's thought (Ms XI 118).

[39] The saints were men filled with the spirit of God (Ms XI 239).

[40] It is very important to unite this propostion with the following one. It is always a duty to seek the spirit of God in one's superior. The superior should not presume that he has the spirit of God (cf. p. 192, note 25; p. 223).

How necessary it is that our superiors have the spirit of God.

The need to choose superiors only from among those who have the spirit of God.

For that we must not consider science, skillfulness, talent, wealth, but we must consider strong and enlightened charity. *Do you love me*, Jesus asked of Peter before giving him the government of his Church[41].
As I hear, I judge, and my judgement is just because I do not seek my will but the will of the one who sent me (Jn.5,30).

How to acquire the spirit of God[42]. By studying the Holy Gospel and praying a lot.
First we must read and reread the Holy Gospel, be penetrated by it, know it by heart, study each word, each action to grasp the meaning and have it pass into our thoughts and actions[43].
It is in the prayer of every day that this study must be done and make Jesus Christ pass into our life. Recite the Rosary, make the Way of the Cross, study our Lord's teaching: that is where we find each day the light of the Holy Spirit and we arrive, little by little, at conforming our life to that of Jesus Christ.
It must be an assiduous prayer, perform our devotion to the Holy Spirit every day, that is, after breakfast, recite the Veni Creator, 7 Aves in honor of the 7 gifts and prayer, repeat often this invocation: My God, give me your spirit! so that we may always act in union with this spirit of Jesus Christ, our Master and our light[44].

Who are those who have the spirit of God? They are those who have prayed a lot and have asked for it for a long time.
They are those who, for a long time, have studied the Holy Gospel, the words and actions of our Lord, who have seen how the saints acted and how they conformed

---

[41] In the manuscript, there is a blank page between this paragraph and the following.
[42] Cf. Introduction, p. 183.
[43] Cf. annex II, p. 461.
[44] Ms XI 546 - But we must ask it with the real intention of receiving it, with the will to do everything possible to acquire it, with the will to make every possible and required sacrifice to have it and receive it. Otherwise we will not be able to receive it and God will not be able to give it to us.

their lives to that of Jesus Christ, who have worked a long time to reform in themselves what is opposed to the spirit of our Lord[45].

The one who has the spirit of God says nothing of himself, does nothing of himself. Everything he says, everything he does rests on a word or an action of Jesus Christ whom he has taken as the foundation of his life. Jesus Christ is his live, his principle, his end.

It is not I who live, it is Jesus Christ who lives in me. He does not allow himself to be led by science or reasoning but by faith and the spirit of God who acts in him.

And often we do not understand because the ways of the Holy Spirit are often unknown to men. The spirit blows where he wills, we do not know where he comes from or where he goes; he comes from above.

And the saints often did admirable things that men did not understand, because they were led by the spirit of God and often became the object of the scorn and insults men because carnal man does not conceive of what comes from God, one needs a supernatural light to judge it. They drew all their inspiration and thoughts from the infinite love of God. Deus caritas est[46], in the crib, on Calvary and in the tabernacle, which are the three great torches by whose light a true disciple must be lead.

The spirit of God is rare. Yes, the spirit of God is rare because it is very difficult to set aside totally one's reason, science, natural life, faults of the spirit to be filled with the spirit of God and act only according to the spirit of God[47].

It is difficult to be so united to God that we become only one with him; it is difficult to be so humble, so small, so docile, so silent in order to be always able to receive and follow his inspirations. His inspirations are so soft, so fine, so imperceptible at times - not to say always - that it is difficult to grasp them, understand them and accept them.

---

[45] Ms XI 121 - We know that someone has the spirit of God by his words. The mouth speaks from the abundance of the heart. Jesus Christ said to Peter: It is neither flesh nor blood that have revealed these things to you, but my Father who is in heaven. In this instance, he had the spirit of God, but he did not have it in the other instance when, reproving Jesus Christ, his Master, who was speaking of his passion, he said that it would not happen; nor did those apostle who wanted to call fire down upon Samaria have it. Jesus told them: you do not know of what spirit you are. (This part from Lk. 9, 55, is considered as an inauthentic variation by many exegetes.).

[46] God is love (1 Jn. 4,16).

[47] Ms XI 18 - How rare it is! How sad it is to see so many souls, especially religious and priests, so little animated by this spirit, so susceptible, jealous, bad, spiteful, angry... seeking only their own interest and not that of their neighbor; acting from natural, and not at all supernatural, principle, full of themselves, gluttonous, lazy, following only their own ideas.

On the contrary, science, reason, the world, the habits of life make so much noise around us that it is difficult to hear him and follow him perfectly.

To have the Holy Spirit, we must have set aside our natural life which envelops us and leads us. We must have struggle a long time against our spiritual and carnal faults, we must have studied the Holy Gospel a long time, we must have prayed for it.

How rare are those who fulfill all those conditions. Besides, natural life is so strong in us, and spiritual life so elevated, so opposed to our nature, that we are tempted to look upon the inspirations of the Holy Spirit as impossible and often treat them as fantasies. The great teachings of the Gospel, the counsels are considered impossible and we prefer to follow the usual, ordinary ways rather than embrace the elevated ways, often arid to nature, that come from the Holy Spirit[48]. And then, through reasonings we destroy the whole Gospel, we always find ways of arranging things to keep the natural life. Reasoning kills the Gospel and destroys all that is elevated, great, spiritual in the precepts and counsels of our Lord; like in what concerns poverty, detachment, charity, renunciation, mortification, penance.

Thus, when we find someone on earth who has the spirit of God, how we seek after him! how we run to him! We come to seek this spirit, his counsels that come from above. Then it seems that we are with God and it is heaven on earth. It is rare and yet, it depends only on us to have it by filling ourselves with the Gospel and putting it into practice.

The spirit of God! It is the greatest treasure that God can give to someone. It is also the greatest treasure that God gives to the earth by giving his spirit to a few men so that others may see him, consult and follow him, profit by him. Let us ask it of God and let us not cease asking it for us and for others.

It is difficult to acquire and difficult to conserve. Because we must constantly struggle against nature, our inclinations, our reason, sometimes our science and also against the world that does not understand it and constantly characterizes as senseless and foolish those who act in opposition to it[49].

---

[48] Ms XI 241 - What a difference between this natural life and the superntural life. Opposition between nature and the spirit of God; most people find the Gospel impracticable, exaggerated, utopian, from the other world. That is how many struggle against the spirit of God, sometimes even good priests. They prefer to keep to a routine, a habit, the ordinary; they dislike persecution. Via trita (the beaten path).

[49] Ms XII 18 - We must resurrect the spirit of Jesus Christ in us and in the world. The flesh struggles against the spirit and, unfortunately, the flesh almost always wins the fight. It is easier to obey the flesh, to serve the flesh than the spirit. This spirit is conserved in fervent communities where poverty and suffering are maintained; but it is quickly lost as soon as these two marks disappear and, in the world, it is more difficult to regain.

230 Those who follow the spirit of God are often persecuted, exposed to scorn, to the hatred of others, and to struggle constantly against ourselves and others we need a great dose of strength and energy and grace in order not to weaken and grow slack in the ways of the Holy Spirit. And the spirit of division which insinuates itself everywhere and fights against those who act uniquely for God!

Signs by which we know that a soul is filled with the spirit of God.

St.Paul tells us that the spirit of God bears particular fruits in us and that they are easy to recognize.

The fruits of the spirit, he says, are: *charity, joy, peace, patience, humility, goodness, perseverance, kindness, faith, modesty, continence, self-control, chastity* (Gal. 5,23).

Explanation of each of these fruits:
    discretion, prudence.
    A word on discretion:
    presence, reserve in words,
    the one who is indiscreet, who speaks thoughtlessly, who reveals useless things, causes much trouble.

Put on then, as God's chosen ones, holy and beloved, compassion, kindness, lowliness, meekness and patience, forbearing one another and, if one has anything against another, forgiving each other; as the Lord has forgiven you, so you also must forgive. And above all these put on love, which binds everything together in perfect harmony (Col. 3,12).

Let all that is true,
    all that is honest,
    all that is just,
    all that is holy,
    all that is lovable,
    all that may give a good reputation,
    all that is praiseworthy in the regulation of morals, occupy your mind
    (Phil. 4,8).

Such are the fruits that the Holy Spirit produces in us. Our words and actions are so many holy and blessed fruits that come out from within us and produce good effects, like a good tree produces good fruit and a bad tree bad fruit. So it is for those who have the Holy Spirit and those who do not have him: one produces good fruit and the other bad fruit.

231 No man has ever seen God, but if we love one another, God is in us and his love is perfect in us; the way we know that we are in him and he in us, is that he has given us his spirit (1 Jn. 4,12). We have all been baptized in the same spirit, to be together in the same body (1 Cor. 12,13).

How much the spirit of God is necessary in a community.	If the spirit of God is necessary for oneself in particular, to have wisdom and love, all the more is it necessary in a community.

To have the spirit of God is everything.
It is everything for oneself.
It is everything for a community.
It is the spirit of God that forms unity in a house, that fuses minds and hearts, that makes all into one.
Ut unum sint.
That was the ardent and often repeated prayer of our Lord Jesus Christ after the last supper. That they all may be one in the same spirit. True unity is neither in prayers, nor money, nor in houses, nor in habits, nor in cohabitation, nor in the title of brother or sister that we give each other; all that supposes unity but does not make it; basically, all that is nothing.
How ridiculous and false those titles of brother and sister often are! True unity is in union of the same spirit, the same thought, a same love and it is Jesus Christ who is the center through the Holy Spirit.
Remain in me and I in you, that we all, so to speak, may be in one another and that in seeing one we may see the others as well: that is the true family, the true community, the true union: the same thoughts, the same views, the same inspirations in Jesus Christ.
The Gospel gives us a true example of this union of spirit and heart in the first Christians who were of one heart and soul.
How harmful are those who do not have the good spirit, and to be feared in a house, a community! How much harm they do to others by their words and examples! They are constantly speaking ill of one or the other; they are, as our Lord says, like those little vipers, those snakes who watch for the moment when they may bite to spread the poison that they carry constantly within themselves.
> Words of blame, criticism, thoughtless and useless words, loss of time, jestings, etc. etc. They should be gagged until they reform.

Brood of vipers, said our Lord in speaking to the Pharisees, because their heart was bad and they sought only to bite and spread their venom on him and his apostles.
And usually, they are the ones who wish to dominate and who seek to dominate by their evil and critical spirit; they are proud and always want to lord it over others.
We must beware of those evil spirits and not keep them because they are a plague and a venom who will always be harmful and fatal and not only prevent good but ruin houses and destroy them. In a house, those people are like wreckers; they do more work in one moment than thirty others do in a whole morning. When some seek to build and others demolish continually, it is useless to waste our time in trying to build; the wreckers will always go faster than the builders.

The best way to obviate these grave inconveniences would be to put them in solitude and make them keep the most perfect silence; that is the one and only remedy. But, since those people are always very proud and domineering, they always want to talk and talk louder than the others and they want to dominate everybody and be submitted to nobody[50].

The best means is to dismiss them; it is better to sacrifice a person than to sacrifice the whole community and to see a house always going badly, living without union and charity because of some bad heads. They should be gagged every day until they have lost their bad spirit. Our Lord says: Every kingdom divided against itself will fall in ruins. The one who is not with me is against me, the one who does not gather with me, scatters (Mt. 12,30).

The one who is not with his superior, even if outwardly he does nothing against him, who is satisfied with being indifferent, of not approving, is against his superior. The one who works outside his superior, good works, it is true, but if these works are not done by the superior himself, seen and sanctioned by him, in union with him, you are not gathering with him, you scatter, that is, you work outside and you scatter the good and the works.

In a house it is very difficult not to have little divisions, little oppositions of minds and views and ways of doing; each one has his mind and view, like each one has his face. But we must melt everything, our mind, our particular views, in the general views of a work, a house, and be able to sacrifice our thoughts, our views, for the good and never put ourselves outside of those with whom we are and must be; unless we leave entirely those with whom we should be and form a society apart, outside the community but never within. And when we cannot unite ourselves, it is better to part; that avoids a lot of suffering on both sides[51].

Seeing the quarrels and divisions among the Corinthians, St. Paul told them: *adhuc carnales estis* (1 Cor. 3,2); you are still carnal. This could be said of many others; you let yourselves be led by the flesh and not by the spirit of God.

Summary: What is renouncing one's spirit.

To renounce one's spirit is to be convinced first of all that we have many spiritual faults and that,

---

[50] Ms. XI 723 - How we must keep silence and make those who do not have the spirit of God keep it! and not allow them to talk, for the babblers, the talkers, do not have the spirit of God. Quick to listen, slow to speak. We must beware of those people who talk a lot, who know everything, who discuss everything, who have no doubts about anything; what spirit makes them talk and act? Their own spirit, pride and not the spirit of God.

[51] Ms 244 - This fusion of spirit and heart is achieved in the knowledge and practice of the same rule of life based on Jesus Christ which must be the center of our love; walking toward the same end; same means.

if we act and judge according to our thoughts and ideas, we can only be mistaken very often and do a lot of harm.

(It is to keep silent for fear of saying things that are not according to the spirit. It is to renounce one's "head", one's ideas, judgements, thoughts, to submit to the judgements and thoughts of another.)

It is to say nothing and do nothing by ourselves, after the example of our Lord; but before saying or doing anything, to see if what we say and do is according to the thoughts and ideas of Jesus Christ, our Master, his humility, his kindness, his poverty, his charity[52].

It is asking advice from superiors when we are in doubt and fear action by ourselves. It is submitting in mind and heart to all the decisions of the Church and the Pope. It is submitting our mind and judgement to the decisions and judgements of our superiors. It is to be one with them, since they represent Jesus Christ on earth and that we must be with them and for them in all circumstances. It is always basing ourselves on a word or action of our Lord Jesus Christ to speak and to act.

Practices. We will always be wary of ourselves, of our thoughts, our judgements, our ideas[53].

We will keep silent for fear of saying things that are contrary to the spirit of God, especially if we are young. We will study the Gospel which encloses the actions and words of Jesus Christ in whom the Holy Spirit resided fully. Every day after breakfast, we will recite the *Veni Creator*, 7 Hail Marys and the prayer to the Holy Spirit, to ask for the gifts of the Holy Spirit. (The Veni Creator is ad libitum, to be recited on Sundays, feast days and during retreats.) We will submit in mind and heart to all the decisions of the Church and the Pope. We will submit to the decisions and judgements of our superiors in whom we must recognize the spirit of God. We will avoid all schism and division among us, working to have but one heart and one soul, one spirit in Jesus Christ who must be the center of all our thoughts and all our affections, remembering these words that we say every day during the Mass: *per ipsum, et cum ipso, et in ipso*[54].

---

[52] Ms XI 247 - Avoid affirming things that we do not know for sure; always base ourselves on a word of Jesus Christ or a decision of the Church or of our superiors.

[53] Distrust of ourselves in the spiritual sense, that is base ourselves on God rather than be closed upon ourselves. Thus we trust the nature that God has given us, we think our intelligence capable of communing with God's thoughts. That is totally diffrent from an unhealthy distrust.

[54] Through him, with him and in him.

Renunciation of oneself 235
3. One's heart[1]

---

[1] *Here, the principal manuscript is interrupted; it continues in the next chapter. Nevertheless, there are several studies concerning renunciation of one's heart in the plan for* The True Disciple; *we have chosen this one even though it remains unfinished. XII (39-44).*

The renunciation of one's heart concerns particularly what we call today the affectivity. However, in this chapter there is a certain confusion because the word "heart" has many meanings.
In French, for example, we say "take one's work at heart" which means that we apply ourselves to it courageously. We can also say that someone has a good heart, which means that he is affectively sensitive to the happiness or sadness of others, or we may talk about having heartburn to say that one is nauseous; that is a physiological state.
In the Bible, the word "heart" is used often, but with yet different meanings. It may mean what is most intimate, profound, as when we say "going to the heart of a question", that is, to the essential. Man's heart is his most intimate and personal secret, as in the word of Jesus: "Where your treasure is, there will your heart be also"[2].
Father Chevrier felt this multiplicity of meanings. For a time it seems that he had thought of putting all the renunciations under the title of "renunciation of one's heart". In fact, if the four objects that can attract our heart are the goods of the earth, creatures (that is men), oneself and God, then in dealing with the renunciation of one's heart, we can talk about poverty, renunciation of family and the world and renunciation of oneself.
Finally, Father Chevrier chose to introduce renunciation of one's heart simply as a part of renunciation of oneself. Therefore, it is a matter especially of our affective life, called here "love of creatures". The subject is only sketched. Besides, the question was approached under another aspect concerning chastity[3].
We note that to renounce one's heart is not to renounce love, but it is to pass from a natural love to a supernatural love.
Unfortunately, here again we have a source of confusion for Father Chevrier does not use the words "natural" and "supernatural" with a rather precise theological meaning.
Natural love denotes the spontaneous inclination, the sympathy that may carry us toward others, especially the spontaneous interest of a man for a woman and vice-versa. This natural love, says Father Chevrier, is permitted for the people of the world because it has an honest end which is marriage[4]. We should add that, according to the will of God, this natural inclination can be lived in a supernatural manner, especially when there is the grace of the sacrament of marriage[5].
In all this, Father Chevrier is dependent on his time. The people of the world seem to be reduced to a sorry condition not favorable to the supernatural life.

---

[2] Mt. 6,21.
[3] P. 154.
[4] P. 213.
[5] Cf. P. 132, note 1.

Fortunately, we have learned to discover the supernatural grandeur of the lay condition and of marriage. The lay Christian, like the priest though in another style, is in the world without being of the world, like Jesus is not of the world.

But Father Chevrier's concern remains true: whoever renounces marriage because of the kingdom of God, renounces a certain type of relationship between men and women for the dynamics of that relationship lead to marriage. We must be logical with what we have chosen.

However, supernatural love does not consist in an inhuman, coldly rational love, deprived of all affective impulse. We have already found this supernatural love described in the part on sensitivity[6]. We will find it again in another chapter[7].

---

[6] P. 133.
[7] P. 373.

When Our Lord Jesus Christ says that we must renounce ourselves, he makes no 239
exceptions: the heart, being an integral part of ourselves, is naturally included in that
renunciation that Jesus Christ demands of those who wish to belong totally to him.

The heart is the seat of love. The heart is the seat of love; it is with the heart that we love.

Love is an attraction, an inclination which carries us toward creatures or toward God. This inclination, this feeling, this attraction can be good, and it can also be bad. This attraction has to be guided, directed and it has its faults, like the spirit has its faults. By the fact that the spirit has its faults, the heart has its faults also because the heart follows the spirit and usually loves only what it knows, what it sees. Thus the heart also has its faults, very serious faults, and it is these faults that we must avoid and to which we must renounce in order to become a true disciple of Jesus Christ. The heart sins through lack of knowledge of the spirit and also by attraction. The heart needs to love; it is its life. It needs to love, it is its life like it is the life of the spirit to think and the life of the body to act. Therefore we must guide the heart in its affections and make it renounce all affections that are not according to God.

The four objects of the love of our heart. Our heart has four objects toward which it can be carried. It can be carried:
    toward money, the goods of the earth,
    toward creatures,
    toward oneself,
    toward God.

Those are the four objects that can attract our heart and become the object of its love:
    love of money,
    love of creature,
    love of oneself,
    love of God.

We must examine the faults that can insinuate themselves in the love of these objects in order to renounce them and make true love reign in us.

1. Love of money. Under this word, we include love of the goods of the earth.

Our Lord condemns this love of money and the goods of the earth when he says that 240
no one can serve two masters; either he will love one and hate the other or cling to one and despise the other; no one can serve God and money. This can also be applied to the love of creatures and of oneself. Because where your treasure is, there will your heart be also.

How to recognize that we love money.	We recognize it when we are anxious and avid to acquire it; when we are worried about our possessions and sad, desperate when we lose them.
Explanation.	Anxious to acquire. Worried in possessing. And sad in losing.
Bad effects that this love has on ourselves.	The miser who is possesed by the love of money is worried, somber, concerned; therefore cold and insensitive to the misfortunes of others.
Excuse of the miser.	Economy, prudence.
Other fault opposed to the love of money.	The fault opposed to the love of money is lackof concern, prodigality;

without economy, without order, dissipates God's goods, abuses God's gifts. People who have never earned their living, who do not know what it is to live, as they say in the world. They are spendthrifts, prodigal without reason; they ruin houses, they bring their fault of prodigality in the houses where they are and they ruin the houses where they are, like they ruined their own, if the superiors do not stop them: prodigal with the money, prodigal with food, clothing, heating, lighting; prodigal with the workers, make them do and undo without reason, or for a small appearance at the most. They call that largess, charity; it must be called disorder and prodigality. Leaves things lying around, cares for nothing, picks nothing up; unconcerned, the opposite of the miser. *In medio stat virtus*[8]. The virtue of poverty must direct our conduct with regard to the goods of the earth[9].

241 **2. Love of creatures.** By the word creature we mean the neighbor, that is, the beings that God has created like us and that we must love as ourselves and in relation to God. Many faults can slip into the love of neighbor. We may love our neighbor in

>a natural manner,
>passionate manner,
>interested manner,
>supernatural manner.

---

[8] Virtue is in the happy medium. (an adage).

[9] Ms XII 46 - In evangelical poverty we will find the rules to follow to destroy the love of money.

From which flow four types of love:
- natural love,
- passionate love,
- interested love,
- supernatural love.

Natural love. It is to love somebody for his natural qualities.
There is the love of family, of the father and mother for their children and the children for their parents. To love somebody for his interior or exterior qualities. The natural love of creatures among themselves and who are of the same species and family. Natural love for the unfortunate. Love [...of gratitude][10]. Natural love that slips into people who live together. Natural love that slips in especially between persons of the opposite sex.

Uselessness of that love. That love is not bad in itself; on the contrary, it is good, natural, honest.
But it is useless for salvation because it does not proceed from a principle of faith and charity and as long as it remains in the natural state, it is useless for heaven[11].

Dangers of natural love. It may even be dangerous, especially when it exists between persons of different sexes,
because of our tendency to evil and natural love, not being guided by faith and true charity, can only degenerate and become progressively a passionate love, if we are not careful and beware of the temptation that it can give rise to in us.

1. Between persons of the same sex.

---

[10] The text is unclear.

[11] For the difficulties that this paragraph and the next might cause, keep in mind that Father Chevrier addresses himself to people who have made profession of consecrated celebacy. (cf. p. 210)

2. This natural love slips in easily between persons of different sex, in the line of duty: confessor and penitent, *reciprocal attraction*; priest and religious woman, persons who have the opportunity to see each other often; relatives, direction; that time to an employment: master and domestic servant; afflicted person and comforter, natural attraction, persons who follow: relationships of character, *natural qualities*, superior and inferior, service; signs of this attachment: thought, exterior manifestation, frequent letters, temptations, emotions. To obviate all temptation, avoid danger: practical means.

False excuses that we find to justify this natural love; spiritual good of souls. We know that natural love degenerates and becomes too natural, that passion comes when we think too often of the same person, when we like to be together, when we seek their company, that time seems to drag when we are not with the person, that we are too concern about what the person does. Therefore we must watch over this natural love and render it supernatural in order to render it useful for salvation and avoid the pitfalls into which it can lead us when we let it grow too much in us. This article is very important. It is because they are not careful enough on this point that many fall into evil ways. This natural love which can be permitted to people of the world because it may have an honest and legitimate end which is marriage, is not permitted to priest and religious who have renounced marriage and who, consequently, must suppress all natural feelings which could result in such an end. We may say what we want, natural love tends toward a more sensitive live; we cannot stop the progress of love.

243 **Rules to follow in order to avoid, not to fall into this natural love.**

Passionate love.

It is a love that seeks the satisfaction of the senses. It is a love that cannot exist without sin.

Sensitive and passionate love.

Renunciation of oneself 245
4. One's will

Why is obedience so important in communities. Father Chevrier seems to have asked himself the question[1].
In fact, it is very prevelant in communities of priests and religious to make obedience the central theme. We even have the tendency to deal with this topic by isolating it from the rest of Christian life, to the point that obedience may have seemed to supplant or purely and simply replace charity.
Two main arguments have been given to explain the importance given to obedience: it is the shortest path to spiritual perfection and the one who obeys never goes wrong. Father Chevrier takes these explanations without discussing them[2].
Today we cannot support such a simplistic explanation. We know only too well how we have maintained that "truth is captive of injustice"[3] *by demanding of unfortunate people an unconditional submission, supposedly willed by God, to those who hold power. We know only too well also that some have committed crimes against humanity and tried to excuse themselves by claiming that they were only following orders coming from higher up.*
Besides, the situation has changed. For example, the cloistered nun goes out from time to time to exercise her right to vote. In so doing she does not obey the superior, she exercises the authority that she has as a citizen according to the constitution of her country. In the determination of her vote, she is responsible to her conscience of citizen and Christian. Her fidelity cannot be reduced purely and simply to religious obedience.
The times have changed also in another respect. Today, as yesterday, an apostle must take initiatives, but the coordination, the harmonization of these initiatives cannot be done simply by observing the laws of the Church and the directives of superiors. All those who work in the same field must work together to discover the steps and initiatives to be taken.
In such conditions, is this chapter of The True Disciple *devoid of interest for us? No, for it is centered on seeking the will of God and obedience as such is placed in the global context without which it is not authentic*[4].
For Father Chevrier, the decisive importance is not in obedience but in a willed and sought dependence on the spirit of God. If someone lives in this dependence, he will follow, in obedience, in the footsteps of Jesus Christ; that is why the most important article remains the one on renunciation of one's spirit.
It is a matter, therefore, of seeking a spiritual understanding of obedience whose principal aspects are the following.
Obedience is situated in the wider search for the the will of God. It is not the sole means for God's will is manifested in other ways. But obedience has a privileged

---

[1] Pp. 220.
[2] Pp. 220; 226-227.
[3] Rom. 1,18.
[4] Cf. P. 219, note 1.

place because it guarantees the sincerity and truth of our search, the authenticity of our charity. Obedience is the greatest mark of our love of God[5].
Obedience is the adherence to God and to the authority of the superiors because of God, for love of God and not through affection or fear of the superiors themselves. We must obey with faith[6].
We must put proper order in the various types of authority for only one authority is total and absolute, that of God, and in each situation we must ask ourselves whom we are to obey[7].
We do not submit to God if we give a superior more authority than God has given him. But in these conditions we could well say that the duty of obedience must come before everything[8]. *In fact, we cannot behave as if God had constituted us the supreme authority to judge all others.*
We must always keep in mind the end of obedience, especially in apostolic life: it assures the cohesion of forces for the service of God's work, it gives us the assurance of being God's collaborators. That is the meaning of what Father Chevrier calls a regulation[9]. *Besides, this concept of obedience is primarily a call to those who hold authority. They are at the service of Christ's authority and at the service of each one. They must be much more concerned about submitting themselves to Christ than of obtaining the submission of others.* How difficult it is to be superior[10].
Finally we must not forget that some days obedience will always be more or less costly, painful, even crucifying for the one who truly seeks to accomplish the will of God. As it was for Jesus who obeyed his Father unto death on the cross, *not wanting to please the high priest or Pilate or himself, but only the Father*[11].

---

[5] P. 226.
[6] P. 225.
[7] P. 224.
[8] P. 224.
[9] P. 224.
[10] P. 224.
[11] Phil. 2,8; Jn. 8,19; Rom. 15,3; P. 222.

It is the fourth act of renunciation that we have to do to arrive at a perfect renunciation of ourselves.

Doctrine of our Lord Jesus Christ on this subject.   If anyone wishes to come after me, let him renounce himself, take up his cross and follow me!

What is there more ourselves than our will, since our will is the expression of our thought, our judgement? It is the exterior translation of our soul. In commanding us to renounce ourselves, our Lord demands the renunciation of our will.

What is renouncing one's will?   It is not acting according to our own will but of submitting our will to that of another[12].

Why must we renounce our will?   Because our will is subject to all the faults of our spirit, to all the passions of our heart;

we want and do only what our spirit knows, understands and what our heart desires. And since our spirit and our heart are filled with faults, it follows that our will conforms to our spirit, our judgements and desires.

As long as our heart is not entirely pure, that our spirit is not entirely enlightened by divine light, our will is evil and subject to all the errors of the spirit and all the passions of the heart, and our actions are in relation with these different passions. Therefore we must submit our will to a superior will in order not to be exposed to many faults and failings.

What are the faults of our will?   Since our will is subject to our spirit and our heart, we can say that it has

all the faults of the heart and spirit, since the will is the spirit acting, the heart acting. If the spirit is bad, the will is bad; if the heart is bad, the will is bad. If our spirit is proud, frivolous, inconstant, evil, narrow, exaggerated, false, capricious, our will is likewise. If our heart is jealous, susceptible, passionate, selfish, our will acts according to the passions of our heart.

However, among the faults particular to the will we may note those of weakness, stiffness, inconstancy, domination, self-will, vacillation, wavering, indecision.

Faults of the will:

---

[12] Ms XI 124.

In what does this renunciation of one's will consist? In no longer doing what I want but what God wants.

weakness, inconstancy, indecision, stiffness, domination, softness[13].

Importance of this renunciation. It is very important to renounce one's will, because renunciation of the will brings with it the renunciation of the spirit and the heart. When we submit our will entirely to our superior, to somebody, we submit, by the very fact, our spirit and our heart and the renunciation then becomes complete and perfect by the fact of the renunciation of our self-will. It is the shortest way to arrive at perfect renunciation, but it is also the most difficult because we do not easily make the perfect sacrifice of our will. Yet that is what we should do to arrive surely and more quickly at perfection. That is why also, in community, we hold so much to obedience, because it is the shortest way to arrive at perfection. But we must say also that we are merely slaves and.........[14] if there is not, above all, a knowledge of Jesus Christ, faith and love of God. But when there is faith, love of God and true Christian submission, then there is true obedience[15].

In what does obedience consist? True obedience does not consist only is saying but in doing[16].
Not every one who says to me, Lord, Lord, shall enter the kingdom of heaven, but he who does the will of my Father who is in heaven. On that day many will say to me, Lord, Lord, did we not prophesy in your name, and cast out demons in your name, and do many mighty works in your name. And I will declare to them, I never knew you (Mt. 7,21). Be doers of the word, and not hearers only, deceiving yourselves. For if any one is a hearer of the word and not a doer, he is like a man who observes his natual face in a mirror, for he observes himself and goes away and at once forgets what he was like. But he who looks into the perfect law, the law of

---

[13] Ms XI 254 - Faults of the will:
Stiffness, not of submission, doing only what we want; caprices, act through caprice; want to submit to nothing; say I want, I do not want.
Our will must be submitted to that of Jesus Christ, the Church, our superiors.
Self-will which does not yield to the common good.
Weak: which bends with every wind, to please, firmness, inconstancy.

[14] Blank space in the manuscript.

[15] Cf. p. 218.

[16] Ms XII 24 -
In what does obedience consist?

In the entire offering of one's will.

Sacrifice of the will...entire
Not what I want, but what you want (Mk. 14,37
Your will, not mine be done. Here I am, O God, I come to do your will (Heb. 10,9).

liberty and perseveres, being no hearer that forgets but a doer that acts, he shall be blessed in his doing (Jas. 1,22). For it is not the hearers of the law who are righteous before God, but the doers of the law who will be justified (Rom. 2,13). The parable of the two sons: one says yes but does nothing, the other says no but does something; it is the latter who did the will of God and will be rewarded.

How our Lord Jesus Christ himself practiced obedience.	Our Lord himself gives us the greatest example of obedience and teaches us how we ourselves must obey.
He did not come on earth to do his will.	I came down from heaven, not to do my will but to do the will of the one who sent me (Jn.6,38).
He offered himself to his Father to do his will and not his own.	Here I am, O my Father, to do your will (Hb. 10,9). You did not want sacrifices or holocausts

or oblations offered for sin according to the law, so I said: here I am, O my Father, to do your will. Erat subditus illis[17]. My food is to do the will of my Father.

He does not seek to do his will.	I do not seek to do my will, but the will of the one who sent me (Jn. 5,30).

It is difficult not to seek to do one's will, even in asking permission; we seek, we ask in such a way as to obtain, to be allowed to do as we please.

He did nothing of himself.	The Son does nothing of himself, except what he sees the Father doing (Jn. 5,19).
I can do nothing by myself (Jn. 5,30).	
He submits totally to the will of his Father.	Your will, not my be done. Not what I want, but what you want.
He obeys without reasoning.	As my Father commands me, I do (Jn.14,31).
He does not seek what pleases him but what pleases his Father.	I always do what is pleasing to him (Jn. 8,29)
He always acts in union with the Father.	My Father acts constantly, and I act with him (Jn.5,17).

---

[17] He was submitted to them (Lk. 2,51).

He is always with me because I always do what is pleasing to him. He who is not with me is against me. He who does not gather with me, scatters (Lk. 11,23).

Obedience has become his food. To his apostles who were telling him to eat, he answers: I have a food that you do not know, it is to do the will of my father (Jn. 4,32).

255 **He puts obedience to his Father before everything else.** Why are you looking for me? do you not know that I must be about my Father's business (Lk. 2,49).

He is obedient even in the smallest things. I did not come to abolish the law, but to accomplish it. Not one iota shall pass before it is accomplished (Mt. 5,17).

He carries obedience as far as doing things at the hour and the moment indicated by his Father. My hour has no yet come. The hour has come. It is your hour.

He does not seek to be exempt from obedience because of the sufferings that will ensue. He willingly goes to the Garden of Olives, although he knows full well that he will suffer there. He strongly rebukes Peter who was trying to defend him, saying that, if he wished, he could summon twelve legions of angels to defend himself; but it must be like this. As my Father commands me, I do.

In his judges and executioners he sees the action and authority of his Father. To Pilate who tells him that he has the power to deliver him to be crucified, he answers: You would have no power over me if it were not given to you from above.

And he carries obedience unto death on the cross. He was obedient unto death, death on the cross (Phil. 2,8). He lays down his life by himself, no one takes it from him, it is the commandment he has received from his Father.

| He knows better than anybody what obedience costs. | Even though he was the Son of God, he learned what obedience costs, because he suffered (Heb. 5,8). |

Saint Paul said [to the Hebrews]: You have not yet resisted to the point of shedding your blood (Heb. 12,4).

| Rules of obedience. | In the words and examples of our Lord Jesus Christ, |

we see how the true disciple of Jesus Christ must practice obedience and we cannot establish any surer and more just rule that those he himself practiced. Therefore, in following our Lord, our Head and Model, we must know and engrave these things in our heart.

That we did not come here to do our will but the will of God and our superiors.

That after the example of Jesus Christ, our Master and Model, we must offer ourselves and be devoted in doing the will of God and our superiors.

That we must do nothing by ourselves.

That we must submit our will totally to that of God and our superiors.

That we must obey without reasoning.

That we must not seek to do what pleases us but what is pleasing to God and our superiors.

That we must always act in union with our superiors.

That obedience must be our spiritual nourishment.

That the duty of obedience must come before everything else.

That we must be obedient even in the smallest things.

That we must be obedient even to doing things at the hour and moment indicated in the rule.

That we must not seek to be exempt from obedience because of the sufferings that we may meet.

That we must carry obedience unto death, in cases of persecution and salvation.

These are the different rules of obedience that we deduce from the conduct and words of our Lord Jesus Christ.

| To whom should we obey?[18] | To Jesus Christ, the Church, our superiors and our regulations. |

---

[18] Here it is a question of obedience in the Church only, since it is a matter of apostolic work. Elsewhere Father Chevrier evokes the question of obedience to our "civil masters". (Ms XI, 125).

Jesus is the great Master, it is he who has shown us the will of God on earth and had it consigned to the Gospel. He is our King, our Master, our Head, our Model[19].

The Church, composed of our Holy Father, the Pope, infallible in his decisions and to whom we owe obedience because he represents Jesus Christ himself and communicates to us the decisions from heaven; our bishops who are God's representatives on earth and who, united with the Pope, also manifest the will of God on earth[20].

Our legitimate superiors. Our legitimate superiors, that is those who have been named by the authority of the Church, of the bishop and the Pope, have the power to command in her name and we owe them obedience because they represent the Church and Jesus Christ himself who commands us through the mouth of his representatives: *he who listens to you listens to me, he who despises you despises me.* How difficult it is to be superior. The superior must be filled with the spirit of God, a superior must know the will of God in every instance and have it accomplished by his inferiors. What a task! What a responsibility! What union this man must have with Jesus Christ, in order to say and have others do only what Jesus Christ wants and desires to be accomplished in his members![21-22]

The regulation[23]

A regulation drawn from the Gospel and approved by the Church is again the expression of the will of God for us.

There is the general regulation of the Church which is for all the faithful and which is found in the commandments of God and the Church; every Christian is obliged to follow this rule of conduct imposed by God under pain of damnation.

---

[19] Ms XI 125 - For us, it is especially important to know the will of Jesus Christ, our Master; he manifested it in his gospel. That is where he dictated all that we had to do. With what respect, submission and love should we not read and study the Holy Gospel, to accomplish it!.

[20] Obedience to the Church. The text gives the impression that the Church is composed of the Pope and the bishops. We should say obedience in the Church to those who have received authority, the hierarchy. This manner of speaking of the hierarchy by saying "the Church" was very prevelant in Father Chevrier's time.

[21] Ms XI 722; XI 256.

How difficult it is to be superior of a community! to be priest to give the good spirit to others, to command according to Jesus Christ, to direct according Jesus Christ, to lead according to Jesus Christ: each house, each person, each soul in particular. Everything that we say, command must conform to the thought, the spirit of Jesus Christ. How a superior must study our Lord, his spirit, his doctrine! (MS XI 722). To become like little children who have no other will but that of their father (Ms XI 256).

[22] Cf. P. 198 (note 40).

[23] On this question of the regulations cf. P. 231.

But, besides this general regulation, each order, each house, each community has a particular regulation, because each house, each community has a particular end which tends, in a different way, to the glory of God and the salvation of souls.
Therefore, when we leave the world to enter into a community, while keeping the obligation of the commandments of God and the Church, we take on the obligation of following the regulation in use in the house. It is a serious and important obligation, and even though this obligation is not under pain of sin, it is nevertheless indispensable for our sanctification, for good example, and the non accomplishment can only entail the ruin of the house and all those who are in it.
We must look upon the regulation as the expression of God's will for us. And in obeying the regulation of a house, from morning to night, we are sure of doing the will of God and our superiors, of achieving our salvation and walking in the way of perfection, because the regulations of the communities are all made to make us walk in the way of evangelical perfection.
Therefore let us have great respect, great affection, great love for our rule; let us look upon it as the expression of the God's will for us. To have the spirit of our rule, not to be satisfied with the letter, that is to act through love and not through fear or constraint, in the fear of being punished.

How should we obey? We should obey with faith, submission and love.

With faith. Remember that our superiors hold the place of God, that they command in the name of God and that in obeying them or our rule, we obey God himself. He who listens to you, listens to me; he who despises you despises me.

With submission. Interior, prompt and total submission. We must submit our spirit and our judgement to our superiors; not only an exterior submission, but an interior submision of our soul. Prompt submission that does not argue, that does not seek to escape, to find means of not submitting. Total submission, by doing everything that is commanded, the way it is commanded and at the time it is commanded.
To become like little children: If you do not become like little children, you will not enter the kingdom of heaven. St. Paul says: Obey your leaders, remain under their orders, so that having to watch over your souls as having to give an account of them to God, they may fulfill their duty with joy and not with groanings, which would not be advantageous for you (Heb. 13,17).

With love. That is what Peter recommends when he says: Purify your souls by your obedience to the truth for a sincere love of the brethren, love one another earnestly from the heart (1 Pt. 22). It is for our good that we receive orders. It is for our good that we must obey.

Excellence of obedience. Obedience is better than sacrifice and holocausts (Mt. 9,13; 4 Reg. 15,22).

Obedience is the greatest sign of our love for God. Our Lord himself assures us: He who has my commandments and keeps them is the one who truly loves me (Jn. 14,21).
Love of God consists in keeping his commandments, we know that we love God when we keep his commandments (Jn. 5,2). The one who keeps the word of God, does what it commands, truly has the perfect love of God in him (1 Jn. 2,5). And our Lord himself says: So that the world may know that I love my Father, as my Father commands, I do (Jn. 14, 31).

Obedience is also the surest sign of the love and respect that we have for our superiors.

Obedience is the shortest way to arrive at perfection and renunciation. In sacrificing our will we also sacrifice our spirit and our heart, since the will is the expression of the thoughts of the spirit and the attachments of the heart.

Obedience is the shortest way to establish order and unity in a house, and also strength.

Strength. The one who listens to the word of God and puts it into practice is like a man who builds on rock; nothing can shake him. The one who listens and does not do builds on sand (Mt. 7; 24). The same goes for communities. Funis triplex non rumpitur[24].

---

[24] The triple cord does not break (Qo. 4,13).

Obedience is the only true sign of salvation.	It is not all those who say Lord, Lord, who will enter the kingdom of heaven, but the one who does the will of my Father in heaven,

he will enter the kingdom of heaven. On that day many will say to me. Lord, Lord, did we not prophesy in your name, and cast out demons in your name, and do many mighty works in your name? And then will I declare to them, I never knew you; depart from me, you evildoers (Mt. 7,21).

Obedience is also the surest means to have peace, serenity of spirit and of heart.	Peace to men of good will! The one who sent me is with me and he never leaves me alone, because I do always what is pleasing to him (Jn. 5,29).

The obedient man will meet many victories (Prov. 21,28). As I hear, I judge and my judgement is just because I do not seek my will but the will of the one who sent me (Jn. 5,30). The one who obeys is sheltered from all responsibilities to God and his conscience[25].

Obedience is also the means that God uses to raise us to higher degrees[26].	Have courage, good and faithful servant, because you were faithful in little things, I will put you over greater things (Mt. 25, 23).

The most beautiful promises are given to the obedient man.	He who has my commandments and keeps them, he it is who loves me;

and he who loves me will be loved by my Father, and I will love him and manifest myself to him (Jn. 14,23). If you keep my commandments, you will abide in my love, just as I have kept my Father's commandments and abide in his love (Jn. 15,10).

It is the meditation of the just.	Mens justi meditabitur obedientiam (Prov. 15,28).[27]

Practical conclusions.

---

[25] To be sheltered from responsibilities. That is, God does not hold guilty the one who obeys, even if the latter has the feeling that, had he been in the superior's place, he would have given a different order.

[26] Ms. X 253 - We will make of obedience our principal virtue and the one which contributes the most to the glory of God, the good order of a house and the sanctification of our souls.

[27] The spirit of just will meditate obedience.

(conclusion of renunciation of oneself) 263

With the concluding pages on the renunciation of oneself, the tone does not soften. The word from the Gospel, "to hate one's life" is maintained.
It would be a gross error to understand that we have to have feelings of hatred for ourselves. Such morbid behavior would achieve nothing good for God's work.
Someone's abnegation is not judged by the level of feelings that he has for himself but in the manner he goes his way[1]. *The one who has flattering or hateful feelings for himself is folded upon himself. That is contrary to what the Gospel demands. It is the unfortunate state of those who have not renounced themselves*[2].
Father Chevrier gives a number of means to take to arrive at this renunciation[3]. *He only takes the means usually prescribed or recommended at the time, especially in the seminaries and especially in religious communities. Some of those ways of doing are hardly in use today. Other have been implemented, that aim at the same end; but they are more adapted to what we are.*
We note the special attention that Father Chevrier gives to a community effort to progress together in evangelical life. For this he sought to make the classic Chapter of Faults efficacious for the progress of a house[4].
As for the regulation[5], *it is useful to know that Father Chevrier composed and recomposed many regulations for his house. He was not seeking a definitive regulation. He wanted, as much as possible, that everything run smoothly in unity and that each one should know what he had to do. But he thought it was normal that the organization of a group be left up to the group itself. He did not hesitate to write to the four Prado seminarians living alone in Rome:*

> I have received your regulation; try to be faithful to it; modify it according to necessity and let charity be your great rule[6].

---

[1] Cf. p. 235, note 10.
[2] P. 236.
[3] P. 238.
[4] P. 239.
[5] P. 224.
[6] LP n. 106, end of November 1876.

Our Lord wants us to carry this renunciation of ourselves even to hatred of ourselves.	Whoever comes after me and does not hate his father and mother...... and even his own life, cannot be my disciple (Lk. 14,26).	267

Therefore we must hate ourself. We must hate our body, worldly thoughts, affections, perverse will: hate everything that comes from self and not from God.

The one who loves his soul will lose it. (Jn. 12,25).	The soul and the spirit, difference between the two, according to Scripture.

The spirit comes from God. The soul is what is in us, holds to us, participates in our miseries, inclinations, passions; it is the animal, terrestraial life. The soul is ourselves, with its miseries, passions; the soul participates in Adam's sin, it receives from Adam the stain of sin and has all its disastrous effects. The spirit is the spirit of God that we receive in baptism and confirmation which makes us live from above.

He who loves his soul, that is loves his soul by following its desires, inclinations, passions; loves his soul by holding to his ideas, caprices, terrestrial judgements, will lose himself. Those who love themselves lose themselves because they love themselves against the will of God, against duty, in spite of the conscience and prefer their pleasure, the satisfaction to the will of God.

He who hates his soul in this world keeps it for eternal life. (Jn. 12,25)	Hates his soul in this world, that is, his passions, inclinations,	

terrestrial and worldly ideas opposed to the Gospel and Christian virtues, everything that comes from oneself, one's spoiled, corrupt heart; who makes his body walk in 268
penance, fasting and prayer, who commands his body and makes it obey...

He who wants to keep his life will lose it.	He who wants to keep his life at the expense of the law of the Gospel, of God,

religion, the rule of life, for the useless care of his body through softness, negligence, laziness, gluttony, excessive cares, will lose his soul.

He who loses his life because of me will keep it.	Through work, penance, mortifiction, suffering death,

like so many Saints who were martyrs at every instant through the continual sufferings of life which they endured for God and for souls. They will find the life that they have lost, a better, more happy life.

Happy effects that renunciation produces in us.	It purifies us of our faults. Renunciation of ourselves rids us of everything that is evil in us;

it purifies us first of our faults, our passions: strip yourselves of the old man. It is the primary work that is the essential base of evangelical life, without which there can be nothing good in us.

It makes us capable of practicing virtue.	Through renunciation of ourselves, we become capable of practicing virtue, virtue no longer finds obstacles in us.

With the grace of God, we can easily practice humility, meekness, charity, poverty. He who has renounced himself and carried renunciation to hatred of himself, will have no difficulty in abasing himself in his eyes and the eyes of others, he will have no difficulty in bearing humiliations, the scorn of the world, to be look upon as trash in the streets, dust, since he already hates and despises himself. He has renounced all that may honor him, be agreeable to him; if he is struck on the left cheek, he willingly presents the right. The one who has renounced himself will not find it difficult to practice poverty; on the contrary, he will like to be poor, small, deprived of many things, to be among the poor; he has renounced glory, the respect of the world, everything that shines in the world.

The one who has renounced himself will not find it difficult to practice charity; not holding to himself, he will not fear to be disturbed, devote himself to others, to take two thousand steps when a thousand are asked of him, to serve others since he considers himself the least of all.

269
It makes us new men.	If anyone is in Jesus Christ, he has become a new creature;

what was old has past, everything has become new (2 Cor. 5,17).

Renunciation makes us capable of receiving the abundant graces that we need to become other creatures in Jesus Christ, little by little, the old man is destroyed, the new man is formed by the grace of the Holy Spirit[7].

True children of God.	Because, in destroying the old man, we are born to a new life and this word of the Savior is accomplished:

---

[7] Ms. XI 131 - Ms XII 19.

Strip yourself of the old man and put on the new man who, in the knowledge of God, is renewed in the image of the one who created him (Col. 3,9). Before putting on, we must be stripped (Ms XI 131).

Once we are stripped, we can put on the new man (Ms XII 19).

If you do not become like little children, you will not enter the kingdom of God. What prevents us from becoming little children is our natural faults; in destroying them, we are reborn. What is born of the flesh is flesh; we destroy what is flesh in us to acquire the spirit of children of God.

Totally Celestial men[8].   As the first man is terrestrial, says St. Paul, his offspring is terrestrial,
and as the second man is celestial, his offspring is celestial; as we have borne the image of the terrestrial man, let us now bear the image of the celestial man (1 Cor. 15,47).
I have been crucified with Jesus Christ and I live now, no longer I, but Jesus Christ lives in me; for if I now live in this mortal body, I live in the faith of the Son of God who has loved me and gave himself up for me (Gal. 2,19). Consider yourselves as dead to sin and living for God alone in Jesus Christ, our Lord (Rom. 6,8). As for us, we are already living in heaven.

Nostra conversatio in caelis est (Phil. 3,20)[9].

When we have rid ourselves of ourselves we are light and rise to heaven in spirit and in heart, no longer held by terrestrial thoughts and affections.

Our conversation is all celestial.

What a difference in ideas, thoughts, conversation between a soul that has renounced itself and a soul that is full of itself. You are dead and your life is hidden with Jesus Christ in God, and when Jesus Christ will appear, you also will appear with him in glory (Col. 3,4).
If you live according to the flesh, you will die, but if by the spirit you put to death the deeds of the body, you will live, for those who are led by the spirit of God are children of God (Rom. 8,12).
The one who has renounced himself is not troubled about anything; he does not pay attention to insults, scorn, neglect, all those things that so trouble the soul that is full of itself[10].

---

[8] On the meaning of the word "celestial", see page 124.

[9] Father Chevrier himself translates: Our conversion is all celestial (cf. p. 235). This restricts considerably the meaning of this phrase from St. Paul. A better translation today is: our city is in heaven.

[10] Ms XI 132 - Ms X 193 - The one who has renounced himself is not troubled by anything, he does not pay attention to all those adversities of the world, to insults, scorn, even blows. He goes his way (Ms XI 132).

Nor is he effected by praise and honors; he is indifferent to all that and always keeps peace and tranquility of soul and heart. He holds to nothing, not to himself or creatures or the goods of the earth; he lives in complete freedom vis-à-vis everything and he has the total liberty of the children of God.

Ubi Spiritus ibi libertas[11].

Happy the house where the subjects have renounced themselves.

When this true renunciation reigns in a house, we no longer find souls who are concerned with themselves and others; everybody is concerned with God and souls to bring them to God and save them; there reigns peace, joy, charity, unity, strength and a thrust toward good and love.

On the contrary, when this renunciation is not found in a house, then there are the works of the flesh of which our Lord and St. Paul, his apostle, speak. Those works are: impurity, indolence, greed, theft, nastiness, fraud, evil eye, pride, folly, enmities, divisions, jealousy, animosity, quarrels, divisions, dissentions, heresies, envy and still others that make of this house a house of the world and not a house of God, because it is no longer the reign of God that exists but the reign of oneself, and when we see this we can say with St. Paul to the Corinthians: *Adhuc carnales estis. You are still carnal*, that is, you behave according to the flesh and not according to the spirit of God. That house is not the kingdom of God.

Unhappy state of those who have not renounced themselves.

The one who has not renounced himself is always troubled, agitated, worried; he is always thinking about what is going on around him, of what is being said, of what was done to him and he always thinks that something is being said or done against him. He is always in a state of jealousy, susceptibility, suspicion; he always thinks that more is being done for others than for him; he is always concerned about others and himself; he is always up and seeking consolation and satisfaction, because he is always worried, troubled. These troubles and worries are basically only little nothings that could be dissipated by only one thought of faith and love of God, of humility, but because there is in these souls neither faith nor humility, neither love of God nor strength nor action, they cannot endure anything and these little nothings are mountains for them and they consider unbearable what others would pay no attention to. All that comes from love of self, attachment to self.

It is because we have not renounced ourself that we are always sad, worried, discouraged (Ms X 193).

[11] Where the Spirit is, there is freedom (2 Cor. 3,17).

How unhappy are those souls who constantly seek themselves, who are concerned only with themselves!
What an unbearable life for themselves and for the others and for those who govern them![12]

---

[12] Ms XII 51.

Love of oneself.
> The true love of self, for one's good, for the glory of God; we belong to God and neighbor, we are not ours exclusively.
>
> Love of self, when it arrives at the degree that is called egoism, is the most terrible of sicknesses.
>
> The great fault of this love is egoism.
>
> There is the egoism that comes from the heart and the egoism that comes from pride of the spirit.
>
> Egoism relates everything to itself, sees only itself, seeks only itself; it wants everything to revolve around it, it is jealous, susceptible, evil, demanding, spiteful, suspicious, curious.

The cult of self.
> He is always looking to see if he is loved or not; he is sick over a lack of consideration, an attention paid to another; he does not want others to make any effort for fear they may be rewarded.

No devotion.
> He cannot bear that others work for him.
>
> He complains of everybody for fear of being blamed himself or that others be thought better of than himself.
>
> He loves nobody; he loves only himself.
>
> He seeks only himself in what he does, what he says; he seeks himself, he seeks only satisfactions of the heart; he is happy to see others humiliated because that seems to elevate him; it saddens him to see others honored and do well because that seems to abase him.
>
> He is happy with the evil that befalls others and sad at the good that befalls them.
>
> What a sad state is the love of self, to be egoistical! what misfortune! what a sad life he leads! always worried and sad. And he is never still, he is always running, he is always worried, unhappy.
>
> *He who loves his soul will lose it, he who hates his soul will keep it, he who loses his soul will find it.*
>
> Those people always want to hear beautiful things; we cannot tell them the truth because the truth would kill them; they think we exaggerate, that we do not know them; it is always the others who are wrong, never themselves; they never have the time to be concerned about

272   A bit of renunciation of themselves would make all this disappear and put peace and serenity in their souls, which will never exist as long as they allow themselves to be led by attachment to themselves.
It is God who has taught us this and when the Master speaks, he says the truth. My God, give us all this true renunciation of ourselves so that, detached from ourselves, we may love you and serve our neighbor and never be hampered in the ways of justice, devotion and charity.

Means to arrive at renunciation of ourselves.

We must:

1. Ask God sincerely for the grace to know ourselves, our dominant fault, our particular faults, and have a true desire to correct them.
2. Choose a true friend who will tell us our faults and tell us charitably when we fall into any fault.
3. Make a daily examination of conscience on our dominant fault, on the part of renunciation that concerns us and on the opposite virtue.
4. Admit to our superior (or the one we have chosen as mentor) our principal faults of this nature and always ask a penance.
5. Make a public declaration of our exterior faults every week.
6. Have the Chapter of Faults every month where we receive humbly the reproaches and remarks that may be made on our exterior behavior.
7. Go to confession every week and prepare for it seriously in order to obtain perfect contrition and true change of one's life.

273   **The Chapter of Faults.**

The Chapter of Faults is the public avowal of one's exterior - *not interior* - faults; the interior faults concern the confessor.
The exterior faults that are matter for the Chapter are the faults:
    against the regulations,
    against one's work,
    and the character faults.
There is certainly a great grace attached to the public accusation of one's exterior faults, if it is done properly.
To do it humbly and fruitfully, it must be done kneeling down and, after having said what we know, pray our brothers or superiors to tell us what they may have noticed

anything but themselves; their duty is neglected. The remedy for all this is humility and charity.

in us which would be contrary to the good example and the edification that we naturally owe one another for the glory of God and the salvation of our neighbor, and ask a penance.

We must accuse ourselves every week and fix a day and hour for this exercise so that it may be done regularly, because it is very important. This exercise prevents us from falling into laxity, forces us to pay attention to ourselves and puts a public sanction on our faults, which is no little stimulus for the weak so that they may pay more attention to themselves.

To make the accusation and particular examen easier, we have made little cards on where the different articles of the regulation and the various points which could be the subject of our examen and accusation are indicated. We can and must use these cards to note our failings each day and accuse them on the day of the Chapter. That is the last means; it must be used only when the house is running well.

Other means, longer but more efficacious:

Before the accusations, begin with the reading of the summary of the regulation, in order be renewed in the spirit of the work, to get a quick view of our obligations and thus prepare ourselves humbly to admit our faults and to accept the penance that will be imposed for our failings.

Means to make the Chapter of faults fruitful for the individuals and efficacious for the progress of the house.

Means to make the Chapter effective and useful for the house. Besides the general regulation of the house, its use and character which must be the ordinary subject of the Chapter each week,

it would be good to fix for a month, or longer, a particular subject beginning with the first article of renunciation of the family and the world, followed by oneself, that is one's body, spirit, etc... We stay with the same subject until we have obtained a good general result, and when that result has been obtained, we go on to the next. We can thus cover all the articles of The True Disciple of Jesus Christ and arrive at some happy result for the whole community.

This means seems long and laborious but it also seems more sure and easier. The superiors must be firm and persevering; begin by showing the need for a virtue, a specific act of renunciation and when everybody feels the need, each one must work courageously to achieve it.

We may, we must read the article related to the subject of examination before the Chapter, every time and as long as we have not achieve perfect observance. Without that we will never arrive at anything solid and lasting. Things are not done seriously enough and we can never achieve this union of spirit and of heart which is found in the pursuit of the same virtues, the unity of a same life[13].

---

[13] This is the end of the main manuscript of The True Disciple.

THIRD CONDITION 275

RENOUNCE THE GOODS OF THE EARTH [1]

---

[1] Ms XII 71-128

This chapter is one of the most extensive of The True Disciple. Later, the subject will be approached again under the title of "Follow in my poverty"². In the annex we find still another text: Thoughts on poverty - the priest, a man stripped of everything³.
This corresponds to the place held by poverty in Father Chevrier's thought and life. At one time, he had thought of speaking of poverty in the broader sense, in the sense that is found in the Gospel: Blessed are the poor in spirit⁴. Under the general title of poverty we find this fragment:

> We possess three things:
>> the goods of the earth,
>> creatures,
>> ourselves.

To belong to Jesus Christ, we must renounce these three things⁵.
Some notebooks were prepared in this perspective but Father Chevrier corrected them and the general title of poverty disappeared. The word is reserved to the strict sense, in relation to material goods.
Why did he do this, when the Gospel invited him to keep the broader sense? It is that Father Chevrier felt a danger strongly. By dint of speaking of poverty in the broad sense, of interior *poverty, Father's first disciples came to the conclusion that they could very well live like the clergy of their surroundings. But Father thought that God had made the Prado so that there would be poor priests⁶. Priests truly and visibly poor, because there are always poor people among us, poor people who have neither the leisure nor the desire to cultivate an interior poverty, poor people who are deprived of their share of the goods of the earth and whose cry reaches the Lord's ears⁷.*
In April 1877, he writes from Rome:

> As for our young priests, I feel that my authority is very weak. Duret and Delorme seem better able to enter into our thoughts and better understand poverty and the life of the Prado. Broche and Farissier have many reasonings, especially Broche, who says nothing but seems to have other fixed ideas; he reasons, he is clever. The authority of Messers Jaillet and Dutel and of the seminary weigh on them. We must pray⁸.

---

² P. 355.
³ Appendix III, p. 464.
⁴ Mt. 5,3.
⁵ Ms XI 609.
⁶ LP quoted P. 12.
⁷ Cf. Jas. 5,4.
⁸ LP N. 82.

At the beginning of the manuscript entitled "Follow me in my sufferings" *we find these lines:*
> Our Lord bore exteriorly the marks of poverty and suffering[9]. Those who only have it interiorly run the great risk of not having it at all[10].

Finally, in the notebook in which he deals with "renunciation of the goods of the earth", *he scribbles a few words at the beginning of the notebook. These words are the sketch of a prior discussion which probably could be summarized as follows:*
> We must agree on an orientation of life in order to act in unity; it will be our strength.
> What we will say about poverty rests on the knowledge of Jesus Christ, his word and example. In proceeding thus we build on rock.
> This practice of poverty may not be very widespread but it must. be precisely the characteristic of our family, like other things may characterize other groups[11].

We can imagine that, at the moment of approaching this thorny question of poverty with the seminarians, "feeling his authority very weak", he experienced the need to come back with them to the fundamental convictions which alone can draw a deep adherence to the life of poverty.

Father Chevrier felt his authority over his first disciples to be very weak. Yet, on this question of poverty, he speaks with authority. He speaks frankly about the lack of poverty among the clergy. He deplores the fact that a slavery to little things such as "style in dress, even ecclesiastical" prevents them form going generously[12].

He does not mince words to say that a beggar who becomes rich in this manner is a fraud and even that to beg without necessity is stealing[13].

He denounces the apostolic consequences of this situation: *It creates an obstacle to the proclamation of the Gospel to the poor who see* in religion a religion of money[14]. Where does he get this authority. He gets it from experience. He has lived everything that he recommends. He has tested this style of life before proposing it to others. Here he applies the principle of education that he has given: Follow me, do as I do, I do not ask you anything more difficult than I have done myself[15]. The best description that we have of Father Chevrier's life among the poor in the Prado quarter is in this chapter.

And at the same time we find the life that the poor people of that quarter led. He speaks from experience because he was able to be close to the poor, to listen to them, love them, understand them. He knows that there are things that make the

---

[9] P. 425.
[10] P. 429.
[11] P. 249.
[12] Cf. P. 258, note 60.
[13] P. 273.
[14] P. 277.
[15] P. 194.

poor cry out and he is sensitive to that cry[16]. He knows that a voluntarily poor religious will never suffer as much as the poor of the world[17]. *He knows that, for the people of his neighborhood, to wear rubber shoes, even a gold medal, is a luxury reserved to the privileged ones*[18]. *Times have changed but the lesson remains.*
So Father Chevrier speaks forcefully because he defends the rights of the poor to hear the Gospel. *It is in order not to put any obstacle in the way of the Gospel that he wants to be satisfied with what is* necessary in the churches *and to* exercise the minstry without charge[19].
Antoine Chevrier's authority comes from experience; it comes even more from his faith. He speaks because he believes[20]. *Everything that he says about the poverty of the priest shows how seriously he counts on the wages promised to the Gospel worker who has done his work:* God has promised it[21]. God's word is there and he wants us to have confidence[22].
Antoine Chevrier's faith is simple. *It is great. It sees the greatness of the apostolic mission, of the priest's ministry*[23], *the greatness of the work to be done, which must be appraised, not according to the* amount of income, *but according to charity*[24].
This faith engenders a generous poverty for others, the poverty of the one who thinks that the sweat of the worker and the poor is never sufficiently paid[25].
A poverty respectful of the justice, that will not buy or make others work unless it can pay immediately[26]. *A realistic poverty which does not causually proclaim that God will see to the payment*[27], *which knows that a bird in hand is better than two in the bush*[28]. *A poverty which is a source of peace and equilibrium because it unifies life around the One necessity, the important thing, the essential thing that must be well done, after which the rest goes well*[29].
Father Chevrier speaks with authority also and especially because he speaks for the Prado. It is very clear that his spiritual authority is not committed in the same way in all he says. It is one thing to know if we must wear a gray or brown woolen

---

[16] Ms XII 184.
[17] Appendix 469.
[18] P. 258-259.
[19] Pp. 261, 273.
[20] Cf. 2 Cor. 4,13.
[21] P. 272.
[22] Cf. P. 280, note 97.
[23] P. 272-273.
[24] P. 280.
[25] Cf. P. 266, note 63.
[26] P. 265.
[27] Cf. P. 282, note 101.
[28] P. 281.
[29] P. 263.

sweater, it is another to know that we must be satisfied with the necessary dress[30]. However, even the details of application not adapted to our present situation have a meaning that we must discover and keep. A priest who wished to live, not in the suburbs of Lyons but in the suburbs of a large Asian city was able to write: "How much I rediscovered all the force and the pertinence of The True Disciple, even in the details. The details on poverty in lodgings, dress, which appear insignificant in Europe where we are used to a high standard of living, find their realism here."

To understand the depth of Father Chevrier's thought, we must know something of the life of the poor that surrounded him. J.F. Six's contribution on this point is invaluable[31].

Father Chevrier's judgement on the "Providences"[32], those workshops that cry out in the world[33], are easily understood when we know what they were all about. Those types of workshop-convents that received children, young delinquents or repentent girls, work for very inferior wages and thus took the work away from workers.

When it is a question of temporal things[34], it is a matter of depicting the real aim of an enterprise. God knows if Father knew the work and worries of a bursar! He did not shirk anything that had to be done to feed, lodge and clothe all the people who lived at the Prado, who numbered about one hundred. But he never forgot the aim of the Prado: to teach catechism well[35], that was the aim of the House of the Prado, to evangelize the poor[36], it is the aim of all the communities of the Prado.

To hold firmly to this orientation, he thought of instituting the "temporal fathers and mothers" whose role he sketched out[37]. The idea had come to him during his stay at the City of the Child Jesus where he had seen an apostolic work threatened with becoming an enterprise of cheap housing. This project does not seem to have been developed. What is sure is that he wants to keep all his freedom of apostle in the use of the revenues[38], and that he uses some revenues solely for the houses of formation which he called "schools and choirs"[39].

The question of "free ministry" was not without difficulty. He saw the importance of it, he found clear directives in the preface to the Roman Ritual, a document coming from Rome, and in practice he came up against a contrary custom[40]. Perhaps the

---

[30] P. 258.
[31] Cf. P. 6.
[32] P. 268.
[33] Ms XII 184.
[34] Pp. 267-268.
[35] P. 263.
[36] LP n. 117, May 22, 1877.
[37] P. 269.
[38] P. 269.
[39] P. 281.
[40] P. 275.

precise contradictions between the Ritual and custom have not been sufficiently clarified. According to the Ritual, the minister may receive an offering on the occasion of a service accomplished, but the bishop has the right to prohibit even this concession and thus impose a rigorous gratuity.

On the contrary, the custom encountered by Father Chevrier established the general principle of the offering according to an offical scale. Here, the bishop's power imposes the non-gratuity and one must have a special permission to exercise the ministry free of charge. Abstractly, moral theologians managed to show that there was gratuity in any case. It was less clear in the minds of the users - or rather it was too clear. For every act of ministry, they had to pay.

In practice, when Father Chevrier tried to exercise his ministry free of charge in the parish that had been entrusted to him in the area of Lyons, the bishop of Grenoble, on whom the parish depended, refused the permission. It was in 1869[41].

That might be why Father Chevrier modified the plan of the chapter on poverty. Originaly he had planned a special part entitled: "4. To exercise the ministry free of charge"[42]. This title was crossed off in various plans and the subject was introduced under the more general title: "To ask nothing of anybody". It is more discreet. But Father does not renounce his idea and he makes sure that he tells us the Pius IX had found it good[43].

Antoine Chevrier's word still holds authority for the Prado today. We are told clearly that in this vocation, "wealth and treasures lose houses, poverty conserves them and maintains them in strength and charity"[44].

The general rise in the standard of living is not a reason to turn away from poverty. On the contrary, when "luxury is at its height, when everybody seeks their well being, comfort, ease, priests must seek poverty"[45].

At all times and in every latitude, it remains true that "to be satisfied with the necessary.... is the whole of evangelical life"[46], that the spirit of poverty consists in considering ourselves "masters and proprietors of nothing", but in "considering all things as belonging to God and the poor"[47].

The directives were summarized in such a way that they are engraved in our minds forever:

> If you do not follow the rules of poverty, wisdom, prudence, God owes you nothing. He will take care of you as long as you are really poor and suffer in

---

[41] Six, 294.
[42] Ms 175.
[43] P. 276.
[44] P. 280.
[45] P. 256.
[46] P. 255.
[47] P. 254.

silence. To be called by God. To seek the kingdom of God. To work. To be poor. Not to be imprudent[48].

The directives are clear. But Father Chevrier's word is always true: "We will begin to see the practice; that is where there probably will be difficulties."[49]

There is also another difficulty. In giving these directives to the public, everybody may then ask an account of the Prado; all the poor especially, if they are aware of these directives, may ask us: Where are you at? What are you doing? Alas! we are far from the mark; but God has been extraordinarily faithful with workers who have not been very consciencious.

---

[48] Ms XII 199.
[49] Lp. n. 83, April 1877.

Necessity for a rule 283
Union
Strength

Our Rule is Jesus Christ
His word, his examples.
Solid, unshakable foundation.

That is what characterizes a work,
a congregation.
....

True Disciple of Jesus Christ,
basis...[50]

---

[50] To understand this page see P. 244.
    There follow 4 pages which reproduce the text on the 5 conditions that are found pp. 115-119.

How we must renounce the goods of the earth.

By studying seriously the doctrine of Our Lord Jesus Christ and the apostles on renunciation of the goods of the earth.

We find that, to practice evangelical poverty we must:

1. Renounce, in spirit and in heart, the goods of the earth.
2. Be satisfied with what is necessary.
3. Give to whoever asks.
4. Not be concerned with temporal matters.
5. Ask nothing of anybody, except in cases foreseen by the regulation.
6. Not be worried about the future.
7. Count on God alone.

1. Renounce the goods of the earth, in spirit and in heart.

That is the formal condition that Our Lord demands of whoever wishes to follow him. Whoever among you does not renounce everything he possesses, cannot be my disciple (Lk. 14,33). It is the express condition that he demands of that rich young man of the Gospel who wanted to be perfect; he had accomplished the whole law and Our Lord told him: You are lacking one thing, if you wish to be perfect, go, sell what you have and give it to the poor and you will have a treasure in heaven; then come, follow me (Mk. 10,21). But, on hearing those things, he became sad for he was very rich and had many goods. And seeing him become sad, Jesus looked around him and said to his disciples: How difficult it will be for the rich to enter the kingdom of heaven!

(Riches make salvation very difficult, almost impossible; that is why we must renounce in spirit and in heart, if not in reality.)

Truly, I tell you, it will be difficult for a rich man to enter into the kingdom of heaven. The disciples were stunned by this language. But Jesus, speaking again said:

I tell you again, my well-beloved, that it is difficult for those who trust in their wealth to enter the kingdom of God. For it is easier for a camel to pass through the eye of a needle than for a rich man to enter the kingdom of God. On hearing this his disciples were greatly astonished and asked: Who then can be saved? And looking at them, Jesus said: For men, this is impossible but what is impossible to men is possible for God, because for God everything is possible (Mt. 19,21).

We cannot serve two masters.	No one can serve two masters, for either he will hate one and love the other or serve one and despise the other (Mt. 6,24).

Thus you cannot serve God and money (Mt. 6,24). Where your treasure is, there is your heart also (Mt. 6,21).

Thorns.	Richess are thorns that choke the good seed of the word of God (Mt. 13,22).
Source and root of all sorts of evil, afflictions and sorrow.	Those who wish to become rich fall into the temptation and traps of the devil and into useless and pernicious desires that hurl men

into the abyss of perdition and damnation. The love of riches is the root of all evils and some who have been possessed by them have strayed from the faith and have become involved in an infinity of afflictions and sorrow (1 Tim. 6,9)[51].

Sell what we have and amass a spiritual treasure.	Fear not, little flock, for it has pleased your heavenly father to give you the kingdom.

Sell what you have and give it to the poor. Provide yourselves with purses that do not grow old, with a treasure in heaven that does not fail, where no thief approaches and no moth destroys (Lk. 12,32). That is why our Lord asks of those who wish to follow him this great renunciation of all the goods of the earth and to be ready to follow him; he who does not have a stone on which to lay his head[52].

The Son of man has nowhere to lay his head.	A young man, full of admiration for Jesus Christ, had the desire to follow him and said to Jesus:

Lord, I will follow you wherever you go. Jesus answered: The foxes have their dens and the birds their nests, but the Son of man has nowhere to lay his head (Lk. 9,58).

---

[51] Ms. XII 243 - In a religious or a priest, luxury and richess are a scandal for the people, the ruin of souls and the greatest obstacle to salvation.

[52] Ms. XII 160 - If we cannot sell our goods, we must at least renounce them in spirit and in heart; consider our goods and all we possess, even the smallest things, as not belonging to us but to God and the poor, putting in practice what St. Paul says: the time is short; let those who weep be like those who do not weep, those who rejoice as those who do not rejoice, those who buy as those who do not possess (1 Cor. 7,30).

We must no longer think of going back into the world, even for business.	To another who asked permission to go settle his affairs before following him, Jesus says: Whoever puts his hand to the plow and looks back is not worthy of the kingdom of God (Lk. 9,62).
Saint John.	It is the practice of St. John in the desert.

What real poverty he had, living in the desert! He had a cloak of camel hair, a leather belt around the waist and his food was grasshoppers and wild honey; and all the inhabitants of Jerusalem and Judea came to him (Mt. 3,1).

The apostles.	It was the practice of the apotles who had left all and followed him. We have left all and followed you (Mk. 10, 28).
First Christians	It was also the practice of the first Christians.

In the Acts of the Apostles we see that the multitude of believers were of one heart and soul, and no one said that any of the things which he possessed was his own, but they had everything in common. There was not a needy person among them, for as many as were posessors of lands or houses sold them, and brought the proceeds of what was sold and laid it at the apostles' feet; and distribution was made to each as any had need (Acts 4,32). It was also Paul's advice to the Christians when he said: the time is short; let those who weep be as though they were not weeping, those who rejoice as though they were not rejoicing, those who buy as though *they had no goods*, those who deal with this world as though they had no dealings with it, for the form of this world is passing away (1 Cor. 7,29).

All that I have is yours.	And our Lord expresses very well in two words how we must behave toward the things of the world when,

in speaking of the relationship of goods that he has with his Father, of this community that exists between him and his Father, he says: All that I have is yours and all that you have is mine (Jn. 17,20). To enter into this disposition of mind, we must consider all things as belonging to God and the poor; we are not masters of anything, owners of nothing before God, we are only the stewards of God and the distributors of goods to the poor. We may use them according to our needs, but we must be ready to give them to whoever has need of them. It is this first attitude of the soul that destroys in us this spirit of ownership which is so opposed to charity, poverty, devotedness and sacrifice.

In fact, what is more shocking than to hear at every moment, in a house of brothers in Jesus Christ and truly poor people: this is mine, it is my room, my bed, my watch, my table; it is mine, don't touch it.

On the contrary, the one who enters into this spirit of Jesus Christ holds to nothing, not to his goods or his lodgings, his furniture or his dress, his money or his purse, nothing; nor to the terrestrial things to which the world holds so much. His motto is: all that I have is yours. If a poor person comes and needs something, he says: here it is, here is my room, my bed, my cloak, my purse; all that I have is yours.

How beautiful is this man who holds to nothing and who says to God's poor: all that I have is yours! and who strips himself to the point of becoming as poor as the poorest; like the Saints who could not bear to see any man poorer than themselves and who gave everything until they had nothing left to give, then they gave themselves.

289 **Rules concerning this first article.** Therefore, to put this first evangelical counsel of poverty into practice, we do not consider ourselves masters or proprietors of anything but we consider all things as belonging to God and the poor. We will put everything that we have in common to use it or give it to the poor according to the will of the superiors. There will be a common room where we will put everything that we have and, when we need anything, we will ask the one who has the charge of giving it to us. We will not have an individual purse, we receive nothing for us personally; there will be a common chest where we will deposit everything that we receive.

(Every month.[53]) We will take nothing without permission; we will keep only what is necessary for our personal use and, from time to time, we will go through our room, closet to see if there is anything contrary to poverty and detachment[54]. We keep the ownership of real estate, lands, houses, but we lose the use of the income.

---

[53] Marginal note. This is to establish a schedule for checking on one's personal things.

[54] Ms XII 251 - Ready to change lodging, books, clothes if it is judged appropriate, if it useful to others, through charity and if it is suitable; to be attached to nothing in order to be all to God. We are often attached to mere nothings, we do not want toslet go, we hold to them. In accomplishing this article, we destroy in us every attachment to little things and we are ready to give, lend, render service to anyone in need and practice that community of goods that existed among the first Christians and that we must revive in our houses.

At the age of 40, or after 10 years of religious life, we may distribute our goods and divide them in three parts: one to the family, the second to the poor and the third to the works.
We put in common the revenue that we may draw from our patrimonial goods or others.
The community must see to the personal and exterior needs of each member and it must be our joy and duty of charity to help each other, to see joyfully to all the needs of our brothers, and even to those of the immediate family, if this is judged necessary. Our motto is that word of our Lord: All that I have is yours and all that is yours is mine, according to the rules of charity, prudence and obedience. We may have for others but never for ourselves. Priests will keep their Mass offerings, not for themselves but for the poor; because it is appropriate that priest give something to the poor when they are asked.

N.B. Priests may keep their Mass offerings for the needs of their family when they have poor parents to support. If those offerings do not suffice, the community will furnish the necessary; if it is more than enough, the surplus is given to the community; they may not use it for themselves, but for the poor. Blessed are the poor in spirit, for the kingdom of heaven is theirs!

2. Be satisfied with what is necessary.   This is a very important article: it includes the whole evangelical life.
That is what our Lord recommended to Martha when he was in her house. She complained that her sister, Mary, was not helping her to prepare the meal and Jesus reproves her by saying: Martha, Martha, you are troubled over many things, but only one is necessary; Mary has chosen the best part and it will not be taken from her (Lk. 10, 38), thus making her understand that we must not be worried about the things of the earth, but rather be concerned with the things of heaven; for the things of the earth, we must be satisfied with what is strictly necessary. Unum necessarium[55].
That is also what St. Paul says clearly when, writing to his beloved son, Timothy, he tells him: We brought nothing into this world and it is certain that we will take nothing out of it; if we have what is necessary to eat and clothe ourselves, we should be satisfied (1 Tim. 6,7). To conform to this teaching of our Lord and St. Paul, we must be satisfied with the necessary. This necessary refers to lodgings, food, clothing.

---

[55] This passage from St. Luke causes difficulties to the exegetes. Various translations are proposed, for example: "You are worried and troubled about many things; yet very few are needed, even only one."

What is necessary in lodgings. At the birth of Jesus, the stable of Bethlehem could not have been a poorer lodging.

The house of Nazareth, as it is seen in Loretto, was poor. During his public life, our Lord often had no other lodging than the solitude of the mountains, the garden of olives; and he says that the foxes have their dens, the birds have their nests, but the Son of man has nowhere to lay his head.

St. Paul says that he has no permanent lodgings. *Non habemus hic manentem civitatem sed futuram inquirimus* (Heb. 13,14).

To enter into this spirit of poverty of our Lord's we strip from our lodgings all that smacks of luxury, vanity, superfluity, uselessness. We do not admit in our rooms any tapistries, woodwork, mirrors, armchairs, marble, gold trimings, paintings, or any ornaments that may be pleasing to the eye or esthetics or please vanity, self-love or well-being. Everything must breathe the simplicity, poverty and suffering of the stable[56]:

  roughcast or plaster walls,
  two or three wooden or straw chairs; a table, a simple wooden desk without ornament
  a crucifix of painted wood,
  a simple prie-dieu which could serve as a cupboard, if needed,
  a simple closet if it is necessary or a few wooden shelves covered with a curtain, or even without a curtain,
  a bed composed of two trestles supporting three pine boards,
  a straw mattress or one or two sheets and a head rest; but never silk or embroidered cloths; we may add a head board to support the head rest; we may put a blanket on the straw mattress, if necessary; in case of sickness, we may have a regular mattress,
  a few pictures in wooden frames without color or glass or paint,
  a few shelves on the table to put books and notebooks,
  if necessary, green or blue curtains on the windows.

On entering our rooms, people should find and breathe poverty, simplicity and suffering. We must take away all that is bourgeois, well-being, comfort; on entering our room, people must not be able to say: *it is good, it's not bad*; they must be able to say: *he suffers*[57].

Today, when luxury is at its height, when everybody seeks their well-being and comfort, the priest must, on the contrary, seek poverty and suffering in order to be an example in the midst of people.

---

[56] The stable: understood, of Bethlehem. It is a reference to the Crib, the mystery of poverty.

[57] Ms X 249 - We will see to it that our room resembles as much as possible that of the poor.

Vos estis lux mundi. 292
Ut videant opera vestra bona et glorificent Patrem[58].
We must become and remain poor to be seen by men and attract their compassion and appear wise; woe to the one who would have such intentions! But we must do that for the love of our Lord, to imitate his holy poverty and go against the world, since we are there to enlighten the world and be opposed to its maxims and customs.

The necessary in food. It is rather difficult to deal with this article since the needs of each one vary according to their age, temperament and circumstance, appetite. Each one must have what is necessary and take it with simplicity and freedom of conscience.

Charity makes it a duty to give it and wisdom forbids us from judging anybody in what concerns the needs of our brothers; one may take more than another, each one must consult his conscience and his needs and keep the rule of the necessary according to his temperament.

In general, to observe the rule of the necessary, we will strip from our table everything that smells of luxury, good eating and gluttony. The utensils will be of ordinary metal, never of gold or silver, nor silver plated. The plates and dishes will be of earthenware or crockery, never of porcelain. The table will be even and clean without tablecloth or ornament, except when we receive a bishop at our table. As much as possible, the wine and water will be served in earthenware pitchers and not in bottles. Each one will have his utensils and napkin.

In the morning: a soup with one or two desserts.

At noon: [two][59] dishes and two desserts; a soup may be served before, but it is not the rule.

At night: a soup, a dish and two desserts.

We must abstain from liqueurs, coffee and fine wines. Those things are only permitted in extraordinary cases: cases of necessary receptions and invitation.

(This article may be place in that of charity.) It must be an honor and a joy to receive the poor, the needy at our table, remembering the word of the Master: when you give a banquet, do not invite your friends or your relatives or your rich neighbors lest they invite you in return and repay what they have received from you. 293

---

[58] You are the light of the world. (Let your light shine in the eyes of men) so that they may see your works and glorify the Father (Mt. 5,14).

[59] The manuscript has TWO which is crossed out and THREE written above it, which is also crossed out.

Instead, when you give a banquet, invite the poor, the lame, the blind and you will be blessed because they cannot repay you and it will be repaid in heaven.

(This article may be found in the renunciation of creatures and the world.)

We must avoid going to dine with others, without grave necessity, and giving out invitations because those dinners are always occasions for a waste of time, useless, conversations - often evil and uncharitable - and of foolish expenses and gluttony that a true poor of Jesus Christ should not allow himself.

To give hospitality and table to those who present themselves, who need it, to tired travellers, to the poor, yes; when charity is our motive, we can always do it, but when there is no other motive than our glory, our satisfaction, our gluttony or an amusement, *never*. See the article on gluttony... *simplicity and poverty*.

What is necessary in clothing.

In the beginning, grace alone was our clothing. But, after the sin, shame became our lot and, to humiliate us, God gave us a cloak of animal skin.

Therefore, clothing was given us to cover us, not to enhance our pride. Unfortunately for the greater number, clothing has become an occasion and a source of vanity, self-satisfaction, self-love, ostentation, pride[60]. To avoid all this and enter into the spirit of our Lord, we must be satisfied with what is necessary in clothing, as St. Paul says, and not make of it an occasion of vanity and self-love.

Be satisfied with a poor and simple cloth.

Not put refinement in the form, avoid all that appears refined, good taste, beauty, elegance; all that is useless and serves only in pleasing self-love and men. Therefore, to avoid all that and please the poor Jesus Christ, imitate the Saints, in particular John the Baptist and Francis of Assisi:

We remove from our clothing all that smells of luxury and vanity.

We do not wear find or precious cloth, no silk or velvet, no embroidery, lace or fringes, no fancy trappings of the world.

Our cassocks are of serge, ample and large, without tail and pronounced tailoring; buttons of the same material and far apart.

---

[60] Ms X 646 - It is luxury and vanity that have invented all that seeking, all those styles in dress, even ecclesiastical. We must seek what is most simple, most easily made and in nothing seek vanity, self-seeking, good appearance, the refined. The people of the world, tailors always put something of this world in what they do: a little color, a little decoration, a little seam here, a little tuck there, for a better fit. Must a man of God seek all this? We must avoid all that and go openly, not be attached to little things, remembering that the clothing is to hide ourselves and not to seek ourselves.

Our cincture is of wool, without fringes; or better still, if we are allowed, a heavy black cord like the cord of St. Francis.

A coat of the same material as the cassock, with a straight collar and sleeves, that goes down to the knees.

A simple hat.

A gray or brown woolen shirt, to conform to the regulation of St. Francis[61].

All the other articles of clothing will be of gray or brown wool or serge.

We do not wear any exterior ornament such as watch chain or even exterior objects of devotion.

We will have a little pocket on the left side to carry our crucifix and use it when we need to.

In summer we may wear a little cape of the same material.

We must avoid wearing cloth, velvet, embroidered shoes or slippers, etc... such shoes breathe delicacy, pretention, refinement; ordinary laced shoes, without rubber; sandals would be much more preferable.

Each one's wardrobe:
two cassocks,
three shirts,
a dozen hankerchiefs.

Be satisfied with the necessary. Blessed are the poor in spirit for the kingdom of heaven is theirs (Mt.5,3).

Piety and moderation are a great wealth for a spirit that is satisfied with what suffices for the needs of the present life (1 Tim. 6,6). It is a very important article with which we must be well penetrated in order not to leave true poverty, because true poverty and the spirit of poverty are found in these words: to have the necessary and to be happy with it. It is because we are not satisfied with the necessary that we fail in poverty[62].

We do begin with poverty but, little by little, we find that things are not useful enough, not sufficient, not solid enough, not clean enough... that they do not last long enough, and a thousand other specious reasons; so we make a little change, a

---

[61] Father Chevrier belonged to the Third Order of St. Francis. He had found no other juridical framework for the Prado which was as a whole attached to the Third Order.

[62] Ms X 698 - To be satisfied with the necessary, an important article. Reflection on that article. How difficult it is to be satisfied with the necessary! We are always seeking to embellish, to decorate, to make easier. What makes easier is no longer the necessary and it is easier to embellish than to remain in the necessary, in that happy medium that constitutes virtue, than to elevate ourselves. The necessary in clothing, lodgings, food; it is better to remain below than go beyond, it is better to suffer than to be at ease... in the decoration of churches and locales... Regnum Dei intra vos est (The kingdom of God is within you (Lk. 17, 21). The poor often lack the necessary.

little embellishment, we find it more convenient, that it lasts longer, and little by little we end up with a comfortable room, at ease, with nothing lacking; a comfortable table with more than the necessary; suitable habits that last longer, more solid and more according to the tastes of the world. From change to change we arrive at doing like the world and losing the spirit of poverty.

The world does not stop telling us: how badly housed, badly fed, badly dressed you are! do this, do that. It is up to us to answer as our Lord answered Peter: Get behind me, Satan, you are an object of scandal for me because you do not taste the things of God but those of men (Mt. 16,23).

The one who has the spirit of poverty always has too much, he is always taking away; the one who has the spirit of the world never has enough, he is never happy, he always needs something more. The real poor of Jesus Christ is always taking away, decreasing. The one who has the spirit of poverty within himself says to himself: I still have more than I need, there are so many poor people who do not have as much as I do, so many people who suffer and do not have what is necessary; and I, what right do I have to be better lodge, better fed, better dressed than God's poor?

Where there is nothing to suffer, there is no real poverty[63]. It is in penetrating ourselves with this spirit that, little by little, we are stripped of all that is not necessary; we are horrified with all that smells of luxury, vanity, brilliance and we always choose what is poorest and simplest. As long as it covers me, that it maintains me, that is all I need. If it can still last, lets keep it[64].

---

[63] Ms XII 248; X 721.

Observation: It is because we do not want to be satisfied with the necessary that we often fail in poverty and we make or require many useless expenditures. How many useless things that are not necessary and that we could do without! But unfortunately, we seek our comfort, our ease in lodgings, clothing, food, and then we come out of the path of poverty so pleasing to our Lord. Under light pretexts we enlarge, embellish, rearrange, and then holy poverty disappears and it is no longer the necessary, it is the beautiful, the comfortable, the pleasing. Before doing anything we must always ask ourselves and others: can I do without it? is it absolutely necessary? Then, if we can do without it absolutely, don't do it. Do the poor of the earth always have the necessary themselves? Don't the poor have to suffer? Where there is nothing to suffer, there is no poverty; true poverty is a suffering (Ms XII 248).

Rules of poverty: The disciple is not greater than the Master. What right do I have to be better treated, better lodged, better fed than Jesus Christ and his apostles, the poor themselves? Don't the working poor shame us? What! We eat choices pieces while the others only have black bread; by what right? The others will work arduously all day and you will do nothing; what right do you have before God? (Ms X 721).

[64] Ms XII 249 - We will not be afraid to mend clothing, to make do with what is poorest and simplest.

It is a mistake to think that exterior, big, beautiful, distinguished, flashy things, of themselves give respect, confidence or authority; that it is by such things that we draw people, win souls for God or ourselves. It is a mistake!
Those exterior things may strike for a moment, designate exteriorly those who command, those who have authority and those to whom we owe respect and obedience, but those things do not give it of themselves.
It is virtue, it is charity that really inspires the confidence and love of the people. We must not think that because we have nice dresses, beautiful coats, nice houses, beautiful furniture, beautiful decorations, we will draw people or gain their confidence. No, it is virtue that does it.
If those exterior things had been necessary, Our Lord Jesus Christ would have used them; but no. He rejected them far from him. For a house he had only a stable, for a bed he had only straw, for parents he had only poor people and a rough cross to die on. And he said: when I am raised on the cross, I will draw all things to myself. Therefore, it is not by luxury and grandeur that he attracted people but by poverty and suffering.
Did the Saints use other means?
In his desert, John the Baptist had only a camel skin on his shoulders and a leather belt around his waist, and all of Judea came to him.
And did St. Francis of Assisi, who ran barefoot with a sack on his back, attach much importance to those frivolities? And yet, how many souls he drew to him! During his life, he counted ten thousand religious who had embraced his way of life.
It is virtue that draws souls and wins hearts for God.
There are those who speak of rank, dignity and who, under this specious pretext, think they demean and abase themselves by becoming poor, in dressing like poor people, in living like the poor, in associating with the poor, in acting as the poor. They would feel dishonored in taking the form of a poor person, in doing what our Lord did.
He became poor and it is precisely what the Pharisees reproached him of when they said to the apostles: your Master is always with sinners and publicans.

[Necessary in the churches.]

We must carry this spirit of poverty and simplicity and be satisfied with the necessary into our churches and in the objects of worship.

Nothing in our churches and ornaments should excite the curiosity or jealousy of the faithful. Our churches, our altars, our ornaments must be simple and modest.

The most beautiful ornament of a church is the priest.
The most beautiful decoration of a church is the priest.
The most beautiful bell of a church is the priest.
The must beautiful furnishing of a church is the priest.

Put a holy priest in a wooden church, open to the four winds, and he will attract and convert more people in his wooden church than another in his golden church.
It is the priest who gives life; it is neither stones nor chalices, ornaments or beautiful altars or beautiful pulpits that bring about conversions. Those things attract through curiosity but they do not bring about conversions or cures.
Yet, today we work much more at building beautiful churches, beautiful rectories rather than at making saints. That is because it is easier to build a beautiful church than to make a saint. Holiness can never be replaced by the most beautiful exterior things.
One day the apostles showed the temple to our Lord to make him admire the beautiful stones with which it was made and our Lord told them that this temple would be destroyed and that not one stone would remain on the other. That is the destiny of all great things. The only thing that remains is the virtue that has good roots and produces good fruit.
Our Lord had none of those exterior things, neither temple nor house. The trees, mountains, sea shore were his shelter and yet everybody ran to him to see and hear him. That is because *virtus de illo exibat et sanabat omnes*[65]; he drew all his strength from himself, his virtue, his holiness; *virtus de illo exibat*.
Therefore, let us not attach any importance to all those exterior things; let us use them without attaching too much importance to them and let us not put the accessory before the principal; stones before virtue, ornaments before holiness.
Martha, Martha, sollicita es et turbaris erga plurima[66].

We will be satisfied with what is necessary, even in the objects of worship; poor, simple and clean; nothing showy, brilliant, elegant, which arouses curiosity; everything must be grave, modest, solid. The beautiful and the great can be simple: a gold chalice may be very simple and yet it will be beautiful and great. Especially, nothing that can excite the curiosity and envy of the people, nothing that smells of profusion.
We easily put a lot of vanity, self-seeking, elegance in albs, surplices, ornaments and ornamentations. We seek what is nice, graceful, and quickly leave simplicity aside because those who work at those things, not having the spirit of poverty, put all their taste, their worldliness in them. If we are not careful, we immediately leave the spirit of poverty and simplicity and become dominated by the ideas of the merchants or the world. The surplices and albs should be of a strong and solid fabric, very lightly starched with only a few pleats; very rarely should we use embroidered albs: only on great solemn days, and even then it is not necessary. We always say: it is for God, it has to be beautiful: illusion! God scorns all our beautiful things and especially our baubles; we must serve God in *spirit* and in *truth*, that is

---

[65] A strength came out of him that cured them all (Lk. 6,19).
[66] Martha, Martha, you are worried and troubled about many things (Lk. 10,41).

the essential and usually, the more we put exterior things, the less interior there is; the more we are concerned with exterior things, the less interior foundation there is. To instruct people, that is the essential.

We must represent the crib and Calvary; let us leave to others the care of representing the glorious mysteries.

As for us, let us be satisfied with littleness and poverty, that is our lot and we must not come out of it; the poor must not come out of their rank, even for God. Let us not expose ourselves to acting through ostentation and pride and to satisfy our vanity rather than to please God.

Let us become saints, that will be worth more than anything else. And in becoming saints all the rest will come without our having to worry about it.

There is great gain in godliness and moderation of a spirit that is satisfied with what suffices for the needs of this life (1 Tim. 6,6).

| Unum est necessarium. | Mary has chosen the best part which will not be taken away from her. That unique necessary for us is to catechize and pray well, the rest is nothing. |

We attach a lot of importance to mere nothings and those exterior things always become cause for disputes and quarrels: one wants to do things one way, the other in another way; what difference does it make. Oh! how we could maintain peace and union and charity if we strove above all for the unique necessary, the love of God.

Pietas ad omnia utilis est exercitatio corporalis ad modicum[67]; that exterior is very little, *caro non prodest quidquam*[68]; therefore, whether it is black or white is of little importance, as long as it does not prevent us from loving God.

We must remember that we are poor, that we live on alms; we must not act like the rich who can spend without wounding poverty. To wish to act like the rich would be to come out of our rank, we would be like those poor people who wear beautiful clothes but have nothing underneath. We must keep our rank and glorify our Lord in our poverty, as the rich must glorify him in their greatness and opulence. Let us always take and keep what is the most simple and poorest; between two things, let us always choose what is most simple and poorest. Let us not have that manner of always wanting what is new, always seeking to embellish, decorate; we waste our

---

[67] Godliness is useful to everyone, corporal exercises are not worth much (1, Tim, 4,8).
[68] The flesh is worthless (Jn. 6,63).

time with those things and leave aside the solid and the unique necessary: to become saints and instruct people.

Only one thing is necessary: to love God, for each one of us and, for the priest and those who are destined for the priesthood, to instruct the poor. To instruct and to heal; the rest is nothing. We worry, we become upset over nothings. One wants one thing, the other another thing; one wants to do things one way, the other another way and we quarrel and pout over nothings.

Let us not be worried over those worthless things, one thing only is necessary: to teach catechism well. When an important thing is well done, the rest goes well also.

300 **3. Give to those who ask.** In his instruction to his apostles, our Lord, wishing to teach them charity as much as detachment from the things of the world, told them: if someone takes your coat, give him also your cloak. Give to all those who ask and do not claim your goods from those who have taken them. Lend without expecting any return and you will be the children of the most high who is good toward the ungrateful and the evil ones (Lk. 6,27; Mt. 5,40). That is the extent to which our Lord wants us to carry detachment from the things of the world; to giving to those who ask as long as we have something to give, to not claiming the return of what was taken from us. Could the spirit of detachment and meekness be carried any further?

How much detachment, meekness and charity those words enfold! How the accomplishment of these words, or rather the spirit, shelters us from all feelings of trouble, rancor, worry of lawsuits, agitation, hatred, and maintains us in serenity and peace of soul!

It is almost always attachment to the goods of the earth that make us refuse alms to those who ask. Among those who ask we can distinguish: the poor, the workers who have worked for us, merchants, borrowers, quibblers and thieves. Our Lord himself goes into all these details and traces the conduct that we must have in these circumstances in order to be a true disciple of Jesus Christ.

(The poor in the parishes not in our charge.)[69]

As for the poor, we must never refuse to give to all the poor people who ask alms and give them all that we can in money, clothing, food and also lodging if necessary. Our Lord makes no exceptions: give to those who ask.

---

[69] This practical question came to Father Chevrier's mind; he noted it in the margin without any further comment.

The pretexts that we often take in order not to give, by saying that they are lazy, that they could work, that we do not know them, are only pretexts to disguise our attachment and our greed; give to those who ask, according to your power, according to your means, but do not refuse anybody, and if you do not have money or anything else to give, we must give spiritual alms and, like St. Peter, say: I do not have any gold or silver, but what I have I give you, and give them some little thing: a picture, a rosary and pray to God for them.

To accomplish this precept from the Lord, each house will have a priest charged with the distribution of alms, and when we go out, we will always have a few coins in our pocket to give to the poor that we may meet.

As for *creditors* and *workers* who have worked for us, it is justice to pay them, not only when they ask but immediately after their work: *Dignus est operarius mercede sua*[70], and it is a fault to make them wait; and we must never buy or make anybody work if we cannot pay them immediately. It is better to suffer and wait ourselves than to make others wait and suffer[71].

As for *borrowers*, we must lend them what we can without interest. Lend without interest, says our Lord.

But it is better to give than to lend. We give what we can and that is the end of it, especially when it is a question of money. Usually, the people who borrow cannot repay and there follows a thousand complication, a thousand difficulties.

If we count on what we have lent to pay or settle some business, we may find ourselves in difficulty and do harm to others for having rendered a service to somebody. This service that you have rendered to your neighbor often becomes a source of coldness and separation, if it does not go as far as quarrel and spite; if you request what you have lent and he cannot repay it, as almost always happens, he receives you badly and thinks ill of you for asking so soon... and people become bitter.

When they ask to borrow 100 francs it is better to give 50 or 20 francs, if you can, and have nothing to claim afterwards. This way you do a good action, you are not obliged to claim anything from those poor people who cannot repay and you maintain friendship and charity with everybody. If it is not a question of money but of some object such as tools, clothing or other objects, it does not cause the same inconvenience, but again we must lend only what we have the real intention of giving in order not to be disappointed if we do not see it again.

At any rate, the accomplishment of this word helps greatly in the perfect practice of poverty and if you really want to become truly poor, you need only lend to

---

[70] The laborer is worthy of his wages (Lk. 10,7).

[71] Ms XII 253 - It would be a great lack of poverty to refuse to pay our debts, to put them off to another day (...) we must try to always pay in cash for what we have bought, because the supplier may need his money; and not paying immediately, when we can, is to keep money that does not belong to us and failing in poverty and charity because the supplier may need it.

everybody who asks and to give all that is asked, and you are sure of soon not having anything for yourself.

302 As for the quibblers, our Lord tells us: if someone wants to take your coat from you, let him have you cloak as well. That is how far we should carry the spirit of detachment in the world to avoid all contentions with the world for the things of the earth. Nothing is more opposed to the spirit of poverty than those daily contentions that occur in the world, and very often even among pious and Christian persons. They quarrel over nothing, over a rag, for a coin; they quarrel, hold a grudge, hatred until death; is that not what happens in many families, especially when dividing goods?

Oh! let us avoid that grasping and greedy spirit and in those cases always remember these words of the Master: *if somebody wants to take your coat, give him also your cloak*, rather than quarrel, dispute over such petty, vile and terrestrial things.

Great and spiritual souls have their spirit above the earth and their heart is in heaven: where your treasure is, there your heart is also. To enter into this spirit of detachment and scorn for the things of the earth, we will avoid all contention, all disputes in what concerns the things of the earth; no quarrels with anyone[72].

It is also against the spirit of detachment to argue too much with merchants, to bargain too much; don't the worker and the merchant have to earn their living? Let us ordinarily give what is ask[73]; we should have enough confidence in those who sell to us and supply us. If you do not trust them, don't deal with them. If you know that they are cheating you, don't go back to them. Try to always deal with honest people. There are some also who never trust workers, they always have to have a third person examine, measure; would it not be better to come to a friendly understanding and do things in good faith? All those precautions only come from a lack of trust and good faith; too bad for those who cheat us, they will bring nothing to the other world.

Let us act with simplicity and good faith; let us have a little confidence in others, even if they don't deserve it.

303 It is better to let people say of us: he is a fool, I caught him, he paid well; rather than: he's a miser, a quibbler, we can never deal with him; he could be had for a penny.

How those reflections that are made unfortunately too often about religious persons are harmful to religion and opposed to the spirit of Jesus Christ!

In everything we must be open and generous and not lack charity.

---

[72] Ms XII 254 - Never go to court for such things, unless the things demanded are evidently unjust and to which they have no right. But never take anybody to court yourself; wait until you are taken to court.

[73] Ms XII 253 - To save a few pennies we lose respect and charity and people call us misers, ambitious and selfish. Let us be generous with the laborer who works; he has his troubles; we never pay enough the sweat of the worker and the poor.

There are some who, under the pretext of a spirit of poverty, frugality, good administration, know-how, good management, are always bargaining, calculating, running from one place to another. All that is often a pretext to hide the greed, attachment to the things of the earth or a fear of lacking anything and a distrust of Divine Providence. Let us be for others the way we want God to be with us: generous and merciful.

It is the wisdom of the Holy Spirit that gives to souls this wisdom to maintain a happy medium that allows us to practice detachment and at the same time keep the interests of God and his poor.

As for thieves, one cannot take away too much from the one who has nothing and holds to nothing. This advice of our Lord: do not claim your property from the one who has taken it, is to make us avoid law suits, hatred, tribunals, disputes, unjust suspicions, false witnesses; to make us maintain inner peace and make us practice meekness and charity and detachment, even if our property is taken away. That way we avoid troubles of the spirit, useless seekings, loss of time, lies, for the one who has stolen will not admit it.

If something is stolen from us, we must think that those who have taken it needed it more than we did, that they did not dare ask for it and that God allows it to force us to practice detachment and charity.

Everything should work for the good of the one who is just.

If we catch a thief, we must give him what he has stolen, if we can, and especially if he cannot return what he has stolen, telling him that it would have been better if he had asked for it, that we could have him punished but, through love of God and for the good of his soul, we forgive him and that we give him what he took so that he will not be damned for it.

That way we avoid a lot of trouble and worry, the Lord is glorified, we have done a great act of virtue and we probably have won our brother for God because the examples of kindness, detachment and charity convert far more souls than pursuit and severity.

After having given such elevated rules of conduct, so opposed to our terrestrial ideas, to his pupils, our Lord adds: If you do these things, you will be the children of the most high who is good to the ungrateful and the evil ones and makes the rain to fall on the just and the unjust (Mt. 5,45).

4. Not become involved in temporal affairs.

The priest's ministry is entirely spiritual. When our Lord sends his apostles, he does not send them to take care of people, to work, build, run a business; rather he sends them to preach and heal. Those are the two great missions that he entrusted to them: *preach and heal*. I send you as my Father sent me. The apostles who had received our Lord's teachings give us the example of this duty, as we have in the Acts of the Apostles concerning the care of the poor as an occupation that was too absorbing and took too much time that should have been spent on spiritual matters. So they ordained deacons to take care of the poor and they kept for themselves the prayers and preaching as their only and true occupation: *nos vero oratione et praedicationi instantes erimus* (Acts. 6,4).

St. Paul says it explicitly in his epistles to Timothy: Let the one who has entered the service of God not become involved in the affairs of this age, so that he can be concerned with pleasing the one to whom he has given himself (2 Tim. 2,4)[74]. Therefore, we must not become entangled in temporal affairs. That is, we must put aside all concerns with goods, lands, farms, business, buying and selling, trading, everything that smells of commerce or that is done to earn money; everything that puts us in relation with business men; we must leave those things to lay people: priest must not touch them with the tips of their finger[75].

We must hire good lay people for all that concerns temporal affairs. To conform to this spirit of the Gospel, we will avoid creating those houses or providences[76] where they are concerned with manual work; the priest at the head of such work houses has to be concerned with all sorts of things, carpentry shop, forge, cobbler, buying and selling, have contacts, relations with business men, have stores, depots; on entering the house or room of those directors, one would think he were in the room of a real businessman.

305 Our aim must be entirely spiritual and we must take the children and the adults only to instruct them, teach them their religion, and not to make them work. We find nothing wrong with the child of a good family, or even of simple workers, spending three, four, ten years in a boarding school doing nothing but being educated, but we would think it wrong for us to keep poor children for five months to form them in Christian life, teach them their duty, without making them work![77]

One would have to have very little understanding of the importance of education and instruction to begrudge us the short time they spend with us without working; a time that we ourselves find not always sufficient. However, we do not disapprove of a little occupational work of a moment during the course of the day, a work of

---

[74] This translation of 2 Tim. 2,4 is no longer admitted today. This text from St. Paul is only remotely related to Father Chevrier's concerns; at most, it can give a comparison. In fact, the translation is: No soldier in service gets entangled in civilian pursuits, since his aim is to satisfy the one who enlisted him.

[75] In Father Chevrier's mind, it is a matter of business, properties that would have been given to him and that he had to exploit so that the revenues might support the Prado. He did not refuse to take a hand in running the Prado; his life proves it (cf. p. 246).

[76] Concerning providences, see p. 246.

[77] Why did Father Chevrier not transform his Prado into a convent-workshop? He would have had an assured income, we would joyfully have found him work (... for starvation wages!). He knew that such criticism were made against him.

useful occupation... useful for the house, morale, to occupy their body and teach them to fend for themselves, such as mending their clothes, preparing meals, cleaning, washing, making rosaries, digging a little garden, etc... we do not have domestic servants so we must do our work, that is our work: to be carpenter, mason, plasterer, sweeper, to wash, mend; but we reject all trade: factory, work for the outside, all work that smells of commerce, which is done to earn money. All that is the concern of good lay people and not of priests.

It is also to conform to the spirit of poverty and separation from all that smells of the world that we do not possess lands, goods, houses, other than the houses in which we live. We will see to it that we have only what is necessary in lodgings: house, yard and garden, in order not to have to be concerned with cultivation, farms, workers, servants or farmers. All those things always entail a lot of inconvenience and worry and are opposed to evangelical poverty and throw us into all sorts of worry that we must avoid.

If God sends us goods for our Providences, our schools and our works, we will establish temporal fathers and mothers who will own those goods, exploit them in their name, direct and administer them, and give the revenue to the superior general who will distribute them to the different works, without anyone having to be concerned with the use of these revenues[78]. All this must be done under the general direction of the ecclesiastical superiors of the congregation.

We must distinguish between work that we do through humility, obedience, necessity, to earn our living, as St. Paul did, and work that smells of commerce, done to earn money and entails involvement in business affairs, relations, displacements totally opposed to ministry[79].

There is work that is in the spirit of poverty, which is even necessary, useful and conformed to the evangelical spirit, since Jesus Christ says that he did not come to be served but to serve; the poor person must work and do what he can to earn his living[80].

5. Ask nothing of anybody.

When Our Lord Jesus Christ sent his apostles into the world, he told them:

---

[78] On this idea of Father Chevrier, see p. 246 and LP n.22, June 1859.

[79] Ms XII 185 - Thus make the Latin students work to teach them humility, make them understand what it is to earn a living, the trouble that others have to make fruit grow, keep their clothes clean; all the work of the house must be done through humility and poverty: cleaning, washing, whitewashing the walls... use outside labor as little as possible, do the work ourselves.

[80] Ms XII 151 - But we wished to give ourselves as model so that you might imitate us and work for your food (2 Tim. 3,7). Little humble jobs, useful to the houses, to give the example of work and humility. Jesus worked.

Go teach all nations, baptize them in the name of the Father and of the Son and of the Holy Spirit. Have no gold or silver, no money in your belts, no spare tunic or shoes or sandals. In whatever house you enter say: Peace be to this house! Eat and drink what is offered you, for the laborer is worthy of his wages and his food (Mt. 10,10; Lk. 9,1; 10,4). And elsewhere: Do not be troubled saying: what shall we eat, what shall we drink, or what shall we wear? Your heavenly father knows what you need (lk. 12,30). Seek the kingdom of God and all the rest will be given you besides (Mt. 6,33).

When the Master sends his laborers, apostles into the world, he does not send them to beg, ask, build, erect, settle in the world; he sends them to teach, instruct, baptize. That is the great end. And if they work, he promises to give them a salary. When we make a laborer work, we must pay him; the worker is worthy of his salary. Since it is God who sends, he takes care of his workers. Therefore, when we go anywhere, the first thing to do is to instruct, teach catechism, baptize, heal, render service to everybody; that is our first mission. If we begin by building, fixing, alining, buying, asking, begging, we do not do the work of God: we do material work.

We must begin with the spiritual work. The material work comes only later[81].

When the apostles went around the world, they did not begin by begging, asking, building houses and churches. No. They began by planting a cross and, at the foot of that cross, they instructed the people; or they taught in the synagogues and houses, and when the people were converted, the faithful themselves built the churches because they felt the need[82].

The conversion of the world comes before everything else. We must not leave souls to run after stones; of what use are stones when there are no souls? Therefore, we must put the spiritual work before everything; to instruct, catechize, that is our first duty to fulfill[83].

---

[81] Ms XII 262 - Therefore, we musts begin works and parishes by evangelizing, cathecizing, praying, spreading spiritual life, leaving it up to God to send us money or houses. What would be the use of having houses and money if we do not do God's work? Is it not putting the accessory before the principal to begin with houses, collections, visits? How do you know God is calling you to this work? How do you know God wants that work that you are contemplating? If you are worthy of this church that you want to found, this work that you want to build? Begin first with souls.

[82] The description is rather quick and romanticized. Father Chevrier has in mind those popular pictures showing the apostles at the foot of a cross. We must not forget the place that the collection has in St. Paul's epistles... but nevertheless Father has understood well the example of the great Saint Paul (cf. p. 274).

[83] Ms XII 264 - What should we think of those who think only of building, embellishing their rectory, their church? and in order to do that are always running to the mayor, the prefect, ladies and gentlemen. Alas! they leave souls to run after stones. We do not need so many things to obtain conversions. We are not sent to build but to convert. Today we have never

So what if we do not have what is needed? Did our Lord have what was needed when he came on earth? Did he have what was needed in his journeys in Galilee, Judea, the Decapolis? Did he have what was needed when he was on the cross? If there is something to be suffered from it, so much the better! God's work will be all the more solid and succeed all the more. We attract and gain more souls for God by poverty and suffering than by well-being and riches. The faithful will give much better, or rather will be better disposed to give, when they see us poor and suffering. If God does not send us any resourses, it is a sign that he wants us to suffer and earn whatever we need by our suffering.

How we lack prudence and wisdom by going too fast! Presumption.

It may also be a proof that God does not want this work or that we are not worthy of doing it, of establishing it, of directing it, and that it would be better not to undertake it than to want to do it through force. All of God's work must first bear the stamp of poverty and suffering.

Besides, don't collections entail a lot on inconvenience? Don't we have to lose a lot of time to go see one, the other, Mister somebody, Mrs. another, sit in parlors, say many useless words, even lies perphaps; boast about what we do, and often about what we do not do? talk about the worries that we have or don't have, hear flattering words of praise? And often, we come back with the spirit of the world and full of empty phrases. Is that doing God's work? And does God attach the success of his work to such vain and puerile things?

Some might say that there is a lot of merit in taking up a collection. Yes, no doubt, there is pain, insults, humiliation; but there is also merit in suffering and waiting for everything from Providence.

And aren't the people of the world tired of always having beggars at their door? And very often the give only reluctantly with severe criticism for those continuous beggars.

Besides, it is not lands, houses, gold, silver that make God's works; it is men, generous, devoted men who know how to suffer, animated by the spirit of God. That is what is necessary to accomplish good works.

Give me a soul that is generous, devoted, that knows how to suffer; it will be worth more than a *million*; and when that soul is joined by another with the same desire and walking toward the same end and united in the love of God, then the work is well founded[84].

It is the Holy Spirit who says it: Happy the pure man without stain, who does not run after gold and has not placed his trust in money and treasure; he will do admirable things during his life (Eccli. 31, 8).

---

built so many churches and rectories and never has there been so little faith and religion. We must build and do exterior things only when we are forced to do so and when we have ample means to do so without upsetting ourselves.

[84] A beautiful phrase that expresses a deep conviction.

309 When we do the spiritual good, the temporal always follows. God has promised it. If we give an ounce worth of spiritual good, God will give us a hundred pounds of temporal good. That was our motto at the beginning of the Prado.
We understand that lay people, doing some work, will ask alms to do it, continue it and enlarge it. But does the priest, so rich, so powerful, who possesses all the heavenly treasures, who distributes God's gifts, need to go running around seeking money for himself and for others? Everybody needs him, the poor, and the rich even more than the poor. He is the doctor of souls, everybody's consoler; he gives God's gifts to everybody; people have more need of him than he has of others; he gives much more than anybody will ever give him; what is given to them is nothing in comparison to what he himself gives; he is richer than all the rich of the world and the rich have more need of him than he has need of the rich.
Therefore, if the priest knows his riches and how to properly distribute God's graces, he will never lack the goods of the earth.
And to run after the goods of the earth is to announce publicly his spiritual misery, it is to admit that he is not working according to God, since God does not pay him; it is to admit that he gives nothing to the world since the world gives him nothing. The priest who gives spiritual life to the world need not be concerned with temporal things. God will send him all that.
Seek the kingdom of God and its justice and the rest will be given to you (Mt. 6,33). The priest who works for God will be maintained first by the poor, then will come the rich, it is *the rule*[85].

Practical directives. To observe this rule of poverty, faith and trust in God, we propose, first of all, to be concerned exclusively with God's works and to put God's work before everything; never begin with the temporal but always with the spiritual, never ask the people of the world for anything, never use those means of collecting money in current usage in the world such as lotteries, concerts, evenings, meetings, sermons and others where money is collected. All those means of collecting money do not smell of charity, confidence, humility; we must not draw money nor force people to give us some.

310 On the contrary, all the money or goods that we receive must be entirely that of Providence and the faithful must give it freely, voluntarily, affectionately, spontaneously. We may make our needs known to those who ask, but not to those who do not ask. We may visit those who have asked us to go get something[86], but not

---

[85] Ms XII 266 - Is the priest not sent to comfort and heal? Yet, how many sick people, poor people in the world...(...) Let us seek God and not worry about the rest; let us live poorly and in charity and we will become far too rich...

[86] Ms XII 164 ...and it would be better to send someone else.

those who do not know us and do not ask us. We may take up the collection in church and say for what purpose; each one then gives what he wishes. We may go to the door of the church, like the poor, to ask for alms.

(It is absolutely forbidden to charge for services, to sollicite the children's parents to ask them anything; we would lose our freedom of action, expose ourselves to baseness, lose our dignity and go against the spirit of Jesus Christ. We are happier in giving than in receiving, in rendering disinterested service to everybody.)

In any case, it is Providence's money and not a sollicited money, given reluctantly to get rid of us. In a spirit of poverty, humility and penance, we may, like a poor person, go from door to door or in the street, to beg for alms for ourselves.... There is the begging of the poor person who asks for bread when he is hungry. That type is not forbiddeen when it is really necessary and for us.

When we have nothing, we must first work, like St. Paul, in order to be a burden to no one, and when we cannot provide for our needs, we must decrease our expenses and sell what we do not need.

It often happens that we have many useless things, that we are not really poor and that is why we do not receive; therefore, sell what you do not need and work to earn your living and God will send you what is lacking. It is only when we have sold all our superfluities and work as the really poor that we may go and beg, if we really lack what is necessary.

And when we ask, always do it with humility, reserve and prudence and remember that nobody owes us anything. Unfortunately, there are those who think that, because they are doing some work, that they have such and such a charge, everybody must help them, receive them well, give to them. Those are only proud people; they only deserve the stick and are not worthy of doing God's work. Beggars are often people who have sacrificed themselves for the spiritual and for their vocation.

It also happens that we become used to taking up a collection and often we do not collect for what is strictly necessary but to enlarge, fix, improve, enrich. That is no longer God's work; it is the work of the devil because God has said: Woe to the rich! and the one who becomes rich by taking up collections is a fraud and falls into the devil's trap[87].

Receive only those things conformed to poverty.

Receive nothing for yourself, but only for the works and the houses.

Receive nothing without permission, and if you receive something, give it to the superior who will dispose of it as he sees fit and give it to whomever he thinks he should give it.

---

[87] Ms XII 210 - To beg without necessity is to steal, it is to enrich oneself, to build. To beg through habit: it becomes routine.

Ask nothing of anybody in the exercise of the ministry. In giving his instructions to his disciples, our Lord also said: you have received freely, give freely. This counsel of perfection that our Lord recommends to his apostles, St. Peter also recommends to the priests of the Church and St. Paul practiced it in all its rigors in his behavior with the faithful of Corinth, Thessalonica, Ephesus and all Achaia, and the Roman ritual speaks of it in the prefaced addressed to priests. Writing to priests and bishops, St. Peter tells them: Tend the flock of God that is in your charge, not by constraint but willingly, not for shameful gain but eagerly, not as domineering over those in your charge but being examples to the flock (1 Pt. 5,2). St. Paul expresses himself forcefully and clearly on this point and shows us to what point he pushes detachment and charity. This is what he says to the Corinthians: If we have sown spiritual good among you, is it too much if we reap your material benefits? If others share this rightful claim upon you, do not we still more? Nevertheless, we have not made use of this right, but we endure anything rather than put an obstacle in the way of the gospel of Christ. The Lord commanded that those who proclaim the gospel should get their living by the gospel. But I have made no use of any of these rights, nor am I writing this to secure any such provision. For I would rather die than have any one derpive me of my ground for boasting of preaching the gospel free of charge (1 Cor. 9,11). At another time, writing to the same faithful, he says: Here for the third time I am ready to come to you. And I will not be a burden, for I seek not what is yours but you; for children ought not to lay up for their parents, but parents for their children. I will most gladly spend and be spent for your souls. If I love you the more, am I to be loved the less (2 Cor. 12,14). In his farewell to the bishops of Ephesus he says: Be alert, remembering that for three years I did not cease night and day to admonish every one with tears. And now I commend you to God and to the word of his grace. I coveted no one's silver or gold or apparel. You yourselves know that these hands ministered to my necessities and to those who were with me. In all things I have shown you that by so toiling one must help the weak, (taking away all pretext that we preach through interest) remembering the words of the Lord Jesus, how he said:it is more blessed to give than to receive (Acts. 20,31). And to the Corinthians he writes again: I think that I am not in the least inferior to these superlative apostles. Did I commit a sin in abasing myself so that you might be exalted, because I preached God's gospel without cost to you? I robbed other churches by accepting support from them in order to serve you. And when I was with you and was in want, I did not burden any one, for my needs were supplied by the brethren who came from Macedonia. So I refrained and will refrain from burdening you in any way. As the truth of Christ is in me, this boast of mine shall not be silenced in the regions of Achaia; and let no one say that I received something from those to whom I preached the Gospel (2 Cor.11, 5).

Writing to the Thessalonians, he reminds them of his conduct when he was among them: We did not eat any one's bread without paying, but with toil and labor we worked night and day, that we might not burden any of you. It was not because we have not that right, but to give you in our conduct an example to imitate and work yourselves in order to eat (2 Thes. 3,7). And elsewhere he tells the Corinthians: To the present hour we hunger and thirst, we are ill-clad and buffeted and homeless, and we labor, working with our own hands. When reviled, we bless; when persecuted, we endure; when slandered we try to conciliate; we have become and 313 are now as the refuse of the world, the offscouring of all things (1 Cor. 4,11). Exposed to all kinds of labors and hardships, through many a sleepless night, hunger, thirst, fastings, the cold and exposure (2 Cor. 11,27).
That is how the great St. Paul behaved.
That is the point to which he pushed devotedness, poverty, charity.
Where are we?
What a difference between our life and his!

Prescriptions of the Roman ritual. In the preface of the Roman ritual, which gives the rules to follow in administering the sacraments, we find these words:
Illud porro diligenter caveat ne, in sacramentorum administratione, aliquid, quavis de causa vel occasione, directe vel indirecte exigat, aut petat; sed ea gratis administret, et ab omni simoniae atque avaritiae suspicione, nedum crimine, longissime absit.
Si quid vero, nomine Eleemosynae aut devotionis studio, peracto jam sacramento, sponte a fidelibus offeratur, id licite pro consuetudine locorum accipere poterit, nisi aliter Episcopo videatur[88]. (Rom. Rit. Preface).

Excercise the holy ministry free of charge. Nothing can be clearer or more precise on this article, and if a contrary usage prevails in France,
it is only because of a concession to the sad circumstances in which the clergy found themselves after the Revolution. When we were in Rome in 1864, we petitio-

---

[88] Among other things, that, in the administration of the sacraments, the minister be very careful not to demand or claim anything, for any reason or occasion, directly or indirectly; but that he administer freely and avoid absolutely all suspicion - and even more, all accusation - of simony and cupidity.

However, after the ceremony, if the faithful offer something spontaneously, as an alms or for a pious intention, it is permitted to accept it, according to local customs, unless the bishop judges otherwise.

ned his Holiness Pius IX for permission to exercise the ministry free of charge. Here is the gist of this request and the reply from His Holiness.

314 Petition to His Holiness

Most Holy Father,

Father Antoine François Marie Chevrier, of the Third Order of St. Francis, humbly prostrate at the feet of Your Holiness, presents the desire that several priests have to come together, as much as the diocesan authority will allow them, to live a regular life and to exercise the Holy Ministry without any retribution except the one that the faithful will spontaneously offer them.

He asks the blessing of His Holiness for himself and his priests.

Rome, October 1, 1864.

And here is the answer that His Holiness sent us through Father Piscivillo, secretary to His Holiness and editor of Civilta Cattolica, who was kind enough to present our petition to the Pope:

Answer from His Holiness, through Father Piscivillo.

My respectable friend,

In the audience of October 12, I presented your petition to His Holiness. He read it attentively. He questioned me on several little things concerning your way of life. I answered as best I could.

After this information, His Holiness said to me: I cannot sign anything, it is a very grave matter in which the Holy See proceeds slowly and prudently.

I wholeheartedly bless Father Chevrier and his companions, and I ask you to transmit my blessing to them.

The work is good, but before approving it, some years have to go by, the bishops must witness to its timeliness and success; for the moment, I can *only approve the intention* and bless the persons, which I do with all my heart.

Rome, November 1, 1864
Charles Piscivillo

The Holy Father says that *the work is good*, but for the approbation, we must find bishops who will receive us and admit us with this way of life and give witness to its success; that for the moment he can only *approve the intentions* and bless the persons.

We could not have a more favorable and at the same time wiser answer. Thus we ask permission to exercise the ministry free of charge and to receive, in our holy functions, only what the faithful will be pleased to give us freely and spontaneously, and never to demand anything for the functions of the holy ministry, in order to practice this word from Our Lord: you received freely, freely give, and to conform our conduct to that of St. Paul who worked with his hands rather than ask, and boasted of evangelizing free of charge[89]. Therefore, we put a coffer in the sacristy of the church, to receive the offerings from the faithful when we administer the sacraments or celebrate the Holy Sacrifice of the Mass[90].

A brother or a sister may pass in the church after the service to collect the offerings and pew rents.

We will avoid putting in our churches and sacristies those posters and notices that fix the price of holy things, burials and pew rents[91].

The faithful who have faith understand this duty toward the priests and easily give to those priests who fulfill their holy function.

But what can you ask of impious people, of those who already despise the priest, who look upon the priest as a miser and a man who lives well, of people who only go to church three or four times during their life: for weddings, baptisms and funerals, and every time they come to church, they hear the priest or the sexton say: *you owe so much*, with authority and insistence.

Those manners of doing only serve to turn people away from the Church and they go swearing and criticising religion, calling it a religion of money. It is a sure fact that very few people give willingly to priests and they usually accompany their donation with injurious words.

That is why St. Paul did not want to receive anything from the Corinthians, Thessalonians and others, and received from the Macedonians; to show us that we must not ask of those who are not firm in the faith, to give them the example of detachment and not put obstacles to the Gospel.

How can we destroy this bad impression in the heart of the people; how can we give rebirth of confidence and respect for the priest? It will be by detachment and poverty that we will rediscover our place in the heart of the people.

How well loved is a disinterested priest, even the worst! and how we despise the miserly, interested priest!

---

[89] Ms X 700...remembering that if we are to be charitable, it is surely in spiritual things and that Our Lord died for everyone.

[90] Ms XII 256 - ... in order to leave the greatest liberty to the faithful and that we may not have to answer their question: How much is it?, removing the signs and price lists that smell of commerce and announce to the people the they have to pay for Masses and the Offices.

[91] Ms XII 257 - Be satisfied with what is given: Eat what is given you, says the Lord. It is those requests from priests in their functions that outrage the people, turn them away from God and the Church.

The more we are poor and disinterested, the less demanding we will be, the more we will be friends of the people[92], and the more doing good will be easy for us[93]. It is better to say: give what you wish, rather than: *you owe me so much*. Does it not look like a business when we say: you owe so much? and when the faithful ask: *how much is it, how much is a Mass?*. And then, how difficult it becomes not to do things for money! not to have more regard for those who give more! not to prefer a Mass or a better paid function over another less well paid function! and to be tempted to ask or to wish to receive more! *I desired neither gold or silver or anything else* (Act. 20,33).

How tempting is money! How it usually gives rise to desire and how difficult it is not to fall into faults of this kind, not to imitate Judas: How much will you give me, and I will *deliver*, give him?[94]

With what force Our Lord chased the sellers from the temple; it is a sin which greatly afflicts his heart. We must take away from holy things all that smells of money, commerce, trade.

Is it not often to punish our greed and attachment to the goods of the earth that God sends revolutions and strips us, by the faithful themselves, of all that we possess? That is the first thing that revolutionaries do: strip us, make us poor. Does it not look as if God wanted to punish us for our attachment to the things of the earth and force us to practice poverty, since we do not want to practice it voluntarily?

It is sometimes very fortunate that this happens because we would fall asleep in our riches and well being and we would no longer care for the things of God[95]. When God says: Woe to the rich, he applies it even more to his ministers than to the others because, if anybody should practice poverty, it is especially the priests, his servants.

---

[92] Another manuscript carries this same phrase with the expression: loved by the people and not: friends (Ms XII 180).

[93] I do not deny the right that God has given priests to live from the altar. But St. Paul gave up that right in favor of the bad Christians of Corinth and he boasted about it, and he loved to remind them that he asked nothing of them, even more, he worked with his hands in order not to be a burden on anybody and put no obstacle to the Gospel. Why, then, could we not see reborn today, men who are detached like St. Paul, animated by his zeal for souls, to the point of yielding their right in favor of the poor sinners, to bring them back to the Church and give them back faith and respect for the priest and love of Jesus Christ? St. Peter told Simon the Magician, who was asking to buy the power of giving the Holy Spirit....(Acts. 8,20).

[94] The comparison is biting.

[95] This opinion about the good results of the dispoilment achieved by revolutionaries must not have been very widespread among a clergy still royalist for the most part.

6. Not to worry about the future.   Our Lord wants us to banish from our heart all worry about the future and does not fear to speak at length about this confidence in God that we must have and he goes into long details in order to show us that God truly wants to be our Father and it would be a great insult to him if we worried when we work for him[96].

Let us listen to what he says: Therefore I tell you, do not be anxious about your life, what you shall eat or what you shall drink, nor about your body, what you shall put on. Is not life more than food and the body more than clothing? Look at the birds of the air; they neither sow nor reap nor gather into barns, and yet your heavenly Father feeds them. Are you not of more value than they? and which of you by being anxious can add one cubit to his span of life? And why are you anxious about clothing? Consider the lilies of the field, how they grow; they neither toil nor spin; yet I tell you, even Solomon in all his glory was not arrayed like one of these. But if God so clothes the grass of the field, which today is alive and tomorrow is thrown into the oven, will he not much more clothe you, O men of little faith? Therefore do not be anxious, saying What shall we eat? or What shall we drink? or What shall we wear? For the Gentiles seek all these things; and need them all. But seek first his kingdom and his righteousness, and all these things shall be yours as well. Therefore do not be anxious about tomorrow, for tomorrow will be anxious for itself. Let the day's own trouble be sufficient for the day (Mt. 6,25; Lk. 12,22).

In the Our Father we say: give us this day our daily bread.

Elsewhere he tells us again: Do not lay up for yourselves treasures on earth, where moth and rust consume and where thieves break in and steal, but lay up for yourselves treasures in heaven where neither moth nor rust consume (Mt. 6,19). Take heed and beware of all covetousness, says Our Lord, for a man's life does not consist in his abundance (Lk. 12,15). Then Our Lord tell us the story of the rich man who had reaped abundantly, enlarged his barns to put all his goods and said: now be at rest, my soul, eat, drink and be merry; and God comes that very night to

---

[96] Ms XII 261; X 650.

He does not want us to distrust him by accumulating treasures for the future; besides, we don't know if we will be able to enjoy them, since God says that he comes to claim the soul of that rich man who had amassed great reserves. And besides, those treasures that are a source of worry and concern for those who have them, expose us to attachment and greed. We become attached to what we have amassed, we like to see it and to think about it and the fear of losing it fills our thoughts and troubles our rest (Ms XII 261).

Poverty of spirit excludes worry about the future; it excludes the desire to acquire, all concern, all envy, all desire; be happy with what you have and don't be troubled for what you don't have. That poverty of spirit gives freedom of soul for good and frees us from all worry (Ms X 650).

take his soul. That is the way it is for the one who amasses treasure for himself and who is not rich in God (Lk. 12,6).

When Jesus sends his apostles on mission, he tells them: Do not take gold or silver or money in your purse, no bag for your journey, nor two tunics, nor sandals, nor staff (Mt. 10,9). Do not bring anything for the road, no staff, nor bag nor provisions, no bread or money, and do not even have two tunics (Mt. 10,10; Lk. 9, 3; 10,4).

By all these words, Our Lord wants to banish from our soul all worry for the future. We are his children, his workers, his servants: he will take care of us. The worker is worthy of his salary. If he takes care of the little birds, all the more will he take care of us who are his privileged creatures, his workers whom he sends to work in his vineyard. We do not make a person work without paying him[97].

In freeing us of all worry about the future, Our Lord preserves us from all greed. It is because we are afraid of lacking in the future that we economize, that we spend only what is strictly necessary, that we seek to earn as much as possible, to set aside, to spend the least possible, to set aside, to amass treasures[98]. The one who fears the future is narrow, stingy, he is always afraid of lacking the necessary later on; he is neither generous nor charitable: he is a miser.

It is precisely against this unfortunate fault that Our Lord wants to warn us when he gives us this confidence in himself.

The miser piles up his gold and silver; he sets something aside every month, every year; he piles up as much as he can in order to enjoy later. He likes to see his treasure; he counts his money from time to time; he invests it to increase the interest. He no longer works for God but to acquire more money. What a misfortune to arrive at that point! When we are rich and self-sufficient, besides losing the spirit of poverty, we no longer count on God as when we are poor, we don't pray as well, we are no longer in the humility of asking for our daily bread; we trust in our treasure, we become negligent, lazy at work. We have what we need to live, we become bourgeois. We sit and count our money, our income; then we regulate our work according to the income and it is no longer charity and devotedness that are the principle of our charitable works but the amount of income that we have.

Poverty maintains us in humility and confidence in God. Riches and treasures lose houses; poverty conserves them and maintains them in the strength of charity[99]. To

---

[97] Ms XII 261 - Can God abandon his servant who works for him? and does he not promise the hundredfold to the one who will have left all for him? Does he not know what we need? and can we think that the one who will have been charitable to others will be deprived of that same charity when he is in need? No. God's word is there and he wants us to trust him.

[98] Ms X 701 -.... and to amass for whom? often for strangers who will enjoy it and laugh at our greed.

[99] Ms XII 219 - Why does Jesus Christ recommend poverty so much? Poverty keeps us under God's hand, in humility, work, submission, fear, piety, prayer. On the contrary, riches put us in well-being, put us at ease, make us live like the bourgeois. Little by little we be-

conform ourselves to that spirit of poverty demanded by Our Lord, who does not want us to amass treasures but that we have confidence in him for the future, we personally renounce all that may create a future for us such as rents, farms, lands, stocks, properties. We will hold strictly to what the Church demands for the clerical title. We will spend what is given to us for the needs of the poor and for the good works of the community, without seeking to accumulate anything. We will live, as much as possible, on the revenues of each day, asking God for our daily bread, to live in poverty and humility. We will avoid having in our houses those abundant supplies that sometimes are a source of profusion and loss. We will possess only those goods necessary for life such as houses, gardens, yards, homes for the elderly and infirm, retirement houses. The houses that the temporal mothers possess are for the schools and not for the priests. The priests must support themselves.

7. Count on God alone.

We must not count on the world: it is for us today and tomorrow it is against us.

The world is wavering and changing: today it promises, tomorrow it withdraws its promise; today you please it, tomorrow you displease it; that holds to nothing, if you do not do what it wants, it turns against you.

Woe to the one who builds on promises, he will find himself in misfortune and ruin. We must not put our confidence in one person or another, whether they be rich or devoted. We must not base ourself on science or wealth. We must not count on anybody in the world, not even on those who are with us, unless they have given certain proof of fidelity and perseverance and that proof is in suffering. *You remained with me in my temptation*, says Our Lord to his apostles. Suffering is the only proof of fidelity. When you have suffered, I will count on you. That is why we must not engage anybody for anything before they have given certain proof of fidelity by suffering.

It is a great mistake to say: such a person is rich, he will give to me; such a person is generous, he will give to me; such a person respects me, loves me, he will give to me. The world loves its money more than you and your works.

Let us not count either on the promises that may be made, nor on the deposits that may be made in our name, even if they say that this will belong to us after their death. The proverb is true: *A bird in the hand is better than two in the bush*.

Do not accept half hearted gifts; they are only a bother and worry, and it can also be an occasion for embarrassment for them and for us.

We must never base ourselves on shaky foundations. We must count on God alone.

---

come used to a comfortable life, we fear being bothered, we need nobody, we have what we need to live. We can do without everybody, even God. Poverty is the strength of the priest, the power of..., a source of good example and encouragement for others.

As long as we are doing God's work, that we have the vocation from God to do his work, God will be for us, it is his promise.

Conditions to have God's support. Seek first of all the kingdom of God and its justice, and everything else will be given to you (Mt. 6,35).
The first condition is to be called by God to labor at his work. Then we must seek the kingdom of God and its justice before everything else.and God will give us the rest.
It is certain that if we seek to establish ourselves, if we seek our ease and comfort, to build, we do not seek God but we seek ourselves, and sometimes the kingdom passes only after ours[100].
We must work and work for God; the laborer must work to gather the grain. God rewards and pays only those who work for him. The laborer is worthy of his wages. We pay only those who work. God also pays only those who work for him. We must work for God and with God, that is, with his spirit. If you go beyond the limits of what God wants; if, instead of remaining in the suffering and poverty that God always asks for in the works that belong to him, you go beyond these limits, you are concerned with too many exterior things, you come out of simplicity, poverty; you dare, you do more than you should, more than you can, you embellish, you spend uselessly. If in blind presumption you say: *God will see to the payment.* No! God does not pay for stupidities, imprudence and sometimes he deserts us and leaves us to ourselves when we try to do more than he wants, especially in material things[101].

---

[100] Ms XII 198; Ms XII 267; Ms XII 266.
We must be truly poor and be concerned only with God's work. Without those two conditions, God cannot use us. If we want to live like the bourgeois: good table, beautiful parlor, nice furniture, ride in a carriage, nice clothes, and do God's work negligently, it is certain that God is not obliged to feed that kind of people (Ms XII 198).
....That is why, supported by those two principles, we do not want to leave foundations, rents, goods. If you are saints, you do not need any of that, you will have more than you want, and if you are not saints, you will have nothing and that will be good because you do not deserve anything and you would use it badly and it is better to let works die if they do not contribute to the Glory of God and if the spirit of God is not there (Ms XII 267).
Therefore, if we are truly God's workers we will receive our salary. God will send it to us. Isn't our house a proof of this great truth? Where are our resources? Where is our income? And yet God feed almost two hundred persons every day; is that not an evident proof of God's Providence over us? And if we continue to live as we have begun, we will always have God's support and help?.
[101] Ms XII 266.
The two life principles for any house are poverty and charity. Join to that prudence which makes us not go beyond what we can do, that we must not tempt Providence, that is, do things

Therefore, we must always act with prudence, moderation, wisdom, know how to be 322
poor, to suffer. When we do not have the means, never engage in useless expenses
beyond our means.
We must count on Providence but not tempt Providence and never undertake
anything without being sure of being able to pay for it. When God sends, to act in
proportion with what God sends. When I sent you without any purse, bag, shoes, did
you lack anything? And they answered: nothing (Lk. 22, 25). God sends his apostles
in poverty and he gives them what is necessary, but they are not concerned with
buildings, temporal things. God promises the hundredfold in this world when we
work for him and we really do God's work. There is no one who has left house or
brothers or sisters or mother or father for the Gospel, who will not receive a hundredfold now in this time, houses and brothers and sisters and mothers and children
and lands, with persecutions and in the age to come eternal life (Mk. 10,29).

How beautiful is that man of God whose feet hardly touch the earth! Quam pulchri
pedes Evangelizantium pacem, Evangelizantium bona[102]! Neither the hands, nor the
heart nor the head touch the earth. And even the feet are beautiful because they only
brush the earth. What freedom, what power this holy and beautiful poverty of Jesus
Christ gives to the priest!
What strength he acquires to struggle against the vices of the world! What an
example he is for the world, that world which works only for money, which thinks
only of money, which lives only for money!
And next to this material, sensual world, a spiritual man who does not live for the
earth, who scorns money and the goods of the world, who wants nothing of those
goods of the world and who says to the world: keep your gold and silver, my treasure is in heaven, my life is Jesus Christ. Who is satisfied with the strictly necessary,
who asks nothing of anybody, who works for God alone, who does not argue for his
tunic or his coat; who lets his coat go and does not claim what was taken from him;
and who abandons himself in the hands of Providence. How beautiful he is! How
great he is! How admirable is that man!
And how people must turn around on seeing him and admire in him the power of
faith, of love and confidence in God.
Where those men are, they will do admirable things, says Wisdom.

The two life principles for any house are poverty and charity. Join to that prudence which
makes us not go beyond what we can do, that we must not tempt Providence, that is, do things
beyond what we are call to do and say: God will see to the payment, as we sometimes hear.
That is tempting God. But the one who waits, who does only what he has the strength to do,
what he can do, without exposing himself; he can go ahead.
See also Ms XII 199, P. 248.
[102] How beautiful are the feet of the messangers of peace, of the messengers of the good
news (Ro. 10, 15; Is. 52,7).

323 O Poverty, how beautiful you are!
Jesus Christ, my Master, found you so beautiful that, on coming down from heaven he espoused you, made you his life companion wished to die on the cross with you.
O my Master, give me this beautiful poverty.
Let me seek it with solicitude,
take it with joy,
embrace it with love,
to make it the companion of my whole life[103] and die with it on a piece of wood, like my Master!

    Hoc fac et vives[104].

---

[103] Ms XII 200 - Like my Father, St. Francis, the true poor of Jesus Christ.
[104] Do this and you will live (Lk. 10,28).

FOURTH CONDITION

TO CARRY ONE'S CROSS[1]

---

[1] Ms XII 277-282.

Father Chevrier calls it the FOURTH CONDITION, *but he sends us back to the preceding conditions: the Cross is poverty, renunciation of creatures and oneself[2]. Yet, in his mind, the cross follows well on the preceding conditions for here he draw our attention to the consequences of renunciation[3]. The stress is on one point: evangelical life tries our patience*
With God's grace it is relatively easy to opt for poverty, for example. In fact, in the beginning we are carried by a certain enthusiasm. We agree with the saying that where there is no suffering there is no true poverty[4], and that if there is anything to suffer, so much the better, God's work will only be the stronger[5]. Those first steps are costly, but they bring their reward.
On the contrary, when the road lengthens, as time goes by, enthusiasm disappears and that is when we must carry our cross each day; that is, be poor every day[6]. Because of that, many accept, take the cross but do not carry it[7]. We must meditate the carrying of the cross in order to have the patience to go to the end. It is constancy in trial, so dear to St. Paul. Thus, tribulation produces constancy, constancy a tried virtue, a tried virtue hope. And hope is not deceiving...[8]
In leading the Way of the Cross in the chapel at the Prado, Father Chevrier liked to say that each one has his cross to take[9]. He recalled it briefly at the second station, the one where, traditionally, we look at Jesus receiving his Cross.

This life is sown with crosses... everyone, in all circumstances; the palace or the hovel.... where we least expect it, wooden cross, gold cross for the rich, but no less heavy, brilliant in appearance. Poverty, work - cross in your spouse, children. Calumnies, slander - loss of goods, parents, disappointments, no success.

It is our human condition - consequence of sin, sickness.

No matter where we go, place of living, inevitable[10].

This type of meditation is often found in his notes on the Way of the Cross or on the mysteries of the Rosary. In The True Disciple, *the conclusion is that the priest, and every apostle in general, must not be surprised at having to share the common lot, on the contrary, for he has wanted to take up the cross of evangelical life[11].*

---

[2] P. 289.
[3] Cf. p. 289, note 16.
[4] P. 260.
[5] P. 271.
[6] P. 292.
[7] P. 291.
[8] Rom. 5,3-5; cf. 2 Cor. 6,4 and 12, 12
[9] P. 290
[10] Ms VI 251.
[11] P. 290.

The end of the chapter may be perplexing. After evoking the apostolic patience and constancy of St. Paul, we fall on a very exterior practice: the use of a crucifix, 9 or 10 centimeters long, carried on the left side[12]. *That is precisely an example of the way in which Father Chevrier procedes.*

He has his fundamental intuition on the priest. In order that this intuition not remain on the level of ideas, it must pass into a way of life. To find this way of life, before having sufficient personal experience, Father Chevrier seeks what could work with others. In this case he thinks of borrowing a custom among certain religious and especially the missionary societies. It is having always with us a crucifix big enough to be of use[13], *that is, an instrument for teaching catechism, proclaiming Jesus Christ crucified. But that cross is also a reminder: to accomplish this ministry, we must resemble Jesus Christ carrying his cross*[14].

In fact, if we do not always carry a crucifix, we often have the opportunity to have one before our eyes, in church, on a work table, on the wall of a room. Is it a routine for us, or a humble apostolic practice?

---

[12] P. 292.
[13] Cf. p. 292, note 28.
[14] Cf. p. 292, note 28.

The fourth condition to be a true disciple of Jesus Christ is to take up our cross[15]. 329

Our Lord Jesus Christ's doctrine on this point. Our Lord says: if anyone wishes to come after me, let him renounce himself, *take up his cross* and follow me (Mt. 16,24). If anyone takes his cross and does not follow me he is not worthy of me (Mt. 10,38). Whoever does not carry his cross and does not follow me cannot be my disciple (Lk. 14,27). If anyone would come after me, let him renounce himself, take up his cross every day and follow me (Lk. 9,23). In these words of Jesus Christ, we see that, in order to be his true disciple, we must first *take up our cross*. That if we do not take it, we cannot be his disciple, essential condition. Not only must we take it, but we must also *carry it*. Thirdly, we must carry it every day. All that is explained well in the preceding texts.

What is the cross? It is the sign of suffering.
General sign that includes all types of suffering. Sign of salvation, sign of redemption, sign of the Christian and especially of the true disciple of Jesus Christ. The cross is poverty, renunciation of creatures and ourselves[16]. It is the pain there is 330 in observing the Lord's law, the Lord's yoke.
It is the yoke of the Gospel that we see in this book. It is the knowledge of this life which is so different from that of other men. It is the cross, it is Jesus who presents it to us and tells us: take my yoke upon you; my yoke is sweet and my burden is light. Ubi amatur non laboratur aut si laboratur labor amatur[17].
It is the regulation of a house. It is the predicted persecution of the world, the hatred of the world, the thorns. The cross is salvation, it is glory. How glorious the cross has become since Jesus Christ took it and carried it!
Jesus presents his cross to generous souls.

---

[15] In going through this chapter we will see that we are still far from a definitive edition.

[16] Ms XI 36-37 - After having followed these three degrees of renunciation, we must take up our cross, that is, we must accept the consequences of these three acts of renunciation. When we have left all our goods, we are poor and poverty is a cross; when we have renounced creatures, the world, we do not have the help of men, their friendship, their protection, their affection - privation - then there is the cross and that isolation from the world, joys and relation with the world, it is a cross. When we have renounced ourselves, that is, the pleasures of the spirit, the affection of the heart, the ease of the body, the acts of our will, we suffer, it is a cross.

[17] Where there is love there is not pain, or if there is pain the pain is loved. This is a deformed quotation from St. Augustine drawn from a work on good widowhood. (De bono Viduitatis XXVI).

We must take our cross. Accept. Take willingly.

When we become priest or religious, it is not to lead a soft life,

easier than the others, than the people of the world. No, far from it. On the contrary, it is to take up a heavier cross than that of the people of the world, to lead a stricter, more perfect life, more painful to nature[18]. We must take our cross, the cross that Jesus gives us. The cross in a strict and rigorous life, evangelical life. And this condition is so essential that Our Lord says that the one who does not accept this cross, does not take up his cross, cannot be his disciple. Thus, if we do not want to accept, take up this cross offered by Jesus Christ, the Master, we must give up. To take up the cross is to take up the evangelical life as Our Lord gives it to us, it is to accept the sufferings that are attached to this life of poverty, renunciation (renunciation to creatures, oneself), sacrifice, devotedness. If we do not accept that, we cannot be his disciple. If a person does not take up his cross, he is not worthy of me. God does not want him for disciple. Our Lord wants courageous, generous souls with him. We must have the courage to accept that cross which Our Lord presents to us or give up because Our Lord does not want us. *Non est me dignus*[19].

Our Lord's invitation to take up the cross.

Our Lord invites us to take up his cross. *Jugum meum suave est et onus meum leve*[20].

He himself took it for us. We must take it up after him. He presents it to us himself. *Ecce ancilla Domini fiat mihi secundum verbum tuum*[21].

Every person in the world has his cross. Different cross for each position.

Each one has his own cross to take. Cross of the Christian, soldier, priest, disciple, worker, father of a family.

We must carry our cross.

It is not a matter of only taking it up. We may take up something and not carry it.

---

[18] Ms XII 288 - When we become priest or religious, disciple of Jesus Christ, it is not to have fun, to live like a bourgeois; to gain status, accumulate money, have a good time, be happier than the rest. No. It is to take up the cross, to suffer, to work, it is to follow Jesus Christ: Jesus Christ scourged, persecuted, poor, crowned with thorns.

Painful to nature. This means conditions of life that are not necessarily in accordance with our spontaneous inclinations. The expression, in this type of expression does not have a philosophical or theological meaning.

[19] He is not worthy of me (Mt. 3,38).

[20] My yoke is sweet and my burden is light (Mt. 11, 30).

[21] Behold the handmaid of the Lord, be it done to me according to your word (Lk. 1,38).

We may accept something and not use it. But Our Lord dots the i's. We must not only accept it but carry it. Many accept, take up the cross but do not carry it. To carry the cross is to really bear the sufferings of the cross. There are some who take up the cross and reject it as soon as it begins to hurt a little. That is not it. We must carry it.

Tollite jugum meum super vos[22]. That is, we must bear the inconveniences of the apostolic life.
We must bear the sufferings that are the consequences of poverty, renunciation of creatures and oneself; the hatred and scorn of the world, persecutions that are the consequences of our life opposed to the world. Consequences of a more serious regulation of life; of a life of detachment, renunciation and sacrifice. We must take up our cross, that is, bear all that with humility, patience, resignation; with joy and love since it is God's cross and it is through the cross that we go to heaven, that we glorify God on earth, that we save our souls. It is in carrying his cross that Jesus Christ saved us and entered into glory. Oportuit pati Christum et ita intrare in gloriam[23]. *When I have been raised on the cross, I will draw all things to myself.* Therefore, we must carry the cross and carry it with joy and love, thinking that it is through the cross that we glorify God and win souls.
We must bend the shoulders and assume it. *Super vos*[24].

Carry our cross every day. Lastly, Our Lord adds: let him carry his cross every day!
He thinks of everything; he defines our duty well! We must carry our cross every day, every day we must begin again. If we leave it at night, we must take it up again in the morning and carry it like the day before, or better than the day before.

---

[22] Take my yoke upon you (Mt. 11,29).

[23] Did Christ not have to suffer those things to enter in his glory (Lk. 24,26).

[24] Ms XII 290 - Our Lord's encouragement to his disciples: Take my yoke upon you... and learn... The disciple is not greater than the Master. Blessed shall you be when...; those who suffer persecution for justice, Jesus carried his cross.

How we must carry it: with submission. It is the will of God... it is our duty of disciple. The one who does not take up his cross (Lk. 14,27); as a duty since we must complete in our flesh what is lacking to the passion of Jesus Christ (Col. 1,24). Sheep among wolves. With patience. When we are struck on the right cheek. Bless those who curse you, pray for those who persecute you. Do not resist evil. Conquer evil with good. Do not fear those who kill the body. With joy. Thinking that it is through the cross that we resemble Jesus Christ, that we gain heaven and that we convert souls. To suffer with meekness, patience and joy (Col. 1,11 Vulg.), thinking of the fruits that flow from the cross. When I have been lifted on the cross, I will draw all things to myself. I die each day to win glory for you (1 Cor. 15,31). Always carrying the death of Jesus in our body (2 Cor. 4,10).

> Every day,
> without getting tired,
> with perseverance,
> if we drop it,
> we must pick it up to the end.

We must not be discouraged on the way of the cross. There is always something to suffer, until death and we will have to die on the cross, allow ourselves to be attached to a cross like Our Lord; to fall sometimes but always get up again through prayer and continue our journey. We need perseverence. Our Lord told us this because our poor nature often rebels and is often weary and wants to drop the cross. But no. Once we have begun, we must persevere and carry our cross every day.

> Teach catechism every day,
> be poor every day,
> bear with our neighbor, the world every day,
> resist weariness of nature, with God's grace.

The cross was the love of the saints, especially of St. Paul who loved it so much he gloried in it. *Mihi absit gloriari nisi in cruce Domini nostri Jesu Christi*[25].
I bear in my body the imprint of the wounds of my Lord Jesus (Gal. 6,17)[26].
He delighted in the cross. He rejoiced in the cross[27].

The cross is the love of the saints.

334 **Practice.** To remember this word of Our Lord Jesus Christ

and the duty that it imposes, we will carry a blessed and indulgenced cross, 9 to 10 centimeters long, on our left side, (Christ) to remind ourselves of the great truth, we will kiss this Christ, especially morning and night, and also during the day[28] [29].

---

[25] But far be it from me to glory except in the cross of our Lord Jesus Christ (Gal. 6,14).

[26] This translation is a bit strained. St. Paul does not necessarily speak of the wounds of Christ. It is better to translate simply: The marks of Jesus.

[27] The parallel Ms, XII-281 quotes St. Paul abundantly: Rom. 8,36; 1 Cor. 4,9; 2 Cor. 4,8; 2 Cor. 5,1; 2 Cor. 6,4; 2 Cor. 11,22 ss; 2 Cor. 12,7; 2 Tim. 4,6. Ms XII-279 sketches a study: "Example of Jesus Christ..."

[28] Ms. XII 287; Ms XII 293.

It is to express this thought, this word of Our Lord that all religious carry a cross exteriorly; to remind them that they must carry it especially interiorly and be like Jesus Christ carrying his cross (Ms XII 287).

Carry a simple cross, but big enough to be of use; have a little pocket on the left side in which to put it and remember that the cross is the sign of suffering and the sight of that cross always brings us to love and bless suffering (Ms XII 293).

[29] Cf. p. 288.

FIFTH CONDITION 335

TO FOLLOW JESUS CHRIST[1]

---

[1] Ms XII 295-299.

Last condition to be fulfilled[2]. *When we speak of following Jesus Christ, can we still speak of condition; are we not at the end itself?* Yes, no doubt, but Father Chevrier does not forget the end to which all our efforts must converge, the end of God's design. That end will not be attained until God is all things to all men[3]. Thus, to follow Jesus Christ in this life is still a condition to attain the end to which God destines creation.

However, the pages that follow describe a summit of spiritual and apostolic life impossible to surpass on earth; it is holiness attained as much as the present human condition permits.

We will often find the previous themes because Father Chevrier never holds to a rigorous plan. Those themes are also repeated because they must be seen in a new light, in the state of the one who is rid of everything that may impede his progress[4], totally free in the Holy Spirit.

Then he can go everywhere, walk, rise *with Jesus Christ, and* never leave him[5]. These pages put us in communion with the mystery of passage, the Passover of the Son of God among us. Having come from God, he returned to God and he draws his disciples behind him. Isn't that the whole Gospel?[6]

What is the use of considering a state to which nobody would dare think he has arrived? That is the point. We must think about it for if we are doing anything good, it is in the measure that we aspire to that state. *Follow me*, said Jesus in calling his disciples[7], and even if he says explicitly: *Sell what you have*, he always adds[8]: *Follow me*[9].

And Jesus also said to his disciples: *You who have followed me*[10]. Yet, many things still needed to be purified in them. But it is true, this state, so perfect in itself, is already at work in us.

Thus, even if it is still very poor exteriorly, we may, without delay, make an effort to follow Jesus Christ, without having fulfilled the other conditions, as long as we have the essential disposition: have firm and efficacious resolve to fulfill them and be disposed to make every sacrifice to accomplish them[11].

For the chapters of this last part of The True Disciple *we may go back to the typical plan that inspired the previous parts of the book.*

---

[2] P. 297.
[3] 1 Cor. 15,28.
[4] P. 297.
[5] P. 297.
[6] Jn. 13, 3.
[7] Mt. 8,9, etc.
[8] P. 297.
[9] Mt. 19,21.
[10] Mt. 19,28.
[11] P. 297.

Example of Jesus Christ.
Teaching of Jesus Christ.
   Summary.
Examples in St. Paul.
Teachings of St. Paul.
   Summary.
Practices, that is, application for us.

This plan is never completely followed because, as we have already said, Father Chevrier does not force himself to hold exactly to his plan. We must also say that most of the chapters that follow remained unfinished. They are rather brief and so will the corresponding introductions be.

The general order of this last part is to be noted. It is not without importance to grasp Father Chevrier's thought.

It begins with the fasting and prayer of Christ. In fact, it is with the period in the desert that begins what we call the public life of Christ. We have to follow Jesus proclaiming the Gospel. Also, this whole last part revolves around the chapter Follow me in my preaching[12]. Fasting and prayer precede the work of the preacher. Meekness, humility, poverty are essential dispositions of the one who wants to proclaim the Gospel to the poor. It is in communion with Christ's love for men that we must accomplish this ministry.

We must also be prepared to bear struggles, persecutions, sufferings which are the inevitable consequences of the proclamation of the word for the disciples will undergo the same things that the Master did[13].

And one day, for the true disciple, all this ends up in following his Master in his death to pass with him to glory with the Father.

---

[12] Pp. 389-403.
[13] Jn. 15,20.

It is the fifth and last condition to fulfill to be a true disciple of Jesus Christ. Our Lord always places this condition last to show us that we cannot accomplish it without having fulfilled the others, or at least having the firm and efficacious resolve to accomplish it and be disposed to make all the sacrifices to accomplish it.

In fact, how could we follow Jesus Christ, so elevated, so perfect, the spiritual and divine man, if we are still all flesh, completely attached to matter? How can we follow a man who walks so fast and who rises so high, if we ourselves are encumbered by all sorts of exterior, temporal things and if we ourselves are not rid of everything that can impede our progress? And he always puts this condition after having pointed out the others, and it is the one that he repeats most often.

Every time he speaks of the others, he always adds this one, to show us that it must always follow the others and that it is the culmination of the others and that it is the principle and the end towards which we must tend:

> To follow Jesus Christ.
> Ego sum via[14].

Follow me - Follow me - Follow me.

It is this condition that glorifies God the most on earth and is the most useful for the neighbor and leads most directly to heaven. Ego sum via, veritas et vita.

When Jesus chose his apostles, he picked twelve, *to be with him*, not to leave him, to follow him everywhere.

---

[14] I am the way, the truth and the life (Jn. 14,6).

What is to follow Jesus Christ?

To follow Jesus Christ is to go everywhere he goes, do everything he does, it is never to leave him.
It is to imitate him in everything possible.
It is to follow his example, it is to resemble him as perfectly as possible in order to become another him: *Sacerdos alter Christus*[15].
It is to be able to say like St.Paul: *imitatores mei estote sicut et ego Christi*[16].
That is what Our Lord means when he says to his apostles: *exemplum dedi vobis ut quemadmodum ego feci ita et vos faciatis*[17].
To follow Jesus Christ is to go with him to the crib to become poor.
It is to go with him to Egypt to share his exile and poverty.
It is to stay with him in Nazareth,in silence to lead an obscure and hidden life.
It is to go to the desert with him to fast and to pray.
It is to go through the cities and towns to instruct the ignorant, console the afflicted, heal the sick and announce salvation to the world.
It is to courageously and firmly fight vice and struggle against evil.
It is to walk amid the persecutions and injustices of the world.
It is to climb Calvary to die.
It is to let ourselves be nailed to a cross and die to obey God and save the world.
It is to go to heaven with him because he said that those who would have followed him on earth would be by his side in heaven.
The servant is not greater than the master; for the servant to be perfect, it suffices that he be like his master. Ego sum via.
It is not only to follow him exteriorly by doing what he did, according to his example, but it is also to be filled with his spirit.
Hoc sentite in vobis quod et in Christo Jesu (Phil. 2,1)[18]
To be filled with his spirit of humility,poverty,meekness and love:qui dicit se in ipso manere debet sicut ille ambulavit et ipse ambulare (1 Jn. 2,6)[19].
Thus it would be very little to be satisfied with the exterior, but we must be filled especially with his interior in order to really walk in his footsteps and act in the same sense and the same spirit[20].

---

[15] The priest is another Christ.

[16] Be imitators of me as I am of Jesus Christ (1 Cor. 11,1).

[17] I have given you an example that you may do as I do (Jn. 13,15).

[18] Have the same sentiments that were in Christ Jesus.

[19] The one who says he lives in him must conduct himself as he did.

[20] Ms XII 315 - To follow Jesus Christ, all we have to do: renounce everything, the earth, creatures, ourselves; take up the cross and follow. Without all these conditions we are incapable of really following Jesus Christ and becoming true disciples. Hoc sentite in vobis quod in Christo Jesu (Phil. 2,5).

How must we follow Jesus Christ?   With faith, love and generosity! It is the Eternal Word, the Word of the living God.

With faith: I am the way, the truth, the life (Jn. 14,16). We can follow someone closely, from afar; *from afar, closely, not at all*. I am the light of the world, the one who follows me does not walk in darkness but he will have the light of life (Jn. 8,12). Verbum vitae. Lux vera quae illuminat omnem hominem venientem in hunc mundum. Splendor patris, candor lucis aeternae. In quo sunt omnes thesauri sapientiae et scientiae. In ipso inhabitat omnis plenitudo divinitatis corporaliter[21]. To whom would wego, you have the words of eternal life (Jn. 6,68)[22].

With love. He is our Savior.
We belong to him, he has called us, he has filled us with his blessings, he has given us everything; he is our Father, our benefactor: follow me. Jugum eum suave et onum meum leve et invenietis requiem animabus vestris (Mt. 11, 29)[23].

To really follow Jesus Christ, we must be rid of everything, we must be light. It is the celestial man. It is only on these conditions that we can really be his disciple.

Follow me in my spirit; it is not a matter of doing as we wish, as we think, but as Jesus Christ thinks, wishes. My way of doing: the spirit of Jesus Christ.

Follow me, that is, do as I do, take the same road I do; follow me in the way that I took to accomplish my mission; do as I did, walk in my footsteps, do not take another road for you could be mistaken and not arrive at the end. You must continue my work. You are my apostles, my [....](a) my successors; you must do as I do to arrive at the end. I converted the universe; I took the way of the crib and the cross. Take the same way to arrive at the same end, otherwise you will not arrive... in the spirit.

I send you like my Father sent me; therefore do as I did, if you wish to fulfill the mission that I have entrusted to you in my Father's name.

(a) illegible word.
[21] Word of life (Jn. 1,1). True light that enlightens all men who come into this world (Jn. 1,9). Splendor of the Father (cf. Heb. 1,3). Brilliance of the eternal light (Wis.7,26). In him are hidden all the treasures of wisdom and knowledge (Col. 2,3). In him the whole fullness of divinity dwells bodily (Col. 2,9).
[22] Ms XII 317 - It is not a man that we follow, it is the Son of God. In following Jesus Christ, we follow the true light. He is the Word of life, he is our Master, our king, our solid foundation; he is the truth, the life, the resurrection.
[23] My yoke is sweet and my burden is light and you will find rest for your souls.

With generosity. The disciple is not greater than the master (Lk. 6,40). It suffices for the disciple to be like his master (Mt. 10,25).
I will follow you wherever you go,
I am ready to die for you,
I will give my life for you,
Let us go and die with him.
There are three types of disciples: the good, the bad, the perfect. The good do what is necessary: law; many good pastors, good curates.
The bad do nothing; scandalize.
The perfect who feel the need to follow Jesus Christ more closely, who are touched by his poverty, charity, devotedness, his sacrifice and who seek to resemble him as much as possible; more than ordinary life: that does not suffice for them.
What a difference between these holy souls and the others! How much more they glorify God! A true disciple gives more glory to Jesus Christ than one hundred other good ones[24].
No lagging, distaste, negligence. Not from afar but closely.   344
It is for the glory of God that you become my disciple and that you bear much fruit.

How we must follow Jesus Christ.

If we study the principal actions of Our Lord Jesus Christ, we find that to imitate Jesus Christ we must follow him:
  in fasting and prayer,
  in his meekness, humility, poverty,
  in his love for mankind,
  in his preaching,
  in his struggles,
  in his persecutions,
  in his sufferings,
  then we will follow him in his glory.

> Ego sum via.
> Exemplum.
> Let us follow Jesus Christ.

---

[24] Ms. XII 318 - Those who feel the need to follow Jesus Christ more closely in poverty, humility, suffering; many good ones but it seems that it does not suffice, that they can do better, that we must have more life, that this ordinary life does not satisfy the souls, does not satisfy the desire to belong to God, that we can do better, that Jesus Christ asks something more of us. Follow me.

1. Follow me
in my fasting.[1] 345

---

[1] Ms XII 299-305.

Father Chevrier sees fasting in relation with the apostolic mission, as it is in the Bible. The rules that he gives seem rigorous. We must remember that at the time, the ecclesiastical law on fasting was still demanding. We had to fast every day in Lent, except Sundays. Father Chevrier adds the days of fast prescribed by the Third Order of St. Francis. But he asks that we take the necessary quantity of food in order to be able to teach catechism[2], *and we feel that his preference is for the* fast of charity[3], *when we* do not have time to eat and chose to render service to our neighbor rather than go eat[4].

At the center of everything, he proposes for our meditation, these words of Jesus which so struck Father Chevrier: My food is to do the will of the one who sent me[5]. *What beautiful words!*[6]

For this chapter, Father Chevrier gave a text edited all in following, leaving as usual, a margin in which he no doubt expected to put subtitles, as may be seen in the typographic setting adopted. Practically, he did not do this work, there are only two subtitles at the end.

347

---

[2] P. 310.
[3] P. 309.
[4] P. 308.
[5] Jn. 4,34.
[6] P. 308. See also pp. 159, 164, 430.

It is the first example that Jesus Christ gives us in his life before 349
beginning his apostolic life; before preaching, teaching, he withdraws.
To fast is to deprive ourselves of food, either to obey a precept of the
Lord, or to acquire, buy some particular grace, or to fulfill a precept of
charity which is more pressing than that of going to take food.
That is what we notice in the conduct of Our Lord Jesus Christ, our
Master. Three actions in preparation for his mission.
- Baptism by John. To receive John's consecration, testimony. John's
mission was to show Jesus Christ, to preach Jesus Christ, to announce
him to the world. He comes, so to speak, to receive the mission from
John, since John was his precursor, the angel[7]. We cannot act without a
mission...It was the exterior consecration.
- To fast, dispoilment of the flesh; stripping off of all that is carnal,
coarse, natural[8].
- Prayer, spiritual man by fasting and prayer. And first we see him immediately after having received baptism, led by the Holy Spirit, going
into the desert to spend forty days in fasting and prayer.
He fasts in those circumstances to obey the will of his Father and buy 350
the graces he needs to begin his great mission on earth which is to
evangelize men. We also, when we have a mission to fulfill, must begin
with fasting and prayer. The Holy Spirit himself says: Bona est oratio
cum jejunio[9].
One day, the apostles had not been able to expel an impure demon from
the body of a possessed man and they wondered why. Our Lord
answered that this type of demon is only expelled by fasting and prayer
(Mt. 17,20).
Therefore, there are graces that we can only obtain through fasting and
prayer.
That is what Moses did on the mountain where he fasted for forty days
and forty nights. That is what John the Baptist did in the desert where he
lived on grasshoppers and wild honey (Mt. 3,4). Anna did not leave the
temple, serving God day and night in fasting and prayer (Lk. 2,37). And
the apostles themselves, before imposing hands on Paul and Barnabas,
fasted and prayed: they fasted and prayed and after having fasted and
prayed, they imposed hands on them and let them go (Acts. 13,3). And
St. Paul recommends priests to be worthy ministers of God by bearing
patiently the tribulations and imprisonments and necessities, living in
work, vigils, fasting and chastity (2 Cor. 6,4). We commend ourselves in

---

[7] The word angel, which means messenger, is applied to John the Baptist by Mark (1,2).
[8] Natural in the sense of subject to our spontaneous inclinations.
[9] Prayer with fasting is good (Tob. 12,8).

every way through great endurance, in afflictions, hardships, calamities, beatings, imprisonments, tumults, labours, watching, fastings (2 Cor. 6,4). I was exposed to all sorts of labors, hardships, numerous vigils, hunger and thirst, fastings, cold and nudity (2.Cor. 11,27).

Four types of fasting:
1. We may fast because the law commands it.
2. Or because we don't have anything to eat.
3. Or because we want to do penance to obtain a particular grace.
4. Or because we do not have the time to eat and we prefer to render service to our neighbor rather than go eat.

There is the voluntary fasting in which we deprive ourselves of food to render service to the neighbor. It is love which imposes charity and the love of God and souls by which we prefer to serve God and neighbor to taking food. That is what Our Lord expresses very well when he answers his apostles who are urging him to eat: I have a food that you do not know, my food is to do the will of my Father (Jn. 4,34).
What beautiful words! The will of his Father is his food. When others are thinking only of eating, of buying, of preparing what they must eat, Jesus Christ thinks only of doing the will of his Father and forgets, so to speak, that food of the body which we seek so much. His father's will comes before everything; he leaves everything aside to do this holy will. What a beautiful example for us who so fear to delay a meal, lack one dish, a dessert! How little concerned he was about this bodily food! Seated by Jacob's well, he asks a little water of the Samaritan woman (Jn. 4,7). When the apostles bring him something to eat he tells them that he has a food that they do not know; invisible food that is to do the will of his Father. Walking through a field with his apostles, they started to crush some grain in thèir hand because they were hungry (Mt. 12,1). He sought figs on a tree because he was hungry (Mt. 21,18)[10].
And often they did not have time to eat because the crowd was so great that they could not go out and probably made do with a piece of bread.
On the cross he was thirsty and he got only gall and vinegar to drink.
That is how Our Lord lived. He sought the will of his father and the salvation of the neighbor before his own food. And the fast that charity imposes is not the least pleasing to God and it is as good as the one that is commanded and that we often do only half way and reluctantly.

---

[10] Ms XII 326 - He eats with his apostles in the plain, the desert, the mountains: they bought something to eat and ate it under a tree.

That is the fast of which St. Paul speaks: the voluntary fast of charity (2 Cor. 6,4). The saints did not have an hour for eating; they ate as if on the run, and they ate what they had, what they found, what they could.
And we always want to be well treated, always have a number of dishes, not to lack any desserts. Always have quantity and quality. Always have a well set table, very clean, well prepared, well laden. Our Lord and the saints sometimes had what they needed, sometimes they lack what was necessary and they got along as best they could. Scio esurire. Scio abundare[11]. The merit of fasting is that we make to God the real sacrifice of ourselves, through obedience or voluntarily. And when this privation is done with a motive of charity for our neighbor, it has double merit. As for abstinence, God shows us the need and usefullness of it when he himself imposes it upon Adam to make him earn heaven by an act of obedience and privation; therefore it is just and legitimate[12].

Practice.

To follow Our Lord Jesus Christ in his fasting and enter into his spirit, we will observe, as much as possible, the fasts of precepts, the fasts of the poor, the fasts of charity and abstinence.

Fasts of precepts: the fasts of the Church: Lent, Vigils, Ember Days; fasts of the Third Order, Advent (Wednesdays and Fridays only) Vigils of St. Francis and the Immaculate Conception and every Friday of the year.

Fasts of the poor: learn to fast when we do not have anything to eat; eat what is given us once a month, the day of the monthly retreat.

Fasts of charity: that we not be afraid to delay our meal, *when necessary*, to exercise charity, of leaving the table to go fulfill a charitable duty for the neighbor. We must forget ourselves for others. In this case, in order not to disturb anyone and not to be a source discontent and hardship for others, we will eat our portion that will have been left on the table and that we will have been careful not to bring with us; no matter if it is cold. And, if we wish, it would be good to wash our own dishes in order not to disturb anyone else. We must be able to suffer without making others suffer.

Abstinence: Wednesday, Friday and Saturday.

---

[11] I have learned the secret of facing plenty and hunger (Phil. 4,12).

[12] This interpretation of the "forbidden fruit" in Gen. 3,3 is not Father Chevrier's alone. It narrows considerably the meaning of this passage of Scripture.

Remarks on fasting.

354

On fast days, we will take the frustulum[13] permitted by the Church.

On fast days, in the morning we will serve bread, wine and fruit and each one will take what he needs to be able to teach catechism. The weaker, more delicate stomachs may take chocolate or coffee in sufficient quantity to permit them to accomplish their duty, because the duties of charity are more excellent than fasting. If we cannot fast materially, we can always do so spiritually.

If we are not able to fast, we will kneel down in our room or in the refectory, if that can be, and say a Pater and an Ave with our arms in the form of a cross, to remind ourselves that if we eat it is through grace and necessity and that we have to ask pardon of God before doing so.

We must see to it especially that there is a difference between the fast days and the ordinary days; that the morning service be very different and a sign of penance.

If health does not permit fasting, we may take the same quantity of food but that it be different, that is, poorer, more simple, coarser: bread, wine, fruits, but nothing cooked, specially prepared; then we will enter into the spirit of penance.

---

[13] A Latin word which means to take a light meal: take just a bite.

2. Follow me
in my prayer[1]   355

---

[1] Ms XII 305-313.

Father Chevrier never gave many explanations on what prayer in itself is, in The True Disciple or elsewhere. He prefers to show the results, the good effects of prayer[2]. *These effects culminate in the transformation of the one who prays; he is transformed more and more into the image of Christ*[3]. *Thus we are placed in a perspective both apostolic and contemplative.*
How do we learn to pray? Father Chevrier puts us simply before the examples and teachings of Jesus Christ. It is by looking at, listening to Jesus praying that we can discover prayer in us.
Another of Father Chevrier's concerns was to vivify the usual prayer exercises. That is what he sought to do whether with the First Communion children, the public in the chapel of the Prado or the priests and seminarians of the house. He did not try to create new prayer formulas but he made many attempts to adapt the formulas in current use, particularly the Rosary and the Way of the Cross. In his effort of adaptation he highlights the knowledge of Jesus Christ, meditation of Christ's mysteries. The prayer formulas are used to help support this meditation and, if need be, they are adapted to that end.
For the celebration of the Divine Office to which the priests are held, we perceive a similar concern. He proposes prayer intentions for each part of the Office[4]. It is an attempt to show the unity that should exist between the priest's prayer and his apostolic activity.
We perceive another concern. At the time of Father Chevrier, it was the custom for priests to say Matins and Lauds in the afternoon or evening of the previous day. At the beginning of the day he said, in one sesion, Prime, Terce, Sext and None,that should have been spread out over the day, and at the beginning of the afternoon he said Vespers and Compline, two night prayers. Father Chevrier does not think of going against this abnormal discrepancy, but the prayers that he proposes for the morning, the Canticle of Creation[5] and Psalm 50, are a kind of summary of the Office of Lauds and the bedtime prayers are various parts of the Office of Compline.
In other places in Father Chevrier we find this desire for an adapted liturgical life. To initiate the seminarians to a personal study of the Gospel, he proposes that it be done within the annual liturgical cycle. In the catechetical formation of the children of the Prado, he wished to make them participate in the Mass in such a way that they would not be bored (at least not too much!), and especially that they discover in the Mass the presence of all that they were studying in catechism class.
It is a very sure apostolic instinct that gave him those concerns, but the liturgical life of the time gave him practically no adapted means and he was unable to be a precursor in this area, execpt in desire.

---

[2] P. 317.
[3] Cf. 2 Cor. 3,18.
[4] P. 318.
[5] Dan. 3,57-58.

Prayer is one of the most important duties of religion. Therefore we must examine
well how Our Lord fulfilled it in order that we may do likewise.

He withdrew to the desert for forty days to fast and pray.
And Jesus, full of the Holy Spirit, returned from the Jordan and was led by the Spirit to the wilderness to be tempted by the devil and he was among the animals and remain there for forty days and forty nights (Lk. 4,1).

He rose early in the morning to go pray in a desert place.
And in the morning, a great while before day, he rose and went out to a lonely place to pray. And the apostles looked for him and when they found him, he went with them (Mk. 1,35).

He withdraws from the crowd and goes to a lonely place to pray.
After his miracles, when the crowd was pressing on all sides, he withdrew to the wilderness to pray (Lk. 5,16).

He prayed on the road with his disciples.
When he was on the road, even with his disciples, he sometimes went apart by himself to pray (Lk. 9,18).

He went at night to the garden of olives to pray.
During the day, Jesus taught in the temple, but at night he withdrew to the mountain of olives to pray, and all the people came early in the morning to the temple to hear him (Lk. 21, 37).

He withdraws to a high mountain to pray.
Jesus took Peter, James and John and led them to a high mountain to pray and while he was praying, his face became radiant and he was transfigured before them (Lk. 9,28).

His apostles, seeing him always in prayer, asked him how to pray.
When he was praying in a certain place, one of his disciples ask him: Lord teach us to pray as John taught his disciples to pray (Lk.11,1,).

He prays after his baptism.
And behold, while Jesus was at prayer after his baptism, the heavens were open (Lk. 3,21).

He prays after the Holy Eucharist. In the Garden of Olives, he prays a long time, on his knees, with his forehead to the ground, shedding tears of blood and always repeating the same prayer. And, having gone forward a little, he withdrew from his disciples, about a stone's throw, and kneeling down, he prostrated his face to the ground and he ask that, if it were possible, this hour be put far from him.

Then an angel appeared to Jesus, an angel from heaven, and comforted him. And he, entering into an agony, prayed all the more. And his sweat became like great drops of blood falling upon the ground (Lk. 22,43).

He prays with his arms extended on the cross. For three hours, he prays with his arms extended on the cross.

Instruction that Our Lord Jesus Christ gives to his apostles on prayer. When you pray, you will not be like the hypocrites who like to pray standing in the synagogues and at the street corners to be seen by men.

In truth, I tell you, they have received their reward.

To pray in secret. But you, when you pray, go to your room and shut the door,

pray your father in secret and your father who sees in secret, will repay you (Mt. 6,5).

and without many words. When you pray, do not multiply words as the pagans do,

for they think that it is by dint words that they will be heard. Do not be like them, for your father knows what you need before you ask him. Here is how you are to pray: Our Father who is in heaven..."Mt. 6,7).

We must pray always. Again, Jesus said to his disciples that we must pray always and never tire of doing so (Lk. 18,1).

To the Samaritan woman who questioned him on the place to worship, Jesus said:

To worship in spirit and in truth. The hour is coming and is already here when the true worshipers

will adore the Father in truth, for the Father seeks such worshipers. God is spirit and those who adore him must do so in spirit and in truth (Jn. 4,23).

That common prayer is very powerful.	I tell you again that if two of you agree on earth on something to ask for,

it will be given them by my Father in heaven. For where two or three are gathered in my name, I am in the midst of them (Mt. 18, 19).

Pray in the name of Jesus Christ.	And all that you will ask the Father in my name,

I will do it so that the Father may be glorified in the Son (Jn. 14,13). You have not ask anything in my name; ask and you shall receive.

Jesus' reproach to his apostles.	Simon, you sleep! So you were not able to watch one hour with me,

why do you sleep? Rise, watch and pray that you may not enter into temptation. The spirit is willing but the flesh is weak (Mt. 26,40).

Good effects of prayer.

It strengthens us, preserves us from temptation.	Watch and pray that you may not fall into temptation (Mt. 26,41).
It expels the impure demon.	This devil is expelled only by fasting and prayer, said Our Lord to his apostles.
We obtain everything through prayer.	Everything you ask the Father in my name, I will do.
It gives us the Holy Spirit.	After his baptism, while Jesus was in prayer, the Holy Spirit came and rested on him.
It transfigures us.	While Jesus was in prayer on Mount Tabor, his face was transfigured and he became different.
Examples of the apostles and the saints.	The apostles left everything to attend to the prayers and preaching.

St. Paul prayed night and day, for himself and for the faithful.

Summary of this chapter on prayer.	Our Lord Jesus Christ withdrew to the desert for forty days to fast and pray.

He rose early in the morning to go apart and pray.
He withdrew from the crowd to go to the desert to pray.
He prayed on the road, a little apart from his apotles.
From time to time, he went to the garden of olives at night to pray.
He went to a high mountain to pray.
Seeing him pray, the apostles asked him to teach them how to pray.
He prayed after his baptism.
He prayed after the Holy Eucharist.
In the garden of olives he prayed with his forehead to the ground, repeating the same prayer.
He prayed with his arms outstretched on the cross.
He teaches us that we must pray in silence and in secret.
We must pray always.
We must pray in spirit and in truth.
We must pray in the name of Jesus Christ.
Common prayer is very efficacious.
He reproaches his apostles for not praying.
Prayer strengthens us against temptation.
Prayer expels demons.
It obtains everything.
It gives us the Holy Spirit.
It transfigures us.
The saints did not stop praying, after the example of Our Lord.
From time to time, he invites his apostles to come away to rest and pray.
We must not be surprised if we see Our Lord Jesus Christ praying so often, so long and withdrawing often to pray, to give us an example of assiduous prayer. Supernatural virtue is so high, the practice of evangelical virtue so difficult to nature, we need so much grace to practice it, as we will see in the sublime virtues of meekness, humility, charity, [poverty][6], we need many graces to achieve it.

Practice.

On rising in the morning, we will recite the Psalm: *Benedicite omnia opera Domini Domino*[7].
On rising, the Psalm: *Miserere Mei*[8].
We will do an hour of meditation a day; three quarters of an hour in the morning and a quarter of an hour in the evening.

---

[6] Illegible word. We suggest poverty, according to the plan of this section.

[7] All you works of the Lord, bless the Lord (Dan. 3,57).

[8] Have mercy on me (Ps. 50).

We celebrate Holy Mass with the greatest respect, never omitting the preparation and thanksgiving, without a serious reason, and we will make it up during the day if we have not been able to make the thanksgiving immediately after Mass.

We recite the Divine Office with *dignity, devotion, and attention*[9], together or alone according to the possibilities, fulfilling exactly the rubrics of the breviary, rising or kneeling at the places indicated, pausing in the verses and having a particular intention for each canonical hour:

>Matins, to adore the Blessed Trinity: infidels. .
>Prime, Incarnation: family.
>Terce, Holy Spirit: Church.
>Sext, Jesus Christ teaching: preachers.
>None, Passion: sinners.
>Vespers, Mary, Mother of Sorrows: afflicted and sick.
>Compline, good death: dying, purgatory, agonising.

The Little Hours before 9 o'clock.
Vespers at 2 o'clock.
Matins and Lauds in the evening.

We must not postpone the breviary until evening; that is to neglect the duty of prayer, expose ourselves to saying it badly and to get it over with. How can we say the breviary well when we have worked all day and are tired; we must begin the day with prayer.

After breakfast, at 8:30, we ask for the Holy Spirit by reciting seven Hail Marys in honor of the seven gifts of the Holy Spirit, the Veni Creator to which we will add the prayer.

Prayers before and after meals:
>Pater, Benedicite, Agimus tibi.
>Pater, Benedicamus.

Every day we recite a part of the Rosary.

In the evening, at 4:30, or at another convenient hour, a visit of a quarter of an hour to the Blessed Sacrament.

Every night, the usual prayer, examen, act of contrition, Litany of the Blessed Virgin, De Profundis, three Hail Marys, Memorare, ordinary invocations.

At bedtime: in manus tuas, salva nos, dignare, prayer, benedicamus.

every week

We will recite, alone, the whole Rosary, we will make the Way of the Cross, we will make a holy hour once a week, from 9 to 10 or from 9:30 to 10:30, each one at the hour assigned to him.

---

[9] Dignity, attention, devotion. Father Chevrier took those three words from the prayer that was recited before beginning the breviary.

every month.
We take a day at the beginning of each month for the monthly retreat; we may make it in the house, while continuing our work, or at the chapel of Saint-Fons, or elsewhere while asking for alms.

On the feasts of Our Lord and the Blessed Virgin, we will try to recite the whole Rosary, if we have time.

On the feasts of the Passion, we will make the Way of the Cross.

During the whole month of May, we will try to recite the entire Rosary every day, unless our work prevents us from doing so.

every year.
We withdraw for at least eight days for a serious retreat, in order to be reimmersed in fervor and the love of God and resume our duties with more courage and fidelity. We will sometimes pray with our arms outstretched or with our forehead on the ground, in imitation of Our Lord Jesus Christ, to humiliate ourselves before God and solicite, for us and our neighbor, the so great graces which we need for ourselves and others.

It is the spirit of prayer that we need.

To have the spirit of prayer is to be led to prayer naturally; it is to feel the need for it, do it spontaneously and understand the need that we have of God's grace to fulfill our duty, so elevated and so great and at the same time so difficult for poor human nature.

It is possible to pray without having the spirit of prayer.

3. Follow me
in my meekness[1]

---

[1] Ms XII 331-341.

The chapter on meekness is easy to understand. 369

Meekness is the Savior's particular trait[2], *of the Messiah of the poor. This meekness reveals the strength of a soul capable of rebuking severely, like Jesus, those who, by their harshness and demands, prevent the little one and the poor from finding the way of salvation.* Those who are brusque and impetuous quench the spark of faith[3].

Let us not remain on the relatively superficial level of the quetion of temperament, character. It is a matter of an essential orientation of the apostolic action. Meekness is a necessary aptitude for the missionary. In the proclamation of the Gospel, we must proceed with meekness[4].

---

[2] Cf. p. 325, note 1.
[3] P. 330.
[4] Cf. P. 78.

Examples and doctrine of Our Lord Jesus Christ on meekness.

He calls everybody to himself and tells them not to be afraid.	Come to me all you who are heavily burdened and I will give you rest.
He wants us to know that he is meek and humble of heart[5].	Take my yoke upon you and learn of me that I am meek and humble of heart and you will find rest for your soul,

for my yoke is sweet and my burden is light (Mt. 11,28).

The prophet says in what meekness consists.	In speaking of his Son, God says, through the mouth of the prophet:

This is my servant whom I have chosen; my well beloved in whom I am well pleased. I will make my spirit rest upon him and he will proclaim justice to the nations. He will not quarrel; he will not shout and nobody will hear his voice in the public squares. He will not crush the broken reed, he will not quench the smoking wick; he will be neither sad nor turbulent, until he has assured justice and the nations shall hope in him (Mt. 12,17; Is. 42,1).

He tells his apostles only what they can bear at the moment.	In John 16,12, Our Lord says to his apostles: I still have many things to tell you, but you cannot bear them now.

When the spirit of truth comes, he will teach you all truth for he will not speak of himself but he will say what he has heard and will announce to you the things to come.

At the moment, he demands nothing too hard from his apostles.	To the Jews who asked why his disciples did not fast like those of John the Baptist or the Pharisees:

your apostles drink and eat; Jesus answered: Can you make the guests of the bridegroom fast while the bridegroom is still with them? As long as the bridegroom is with them they cannot fast. But the days will come when the bridegroom will be taken away from them; then they will fast.

---

[5] Ms XII 349 - It is the particular trait of the Savior, a man who is called to heal. Meekness is the magnet that draws, that wins hearts. We draw more flies with honey than with vinegar. Also, Our Lord says that, through meekness we posses the earth, that is, that we win everybody; men, animals, everything lets itself be won by meekness. It is the first quality that we notice in him. Woe to those who are brusque, severe, [haughty], rough...

| Comparison that he uses to make us understand with what consideration we must act in leading others. | And again he gave them this comparison: Nobody puts a new piece of cloth on an old garment for it will tear the garment; |

the new cloth tears the old cloth and the rent will be greater;the new piece is not good for the old. Also, nobody puts new wine in old wineskins, otherwise the new wine will break the wineskins and the wine will be spilled and the wineskins will be lost; but the new wine must be put in new wineskins and both will be saved and nobody who drinks old wine want to taste new wine immediately for he says: the old is better (Mk. 2,18 and parallels).

| How Our Lord answered the Pharisees who were scandalized to see the apostles crushing grain and eating it on a Sabbath day. | On a Sabbath day,the apotles had crushed grain in their hands and eaten it, and the Pharisees were scandalized and came to Jesus and said: your disciples are doing something that is not permitted on the Sabbath. |

And Jesus said to them: Have you not read what David did when he and those who were with him were in need and were hungry? How they entered the house of God, under Abiathar, the chief priest, and ate the bread of the offering which it was not permitted to anyone but the priests to eat, and he gave some to those who were with him.

373 | Not to be severe with others nor condemn the neighbor. | And he said: the Sabbath is made for man and not man for the Sabbath. |

Or have you not read in the law that the priest violate the Sabbath in the temple on the Sabbath day and are exempt from guilt. And I tell you, there is here one greater than the temple.

| It is mercy that I want and not sacrifice. | If you only knew what I mean: It is mercy that I want and not sacrifice, you would never have condemned the innocent (Mk. 12,1). |

| Jesus rebukes the scribes and Pharisees for imposing a heavy and unbearable burden on others. | Jesus spoke to the people and to his disciples and said: The Scribes and Pharisees are seated in the chair of Moses; |

observe all that they will tell you but do not do as they do for they say and do not do. They bind heavy and unbearable burdens to put on men's shoulders but they do not even lift them with a finger (Mt. 23,1).

Jesus rebukes the apostles for pre- | Little children were being brought to
venting the little children from co- | Jesus so that he might touch them,
ming to him. | place his hands upon them and pray.
On seeing this, the apostles threatened those who were bringing them. And seeing that Jesus was angry and called them to him and said: Let the little children come to me and do not prevent them, for the kingdom of heaven belongs to such as these. In truth I tell you, whoever does not receive the kingdom of God like a little child will not enter it and embracing them he put his hands on them and blessed them (Mt. 19,13 and parallels).

* Jesus rebukes James and John who | When the time when he was to be
want to call down fire on Samaria. | taken from this world was approaching,
he started toward Jerusalem *where his sacrifice was to be consumated*. And he sent a few persons before him to announce his coming. Those persons having left, entered a village of the Samaritans to prepare lodging for him; but the people of that place did not want to receive them because it seemed like they were going to Jerusalem *to celebrate the Passover*, which did not please the Samaritans who wanted to adore God on Mount Garizim. James and John, *having seen the insult that was being done to their Master*, said to him: Lord, do you want us to command fire from heaven to come down on those people and consume them? But, turning around, Jesus rebuked them: You do not know to what spirit you are called; the Son of man has not come to lose men but to save them. So they went to another village (Lk. 9,51).

How he receives Judas who comes | The traitor had given them a signal
to betray him. | saying: the one that I will kiss is the one, take him and bring him carefully;
and having arrived, he preceded them. And approaching Jesus to kiss him he said: Hail, Master, and kissed him. And Jesus said: my friend, why have you come; Judas, do you betray the Son of man with a kiss (Mt. 2, 50 and parallels).

How he rebukes Peter who lacks | Then the soldiers and the crowd came
meekness by striking with the | forward and took hold of Jesus.
sword.
Those who were around him, seeing what was about to happen, said: Lord, let us strike with the sword. And Simon Peter, one of the ones who were with Jesus, stretched out his hand, drew his sword and striking the servant of the high priest, cut off his right ear. The servant's name was Malchus. But Jesus spoke and said: Stop. And having touched the ear, healed it. Jesus said to Peter: Return you sword to it scabbard for those who take the sword will perish by the sword. Do you think that I cannot ask my Father and he would send more than a dozen legions of angels. But

how then should the Scripture be fulfilled, that it must be so. And shall I not drink the chalice that my Father has given me? (Mt. 26,50 and parallels).

How Jesus rebukes Peter with meekness and makes him atone for his three denials.

When they had eaten, Jesus said to Simon Peter: Simon, son of John, do you love me more than these? He answered: yes Lord, you know that I love you. Jesus said: feed my lambs. He said again: Simon, son of John, do you love me? He answered: Yes, Lord, you know that I love you. Jesus said: Feed my lambs. A third time he said to him: Simon, son of John, do you love me? Peter was saddened that he would have asked him a third time: do you love me? He answered: you know all thing, Lord, you know that I love you. Jesus said to him: feed my sheep. Truly, I tell you, when you were young, you put on your own belt and went where you wished; but when you are old, you will stretch out your hands and another will tie you and lead you where you would not go (Jn. 21, 15).

Jesus Christ's instructions to his apostles on meekness.

Behold, I am sending you like sheep among wolves. Be prudent as serpents and simple as doves (Mt. 10,16). You have heard it said: an eye for an eye and a tooth for a tooth, but I tell you, do not resist evil. If somebody strikes you on the right cheek, offer him the other cheek to strike, and if anyone would bring you to court to take your tunic, offer him your coat as well, and if anyone would force you to go one mile, go two miles with him (Mt. 5,38). You have heard it said to the elders: you shall not kill, and the one who has killed will be subject to judgement; but I say to you that whoever is angry with his brother will be subject to judgement, and whoever will have called his brother 'raca' will be brought before the council and the one who will have called him fool will be subject to the fire of Gehenna (Mt. 5,21).

Graces, favors reserved for those who are meek.

Blessed are the meek for they shall possess the earth (Mt. 5,4).

Summary of Our Lord Jesus Christ's doctrine and teaching on meekness.

We see by these examples and words of Our Lord Jesus Christ that:

He wants us to know, above all, that he is meek and humble of heart.
He calls everybody to himself so that they may benefit from his meekness.
The Spirit of God rested on him and communicated his meekness to him.
God found him so meek and so lovable that he was well pleased in him.

| In what does meekness consist? | in not arguing, not shouting, not making one's voice heard on the public square, not breaking the crushed reed, not quenching the smoking wick, not being sad or turbulent. | 376 |

Explanation of these words[6].

He will not argue.
He comes to proclaim justice to the nations. He proclaims it with authority and meekness, est, est, non, non[7], everything else comes from the evil one. From arguments there always flow bitterness, animosity, attachment to one's own ideas. All that comes from the evil one and is totally opposed to the spirit of God who is calm and is never troubled and always maintains peace, meekness and serenity.

He does not shout
Meekness in his voice. In his mouth there shall be no outbursts, useless shouts, words of anger; but his voice will always be meek, calm, peaceful, moderated. The spirit of God is not in shouts, noise, outbursts; the noise passes and leaves nothing behind. The spirit of God is in the thoughts, doctrine and virtues; virtus de illo exibat[8]. God's work is done in serenity, peace, meekness. To do without noise, brilliance. Goodness does not make any noise, and noise does not do any good.

Nobody will hear his voice on the public square.
He will not go to the public square to make noice and attract people. He will attract everybody to himself by meekness and not with noise, racket, posters and all these human means that are opposed to the spirit of God which is a meek, serene, peaceful spirit.

He will not crush the broken reed 377

In the natural sense

His manner will be so meek that he will break nothing, not even half broken things. On the contrary, the one who is brusque breaks everything; he acts roughly, he walks hurriedly, he upset, he breaks, he tears.

In the figurative sense

His meekness with sick bodies and souls that, on touching them, treating them, will cause them no harm but, on the contrary, he will comfort them. The one who is brusque does harm, increases the harm; he lacks concern.

---

[6] Manuscript XII 331 only gives the titles; the commentary is taken from Ms XII 352.

[7] Cf. Let your language be yes, yes, no, no. (Mt. 5,37).

[8] A strength came out of him (Lk. 6, 19).

He will not quench the smoking wick.
He will bear the discomforts of life without complaining; he will act with so much attention and meekness that he will rekindle the almost extinguished fire.

He will bear the little inconveniences from the neighbor without complaining. He will not extinquish the small spark of faith and love that is still burning in the neighbor but he will act with such concern and meekness that he will rekindle and revive it, give back grace life. Those who are brusque and impetuous extinguish the spark of faith. What attention, what meekness we must have with souls!

He will be neither sad nor turbulent

Meekness will be etched on his face which will not be sad or turbulent. His face will be meek, affable; everything in him will breathe amiability, attraction and souls will go to him with confidence and joy. A sad, stern mien repels. We must make those sad, stern, austere airs disappear. We must also avoid being turbulent, agitated, hurried, running here and there; this agitation, hurriedness is again contrary to meekness and repels people.

And the nations will hope in him.

How meek he is with his apostles[9].
He only tells them things gradually.
In the beginning, he does not ask things too painful to nature.
He teaches them with what attention they must act with others.
He condemns the severity of the Pharisees who accuse the apostles of sinning because they crushed some grain on a Sabbath day, being hungry...
His principle of conduct is: I want mercy, not sacrifice.
He reproaches the Pharisees of wanting to impose on others an unbearable burden that they themselves would not carry.
He rebukes the apostles who lack meekness toward the little children.
He rebukes James and John who want to call fire down on a Samaritan village.
He receives Judas with meekness.
He reprimands Peter when he strikes with the sword.
How he makes Peter atone for his three denials.
He wants us to carry meekness to the point of being like lambs and not resisting evil, to presenting the left cheek when we are struck on the right, to giving our cloak rather than going to court for it, going two miles with the one who would force us to go one, to never being angry, to not saying any insulting or wounding words.

---

[9] Here Father Chevrier continues the summary of the Gospel begun above (p.328).

Conclusion. To the one who acts like this, God promises the earth.

Rules of conduct with regard to the virtue of meekness.

To conform our conduct to this spirit of meekness that we see in Jesus Christ, we often remind ourselves that meekness is a virtue which is particularly pleasing to God and attracts souls.
We will avoid arguing with anybody; raising our voice when speaking, walking noisily and hurriedly.
We will treat all things with attention and meekness in order to break, crush, upset nothing; support the discomforts of life and also those caused by the neighbor.
We will avoid all bursque words or actions to spare the weak.
We will maintain a joyful and affable face with everybody.
We will not impose on others a burden too heavy or unbearable.
We will pay attention to each person in particular.
We will receive everybody with goodness and meekness.
We will never hit anybody.
We will not harm anybody.
We will look upon ourselves as lambs among wolves.
We will carry meekness to the point of not resisting evil, presenting the left cheek to the one who strikes the right, being stripped of our cloak, walking two miles with the one who would force us to go one, never pronouncing an insulting or wounding word.
May God help us to practice this beautiful virtue.
Meekness is opposed to all bitterness, impetuosity, brusqueness, words, threats, anger, etc..
Meekness is a virtue that bears everything from the neighbor, without becoming angry and bitter and makes nobody bear anything.

Patient. Knows how to suffer.

4. Follow me in my humility[1] 381

---
[1] Ms XII 391 to 410.

Jesus said, "I am meek and humble of heart"[2]. There is no meekness without humility, that is evident. Besides, Jesus expresses himself in the Jewish manner which likes to say the same thing with two different words.
Here we have an abundant study of the Gospel and St. Paul that Father Chevrier did not have the time to put in perfect order.
Jesus frequently called the apostles to humility. Therefore that is addressed also to priests and to all those who are sent in the name of Christ.
This humility is that of Jesus, Son of God, convinced of his mission and happy to be man among men. He loved that kind of life[3]. It is the humility of the one sent by Christ to the poor who will chose the company of the poor and sinners, not by force but by attraction and love[4].

---

[2] Mt. 11, 29.
[3] Ms XII 381; cf. Prov. 8, 31.
[4] P. 352.

Our Lord Jesus Christ's teaching on humility.	See the examples of Our Lord's humility [p. 342][5]	385

We must not act to be seen by men.   Mt. 6,1.
Beware of practicing your piety before men
in order to be seen by them; for then you will have no reward from your Father who is in heaven.

His justice, his religious actions.   Thus, when you give alms, sound no trumpet before you, as the hypocrites do in the synagogue and in the street, that they may be praised by men. Truly, I say to you, they have their reward. But when you give alms, do not let your left hand know what your right hand is doing, so that your alms may be in secret; and your Father who sees in secret will reward you. And when you pray, you must not be like the hypocrite; for they love to stand and pray in the synagogues and at the street corners, that they may be seen by men.
Truly, I say to you they have their reward. But when you pray, go into your room and shut the door and pray to your Father who is in secret; and your Father who sees in secret will reward you. When you fast, do not become sad like the hypocrites, for they disfigure their faces to show men that they are fasting. In truth, I tell you, they have received their reward. As for you, when you fast, perfume your head and wash your face so that your fast will not be seen by men, but your father who is present in hidden things and your father who sees hidden things will repay you.

We must chose the last place.	Lk. 14,7	386
	Now Jesus told a parable to those who were invited,	

when he marked how they chose the places of honor, saying to them. When you are invited by any one to a marriage feat, do not sit down in a place of honor, lest a more eminent man than you be invited by him; and he who invited you both will come and say to you, Give place to this man, and then you will begin with shame to take the lowest place. But when you are invited, go and sit in the lowest place, so that when your host comes he may say to you, Friend, go up higher; then you will be honored in the presence of all who sit at table with you. For every one who exalts himself will be humbled, and he who humbles himself will be exalted. Always *take the last place*, in a spirit of *humility*, thinking that the others are worth more than us and are more worthy than us. For God alone sees and knows men and the interior. Those titles of dignity are nothing before God. *Through charity*: leaving for others

---

[5] Father Chevrier added this note, thinking that it would have been better to put Christ's example before his teaching.

the more convenient, the most comfortable, the most agreeable places, where we can see better...; please our neighbor. Our Lord condemns this eagerness to be well placed; we run to be first, choose... in every place.

Choose the last place on earth to have the first place in heaven.

In the age to come, it will be likewise: many who were first will be last and many who were last shall be first (Mt. 19,30; Mk.10, 31).

Our Lord says this of those who will have left all on earth for him, those who will have been the last in the world, humiliated, scorned; who will have put themselves in the last place in the world, according to the world; they will be first in heaven.

Mt. 23,1.

Then said Jesus to the crowds and to his disciples, The Scribes and the Pharisees sit on Moses' seat; so practice and observe whatever they tell you, but do not practice. They bind heavy burdens, hard to bear, and lay them on men's shoulders; but they themselves will not move them with their finger. They do all their deeds to be seen by men.

Avoid showing off in nice clothes, appearing, showing off, taking the first places.

Beware of the Scribes who like to walk around in long robes, they make their phylacteries broad and their fringes long, and they love the places of honor at feasts,

387 **being greeted,**

and salutations in the market place.

loving names and titles.

And being called Rabbi by men. They eat up the widow's goods

under the pretext of long prayers; they make believe that they say long prayers. Those men will undergo a more rigorous judgement, a more severe condemnation (Mt. 23,14).

Avoid titles of honor, do not accept the title of father or teacher; if we are called thus, think that there is only one Father in heaven and one teacher, Jesus Christ.

But you are not to be called rabbi, for you have one teacher and you are all brethren. And call no man your father on earth, for you have one Father who is in heaven. Neither be called masters, for you have one master, the Christ. He who is greatest among you shall be your servant;

whoever exalts himself will be humbled and whoever humbles himself will be exalted.

It is better to be perecuted, humiliated than to be praised and applauded.

Woe to you when men praise you and speak well of you (Lk. 6,26). Blessed are you when men hate you, and when they exclude you and revile you and cast out your name because of the Son of man (Lk. 6,22).

Parable of the Pharisee and the Publican.

Jesus told that parable to a few who thought of themselves as being just, and who despised other.

Two men went up to the temple to pray: one was a Pharisee, the other was a Publican.

he compares himself to others.

The Pharisee stood and prayed thus within himself:

God, I thank you that I am not like other men, extortioners, unjust, adulterers, or even like this Publican.

He is pleased with what he does, he rests on his actions.

I fast twice a week, I pay tithes of all that I get. But the tax collector, standing far off, would not even lift up his eyes to heaven,

but beat his breast, saying, God, be merciful to me, a sinner. I tell you, this man went down to his house justified, rather than the other; for everyone who exalts himself will be humbled, but he who humbles himself will be exalted. (Lk.18,10).

We are only useless servants.

Will any one of you, who has a servant ploughing or keeping sheep, say to him when he has come in from the field,

Come at once and sit down at table? Will he not rather say to him, prepare supper for me, and gird yourself and serve me, till I eat and drink, then you may eat and drink. Does he thank the servant because he did what was commanded? I do not think so. So you also, when you have done all that is commanded you, say, We are unworthy servants; we have only done what was our duty (Lk. 17,7).

Do not take pride in your power.

The seventy two returned with joy, saying, Lord, even the demons are subject to us in your name!

And he said to them, I saw Satan fall like lightening from heaven. Behold, I have given you authority to tread upon serpents and scorpions, and over all the power of the enemy; and nothing shall hurt you. Nevertheles do not rejoice in this, that the spirits are subject to you; but rejoice that your names are written in heaven (Lk. 10,17).

Jesus' answer to James and John who ask to be first in his kingdom.

The mother of the sons of Zebedee approached Jesus with her sons and, doing him homage, asked for something. Jesus said: What do you want?

Request of a natural mother[6]

She said: Command that my two sons here be seated, one on your right and the other on your left, in your kingdom.

Ruse of the apotles.

James and John, sons of Zebedee, approach Jesus saying: Master, we would like you to do what we ask of you. But he said to them: What do you want me to do for you.

terrestrial ideas, glory.

They said: grant that we may sit, one on your right and the other on your left, when you are in your glory. But Jesus said to them: You do not know what you are asking. Can you drink of the chalice of which I drink? or are you baptized of the same baptism? They answered: we can.

sufferings.

But Jesus told them: in truth, you will drink of my chalice,

death.

and you will be baptized of the same baptism.

But to sit at my right hand and at my left is not mine to grant, but it is for those for whom it has been prepared by my Father. And when the ten heard it, they were indignant at the two brothers. But Jesus called them to him and told them:

How we must be first among our brothers.

You know that the rulers of the Gentiles lord it over them, and their great men exercise authority over them.

---

[6] Request of a mother who remains on the natural level.

difference. It shall not be so among you; but whoever would be great among you must be your servant, and whoever would be first among you must be your slave; even as the Son of man came not to be served but to serve, and to give his life in ransom for many (Mt.20, 24).

The things of God, hidden to the wise of this age, are revealed to the little ones and the humble.

At that time, that is, after the diciples had returned from their mission and were rejoicing that the demons were subject to them, in the name of Jesus. Jesus rejoiced in the Spirit and said: I thank you Father, Lord of heaven and earth, that you have hidden these things from the wise and understanding and revealed them to babes; yea, Father, for such was your gracious will. All things have been delivered to me by my Father; and no one knows who the Son is except the Father, and who is the Father except the Son and anyone to whom the Son chooses to reveal him (Lk. 10,21). Take my yoke upon you and learn of me that I am meek and humble of heart.

Jesus teaches his apostles in what primacy and pre-eminence among them should consist.

A dispute also arose among them, which of them was to be regarded as the greatest. And he said to them, the kings of the Gentiles exercise lordship over them, and those in authority over them are called benefactors. But not so with you; rather let the greatest among you become as the youngest, and the leader as one who serves. For which is the greater, one who sits at table, or one who serves? Is it not the one who sits at table? But I am among you as one who serves. You are those who have continued with me in my trials (Lk. 22,24).

Lesson in humility that Our Lord gives to his apostles who were disputing precedence.

And an argument arose among them as to which of them was the greatest. But Jesus, seeing their thoughts, when they were in the house he asked them: What were you discussing on the road? But they kept silent because they had been discussing who was the greatest among them. And sitting down, he called the twelve to him and the disciples approached Jesus and said: Who do you think is the greatest in the kingdom of heaven? and he said to them: If anyone wants to be first, let him be last and the servant of all. And he took a child and put him by his side and said to them:

We must become like little children. Truly, I tell you, if you are not changed and do not become like little children, you will not enter the kingdom of heaven.
Therefore whoever lowers himself like this child, he is the greatest in the kingdom of heaven, and whoever receives in my name a child like this, receives me; and whoever receives me receives not me but the one who sent me. For the one who is the least, humble among you is the greatest (Lk. 9,46)[7].

How Our Lord Jesus Christ practiced humility.

In his incarnation.
The Word became flesh and dwelt among us (Jn. 1,14).
He emptied himself, taking the form and nature of a slave and becoming like men, being recognized as a man by all that showed of him exteriorly (Phil. 2,7).

In his birth.
And when they were in Bethlehem and the days were accomplished, she gave birth to her first born and wrapped him in swaddling clothes and laid him in a manger because there was no place for them in the inn. The angel said to the shepherds; today, in the city of David, is born to you a Savior who is Christ, the Lord; and this will be a sign: you will find a child wrapped in swaddling clothes, lying in a manger. There is nothing great in this birth, nothing to flatter self love, vanity; nothing that attracts glory. On the contrary, everything is small, contemptible, unworthy; he is rejected, the scum of the earth, the trash in the street[8].
That is where the eternal Word was born.

In his circumcision.
He was circumcised on the eighth day and was given the name of Jesus.
He takes the mark of sinners: he submits to this law of sin[9].

His presentation.
Like the poor, without fanfare, without noise, poor parents, offering of the poor, mixed with everybody. Mary is mixed with the other women and receives the blessing of ordinary women.

---

[7] Ms XII 20 - The more we make ourselves little, the greater we are.
[8] The tone is a bit exaggerated.
[9] Ms XII 282 - No privileges, no exemption, the common law.

Flight into Egypt. He flees like a powerless, defenseless man, no opposition.
What a humiliation to flee before a man, what a sign of weakness, fear, dread. He does not resist: meekness and humility.

His hidden life in Nazareth. In work and obedience. He was submitted to them To be submitted to inferiors,
to pass for a child, ignorant, to have to be minded, commanded, receive lessons, orders from a man; he who commands all of nature, master of nature.

He passes for the son of Joseph. He, the Son of God, conceived by the Holy Spirit, eternal Word, how hidden is his dignity!
The Son of God passes for the son of man, the son of the carpenter. What a lesson for those who hold to their titles and dignity! He asks for neither grace nor privilege; he acted like an ordinary man.

He is baptized by John. 392

Jesus goes to John, his inferior, he recognizes and respects John's ministry although it is inferior to his.

It happened that, while all the people were receiving John's baptism, Jesus came from Nazareth, a city in Galilee, to be baptized by John in the Jordan. But John objected saying, It is I who should be baptized by you, and you come to me!

He does not disdain the grace that comes from John.

And Jesus said to him: Leave it for now.

He mixes with sinners.
He receives the baptism of sinners.

Everything that is just and good must be accomplished.

For thus must we accomplish everything that is just.

Good example. How God honors him afterwards!

He also praises St. John; later, he is not afraid to minimize his ministry to heighten that of John.	So he consented and Jesus was baptized by John in the Jordan and, during his prayer, dove, voice from heaven (Mk. 1,9).

He goes to the desert to fast and be tempted by the devil.

The Holy Spirit led him to the wilderness.
    And Jesus, full of the Holy Spirit, came out of the Jordan and was immediately led by the Spirit to the wilderness to be tempted by the devil. He was with the animals, and he was among the animals.

And he was hungry.	And when he had fasted for forty days and forty nights, he was hungry.
What a humiliation to be tempted by an inferior who comes to see what you are, try to force you, set traps, incite to evil, see if you are able to do anything.	And the tempter, coming close, said: If you are the Son of God, order that these stones be changed into bread. And Jesus said, man does not live by bread alone but by every word that comes out of the mouth of God.
393 Jesus does not show what he is, he does nothing spectacular; he does not answer anything that might attract glory to himself, he doesn't boast of his titles; he does not show his glory; he does not asks his Father for extraordinary things for himself.	Jesus begins his great mission with three great acts of humility: baptism fast temptation, trial he has to be tried.

There was no place for them in the inn[10].

He hides when he does a good act.

After having cured the paralytic at the pool, Jesus withdrew from the crowd. The one who had been cured did not know who he was, for Jesus had withdrawn from the crowd (Jn. 5,13).

---

[10] We do not see why this phrase is noted here. Father Chevrier must have had a thought which he did not want to lose, then forgot to cross it off. Perhaps he saw the refusal of privileges.

He forbids the ones he has cured to speak of it to anybody.	Having cured two blind men, Jesus forbade them strongly to speak of it, telling them,

see that no one knows it (Mt. 9,30). Having cured a leper, he forbade him to speak of it to anyone (Lk. 5,14). After raising Jairus's daughter, he strongly commanded that no one should know about it (Mk. 5,43).

He goes apart to cure the deaf mute.	When Our Lord had cured the deaf mute that he had taken apart from the crowd,

after he had said Ephpheta and the man was cured, he forbade those who were there *praecepit eis*, from telling it to anyone; but the more he forbade it, the more they published it (Mk. 7,36).

He even seeks to minimize the glory of his miracles.	Jesus was on his way to Jairus' house to heal his daughter when they came from the ruler's house to say,

do not trouble the Master, your daughter is dead. However, Jesus ignored them and going with his three disciples, entered the house and said: Why do you make so much noise and why do you weep? *This girl is not dead but sleeping.* And they laughed at him. But he put them all outside and took the child's father and mother and those who were with him and taking her by the hand he said to her, Little girl, I say to you arise. And immediately, the girl got up and walked, and he strictly charged *them that no one should know of this* (Mk. 5,36).

394

He forbids his apostles to speak of his tranfiguration until after his death.	After the tranfiguration, when the apotles were coming down from the mountain,

Jesus commanded them saying: Do not speak of what you have seen until the Son of man is risen from the dead (Mt. 17,9).

He even forbids his apostles to say that he is the Christ.	When Peter had made his profession of faith and said: I believe that you are the Christ,

the Son of the living God, and Jesus had given him the keys of the kingdom, he forbade his disciples to tell anyone that he was Jesus, the Christ (Mt. 16,20).

He withdraws from the crowd that is admiring him and goes to the wilderness to pray.	As his reputation was spreading more and more, the people came in crowds to hear him and be healed. But he withdrew to the wilderness to pray (Lk. 5,15).

When people are in admiration of him, he speaks of his passion.	After his miracles, all were astonished at the great power of God in him

and when they were in admiration at all that Jesus did, he said to his disciples: Let these words sink into your ears, for the Son of man is to be delivered into the hands of men (Lk. 9,43; Mt. 16,21).

He hides his glorious name and titles.	He hides his glorious name and title to call himself simply the Son of man and the envoy of the Father.
He is not concerned about what is said of him.	
He does not answer the accusations against him.	Speaking of John, he said: John came neither eating bread nor drinking wine and they say:

he is a demon. The Son of man came drinking and eating like the others and they say: he is a glutton and a drunkard (Mt.11,19).

395
He makes the poor and sinners chosen companions.	The Scribes and Pharisees reproached Jesus for eating with publicans and sinners and Jesus told them:

It is not those who are well who have need of the doctor, but those who are sick (Lk. 5,31). He goes to the house of Zachaeus, the publican. He goes to be baptized with sinners. He is the friend of publicans and people of evil lives, said the scribes and pharisees (Mt.11,19).

He does not accept the glory of men.

He does not receive glory from men.	I do not receive my glory from men (Jn.5,41).
He does not seek his own glory.	I do not seek my own glory.
He leaves his glory to his Father.	Another seeks it.
and judging what is to be done.	and he will be the judge (Jn. 8,50).
He says that anything he might say for his glory is nothing.	If I glorify myself, my glory is nothing,

that his Father alone can glorify.	it is my Father who glorifies me (Jn.8,54).
He attributes to his Father the good works that he does.	Having proved his divinity to the Jews, Our Lord tells them: I have shown you many good works from the Father, for which of those do you stone me? (Jn. 10,32).
He considers himself the servant of everyone.	Who is the greatest, the one who is at table or the one who serves? Is it not the one who is at table?

Yet, I am among you as one who serves (Lk. 22,27). The one who would be the greatest among you, let him be your slave; as the Son of man has not come to be served but to serve (Mt. 20, 27).

Jesus washes the feet of his apostles.	At the Last Supper, Jesus rose from table, took off his cloak,

tied a towel around his waist, and pouring some water in a basin, began to wash the feet of his apostles and to dry them with the towel around his waist (Jn. 13, 4).

396

He teaches them that they should do the same to others.	When he had washed their feet, and taken his garment and resumed his place, he said to them,

do you know what I have done? You call me teacher and Lord, and you are right, for so I am. If then, I your Lord and teacher, have washed your feet, you also ought to wash one another's feet. For I have given you an example, that you also should do as I have done to you.

The servant is not greater than his master.	Truly, truly, I say to you, a servant is not greater than his master;

nor is he who is sent greater than the one who sent him. If you know these things, blessed are you if you do them (Jn. 13,16).

Jesus prepares the meal on the shore.	The apostles had worked all night and taken nothing.

After the miraculous catch, they came ashore and saw a fire and fish and bread on it. Jesus told them; bring here some of the fish that you have just caught. Then Jesus told them: Come and eat. Jesus took some bread and gave it to them as well as some fish (Jn. 21,9).

The humiliations of the crib,

of the passion.

397 St. Paul's teaching on humility.

We have received everything from God.	What have you that you did not receive from God?

If then you received it from God, why do you boast as if you had not received it from him (1 Cor. 4,7).

Of ourselves, not even able to form a good thought.	Of ourselves, we are not even able to have a good thought, but God makes us able (2Cor.3,5).
Why God chooses what is least in the world to accomplish his work.	But God chose *what is foolish* in the world to shame the wise, God chose *what is weak* in the world to shame the strong,

God chose *what is low and despised* in the world, even things *that are not*, to bring to nothing things that are, so that no human being might boast in the presence of God (1 Cor. 1,27).

We must only boast in the Lord.	Let the one who boasts, boast in the Lord.
Our glory is nothing.	For it is not the man who commends himself who is accepted, but the man whom the Lord commends (2 Cor. 10,17).

398 | **It is God who gives growth.** | I planted, Apollos watered, but God gave the growth. |
|---|---|

So neither he who plants nor he who waters is anything, but only God who gives the growth and *who is all* (1 Cor.3,7).

To lower ourselves in our mind to the most humble persons.	Live in harmony with one another, with the same sentiments and affection;

do not be haughty but associate with the lowly; never be conceited, but lower yourselves to the most humble persons.

and not be wise in our own eyes.	And do not be wise in your own eyes (Rom. 12,16).
Be subject to others.	Be subject to one another in a truly spiritual love, servite invicem (Gal. 5,13).

Do nothing in a spirit of contention or vain glory.

Think the others greater than us.	But that everyone, through humility, believe the others greater than himself (Philip. 2,3).
We are nothing.	If anyone thinks that he is something, he is mistaken, because he is nothing.
We must not compare oureslves to others or think ourselves greater than others because others may have fallen into some fault.	But let each one test his own work and he will find his own glory, that is, *in the merit of his own works* and not in others, in the comparisons he may make with others (Gal. 6,3).
Show honor and deference to one another.	Love one another with brotherly affection; outdo one another in showing honor.

Anticipate one another with marks of honor and deference (Rom. 12,10).

St. Paul warns us that knowledge puffs up.	St. Paul warns us that knowledge puffs up, love builds up.
That knowledge without charity is nothing.	If any one imagines that he knows something, when he does not have love,

he does not yet know how he ought to know (1 Cor. 8,1) nor how to use his knowledge; he does not know how to use his knowledge. 399

God is free to do what he wants; we should not murmur against God.	O man, who are you to argue with God? Does an earthen vessel say to the one who made it:

why did you make me? Does the potter not have the power to make a vessel for an honorable use and another for a shameful use out of the same mass of clay?

Examples of humility.

Abraham.	He calls himelf ashes and dust (Gen. 18,27)
David.	It is you who have made me (Ps. 118).
St. Paul.	I am the least of the apostles, and I am not worthy to be called an apostle because I persecuted the Church of God.

But it is through the grace of God that I am what I am and his grace has not been fruitless in me. I have worked more than the others, not I but the grace of God in me (1 Cor. 15,9). He is in a state of weakness, fear and trembling before the Corinthians (1 Cor. 2,3).

False humility.	People who feign humility but inside are full of deceit and pride (Eccli. 19,23).

Summary of Our Lord Jesus Christ's teaching on humility.

We must not do our actions, our justice, to be seen by men.
We must seek the last places through humility and charity.
Avoid showing off in nice clothes, fine manners.
Do not seek nor accept greetings, titles, flattering names, marks of esteem and respect.
Beware of the applause of men.
Do not put your trust in works or compare yourself to others.
Do not take pride in success; believe that we are useless servants.
Do not desire the first places.
In what manner we are to be the greatest.
Difference between being first among us and being first in the world.
We must become like little children; they are the greatest in the kingdom of heaven.
The Lord reveals himself to the little ones and the humble.

Examples of humility that Our Lord Jesus Christ gives us during his life.

In his incarnation.
In his birth.
In his presentation in the temple.
In his hidden life in Nazareth, where he passes for the son of Joseph the carpenter.

Throughout the beginning of his life, he follows the ordinary laws, he does not ask for graces or privileges or any exemption; the only thing he does not take is sin, in everything else he follows the ordinary laws.
He recognizes and honors the mission and ministry of John, his precursor, by being baptized by him.
He goes to the wilderness where he fasts and prays like a sinner and a poor person who needs grace.
He hides when he does a good action.
He forbids the sick to speak of their cure to anyone.
He often withdraws apart, when he can, to perform miracles.
He tries to minimize the glory of his miracles before performing them.
He forbids his apostles to speak of the transfiguration until after his death.
He even forbids the apostle to say that he is the Christ.
He withdraws for the crowd who admires him to go pray in the wilderness.
When everybody is in admiration of him, he speaks of his passion.
He hides his name and glorious titles to call himself only the Son of man.
He does not answer the accusations against him.
He takes the poor and sinners as his companions of predilection.
He does not accept the glory of men.
He does not take his glory from men.
He does not seek his glory.
He leaves the concern about his glory and the judgement of it to his Father.
All that he can do for his glory is nothing.
Only the Father can glorify him
He attributes to his Father the works he has done.
He considers himself as the servant of all.
He did not come to be served but to serve.
He washes the feet of his apostles.
He tells them that the servant is not greater than the master.
After his resurrection, he prepares the meal on the shore.
Humiliations of the passion.

St. Paul's teachings on humility.

We have received everything from God.
By ourselves, we are not able to have a good thought.
We must glory only in the Lord.
Our glory is nothing.
It is God who gives growth.
Not to be wise in our own eyes.
In our thoughts, we must lower ourselves to the most abject persons.
Be subject to one another, and believe the others above us.

Not to compare ourselves to others.
We are nothing.
Anticipate one another with marks of honor and deference.
Not be proud of our knowledge which only puffs up if it is not based on love.
God chooses what is poorest and smallest to accomplish his works.
God is our master, he does what he wants with us; we must beware of murmuring against him.

Examples of humility:
> Abraham
> David
> St. Paul
> the Saints.

402 **Practices**[11].

To follow Our Lord and imitate his humility.

We will choose, like him, what is most humble and poorest on earth.
We will ask Our Lord for this humility of heart, in order not to do it through constraint but through attraction and love. Humble of heart.
We will prefer the company of the poor and sinners.
We will hide all that might elevate us in the eyes of men.
We will hide in order to avoid glory and honors.
We will prefer the company of the poor and sinners.
We will hide all that might elevate us in the eyes of men.
We will hide in order to avoid glory and honors.
We will do nothing to make ourselves loved, known or glorified.
We will relate everything to God.
We will easily speak of what might lower or humiliate us.
We will not be afraid to perform the lowest and most humiliating actions.
We will support humiliations without complaining and in silence.
We will avoid boasting about anything, making our actions known to men.
We will fear nothing so much as praises and honors.
We will not accept any titles or flattering names.
We will always take the last places in the world and everywhere.
When we have done everything we should do, we will say to ourselves and aloud and sincerely: I am only a useless servant.
We will be very convinced that the servant is not greater than the master and if we want to be first in the heart of God and men, we must be the last, that is, their servant and slave.

---

[11] Manuscript XII 391 gives only the titles. Here we give the development in Ms XII 357.

Qui potest capere capiat[12].
Blessed shall you be if you know these things and practice them.

---

[12] Let he who can understand, understand.

5. Follow me
in my poverty[1]   403

---

[1] Ms XII 411-415.

The topic of poverty has already been dealt with in the chapter on the renunciation of the goods of the earth *to which we may refer*[2]. *Father Chevrier certainly had the intention or returning to this theme, but it seems that the definitive text never saw the light of day. Thus, in the text reproduced here, we find, under the title* Rules of poverty[3], *the draft of the various parts of* renunciation of the goods of the earth.

But the approach to the subject is very much in conformity with the general appearance of the last part of The True Disciple. *It is a peaceful, attentive, prolonged look at Jesus Christ, born poor, who lived poor, and who died poor, and all this for the love of poverty, through obedience to his Father and for love of us*[4].

405

---

[2] P. 241.
[3] P. 359.
[4] P. 359.

How Our Lord Jesus Christ practiced poverty.

It is the first example that Jesus gives us on entering into the world.

> He wished to be poor[5].
> He chose poor parents.
> He was born poor.
> Poverty was his distinctive trait.
> He put himself among the poor.
> He liked to be with the poor.
> He lived like the poor.
> He worked like the poor.
> He suffered like the poor.
> He was despised like the poor.
> He was homeless like the poor.
> He behaved like the poor.
> He lowered himself like the poor.
> He was hungry like the poor.
> He was thirsty like the poor.
> He was abandoned like the poor.
> He died like the poor.
> and all this for love of poverty,
> through obedience to his Father,
> for love of us.

He wished to be poor[6]

St. Paul tells us: You know the grace of Our Lord Jesus Christ, that though he was rich, yet for your sake he became poor, so that by his poverty you might become rich (2 Cor. 8,9).

He chose poor parents.

The angel Gabriel was sent by God to a virgin betrothed to a man named Joseph, of the house of David, and the virgin's name was Mary (Lk. 1,26).

---

[5] In the manuscript, each one of these phrases refers to another notebook whose study of the Gospel we reproduce on page 359-60. The handwriting of this notebook is not Father Chevrier's but he has touched it up and annotated it.

[6] Ms XII 219.

He was despised like the poor.
The Jews despised him and said: Is he not the son of the carpenter? Is not his mother Mary? And they were scandalized because of him (Mt. 13,55).

I was born poor.
Mary in Bethlehem. And her time was accomplished; she gave birth to her first born, wrapped him in swaddling clothes and laid him in a manger.

He was rebuffed like the poor.
Because there was no place for them in the inn (Lk. 2,7).

Poverty was my sign, my distinctive trait.
The angel said to the shepherds: this will be a sign for you, you will find a child wrapped in swaddling clothes and lying in a manger (Lk. 2,12).

I placed myself among the poor.
In choosing a poor mother. Through the family... through religious duty... Presentation... In a life always with the poor. It was the reproach of the Jews.

I lived like the poor.
In humility, meekness, without luxury, in work. I am poor and needy (Ps. 39,18). Crushed grain. From day to day. Mendicus et pauper[7].

I worked like the poor.
I am poor and at work since my youth (Ps. 87). He worked until the age of thirty to earn his living and obey God's command: You will work by the sweat of your brow.

He liked to be with the poor.

I suffered like the poor.
I am poor and suffering. (Ps. 69,30)

He was despised like the poor.
There was no place for them in the inn (Lk. 2,7). In propria venit et sui eum non receperunt (Jn. 1,11)[8].

---

[7] I am begging and poor (Ps. 39,18 Vulg.).

[8] He came among his own and his own did not receive him.

During my life, I was homeless like the poor.
To a scribe who says: Master, I will follow wherever you go, he answers: The foxes have their dens and the birds have their nests, but the Son of man has nowhere to lay his head (Mt. 8,19).

I behaved like the poor.
I am among you as one who serves (Lk. 22,27). The Son of man did not come to be served but to serve (Mt. 20,28).

I humiliated myself like the poor.
He washed the feet of his apostles (Jn. 13,5).

I was hungry like the poor.
In the wilderness, after his fast: esuriit he was hungry. In the morning, passing near a fig tree, he looked for some fruit, because he was hungry (Mt. 21,18). And one day passing near the wheat, his disciples ate some grain because they were hungry (Mt. 12,1).

I was thirsty like the poor.
On the cross, he said: *Sitio*. On the road, tired, he sat by Jacob's well and said: da mihi bibere[9]. Gall and vinegar on the Cross.

I was naked like the poor.
Before being nailed to the cross, and on the cross, he was stripped of his garments.

I was abandoned like the poor
On the cross he says: My Father, why have you abandoned me? And there is nobody to help him...

I died like the poor
On a plank, naked, stripped, abandoned, scorned.

And all that because I wanted it
St. Paul tells us: You know what has been the goodness of Our Lord Jesus Christ who, *rich though he was, became poor for love of us*, in order that we might become rich through his poverty (2 Cor. 8,9).
The devil comes to offer Jesus all the riches of the world, showing them to him and promising them to him, if he will only adore him. Jesus answers; Begone, Satan, for it is written, you shall worship the Lord your God and him only shall you serve (Mt. 4,8).

---

[9] Give me to drink (Jn. 4,7).

Through obedience to my Father
I did not come to do my will but that of my Father.

And for love of you
You know what has been the goodness of Our Lord Jesus Christ who, rich though he was, became poor for love of us, in order that we might become rich through his poverty (2 Cor. 8,9).

Our Lord Jesus Christ's teaching on poverty.

When Jesus sends his apostles into the world to preach and heal, he orders them:
- to give freely (Mt. 10,8).
- to have neither gold nor silver nor bag nor spare tunic, and to eat whatever would be given them (Lk. 9,1; Mt. 10,1).
- not to amass a treasure on earth (Mt. 6,19).
- to sell what they have and give it to the poor (Lk. 12,32).
- to carry poverty to the point of letting their coat go.
- to give to whoever asks.
- not to claim what has been taken away from them.
- to lend without hope of return, give to whoever asks (Lk. 6,27; Mt. 5,40).
- that detachment from everything is one of the essential conditions to be his true disciple (Lk. 14,3).
- when someone asks to follow him, he demands above all that they leave everything (Lk. 9,57).
- that, to be perfect, they must sell what they have, leave all the goods of the earth, follow Jesus Christ (Mt. 19,21).
- that it is impossible for a rich man, attached to goods, to really follow Jesus Christ (Mk. 10,21).
- that no one can follow two masters (Mt. 6,24).
- that God sees to feeding and clothing those who work for him (Mt. 6,25).
- that he has never let anyone who really works for him lack for anything (Lk. 22,35).
- he has promised it: Seek first the kingdom of God (Mt. 6,24).
- that he promised the hundredfold in this world and eternal life in the next to those who have left everything (Mk. 10,29).
- that happiness is attached to true poverty (Lk. 6,20).
- Our Lord cannot tolerate the least little trade in his Church (Jn. 2,15).
- we must be satisfied with what is necessary (Lk. 10,38).
- not even be concerned with money matters (Lk. 12,13).
- that only the poor man is truly happy, according to Our Lord (Mt. 5,3).

- Words of our Lord that can be the motto of the real poor (Jn. 17,10).

How Our Lord Jesus Christ practiced poverty himelf.
   (above)[10]

How the saint accomplished these prescriptions of the Divine Master.
  St. John the Baptist (Mt. 3)
  The early Christians (Acts 4,32).

Example of St. Paul.

- He evangelizes freely (1 Cor. 9,11).
- He gives up his rights in favor of the Gospel.
- He is not a burden to anyone (2 Cor. 12,14).
- He did not desire anybody's goods.
- He worked with his hands (Act 20,34).
- He apologizes for having preached freely, but he does not want to stop doing so because it is his glory (1 Cor. 9,15).
- He does not eat anybody's bread without having earned it.
- He does not even have a maid with him (1 Cor., 9,5).
- He bears all sorts of sufferings (1 Cor. 4,11; 2 Cor. 11,17).
- He makes himself all thing to all men (Phil. 4,11).
- He is satisfied with the necessary in food and clothing (1 Tim. 6,7).

---

[10] Father Chevrier refers to the beginning of the chapter (cf. p.359).

412 **Summary of the example and teachings of Our Lord Jesus Christ on Poverty**[11].

---

[11] Ms. XII-150; 432.

He did not eat anyone's bread without paying for it.

We did not eat anyone's bread without paying, but with toil and labor we worked night and day, that we might not burden any of you. It was not because we have not that right, but to give you in our conduct an example to imitate (2 Thes. 3,7).

We must work to earn our living and not live in idleness, spiritual work especially. People must not see a priest live in idleness, like the bourgeois who live off their income; but they must give the example of work and activity. Make rosaries, little objects of devotion, when we have time, and remember this duty to work. Little humble works, useful to the house, to give work and humility. Jesus worked (Ms XII 150).

What I ask of you, I practiced myself.

    I wished to be poor,
    I chose poor parents,
    I was born like the poor,
    poverty was my sign, my distinctive characteristic,
    I lived like the poor,
    I worked like the poor,
    I put myself among the poor,
    I suffered like the poor,
    I endured like the poor,
    I lacked shelter like the poor (exile),
    I behaved like the poor,
    I humiliated myself like the poor,
    I was thirsty like the poor,
    I was naked like the poor,
    I died like the poor,
    and all that because I wished it.
    As my Father has commanded me, so I do.
Quae placita sunt ei facio. (I always do what pleases him. Jn. 8,19) (Ms XII 432).

Rules of poverty.

We conform to the teaching and examples of Jesus Christ.

1. We renounce all worldly goods, in spirit and in heart.
2. We are satisfied with the necessary.
3. We give to whoever asks.
4. We do not become involved in temporal matters.
5. We ask nothing of anybody.
6. We will not worry about the future.
7. We count on God alone.

Life of the truly poor.

Truly, that is, he has chosen poverty through love of Our Lord,

> he is satisfied with very little (1 Tim. 6,7),
> he does not allow anything to go to waste (Jn. 6,12),
> he receives everything with gratitude (Lk, 10,7,8),
> he has great respect for what is given to him, respect for alms,
> he does not complain about anything (Phil, 4,11),
> he works to earn his living[12],

---

[12] Ms. XII 214.

He works with his hands to earn his living and he does not have ready money to give to workers.

St. Paul, does everything he can. I did not come to be served but to serve. He uses workmen only when he cannot do otherwise.

He hires people to serve him only in grave necessity and when he cannot do the work himself.

The poor person is a jack of all trades: carpenter, painter, tailor, mason; he does not always have workers at his service, like the bourgeois; he does not seek the most beautiful, the most well made; he does the best he can.

He does not travel in a carriages.

He does not have servants.

I did not come to be served but to serve.

He does not fear the most humble tasks.

Serves and washes feet, dishes, sweeping.

414
>he does not have servants,
>he does without everybody,
>he does all his housework,
>he hires workmen only in cases of necessity,
>he does not fear doing the most humble and poor tasks, the lowest,
>he shuns everything that smells of greatness, luxury and vanity (bourgeois),
>he renders service to everybody,
>he takes care of everything he has,
>he avoids profusion, prodigality, he makes no useless expense,
>he is sparing without being miserly.

Happiness to the poor[13].
Power to the poor...
Our Lord's promises to the poor (Mt. 5,3; Lk. 6,20; Mk. 10,29).
Conditions to share in these promises[14].

>He is not bourgeois.

[13] Ms XII 215.
Happines to the poor.

To have no desires is to be rich.	The godlines and moderation of the one who is satisfied with the necessities of life is a great wealth (1 Tim. 6,6).
	It is the desires that make one unhappy.
	Blessed are the poor in spirit for the kingdom of heaven is theirs (Mt. 5,3; Lk. 6,20).
[14] Ms XII - 5m p.54. Condition to have God's promise, the only condition is to seek first the kingdom of God.	Seek first the kingdom of God and its justice and the rest will be given to you (Mt. 6,35).
	God will certainly not give to the one who does nothing or who works for himself, to attract praise, esteem, acquire riches. But the one who seeks only God, sacrifices himself, renounces everything for God, to glorify God, make him loved: he is the one whom God take care of and to whom he gives his goods.

N.B. This commentary was not reproduced in the manuscript copies. It is not in Father Chevrier's handwriting, but somebody who worked for him whom we have been unable to identify. We are morally sure that the thought is Father Chevrier's.

6. Follow me in my charity[1]

---

[1] Ms XII 475-487.

In Father Chevrier's manuscript we find several titles for this chapter. In trying to find the order of succession, it seemed to us that the first attempts were entitled: Follow me in my charity for the neighbor[2]. *Then the title became:* Follow me in my love for men[3]. *And finally,* Follow me in my charity. *That last choice was probably made in a concern to hold more strictly to the words of Scripture. In fact, in the New Testament, we do not find the expression:* charity for the neighbor, *but we do find:* love for men[4], *and more often:* charity[5].

On the whole, it is a matter of the Gospel, pure and simple. A look at Jesus Christ, an attentive ear to his teaching, nothing else. We note in particular the concern to allow ourselves to be taught the motives that may direct us toward charity. In these motives, Father Chevrier does not choose the ones that seem most noble or those to which he would be more sensitive, he wants to give us all those that Jesus Christ gave us[6].

One of the manifestations of charity is highlighted more: compassion[7]. *There is even question of feelings of* tenderness[8]. *Of course, the whole context shows that we must not stop there, but Father Chevrier is clear-sighted. He has seen that often the grace of an active charity insinuates itself through compassion and that we are always tempted to harden ourselves because we have the presentiment that in accepting to be compassionate we may be drawn further.*

These pages make us understand better what renunciation of the heart[9] *consists in and the end to which it tends: to make us really more compassionate.*

In thinking of the house of the Prado where there lived some hundred boys and girls who were not the most restful, Father Chevrier summarized and concretized his thought as follows:

> We ask God to give us a great compassion for the poor and sinners, which is the basis of charity, and without this spiritual compassion, we will do nothing.
>
> We will excite this divine charity in us so that we may go meet the neighbor's miseries and, like Jesus Christ, say: Come to me. We will imitate Our Lord in his goodness toward children, calling them to him and giving them particular proofs of tenderness and affection. We will be mother and father to them, taking care of them with sincere affection to win their souls for God. When the occasion presents itself, we will receive our children's parents, as well as the poor, at our table, happy to serve them and show

---

[2] Ms XII 437.
[3] Ms XII 451.
[4] Titus, 3,4.
[5] 1 Cor. 13.
[6] P. 379.
[7] P. 373.
[8] Cf. p. 373, note 11.
[9] Cf. Pp. 209-210.

them our affection for them. We will be forgiving, remembering those words of the Master: I like mercy better than sacrifice, and that we must win hearts with love rather than rigidity and severity. We will give charity to all who ask for it, even if it is only a holy picture or a good word, remembering that word of St. Peter: I have neither gold nor silver, but what I have, I give you.

We never refuse to render service to anybody. We do so joyfully and happily, considering ourselves, in charity, as the servants of everybody.

Our motto of charity is this word of Our Lord's: Take and eat, considering ourselves as spiritual bread that is to nourish everybody through word, example and devotedness[10].

---

[10] Ms X 261-262.

| In studying the life of Jesus Christ, our divine model, we find first of all, that he felt in his heart a great compassion for the unfortunate. | Then, in those days, since the crowd [did not have anything to eat] (Mt.15,32), raising his eye, Jesus saw [a great multitude] (Jn. 6,5). Jesus went throughout the cities and villages (Mt. 9,35). And they were bringing a dead man to bury him (Lk.7,11). |

419

At Lazarus' death, Jesus was [deeply moved in his spirit] (Jn. 11,33).
The tears over Jerusalem (Lk. 19,41).
He calls Judas: My friend (Mt. 26,50).
He has compassion for the sinful woman at his feet (Lk. 7,38).
On the cross, he forgives his enemies (Lk. 23,34).
He looks with compassion upon all those who insult and scorn him. His compassion is the foundation of charity. It is the first sentiment that should take hold of our soul when we see anybody in trouble. The one who remains cold, insensitive at the sight of evil is incapable of any charity[11].

| **He called all the unfortunate to himself to comfort them.** | Come to me all you [who are weary](Mt. 11,28). You do not want to come to me [to have life] (Jn. 5,40). |

The will of my Father is that he who believes in the Son should have life (Jn. 6,40).
I am the way, the truth and the life (Jn. 14,6).
He who comes to me shall never [thirst] (Jn. 6,35).
I am the living bread (Jn. 6,35).
I am the resurrection and the life (Jn. 11,25).
He who believes in me [even though he die, shall live] (Jn. 11,25).

420

| **He welcomed everyone with meekness and charity.** | He receives the multitude (Jn. 6,5). He welcomed them all and restored them to health (Mt. 14,14). The sick were brought to him and he healed them (Mt. 15,30). |
| **The children.** | Children were brought to Jesus (Mt. 19,13 and par). |

---

[11] Ms XII 492 - What we must admire in Jesus Christ is the feeling of compassion and tenderness that takes hold of him at the sight of our troubles; that trouble in spirit that he experiences in himself; those tears that he sheds over us and the desire that he has to comfort us. It is the foundation of charity, it is the first sentiment that arises in our soul. Those who remain cold, insensitive at the sight of evil cannot have charity.

The poor.

You yourselves give them something to eat.

When it was evening (Mt. 14,15). I have pity on this crowd (Mk. 8,2). He was always with the poor; that was the reproach that the pharisees made him.

The sick.

A blind man sitting by the side of the road (Lk. 18,35).

In the evening, [after sunset] (Mk. 1,32).
He laid his hands on everyone (Lk. 4,40).
Jesus arrived in a level place, the crowd [followed him] (Lk. 6,17).
A deaf mute was brought to Jesus (Mk. 7,32).
Raising his eyes Jesus saw [a great crowd] (Jn. 6,5).
When he arrived in Bethsaida [a blind man was brought to him] (Mk. 8,22).
After he had cured the deaf mute [a] great crowd [came to him] (Mt. 15,29).
Jesus having gone to the sea with his [disciples] (Mk. 3,10).

Sinners

He eats with sinners and publicans (Mk. 2,15). He goes to Zacchaeus' house (Lk. 19,5).

He tolerates the sinful woman who kisses his feet (Lk. 7,37).
He does not condemn the adulterous woman (Jn. 8,11).
The Samaritan woman (Jn. 4,17).

He sends no one away without help and consolation.

All that my Father gives me will come to me (Jn. 6,37). The will of my Father who sent me (Jn. 6,39). The Son of man has come to save what was [lost] (Mt. 18,14; Lk. 19,10).

I have lost none of the ones you gave me (Jn. 18,9).
I have pity on those people for they [have been with me] for three days (Mk. 8,2).

He even sought out the unfortunate to comfort them.

Jesus went through all the cities and villages (Mt. 9,35). A ruler of the synagogue named Jairus (Lk. 8,41). The centurion (Mt. 8,7).

When he goes to the Sheep Gate pool, he asks [do you want to be healed?] (Jn. 5,6).
Ad hoc veni - ad hoc[12].

---

[12] That is why I came (Mk.1,38).

Comparison that he uses to make them understand his zeal and love.	Parable of the Good Shepherd who runs after the sheep (Lk. 15,3). The woman who has lost a coin (Lk. 15,8). The father of the prodigal son (Lk. 15,11)[13].

Parable of the king's wedding feast [no one came] (Mt. 22,1).

He did good in spite of men's jealousy and wickedness.	Jesus went into the synagogue [a man with a withered hand] (Lk. 6,6). And a woman who had an [infirmity] (Lk. 13,10).

A woman caught in adultery (Jn. 8,1).
The sinful woman (Lk. 7,37).
He goes to Zaccheaus' house even when he knows that the Pharisees will criticize him (Lk. 9,5).
Is your eye evil because I am good? (Mt. 20,15).

And he carries charity to the limit.	I am the good shepherd. The Good Shepherd gives his life (Jn. 10,11). No one can have a greater love [than to give his life for his friends] (Jn. 15,13).

422

That is why my Father loves me, because [I give my life]. (Jn. 10,17).
He took our sins upon himself. Ecce agnus Dei[14]. He took upon himself our infirmities (Mt. 8,17).
I must be baptized with a baptism and I burn with desire to see it accomplished (Lk. 12,50).
I have desired with great desire to eat [this Passover with you] (Lk. 22,15).
He loved to the point of supporting his apostles, washing the feet of his apotles, of becoming the servant of others. I did not come to be served but to serve (Mt. 20,28).
Take and eat, this is my body which will be given up for you. Take and drink, this is my blood which will be shed for the forgiveness of sins. He loved until the end (Jn. 13,1).
Father, forgive them, for they do not know what they do (Lk. 23,34).

---

[13] Ms XII 495 - The father of the prodigal son: He waited; his anxiety. He paced to and fro, he ran, he fell on his neck and embraced him. He hardly hears what the son says, he does not even answer to what is said. He orders the servants: Quick, the most beautiful garment, dress him, a ring, shoes; fatted calf, a feast. Rejoice, for my son here was dead and now he lives!

[14] Behold the lamb of God (Jn. 1,29).

Holy Father, keep in your name those [that you have given me] so that they may be one, like us (Jn. 17,11).
And after the resurrection, he prepares a meal on the shore (Jn. 21,9).
Aquae multae non potuerunt extingere caritatem. (Cant. 8,7)[15].
No one can have a greater love than to give his life for his friends (Jn. 15,13).

He invites us to do the same.	Love one another as I have loved you. What I command you is that [you love one another], that is how all will recognize [that you are my disciples] (Jn. 13,34).

Remain in my love (Jn. 15,9)[16]. Therefore be imitators of God as his children and walk in charity (Eph. 5,1).
He prays his Father so that we may all be one (Last Supper) (Jn. 17,21).
I have come to bring fire on the earth (Lk. 12,49).
Exemplum dedi vobis ut quemadmodum ego...[17]
The servant is not greater than the master (Jn. 13,16 and 15,20).
I have come to bring fire upon earth and how I wish it were already lit (Lk. 12,49).

423

Instructions that Jesus Christ gives us on charity.	In his sermon on the mount.
Not only must we not harm our neighbor, but we must not even become angry with him.	You have heard that it has been said to the elders: you shall not kill. But I say to you.. (Mt. 5,21).
We must not pronounce a word of insult or scorn against anyone.	Whoever says raca, fool to his brother (Mt. 5,22).
We must be reconciled with our brother before making an offering.	If you present your offering at the altar (Mt. 5,23).
Not even accept that others may have the least resentment against us.	If you present.... and there remember.... even if we are not at fault.

---

[15] The great waters were not able to quench love.

[16] Ms XII 493 - Remain in my love, he says to his apostles. How he prays that this charity may unite them all to himself and with one another. It is love that makes us leave everything for Jesus Christ: goods, family, parents, friends; that makes us renounce ourselves to follow Jesus Christ. Love is stronger than death.

[17] I have given you an example so that you may do as I have done (Jn. 13,15).

We must come to an agreement with our adversary.	Come to an agreement as soon as possible with your [adversary]...(Mt. 5,25).
Not even resist evil for fear of lacking charity or making others lack it.	You have heard it said: an eye for an eye... (Mt. 5,38).
Be ready to suffer everything rather than lack charity.	If anyone strikes you on the right cheek... (Mt. 5,39).
Give up one's cloak and coat rather than lose charity.	And to the one who would bring you to court... (Mt. 5,40).
Render service to everybody and even double it if they let you.	And whoever would force you to go one mile [step].... (Mt. 5,41).
Give to whoever asks and do not refuse the one who wants to borrow.	Give to whoever asks (Mt. 5,42) and do not refuse the one who wants [to borrow].
Be careful not to scorn anyone.	Be careful not to scorn even one [of these little ones] (Mt. 18,10).
Do good to everybody, even those we meet in the street.	The good Samaritan (Lk. 10,25)[18]. 424
Invite the poor and the lame at our table.	When you give a feast... (Lk. 12,14).
Judge no one.	And why do you see the straw... (Lk. 6,41)[19]. The light of the body is your eye (Lk. 11,34).

---

[18] Ms XII 489 - He got off his horse and went to that man. Compassion. He comes near, sees the wounds, pours oil and wine and binds the wounds; puts him on his mount, takes him to the inn and takes care of him during the day; pays the innkeeper, recommends his poor person and promises to pay and come see him.

[19] Ms XII 489 - Not to see evil in others. We see the sickness in others and we are more sick than they are. We want to correct others and we have more faults than they do.

Rebuke with meekness and charity.	If your brother has sinned against you, rebuke him (Lk. 17,3).
And always forgive.	If you brother has sinned, rebuke him; how many times [must I forgive] my brother who sins against me (Mt. 18,21).
Our charity must be greater than that of the Pharisees and sinners.	If your justice is not greater than that.... (Mt. 5,20).
For that, we must not be satisfied with loving those who love us.	If you love those who love you, [what reward will you have?] (Mt. 5,46).
With doing good to those who do good to us.	And if you do good to those who do good to you what merit [do you have?] (Lk. 6,33).
With lending to those who pay interest.	And if you lend to those from whom you expect... (Lk. 6,34).
With greeting those who greet us.	And if you only greet you brothers who [greet you...] (Mt. 5,47).
425 We must do more.	WE.
We must love our enemies.	And I say to you, love your enemies (Mt. 5,44).
Do good to those who hate us.	Do good to those who hate you (Lk. 6,27).
Bless those who curse us.	Bless those who curse you (Lk. 6,28).
Pray for those who persecute and calumniate us.	Pray for those who persecute you (Mt. 5,44).
Greet those who do not speak to us.	And if you only greet those who greet you (Mt. 5,47).

Anticipate those who have a grudge against us.

Lend without interest.	Lend without expecting any return.
Do good without expecting a reward.	Do good without expecting reward (Lk. 6,35).
Do good to the evil and the ungrateful.	You reward will be great and you will be the children of the Most High (Lk. 6,35).

To the just and the unjust.

and your reward will be great,

and we will be sons of the Most High,

and we will be perfect as our heavenly Father is perfect.

Finally treat everybody as we would like to be treated if we were in their place.	Do to others what you would like others to do to you (Mt. 7,12).
To make us practice this divine charity, Jesus Christ assures us that,	
God will use the same measure with us as we have used with others.	The same measure will be used with you as you have used with others (Lk. 6,38).
If we do not judge, we will not be judged.	Do not judge and you will not be judged (Lk. 6,37).
If we do not condemn, we will not be condemned.	Do not condemn and you will not be condemned (Lk. 6,37).

426

If we forgive, we will be forgiven.	Forgive and you will be forgiven (Lk. 6,37) for if you do not forgive men, [neither will your Father] (Mt. 6,15).

Parable of the servant who could not pay (Mt. 18,23). Forgive us our offenses as we [forgive]. Pater. And when you start to pray...[forgive..](Mk. 11,25). Blessed are the merciful for they [will obtain mercy].

If we give, it will be given to us.	Give and it will be given to you, good measure will be poured into your lap (Lk. 6,38).
If we want our prayers to be answered, we must hold nothing in our heart against anybody.	And when you go to pray, [forgive..] (Mk. 11,25).
That Our Lord considers done to himself all the good that we may have done to the least of his.	Christ's answer to the chosen ones who ask him: when did we feed, cloth you? (Mt. 25,37)

He who receives you, receives me (Mt. 10,40).
And the one who will have given to drink to one of these [little ones]...(Mt. 10,40).
Whoever will have given a glass of water...(Mt. 10,40).
Whatever you will have done to the least...(Mt. 25,40).
The one who receives you, receives me (Mt. 10,40).

427
On judgement day we will be judged mainly on charity.	And when the Son of man comes...(Mt. 25,31).
That charity is his commandment of predilection.	I give you a new commandment. What I command you is that you [love one another] Jn. 13,34).
That charity is the distinctive sign of his true disciple.	That is how all will know that you are my disciples (Jn. 13,35).

I am in them and you in me so that they [also may be in us] and that the world may know [that you have sent me] (Jn. 17,21).

That this commandment contains all the others.	A scribe, coming up to Our Lord... (Mk. 12,28). These two commandments contain all [the others].

The whole law is contained in this one precept (Mt. 22,40; Gal. 5,14).

That charity is the end of all the precepts.	The end of the precepts is charity that comes from a pure heart (1 Tim. 1,5).
And that before entrusting Peter with the government of the Church, he asks for nothing else but love.	When they had eaten, Jesus said to Simon.... (Jn. 21,15).
Charity is recognized by words and works.	A good tree does not bear [evil fruits] (Mt. 7,18).

Paul's teaching on charity. 428

He teaches us that charity is the most excellent of all virtues.	The scribe in the Gospel says so when he repeats what Jesus Christ had said;

that to love our neighbor as ourselves is worth more than holocausts and sacrifices (Mk. 12,33).

It is more excellent than the gift of tongues, than knowledge.	1 Cor. 13. If I spoke all the languages of men and angels... To speak well. Theology. To know all the languages.

Gospel. To be able to speak of spiritual things, preach,
    gift of tongues,
    gift of prophecy,
    gift of knowledge,
If I had the gift of prophecy; discernment, insight, counsel; penetrate mysteries and if I had all knowledge, mystery of nature and heaven.

more excellent than the gift of faith and miracles.	If I had all the faith possible...
more excellent than humanity that gives all its goods,	If I distributed my [goods]...
more excellent than poverty that strips itself of everything,	distributed all my goods,
more excellent than mortification,	If I would given my body to be burned by penance.
and martyrdom.	burned through martyrdom, when I have given my body to be burned in martyrdom.

Charity is patient. The word patient means to suffer, that is, that the one who has charity suffers without complaining the pains and annoyances of others.

It is meek. It is meek, that is, it does not make anyone suffer. What is meek is agreeable, good and does not annoy others. Those are the two main characteristic of charity: suffer what the others make us endure without complaining, and make no one suffer; be agreeable with everybody.

beneficial, It does good to others.

it is not envious,

nor reckless,

nor proud, Be subject to one another (Gal. 5,13).

nor hasty. James and John who want to call fire on the Samaritans (Lk. 9,52).

It is not ambitious,

it does not seek its own interests,

it does not become angry,

it does not think evil,

it does not rejoice in evil;

it rejoices in truth.

it bears all,

it believes all,

it hopes all,

it suffers all,

it will never pass.

We must all consider ourselves as forming one body whose soul and head is Jesus Christ and each one of us is a member. (1 Cor. 12,12).

Before all thing, we must have charity which is the true bond of perfection. (Col. 3,14)[20].

430

The end of the precepts is charity.	The end of the precepts is charity which comes from a pure heart and a good conscience (1 Tim. 1,5).

Thus, give to each one the tribute due him (Rom. 13,7).

In St. Paul we note the love of tenderness and affection.	2 Cor. 6,11-18; 7,2-3,11,2; 12,20. Phil. 1,3-8; 4,1-3. Gal. 4,19. 1 Thes. 1,7-12[21].
The love of zeal and solicitude.	Eph. 1,3-11; 1,15-18; 3,13-18. Phil. 1,2 2 Cor. 11,28-29; Col. 1,9-11; 11, 1-3.
and the love of sacrifice.	1Cor.,9,18-23; 10,33; 15,30-31. Phil.,1,22-25; 2,1-8; 11,17. 2 Cor.,5,1-2; 12,14-15.

St. Paul's exhortations on charity.

Pay all of them their due... owe no one anything except to love one another (Rom. 13,7).

I therefore, a prisoner for the Lord, beg you to lead a life worthy of the calling to which you have been called (Eph. 4,1).

---

[20] Ms XII 456 - Charity must be the principle of our actions, ruled by the Holy Spirit. Some begin their actions by examining, considering: compass, ruler...

If we begin with that, we never finish and we do nothing; we must begin with love and see first everything that may be useful, and then act. Knowledge, reasonings always restrict love, restrict actions.

[21] We give here the references from a parallel manuscript (XII 11 b).

If there is any consolation that I may expect of you, if there is any comfort..(Phil. 2,5).

431 Let us have eyes for one another to animate us in charity and good works (Heb. 10,24).
Be subject to one another in a truly spiritual charity (Gal. 5,13; 26).
May your charity be sincere without dissimulation (Rom. 12,9).
In all things practice humility and meekness (Eph. 4,2).
May all your actions be done with love (1 Cor. 16,13).
As children, be imitators of God (Eph. 5,1).
May the God of patience and consolation give you [grace] Rom. 15,5).
Be good to one another (Eph. 4,31; 5,1).
For, like in one body we have many members...(Rom. 12,4).
Put on [charity], as elect of God, holy and good (Col. 3,12).
Bear each other's burden (Gal. 6,2).
If anyone among you has fallen [in a fault]... (Gal. 6,1).
Let all bitterness, all anger, all recklessness [be rejected]...(Eph. 4,31).
Let each one give what he has decided to give (2 Cor. 9,7).
Everything is permitted but not everything builds (1 Cor. 10,23).
Therefore let us seek what may maintain peace (Rom. 14,19).
Receive and treat kindly the one who is still weak (Rom. 14,1).
Let no dishonest word be heard among you (Eph. 5,4).
Let us not judge one another (Rom. 14,13).
Let each of us please his neighbor (Rom. 15,1).
Renounce anger, bitterness, slander (Col. 3,8).
Therefore, why do you condemn you brother (Rom. 14,10).
Do not judge before hand (1 Cor. 4,5).
O man, who are you to condemn others (Rom. 2,1).
I beg you, my brothers, in the name of Jesus Christ (Gal. 5,3).
I fear that, when I come, I shall not find you such...(2 Cor. 12,20).
There is a diversity of gifts. Finally, my brothers, rejoice, be perfect (2 Cor. 11,13).

St. Peter's exhortations.

Above all, have a persevering charity (Pet. 4,8)
Make your souls pure by a loving obedience (1 Pet. 1,22).
Be hospitable without murmuring (1 Pet. 4,9).
So put away all malice and all guile and all insincerity (1 Pet. 2,1).
Let each one of you render service to the others according to [the graces received] (1 Pet. 4,10).

St. John's exhortations.

Let us love one another for love comes from God (1 Jn. 4,7).
God has shown his love for us (1 Jn. 4,9).
In the love that we have for our brothers we see that we have passed [from death to life] (1 Jn. 3,14).
My child, do not love in word or speech (1 Jn. 3,18).
A man who has worldly goods and who sees [his brother in need...] (1 Jn. 3,17).
The one who loves his brother is in light (1 Jn. 2,10,9).
Love one another. Those were his last words.

St. James' exhortations.

[If a brother or sister is naked and lacks food...] (Jas. 2,15).
Do not speak ill of one another (Jas. 4,11).
The tongue [no one can tame it] (Jas. 3,8).
If anyone thinks he is religious but does not bridle his tongue (Jas. 1,26).

Block your ears with thorns and do not listen to the malicious tongue. Put a door and a lock on your mouth (Eccli. 28,28).[22]
The whole multitude of the first Christians were of one heart and one soul (Acts 4,32).

---

[22] Translation from the Latin text. Our modern Bibles often give a rather different translation for the book of Ecclesiasticus.

433   Ms XII 470.

Rules of charity that a true disciple of Jesus Christ must observe.

According to the word and example of Our Lord Jesus Christ, we see that we must:
- never be angry with anyone,
- never speak a word of insult or scorn to anyone,
- never render evil for evil,
- not even resist evil,
- not fight with anyone, court case, quarrel, better to lose our goods rather than lose charity,
- be careful not to despise even one of the little ones,
- not see the straw in our brother's eye when we have a beam in ours; not try to remove the straw from our brother's eye when we have a beam in ours; we must first remove the beam from our eye before removing the straw from our brother's eye.
- A blind man cannot lead another blind man.
- Judge no one, condemn no one, think no evil of anyone.
- After Our Lord's example, we must feel in us a great compassion.

What we must feel in us.
- Call the unfortunate to us to comfort them.
- Feel in us that divine fire that Jesus came to bring to the earth: igne veni mittere.
- Like St. Paul, say: *caritas Christi urget nos*[23].
- Desire to spend our life for our neighbor, to give our life for him.
- I must be baptized with a baptism and I burn to see it accomplished.
- Feel in us that mission that has been given us to comfort and heal.
- Decry the lot of the unfortunate.

434   *What we must do.*
- Be reconciled with our enemy before going to the altar.
- Seek them out, even if we are not in the wrong.
- Not allow others to have the least resentment against us.
- Come to an agreement with our adversaries.
- Give to whoever asks; lend to the one in need; if a service is request, give double.
- Love our enemies; do good to those who hate us; bless those who curse us; pray for those who persecute and calumniate us.
- Do to others all the good that we would want them to do to us.
- Receive everyone with meeknes and charity: the children, poor, sick, sinners; send no one away without help; even seek out the unfortunate to comfort them.

---

[23] The love of Christ urges us.

- Do good, in spite of the jealousy and wickedness of men.
- Take care of the sick that we find on the road.
- Give dinner to the poor; invite them to our feasts.
- Run after the lost sheep.
- Rebuke our brother with prudence and charity when he falls into some fault.
- Forgive seventy times seven times.
- Not stumble on obstacles.

Our charity must be supernatural.
- Our charity must be greater than that of the people of the world.
- If sinners love those who love them, greet those who greet them, do good to those who are good to them, lend to those who pay interest,
- We must love our enemies, seek out those who wish us ill, greet those who do not speak to us, do good without expecting reward, lend without interest, do good to the good and the bad, the just and the unjust,
- And we will be the children of the Most High, and we will be perfect as our heavenly Father is perfect.

God will treat us as we have treated others.
- We must remember that God will use for us the same measure that we have used with others.
- If we do not judge, we will not be judged; if we do not condemn we will not be condemned; if we forgive we will be forgiven; if we give it will be given to us - much more than we may have given.
- If we want our prayers to be heard we must keep nothing against our neighbor in our heart.
- On judgement day we will be judge mainly on our charity to our neighbor.
- Jesus considers as done to himself whatever we may have done to the least of his little ones.
- Charity is his commandment of predilection,
- It is the mark of his true disciples,
- This commandment contains all the others,
- Before giving the government of the Church to Peter, Jesus Christ demanded only love.

Excellence of charity. 435
- We must remember that charity is the most excellent of all the virtues.
- That it is more excellent than knowledge, faith, poverty, penance.

Qualities of charity.
- Charity is meek and patient; it is not envious, rash, proud, hasty.

- It is not ambitious; it does not seek its interest; it does not become angry; it does not think evil; it does not rejoice in evil; it rejoices in truth, good.
- It endures all, believes all, hopes for all, suffers all, it will never end.

7. Follow me [437]
in my preaching[1]

---

[1] Ms XII 544-559.

To succeed in our life, to be useful to others, we must know what we have to do and the rest will fall in place. When an important thing is well done, the rest goes well also[2].
For Father Chevrier, it is very clear that the priest's great mission is to preach[3]. *The chapter:* Follow me in my preaching, *though unfinished, remains one of the capstones of* The True Disciple[4].
This view is admissible only if we understand the expressions: preaching, teach catechism, *in the sense of* making Jesus Christ known.
Are we not there for that and only that: to know Jesus Christ and his Father and to make him known to others?[5]
The study of the Gospel and St. Paul puts us first of all before the vastness of the ministry of the Word and the many forms that this ministry can take: Jesus preached everywhere and he preached every day[6].
Passing to concrete applications, Father Chevrier camps especially on two areas: catechism *and* the little missions[7]. *In conformity with what we know of him, he limits himself to what he has experienced.*
In the directives that he gives, there are the great ideas that should be retained.
For catechesim, *he does not present the teacher adapted to the various ages, as we would do today. He was concerned about adaptation to the social milieu, to the mentality of the children of the Prado, but he did it with the means of his time.*
Yet he follows the doctrinal principles that should guide all catechetical teaching. He does it with much simplicity but also much precision.
"This Catechism of the Prado, *so remarkable in its simple development, the abundance of pictures or comparisons, the depth of the examination of conscience, has lost none of its actuality. A master could easily transpose it into a 'Catechism for Today'*"[8].
The little missions *are a series of sermons generally called parish missions. The great models of this type of ministry remain those of the XVII century such as Vincent de Paul and his Congregation of the Mission, St. Grignion de Montfort, etc...*
Father Chevrier speaks of little missions. *That is because he renounces* all great and solemn preachings[9]. *According to him, this type of preaching cannot achieve the end*

---

[2] P. 264.
[3] P. 399.
[4] Cf. Pp.55-56 for indications for the study of the topic: The Word, and also p. 296.
[5] Lp n. 231, June 30, 1873.
[6] P. 393-394.
[7] P. 402.
[8] P. Broutin - Le mouvement catéchistique en France au XIX siècle. Nouvelle Revue Théologique, June 6, 1960. P. 632.
[9] Ms. X 275.

it *proposes: make sure that the poor who will come will feel at ease, familiarize them with the Gospel, with Christ. This is seen in the practical advice he gives: do not go into the pulpit, do not oblige people who came in furtively to come up to the front, find an atmosphere that is not intimidating, etc. He would have liked to do the same for the celebration of Mass. He had prepared a petition to the Pope to obtain permission to say Mass in the villages, during the missions, outside the parish church*[10].

We see also how the priest must follow Jesus Christ in his meekness, his humility, his charity, not only outside his ministry, as in preparation for this ministry, but in the exercise of his great function of priest.

The manuscript that we follow here is a copious extracts from Scripture. In fact, it contains all Jesus' preaching and therefore all the discourses contained in the Gospels. This transcription is not in Father Chervrier's handwritting and many pages have no annotations of his. We have chosen to reproduce only those texts written by Father Chevrier himself, giving simply the references of the passages that he comments.

---

[10] Ms X 164.

| It is his great mission. | In Nazareth, he goes into the synagogue (Lk. 4,16). | 441 |

He reads and explains Isaiah's prophecy concerning him: to evangelize the poor. Astonishment of the crowd: they were scandalized saying, we know his father and mother. Jesus Christ's answer: No one is prophet in his own country. They were angry, took him out to the brink of the mountain to throw him down. At the age of twelve, he remains in Jerusalem and teaches the doctors of the law. His answer to his mother (Lk. 1,41). To his apostles who were telling him that the people were looking for him he says: Let us go to the cities and towns so that I may teach, for that is why I came. The crowd wants to stop him because they do not leave him and he says: there are still other cities where I must evangelize the kingdom of God, for that is why I was sent (Lk. 4,42; Mk. 1,35).

| He went throughout the cities and towns. | From Nazareth he went to Capharnaum (Mt.4,13). Accomplishment of Isaiah's prophecy (Is.9). |

He begins to preach. He teaches in the synagogues. He says to his disciples: Let us go to the towns and cities so that I may preach there also, for that is why I came (Mk. 1,38; Mt. 4,23). They try to hold him back: there are still other cities, that is why I came. And he goes throughout Galilee, teaching and healing. He went throughout the cities and towns, preaching and healing (Mt. 9,35); to preach and heal, he does not separate the two actions. And the twelve were with him (Lk. 8,1). When he is expelled from Nazareth, he goes to the neighboring villages (Lk. 4,31).

| He preaches everywhere. | In the temple (Lk. 21,37). Every day in the temple (Lk. 19, 47; Mt. 21,14). |

In the synagogues (Lk. 4,15; Mk. 1,21; Mt. 9,35). He stops in a level place and preaches (Lk. 6,17). And raising his eyes to the multitude and his disciples said: Blessed are the poor! for the kingdom of God is theirs. Jesus went up on a mountain and preached to his disciples and the crowd (Mt. 5,1). On the road, he instructs the Samaritan woman (Jn. 4,4). He takes the occasion of the water to instruct her and speak to her of this living water which gives eternal life. Softly he rebukes her for her life; he instructs her on the manner of adoring God. He goes into Simon's boat and teaches the crowd from the boat (Lk. 5,3; Mt. 13,2). At table in the Pharisee's house (Lk. 11, 37). In houses (Mk. 2,2). On the shore (Mk. 2,13). By the sea. In a boat (Mk. 4,1). 442

| He preaches every day. | (Lk. 21,37; 19,47). |

He speaks with fidelity.   My doctrine is not of myself (Jn. 7,16). If anyone wants to put it into practice, they will see if it comes from God or if I speak of myself. He does not seek his glory. The one who believes in me does not believe in me but in God (Jn. 12,44). I did not speak of myself, but the one who sent me told me... I say what my Father has commanded me. I say what I have heard from my Father (Jn. 8,26). I speak as my Father has taught me. My Father is with me. I speak of what I have seen in my Father (Jn. 8,38).

He speaks with simplicity.   In all his discourses [on the mountain] (Mt. 5,7; Lk.6,20), we see no refinement or preliminaries; nothing that smells of study, research, effort, proclamation, care, high manners. Everything is simple in tone, words, bearing, manners; much doctrine and few words. With us it is the contrary. The comparisons are: salt, light, lamp, bird, lily, straw, beam, sheep, wolves, trees, thorns, briars, houses, the wind, rain, rock: all things that are easily understood. In his parables, all those things are visible, palpable:

the grain that is sown (Mt. 13,1)
the weeds (Mt. 13,366)
the mustard seed (Mk. 4,30)
the seed that grows by itself (Mk. 4,26)
the yeast (Lk. 13,20)
the hidden treasure (Mt. 13,44)
the precious pearl (Mt. 13,45)
the fisherman's net (Mt. 13,47)
the two sons (Mt. 21,28)
the prodigal son (Lk. 15,11)

He speaks with authority.   He bases himself on his Father's authority (Jn. 8,13 ff; Mt. 5,18, 20, 22, 28, 32, 34, 39; Mt. 7,29). What authority of language, what sublime doctrine reigns in this whole discourse [on the mountain]. We need only read it to note that it is a Master who speaks[11].

He speaks firmly.   Jn. 18,37). He rebukes the Scribes and Pharisees on their false maxims (Mt. 15,3).

---

[11] These two sentences of commentary are not in Father Chevrier's handwriting but no doubt copied from another preparatory text drawn up by Father himself.

He calls them hypocrites (Mt. 15,7). To Herod (Lk. 13,32). He rebukes the Pharisees who were observing him (Lk. 14,1; Mt. 22,18; Mt. 23,2).

It is the great mission that Jesus Christ confers on his apostles. Jesus Christ chose twelve men to be with him and to send them to preach (Mk. 3,13).
They first go with Jesus and follow him in his preaching (Lk. 8,1).

Instructions to his apostles when they set out to preach. He sends them two by two (Mk. 6,7). Where they are to go (Mt. 10,5).
What they are to say; what they are to do; all that free of charge. In what condition they must go: poverty.
The worker finds his food where he works.
Where they must live; how they are to present themselves; how those who will receive them will be treated; and those who will not receive them.
In what disposition they must be; what their principal virtues should be (Mt. 10,16).
Warnings that he gives them; persecutions that he foretells; not to worry about what they will say to their judges; terrible wars in families. In persecutions, flee to another city; fear nothing: the disciple is not greater than the Master (Mt. 10,24). Do not let that prevent you from speaking, preaching on the roof tops; do not fear those who kill the body. God watches over you, trust (Mt. 10,29).
Whoever confesses me [before men...] (Mt. 10,32).
I have come to bring the sword of division (Mt. 10,34; 35; 37).
Takes his cross (Mt. 10,38); loses his life .
Reward of those who receive us (Mt. 10,40).
Salt of the earth (Mt. 5,13); light of the world (Mt. 5,14).
We must enlighten others by good example
Good examples.
Strength of this word (Mt. 5,18). Blessedness of the one who has taught; done and taught (Mt. 5,19).
Mission of the seventy two disciples (Lk. 10,1)
He asks for workers for his harvest.
Be like lambs among wolves. In poverty; not spend time chatting with people.
The priest's greeting when entering [peace to this house].
The apostles hold the place of Jesus Christ (Lk. 10,16).
Great mission that Jesus entrusts to his apostles before leaving them (Mt. 28,16; Mk. 16,15).
Preach repentence and forgiveness of sins in the name of Jesus Christ (Lk.24,46).

They must first be filled with the Holy Spirit (Lk. 24,49). When they had received the Holy Spirit, they began to speak Caeperunt loqui (Acts 2,4); ariis linguis, prout Spiritus Sanctus dabat illis eloqui[12].

The mission to preach is the most important of all, it is the one that comes before all others; we must preach before baptizing; preach before hearing confession, enlighten, instruct, fundamental mission; without it, there is nothing in the world. How the apostles fulfilled their mission[13].

Teaching of St. Paul, the great doctor of the nations, on preaching.

St. Paul has to preach the Gospel to everybody (Rom. 14-17). He is not ashamed of the Gospel.

445 To preach without the ruse of words in order not to avoid the cross of Jesus Christ (1 Cor. 17-25). God destroys the wisdom of the wise. Folly of preaching. Preach Jesus Christ crucified. Strength of the wisdom of God. In God, what appears as folly is wisdom; what appears as weakness is stronger than men. Not with elevated discourses, eloquence and human wisdom (1 Cor. 2,1-16). I know only Jesus Christ and him crucified. Not based on the persuasive arguments of human wisdom. That faith not be based on human wisdom but on God. We have not received the spirit of the world, but the spirit of God. Announce the truth, not with the studied discourses of human wisdom, but with those that the Holy Spirit has taught. Give each one the food adapted to him (1 Cor. 3,1-3). The milk of the weak. The one who sows and the one who waters are nothing, everything comes from God. The only foundation to be implanted in souls is Jesus Christ. He teaches free of charge in order not to put the least obstacle in the way of the Gospel of Jesus Christ (1 Cor. 9,9-23). He would rather die than lose that glory. I am obliged to preach the Gospel. Woe to me if I do not preach! willingly, not reluctantly, through force. My reward is to preach free of charge. Free in relation to everybody; he makes himself the servant of everyone in order to gain a greater number. He became all things to all men. Odor of death, odor of life (2 Cor. 2,14-17). Preach with sincerity, coming from God, in the spirit of Jesus Christ (2 Cor. 4,1-13), not altering the word of God. Our credentials are the sincerity with which we preach. To preach Jesus Christ. We are your servants through Jesus Christ. God has made his light shine in our hearts to enlighten others. To preach the Gospel in persecutions and afflictions of the flesh (Gal. 4,11-20). He is like a mother who engenders Jesus Christ in us. May God put his word on my lips (Eph. 4,18-20). To announce the Gospel freely. Freedom and boldness in chains. To preach Jesus Christ to all men, instructing in all wisdom (Col.1,21-29). The end of my labors.

---

[12] They began to speak in other languages, according to the manner in which the Spirit gave them to express themselves.

[13] Cf. p. 398 and 400.

We speak, not to please men, but God (1 Thes. 2,1-13). Neither flattery nor greed nor the glory of men; poorly; like a nurse full of tenderness; ready to give our life for you, in toils and labor. The work, night and day, poor. Irreproachable conduct, like the Father (1 Thes. 4,8). Paul's admonition to Timothy, through Jesus Christ (Tim. 4,1-5). We must speak, preach always, at every moment. Watch, suffer, fulfill the duties of a preacher of the Gospel Preach, exhort, reprove (Tit., 2,15). (Heb. 4,12).

Condition to preach well.

Feed the flock, watch over it, not through force but with voluntary affection;
not with interest but disinterestedly (1 Pet. 5,1-3).
Not as master but as model.
No scandal (1 Cor. 10, 32-33).
Seeking what is useful to others.
Support the weak and not seek self-satisfaction (Rom. 15,1-7).
Seek to please the neighbor.
Need for preachers sent by God (Rom. 11, 13-17).
It is God who exhorts you through us; speak in the name of God (2 Cor. 5,20-21).
Give scandal to no one in order not to dishonor our ministry (2 Cor. 4,1-10) but let patience be our recommendation.
Though young, be an example to the faithful (1 Tim. 4,12).
Model of good works (Titus 2,7-8). Pure and irreproachable words.
The apostles chose prayer and preaching exclusively (Acts 4,4).
St. Paul does not cease preaching in public and in homes. *Publice et per domos* (Acts 20,20).
The apostles did not cease announcing Jesus Christ in the temple and in homes (Act. 5,42).
Qualities of a preacher: not quarrelsome, moderate, capable, patient, meek, full of hope for sinners, their conversion (2 Tim. 2,24-26)[14].

Summary of Our Lord's conduct in his preachings.

It is the great mission that he received from his Father. He goes throughout the cities and towns preaching and healing.

He preaches everywhere.
He preaches every day.
He preaches with fidelity.
He preaches with simplicity.

---

[14] Father Chevrier himself copied this text from 2 Tim. 2,24-26, forgotten by the one who had prepared the notebook.

He preaches with authority.
He preaches with firmness.

Jesus chose twelve apostles to send them to preach. First he brings them with him; he sends them two by two.
First he sends them to the sheep of Israel, and gives them the power to heal.
He sends them in the greatest poverty.
He tells them to preach freely, that the worker is worthy of his wages.
He tells them to live with worthy people.
He tells them to be meek as lambs, prudent as serpents, simple as doves.
He foretells persecutions for them for he has come to bring the sword of division.
He tells them to trust, that he also was persecuted.
Preach on the house tops, fear nothing, God watches over you.
You must be the salt of the earth and the light of the world.

Before going to heaven, Jesus Christ gives them his great powers. All power has been given me. Go teach all nations, baptizing them. *Ite docete.*

How the apostles fulfilled that mission[15]. After having received the Holy Spirit, St. Peter: three thousand, five thousand men converted.

Persecutions, scourgings, prison. *Ibant gaudentes*[16].
They left everything to preach: *nos vero oratione et predicatione instantes erimus*[17].
They did not cease teaching and proclaiming Jesus Christ in the temple and in homes (Acts 5,42). St. Paul: *publice et per domos* (Acts 20,20)[18].

448 **Summary of St. Paul's doctrine on preaching.** We are obliged to preach. We must not be ashamed of the simplicity of the Gospel
and not empty the power of the cross by semblances of human eloquence. In preaching, we count for nothing, God does everything. We must base ourselves on God alone. We must please God and not men. We must make every possible sacrifice to win souls for Jesus Christ. We must find our reward in souls. Pressing invitation to all to preach. One of the great conditions to bear fruit is good example.

---

[15] Cf. p. 396, note 13.
[16] They went away joyful (Acts 5,41).
[17] As for us, we will remain assiduous in prayer and the service of the word (Acts 6,4).
[18] In public and in private.

Practical summary.

To preach is the priest's great mission.

Preach with fidelity. Speak only of what God has taught us, say nothing of ourselves.
Say only what Jesus Christ has taught us, Gospel. If we say anything of ourselves, it is no longer God's word but a human word.
Not preach ourselves, preach Jesus Christ.
We preach ourselves when we seek everything in study, outlines, refinement, satifaction[19].

With simplicity[20].

With authority.

With firmness.

When must we preach? Every day and several times on Sunday. It is especially on Sunday that we must preach, catechize.
At every moment; a priest must always be ready to speak, like Our Lord: he spoke, instructed, rebuked at every moment and in all occasions.
Before Mass, explain Holy Mass and recite aloud the prayers of the Mass.
After the Gospel, simply explain the Epistle and the Gospel.
After Vespers, explain the Rosary.

---

[19] Ms XII 243. Speak with sincerity, from God, in the presence of God and in the spirit of Jesus Christ.

[20] Ms XII 524-534.

The word is the bread of souls; it is the food of Christians; men are well according to the food they take; health and life depend on it. If the food we give is good, our faithful will have life.

The same goes for the instruction that we give as food (non in solo pane). There are the great dinners, there is the ordinary food, there are the pastries, cakes, delicacies, choice bits. It is the ordinary food that is most necessary, the most useful for health and it is on it that our health depends. The ordinary food is simple instruction: catechism. (Ms XII 524)

Simplicity in words, bearing, manners. No refinement no rule; if the occasion presents itself, walking, occasionally... no podium, preparation, sitting on the ground, in a boat (Ms XII 534).

In the evening, explain the Way of the Cross before making it and make it in the form of an instruction.
At prayer, explain a commandment of God.
During examination of conscience
praedica verbum insta argue obscera[21].
Every evening, Our Lord Jesus Christ's teaching to the faithful.
Our Lord told us what to say: we need only open his book and read it to the faithful, with a little explanation.

Whom should we preach?   Jesus Christ. *Haec et vita eterna ut cognoscant te solum Deum verum et quem misisti Jesum Christum*[22].
I know only Jesus Christ and him crucified, it is the foundation of all things. His divinity. That is one of the main points. *Predica, praedicate Evangelium*[23].

A little less devotion, a little more faith in Jesus Christ.

What must we teach especially?   The Rosary, the Way of the Cross, the Mass, the Commandments of God, Jesus' teaching to the faithful: God - Jesus Christ - the Church.

Where should we preach?   Everywhere, like Jesus Christ. Wherever we find the occasion, where we think our word might have an effect, like Jesus Christ.
Like the apostles. *Publice et per domos*[24].
If we were permitted to go into the homes, that is, to set up rooms or places of instruction in the homes of the faithful, and gather the people to instruct them, give religious conferences; the people do not come, we must seek them out.
What would prevent us from dividing a parish into different sections and spending a month in each section? set ourselves up in a convenient place: a barn, a room, a house, and teach the people every evening; how we would fulfill our task of preaching!

---

[21] Preach the word, convince, rebuke and exhort (2 Tim. 4,3).

[22] Eternal life is that they may know you, the only true God, and the one whom you have sent, Jesus Christ (Jn. 17, 3).

[23] Preach, preach the Gospel (Mk. 1,15).

[24] In public and in private (Acts 20,20). Cf. p. 396, note 13.

Example of Jesus Christ in Nazareth.   Our Lord enters the synagogue to read in the scroll; he reads and after the reading he explains the prophecy (Lk. 4,16).

Thus, read first a passage of the Gospel, of Holy Scripture, and explain it; that is the ordinary form of instruction.

Have a desk on which is placed beforehand the book that contains the part that will serve as the topic for the instruction; read that part and then give a practical explanation, this for the Gospel...[25]

the Rosary,
the Way of the Cross,
the evening catechism lesson.

Catechism, simple instruction.   It is the simple instruction, in question and answer form.

It is not the book that instructs, it is the priest. Our Lord did not say: *read, learn*, but he says to the priest: *docete*[26].

How sad it is to see children spending two hours a day learning words, being bored in always repeating the same words, *they* and the *catechist*! for it is *boring*. While we could give them more faith and love and religion in a quarter of an hour than they take in those two hours.

When we instruct adults or ignorant people, we cannot tell them: here, take these catechism and read; we have to do it for them, put ourselves on the level of each one and of the greater number and instruct them with the word. *Fides ex auditu*[27] [28].

Way to proceed.   We must proceed by truths, begin with the fundamental truths

and then to the more remote When we build a house we always begin with the big walls and then we go to the refinement and the ornamentations.

The fundamental questions are: God, sin, Jesus Christ, his teaching and death, his Church, sacraments, the general resurrection, the last ends.

We must put all faith in these great truths and not waste time in all those little instructions that do not hold because the foundations do not exist.

---

[25] Uncertain text, it might be 'and the priest'.

[26] Teach.

[27] Faith is born of preaching (Rom. 10,17).

[28] Ms XII 526 - docete, remember that word of the Master. We must teach, not make them read. Uselessness of books; teaching does not come from books, little. How many books! The Gospel. Not read, they do not understand, understand badly. The book is cold, the word is worth more than the book, the word reaches people better.

in little missions.   Avoid going into the pulpit, or only go up when we cannot do otherwise because of the crowd.

When we go to evangelize a parish, begin with the church.... place ourselves on one side of the church or at the bottom and come up as the people arrive. In the villages, we begin by going every evening. We set up in a barn or the house of an honest citizen; as soon as there are enough people, settle down and say Mass. Go especially in the ignorant villages without religion.

End of all instruction and catechism.   It is to enlighten the intelligence through knowledge, touch the heart through love and strengthen the will to act.

Faith, love and action: those are the three effects that we must seek to produce in every instruction. To give faith through knowledge, reasonings, the view of things. Give birth to love for the truth that we teach. And incite to action in relation with the truth known and loved. To arrive at these three effects, we must take all possible means and, as St. Paul says: we must give birth like a mother, become nurse and father and give his life through charity.

form catechists.

Means to become good catechists.   We must teach catechism often and for a long time, know the method to teach catechism.

Have a big notebook, or better yet, several notebooks to write our own catechism.

> Catechism often, every day. We must make our own catechism, write our own catechism; have a big notebook or several in which are written, in the margin, the titles of each lesson and, each day, note what we learn in our readings, instructions and, at the end of every year, we end up with a complete catechism and in the course of instructions that we ourselves have given and where we can go draw for our catechisms and instructions.

We must begin this work early, as soon as we begin teaching catechism, and add some article every time we teach catechism. As we read or study a question, we note on the page what we have learned in the reading, an instruction, prayer, study or conversation. Thus, you are enriched every day, without effort or labor and, after a certain time, you find that you have, on all religious questions, a complete work to preach and catechize, and you need only consult your catechism to find your topic already dealt with and you need only reflect and pray and arrange your ideas to speak in public, and as that is your own work, you have little trouble to recall it. For this, follow the sequence of questions or lessons that we have given in catechism. Place the title of each lesson and article in the margin, not too spaced out, according to the importance of the subject, so that you may write, in summary form and succintly,the reflections, proofs,stories or indications necessary for the subject; and do this on all the lessons of the catechism.And at the end of a few years we end up with a complete work from which we can draw great profit,without it having cost a lot of trouble and we thus pre-pare ten years in advance the instructions that we have given thoughout our life.

order of lessons[29].

---

[29] The manuscript ends with the announcement of a development which did not see the light of day, or it may be an invitation to refer to the indications given in the notes on the catechism that were drawn up elsewhere. Those notes are rather numerous. (Ms VII)

8. Follow me 453
in my combats against the world[1]

---

[1] Ms XII 609-614.

Father Chevrier had first thought of grouping in one chapter the topics: follow me in my persecutions, my sufferings and my death, *then he thought of three distinct chapters, the first being entitled* "follow me in my combats and persecutions". *Finally he decided to divide that one also into* "follow me in my combats" *and* "follow me in my persecutions".

Thus, the intention is very clear: Jesus's combats are not the assaults that others wage against him, but the assaults that he wages against others.

At first sight we may be surprised to find such a preoccsupation in such a meek and peaceful man as Father Chevrier. And when we consult the manuscripts, we are even more surprised at the number of studies entitled, explicitly or equivalently, "struggle against the Jews". *We wonder what this excessive anti-Semetism means.*

When we look at it more closely, the surprise ceases. A big notebook of more than six hundred pages contains a study of this kind, linked to the study of the Passion[2]. *It can be summarized as follows:*

Struggle between Jesus Christ and the Jews which ends up in the triumph of the Jews when the death of Jesus is decided.

Jesus then freely suffers his Passion and, by his death and resurrection, he wins the definitive victory.

In this we see the connecting thread in St. John's Gospel. Thus, it is the struggle that Jesus waged against the Jews in proclaiming the Gospel. By the very fact of this proclamation, he was going against all those who, in themselves, do not conform to the Gospel. Father Chevrier noted well that Jesus had to wage this combat even against his disciples[3]. *But it is evident that it is the combat against the Pharisees that holds Father Chevrier's attention*[4].

We might think that he was somewhat disconcerted by the opposition he met throughout his life, within or outside the Prado. Precisely because he was not of a combative nature, he had great need to find in the Gospel the light and strength to struggle against those who were putting obstacles.

We sense a dual preoccupation in him. He must struggle against his own collaborators to maintain the true religion and repulse a false religion of a pharisaical spirit, the one that imposes sacrifice before mercy. It seems that this would be mainly the way of treating the children of the First Communion and the young seminarians. Father Chevrier did not accept the too strict ways of some[5].

He must struggle against his disciples. He uses a certain severity, not to punish but to rebuke. To rebuke is not first of all to sanction but it is to enlighten by pointing out what is not according to the Gospel in someone's behavior. In fact, the weapon

---

[2] This notebook has been reproduced in the sixth volume of the manuscript copies, in three different places as if they were three distinct books: Ms VI 535-540; 485-486; 383-385.

[3] Cf. P. 412, note 15.

[4] Cf. Ms VI 527: Words or actions of the Jews or Pharisees against Jesus Christ.

[5] P. 412.

with which we must struggle is the testimony to truth. That is how we fight, not haphazardly but with knowledge, wisdom and charity[6].

---

[6] Cf. p. 414, note 18.

He came to bring war.	He came to bring the sword (Mt. 10,34-35).
Sign of contradiction. Simeon (Lk. 2,34). Bring separation in the house, father against son in the family (Lk. 12,51-53).	
Reason for that war.	It is the eternal Word, wisdom, truth, light.

The reason for this combat is that there is a difference between what comes from heaven and what come from earth. What comes from earth is terrestrial, what comes from heaven is celestial (Jn. 3,30-31). There can be no peace between truth and error; Jesus Christ and the world; I am from above, you are from below. I am the truth. Spiritus domini super me[7]. He says nothing of himself, he says what his Father has told him to say.

He comes to fight against the error, lie and sin that reigns in the world.	Since the first sin, the devil has established his empire on the earth.

He comes to over throw the devil's empire that has been established on earth since sin. He comes to restore faith, justice, truth, worship of the true God, destroy pride, greed, impurity, lies. *Great* warrior: exultavit ut gigas ad currendam viam[8]. Glory to God. Peace to men. He seeks the glory of God. Fight against evil. If I was born and came into the world, it is to give witness to truth (to Pilate); that also is one of his great misions. Through my words and actions[9].

Inevitable war.	The devil's words to Jesus. He asks him to leave (Lk. 4,33-34).

We do not like to be annoyed... dislodge. There can be no peace between Jesus Christ and the devil, truth and error, evil and virtue. Leave me (Lk. 8,27-28). Evil cannot love good, nor error truth, thus he is not welcome or received. The world did

---

[7] The spirit of the Lord is upon me (Lk. 4,18).

[8] He rejoices to bravely run his course (Ps. 18,6).

[9] Ms XII 578-635.

Every time he sees a reform, a lesson to be given, he does it, something that is not right in the soul or the heart (Ms XII 578).

Evil is in the world, our souls, our heart and our spirits. The devil has taken God's place, he is called prince of the world. Darkness, error, lies, pride, cruelty, impurity, envy, homicide. Instruct and rebuke. It does not suffice to instruct, they must be rebuked; it does not suffice to plow a field and plant the seed, we must pull up the weed, cut, prune; without that the initial work is worthless. We must rebuke, fight constantly against evil, pull it up wherever we find it. Important work, more difficult perhaps that the initial one, but just as necessary; the one becomes worthless without the other. It is easier to find people who instruct than people who correct (Ms XII 635).

not know him. The world did not receive him (Jn. 1,10-11). He was a stumbling block for the unbelievers (Rom. 9,33). As soon as a man does not act like the others, annoys the others with his manners, condemns others, he becomes a cause of scandal; because self-love, jealousy is awakened in others. Reason for this hatred between the world and Jesus Christ: because he shows that its works are evil (Jn. 7,7). Our Lord often said: Blessed is the one who is not scandalized because of me (Lk. 7,23) et scandalizabantur in eo (Mt. 13,57)[10].

The fight first against the incredulity of the Jews and their terrestrial and worldly ideas.
The Jews had a very temporal idea of the Messiah: a temporal king who was to deliver them.

Their state favored that idea... with-out a king. The apostles themselves ask when he will establish his temporal kingdom. Terrestrial ideas of the Jews and the apostles so opposed to truth.

459 Temporal kingdom.
Temporal king.
After having read the Scriptures in the synagoge of Nazareth, Jesus closed the book. And he taught. The Jews were scandalized by his knowledge and doctrine, not knowing where he got his knowledge from; it was not from them.
He is the son of Joseph, the carpenter... his mother... his brothers.
No one is a prophet in his own country (Mk. 6,2-4).
After the discourse on the Eucharist, they were scandalized because he said that he came down from heaven (Jn. 6,41).
Various feelings toward Jesus: some say he is the Christ, others say no; we know where he comes from, when he comes, no one will know where he comes from (Jn.7,25-27).
Division among the people over Jesus Christ: some recognize him as the Christ, others refuse; will the Christ come from Galilee? (Jn. 7,37-41).
Their reasoning should have been their precise motive for believing, if they had studied properly (Jn. 7,42).
Answer to the Pharisees' messengers who had been sent to trap him (Jn. 7,46).
How the Pharisees shake the crowds who believe (Jn. 7,47-49).
Nicodemus comes to his defense and he is told that no prophet can come from Galilee (Jn. 7,50-52).

Combat that Jesus Christ waged against the Jews to be recognized for what he is.
The trouble he has to be accepted for what he is (Jn. 8,12). As witness he invokes his origin and his end (Jn. 8, 13-14).

---

[10] And they were scandalized because of him.

He is only the witness of the one who sent him. His Father is with him (Jn. 8,15-19).
He invokes the testimony of his works and that of the Father himself, and the Scriptures...
He comes in the name of the Father.
He gives them the reason for which they cannot believe.
Testimony of Moses.
If you do not believe his writings, how will you believe my word? (Jn. 5,36-47).
They are scandalized because of ahim, especially his compatriots: no one is a prophet in his own country, his house, his family (Lk. 4,23-24).
You have seen me and you do not believe (Jn. 6,35-36).
The Jews murmur against what he says about himself, they point to his birth, his parents and Jesus tells them that no one can come to me unless the Father draw him (Jn. 6,41-44).
To his miracles they oppose those of Moses (Jn. 6,28-33).
They demand a miracle to believe.
How Jesus answers them (Mt. 16,1-4).

460

The struggle against pharisaism, the bad spirit of some. Jesus fights against the bad spirit of the Pharisee who despises the sinful woman who had come to weep at his feet and ask forgiveness, and he shows him that this woman is worth more than he and that she has obtained forgiveness.
They are scandalized at the powers that he gives (Lk. 7,36-50).
Narrow and proud spirit of the Pharisees who despise others.
Against the pride of the Pharisees who were displeased to see Jesus eat with the publicans.
Fight against the Pharisees who reproach him for eating with sinners (Mk. 2,15-17 and parallel).
He combats the severity of the Phariseess' rule on fasting against the apostles, and he opposes a wide, prudent and merciful spirit (Mk. 2,18-22)[11].
And why do you see the straw...? (Lk. 6,41-42).
Bad spirit: they murmured because Jesus went to a sinner's house (Zaccheaus) (Lk. 19,1-10)[12].
False religion: they take it badly that he heals the sick on the Sabbath (Lk. 6,6-8).
False, bad religion: Jesus proves to them that we may do good on the Sabbath; they do not capitulate, they deliberate against him (Mt. 12,9-14).

---

[11] Ms XII 574 - He enlightens the Pharisees and John's disciples on the question of fasting.

[12] Ms XII 576 - He scorns opinion, he blames; he is not concerned about the reproach the Pharisees might make if he goes to Zaccheaus's house; he goes.

They seek to trap him in his words; they seek the means to trip him to be able to accuse him and they bring him the woman caught in adultery (Jn. 8,1-11).

He has to combat the false religions of others[13]. False religion of the Pharisees who do not want the sick man to carry his bed on the Sabbath (Jn. 1-15).
False religion of the Pharisees who reproach the apostles for having crushed grain on the Sabbath to eat it.
Put mercy before the rule, before sacrifice.
Rigid observers who put the rule before everything.

461 I want mercy and not sacrifice; you would never have condemned the innocent (Mt. 12,1-8 and paral.)[14].
Pharisees whose justice consisted in certain exterior practices; Jesus tells his disciples: if your justice is not greater than that of the scribes and Pharisees (Mt. 5-20).
False religion of the Pharisees: they put human traditions before the Lord's precepts. Many similar things replace the commandments: certain practices, customs. Hypocricy: lip service. Human doctrine and ordinances.
Annul the precepts to observe the traditions (Mk. 7,1-9).
Lesson that he gives when he tells them that it is not what enters the body that defiles man but what comes out of it (Mt. 15, 10-20)[15].
Do not judge by appearances (Jn. 7,19-24).
False religion of the Pharisees who made it a sin to eat without washing one's hands. Reproach of Jesus Christ.
We must take care of the interior as of the exterior.
False religion of the Pharisees who paid tithes on the mint, rue and other herbs and neglected justice and love of God.
False religion of the Pharisees who chose the first place (Lk. 11,37-43).
Tomb.
False religion of the doctors who, by their knowledge, impose unbearable burdens on men's shoulders, which they do not lift a finger to ease, building the tombs of the prophets. Exterior glory.

---

[13] Ms XII 586 - Recommendations of our Lord Jesus, especially to us priests; instruction to the Pharisees. Be very careful. Beware of the leaven of the Pharisees (Mt. 26,6). Nothing is more opposed to the spirit and the religion of Our Lord.

[14] Ms XII 589 - Spirit of Jesus Christ. His thoughts on fasting, prayer, almsgiving, exterior worship, his religion, his yoke. Summary of Our Lord's doctrine on fasting, prayer, almsgiving, exterior worship; on what is to be avoided about the Pharisees. The main thing is mercy. I want mercy and not sacrifice. If we begin with sacrifice, how can we succeed?

[15] Ms XII 626 - He is not afraid to reproach the apostles of their ignorance. But Jesus said: are you also without intelligence?

False religion of the doctors who have the Scriptures, the key to knowledge, and do not hear the meaning of Scripture and prevent the others from understanding, prevent them from understanding the meaning (Lk. 11,44-45).
False religion of the Pharisees.
Parable of the Pharisee and the Publican (Lk. 18,9-14).

| He convicted his enemies of blindness, incredulity and homicide. | Bad spirit of the Pharisees and Doctors who scorned God's designs on them; They always found fault with everything; |

whether it was white or black, they always criticized everything.
But the children of wisdom have rendered justice to wisdom (Lk. 7,30-35).
Bad spirit of the Pharisees who are not happy with what they see but demand a miracle as a proof.
We must be happy with what we see in Scripture (Mt. 12,38-42).
He fights against the blindness of men which comes from their passions and reasonings.
Explanation that Jesus Christ gives of this bad spirit that reigns in the Pharisees (Lk. 11,33-35).
Those who see become blind. Blindness: we see and we do not want to see. We want to see only with our eyes and reasonings; we do not want to see things as they are and as God gives them to us, simply and with goodness. The reasoners do not see well (Jn. 9,39-41).
To this blindness he opposes the works he does in his Father's name.
Reason for their incredulity: they are not my sheep (Jn. 10,22-30).
Those who speak and do nothing will be excluded from heaven; those who begin by refusing but then do, they do the will of God.
Those who boast that they do everything and do nothing will be excluded; those who refuse, yet do will be admitted (Mt. 21,27-32).
He is not of this world.
I have many things to condemn in you (Jn. 8,23-26).
We are descendants of Abraham; Abraham is our father. He fights against this blind confidence in their title of Abraham's children, they who do the devil's work; they do the work of their father who is the devil.
They boast of having Abraham for father, that is, the spirit of Abraham; father in the sense that they follow him in his law, his faith, his works.
Jesus proves to them that they do not have Abraham for father because they do not do Abraham's works.
Religious pride that rest on a title, that of child of God, of St. Francis, St. Benedict, St. Dominic; ill-founded trust: we must do our father's works. Titles are nothing, it is the works that do. You have the devil for father, envy, homicide (Jn. 8,37-44).

Bad spirit of the Jews who say that it is by the power of the devil that he expels the devil.
Prejudice, mind set.
Brood of vipers, there is only gall and venom in your heart (Mt. 12,22-34).
Mind set not to believe and to give a contrary meaning to the most evident things.
Spirit of blasphemy: is not forgiven (Mt. 12,31-32).
The evil eye.
How he confounds the Pharisees who were watching him to see if he would cure the man with dropsy on the Sabbath.
Narrow and rigid spirit that puts the law before charity, that carries the law to excess.

463 Reason for his conduct (Lk. 6,6-10).
Mk. 12,1-12) [The murderous vine keepers].

| **He rises against the vice of these men and crushes them with his curse.** | He fights against those who profane the temple (Jn. 2,13-21). Against the proud, the hypocrites (Mt.6,2-6)[16]. Against long and useless prayers. (Mt. 6,7-8). |

Hypocrites... fastings, prayers (Mt. 6,16-18)[17].
Mt. 23,13-31: Jesus said to the Jews: no one can serve two masters, for either he will hate the one and love the other or he will adhere to one and despise the other. You cannot serve God and money (Lk. 16,13).

| **What weapons did he use in this combat.** | His weapons to defend himself: Union with his Father and act with him (Jn. 5,16-17). The works that he does (Jn. 5,36-38). |

Holy Scripture (Jn. 5,39-41). He came in the name of His Father (Jn. 5,43). Reason that they do not believe is that they do not seek God's glory (Jn. 5,44). Moses (Jn. 5,45-47). The prophet Isaiah (Lk. 4,16-19). His future death (Jn. 8,28-29). His innocence (Jn. 8,45-46). The works testify for me; not of my sheep (Jn. 10,22-26; 34-38). I say nothing of myself; believe because of my works (Jn. 14,10-11). Labora
464 sicut bonus miles Christi Jesu[18]. Bonum certamen certavi[19]. How important it is to

---

[16] Ms XII 626 - Exterior religion which seeks to show off.
[17] Ms XII 573 - He condemns the hypocrites, the great prayers, the great fasters.
[18] Work like a good soldier of Jesus Christ (2 Tim. 2,3).
[19] I have fought the good fight (2 Tim. 4,7).

Ms XII 596-626 and 628 - He set us up to continue the war on earth. We are God's envoys. We must not put up with evil. Examples of St. John the Baptist and the Saints XII-

have the spirit of Jesus Christ in order not to go to war against him, but rather to go to war for him[20].

---

595. - We are soldiers of Jesus Christ. Conditions to be a good soldier, doctor, teacher: doctor, heal yourself; if a blind man leads another blind man, they will both fall into the pit; hypocrit, first remove the beam that is in your eye, then you will be able to see to remove the straw from your brother's eye. With attenion and meekness: we do not put a new patch on an old garment nor new wine in old wine skins (Ms XII 626-628).

[20] Ms XII 584 - Follow me in my combats. The false ideas of the Jews and his apostles. He fought against the evil spirit of the apostles and the Jews, follow me in my good spirit. The false religion of the Pharisees, follow me in my true religion. The vices of everybody: pride, greed, impurity; follow me in my humility, poverty, purity. With what weapons he fought.

Ms XII 562 - What weapons he used in his great combat: words, examples, lamb among the wolves, meekness. We fight with the weapons of justice (2 Cor.6,5-10); we do not fight according to the flesh (2 Cor.10,1-5). Conditions to take up the fight: be full of charity and knowledge in order to [instruct one another] (Rom. 15,14). Knowledge, wisdom and charity. He rebukes everybody with meekness and prudence, discernment, prudence, strength and charity; what difference in the manner of rebuking each individual!

9. Follow me in my persecutions[1]

[see] Chapter "*To carry one's cross*"
persecuted unto death
despised, insulted, hated.
Our Lord predicted persecutions for his apostles. Examples of the apostles[2].

---

[1] Ms XII 643-649.
[2] Note scribbled on the cover page.

Persecutions are all the manifestations of men's hostility to Jesus Christ and his apostles. The New Testament speaks of them abundantly.

Here we have only the results of Father Chevrier's preliminary research, the sketch of references in the order that he found them in Les Evangiles Unis. (Only one reference to the Acts of the Apostles at the end).

He notes his intention to come back to the chapter "To Carry one's cross"[3]. No doubt, he wanted to harmonize the study on persecutions to that of the cross. He also refers to the Notebook on the Passion[4]. He wanted to use one of his many works on the topic to draw up his commentary.

The last lines are a sketch of that commentary, they give us his orientation: it is not a question of deploring the hostility deployed against Jesus but of admiring the manner in which he bore persecution.

---

[3] P. 417; cf. pp. 285-292.
[4] P. 423.

Already at his birth, there is no place for them in Bethlehem (Lk. 2.2)
Herod, the hypocrite, tells the Magi to find out about Jesus and come back and tell him so that he may go adore him (Mt. 2,8).
Behold, this child is for the downfall and resurrection and a sign of contradiction and a sword shall pierce your heart, and the thoughts of many will be revealed (Lk. 2,34).
The angel said to Joseph: rise and take the child and his mother and flee into Egypt, because Herod is seeking the child to kill him (Mt. 2,13). .
He came to his own and his own did not receive him (Jn. 1,11).
After Jesus had expelled the merchants from the temple, the Jews asked him why he did that: By what miracle do you show us that you have a right to do it (Jn.2,18).
The light came into the world and men preferred darkness to light, because their works were evil, for every man who does evil hates light and does not come close to it so that his works may not be discovered (and if he comes close to it, he extinquishes it), but the one who acts in truth comes close (Jn. 3,19-21).
Blessed are those who suffer persecution for justice's sake... Blessed are you when men curse you, persecute you, say all sorts of evil against you because of me (Mt. 5,10).
Jesus expels a mute devil. The Pharisees say: It is by the prince of demons that he casts out demons (Mt. 9,34).
Blessed will you be when men hate you, when they separate you (Lk. 6,22).
Blessed is he who will not be scandalized because of me (Lk. 7,23).
The Jews persecute Jesus because he heals on the Sabbath (Jn. 5,15). After which the Jews sought even more to put him to death, because not only did he violate the Sabbath, but he said that God was his father, he made himself equal to God (Jn. 5,18).
When, in spite of them, Jesus had healed a man with a withered hand on the Sabbath, they were full of anger and deliberated among themselves on what to do to Jesus (Lk. 6,11).
After this, the Pharisees held council with the Herodians to see how they could take him; he goes and the crowd follows him (Mk. 3,6). The ones persecute him, the crowd, the people follow him.
His people, having heard this (the cure of the possessed man), said: he is besides himself (Mk. 3,21). And the Pharisees said that it was by the prince of demons that he cast out demons (Mt. 12,24). And others asked for miracles (Lk. 11,16).
How Jesus answeres all these persecutions, Jesus answers: if it is by Beelzebul, prince of demons, that I cast out demons....(Lk. 11,19).
How great is the sin of those who persecute God and refuse to believe in his miracles when they see them with their own eyes, because they said: he has the evil spirit (Mk. 3,30).
They ask for a miracle to jeer. Evil and adulterous generation (Mt. 12,39).

Explanation of this war against Jesus, the heart of these people has become heavy and their ears have been stopped up and they have closed their eyes (Mt. 13,15).
Persecution that he had to bear in Nazareth where he says that no prophet is well received in his own country and he proves it by facts. They expel him and lead him to a high mountain to throw him down (Lk. 4,29).
Jesus' recommendation to his apostles when he sends them on mission: I am sending you like sheep among wolves. Be prudent as serpents and simple as doves (Mt. 10,16).
For they will drag you before tribunals, flog you... Persecutions that they will have to bear because of me. Conduct that they should maintain (Mt. 10,17).
After those things, Jesus went to Galilee because he did not want to go to Judea because the Jews sought to kill him (Jn. 7,1).
Dissensions that arise among the people because of him: some say he is good, but others want to take him but no one dared put hand on him (Jn. 7,43).
The Jews take up stones to throw at him (Jn. 8,59).
After Jesus had said that he was the Good Shepherd, many others said: he is possessed, he is besides himself. Others said that a possessed man could not speak like that. (Jn. 10,19).
Do you think that I have come to bring peace upon earth? No, I tell you, but separation (Lk. 12,51).
After Jesus had said that he and the Father were one, they took up stones (Jn. 10,30-31).
After the resurrection of Lazarus, some Jews went to the Pharisees to tell them what Jesus had done (Jn. 11,46).
The priests and Pharisees gathered their council to order his death (Jn. 11,47).

471 A great multitude of Jews came to see Lazarus and believed and the chief priests plotted to kill Lazarus (Jn. 12,9-10).
The Pharisees' reflection on seeing the crowd honor Jesus entering Jerusalem. The Pharisees said among themselves..... Master, rebuke your disciples (Lk. 19,39).
The Jews ask by what authority he does those things and who has given him the power (Lk. 20,2).
To trap him and give him over to the magistrate, the Pharisees and Herodians ask him if it is lawful to pay tribute to Caesar (Mt. 22,17).
Jesus predicts persecutions for his apostles. They will lay hands on you. They will give you to the synagogues,prisons,tribunals... beaten,testimony (Mt. 24,9).
Jesus promises the hundredfold with persecutions (Mk. 10,30).
The chief priests and the scribes sought to kill him. Council to take him (Mk. 14,1 and paral.).
Satan (Lk. 22,3).
He predicts Judas' betrayal (Mk. 14,18).
Satan entered into Judas and he went out (Jn. 13,27).
Behold that Satan has demanded you that he might sift you like wheat (Lk. 22,31).

Peter's answer:Lord,I am ready to go to prison and to death with you (Lk. 22,23).
And he was reckoned with transgressors (Lk. 22,37).
Jesus foretells his Passion (Mt. 20,17-18).
If the world hates, know that it hated me before you (Jn. 15,18 ff).
You will weep, you will moan, but your sorrow will be turned into joy (Jn.16,20).
In the world, you will have tribulation, but have confidence, I have overcome (Jn. 16,33).
The world has hated them because they are not of the world (Jn. 17,14).
How Jesus behaves when his enemies come to take him (Mt. 26,47-56; Jn. 18,4-11).
With Annas (Jn. 18,13).
Peter denies his master (Mt. 26,69-75; Jn. 18,15-27).
How he answers questions (Jn. 18,19-23).
They seek false witnesses against Jesus (Mt. 26,59).
He does not fear to say what he is (Mt. 26,64).
How Jesus answers the priests (Lk. 22,66-67).
Pilate's accusations (Lk. 23,2).

(Notebook on the Passion)

With what dignity he speaks to his judges and enemies. 472
With what meekness he treats his enemies and surrenders to them.
With what majesty he speaks to his judges.
With what patience he endures all the bad treatment.
His silence before all the accusations.
With what sorrow he receives insults and humiliations.
With what goodness he forgives.

Malice and wickedness of the Jews and priests in the scourging and the crowning with thorns.

Jesus predicts Peter's death and tells him: When you were young, you put on your own belt and went where you wanted. Follow me (Jn. 21,18).

Jesus tells his apostles that they will bear witness to him (Jn. 15,27; Acts 1,8).

10. Follow me in my sufferings[1] 473

---

[1] Ms XII 691-697.

These pages could be entitled: the mystery of suffering in the life of the priest. An important topic in Father Chevrier's mind; there are sixteen manuscripts that testify to his work on the question, but none is a definitive draft.

The chapter should have had the following outline.
    Examples of Jesus Christ.
    Instructions of Jesus Christ.
    Examples of St. Paul.
    How shall we follow Jesus Christ in his sufferings[2].

This is the main idea that seems to emerge when we consult all those papers:

    Suffering is the seal of love and conversion of heart,...
    That trait is the most beautiful, the greatest, the strongest, the most powerful with God and men and it is the one that converts and heals...[3]

We think of the Risen Christ appearing to Thomas and showing him the marks of his Passion to heal his unbelief[4]. We think of Paul, converted to Christ, become apostle and carrying everywhere and always in his body the sufferings and death Jesus, so that the life of Jesus be manifested in his body[5].
This trait, this seal of suffering must not necessarily be understood in the physical, visible sense. On the contrary, several manuscripts highlight the importance of suffering of the heart[6]. This comes especially from the anxiety of the apostle who, with his master, suffers in his heart on seeing the sheep without a shepherd[7].
We have chosen to reproduced the most developed commentary. Other manuscripts surely came later but they only sketch a new plan and do not contain any commentaries.

---

[2] Cf. Ms XII 683-684.
[3] Ms XII 657-658.
[4] Jn.20, 27-28.
[5] 2 Cor. 4,10.
[6] Ms XII 683.
[7] P. 430.

(Our Lord bore exteriorly the trait of poverty and suffering; those who only have it interiorly risk not having it at all)[8].

He was born in a stable.	He suffered from poverty (Lk. 2,6-7).
The angels speak of his poverty as a sign by which the shepherds will recognize him.	Poverty was his particular trait (Lk. 2,12).
He was circumcized on the eighth day.	He suffered in accomplishing the law (Lk.2,21)
The old man Simeon announced to Mary that she would suffer.	He suffered the contradictions of the world. And the Blessed Virgin will be pierced by a sword (Lk, 2,34-35).
He remains seven years in exile in Egypt.	He suffered persecutions. He suffered in exile (Mt. 2,13-15).
He is an occasion of suffering for others.	involuntarialy (Mt. 2,16-18).
He came to his own and his own did not receive him.	He suffered the rebuffs of the world. No place for them (Jn. 1,11; Lk. 2,7).
St. John the Baptist bore on himself the marks of suffering. (Mk. 1,6).	
Jesus Christ goes to the desert, he fasts, prays, is with the animals, he is hungry.	He suffered in the desert. Voluntary penance (Mk. 1,13; Mt. 4,2).
He is the lamb of God who bears the sins of the world.	He suffered because he wished to bear the sins of the world (Jn. 1,29).
The angel tells Joseph that it is he who will save the people from their sins.	[He suffered] because he saved the people from their sins (Mt. 1,20-21).

---

[8] Cf. P. 244.

He had to suffer, as Moses lifted up the serpent in the desert... (Jn. 3,14)[9]. When the disciples urge him to eat, he tells them that he has a food that they do not know.	He suffers fatigue and hunger, when he sits by Jacob's well. He forgets that he is suffering to do his Father's will, which is his food (Jn. 4,31-34).
Blessed are they who suffer.	We will be blessed when we suffer something for God (Mt. 5,10-11).
To follow Jesus we must suffer; that is what he tells that young man who asks to follow him.	He suffers from poverty...(Mt. 8,19-20).
Jesus suffered in his soul on seeing the multitude without a shepherd.	He suffered in his heart on seeing the sheep without a shepherd (Mt. 9,35-38).
How sternly he rebukes Peter who wanted to oppose his sufferings.	He speaks openly of his sufferings, as of something very natural. Suffering is a mystery that we can only understand with the spirit of God (Mt. 16,21-23).
If anyone wishes to be my disciple, let him renounce himself and carry his cross.	To follow Jesus Christ, we must suffer; there are suffering; take up our cross (Mk. 8,34).
He who wishes to save his soul will lose it.	We must lose our life (Mk. 8,35).
In his transfiguration, he speak of his sufferings.	He speaks of the Passion with Moses and Elijah (Lk. 9,28-31).
He suffers from being with this race.	He suffers from being with men who are so far from the truth, so coarse (Lk. 9,41).

---

[9] Ms XII 681 - He did not come to earth to enjoy himself and have an easy life; he came to convert the world, bear the sins of the world, atone for the sins of the world, fight against and give to men the example of virtue; and that could not be done without suffering. To instruct, rebuke, correct, give example; convert, atone; all that could not be done without suffering.

Jesus predict his sufferings to his apostles, but it was a hidden mystery.	He speaks of the sufferings of the passion. The apostles understand nothing, it is a hidden word (Lk. 9,43-45).
I am the good shepherd, I give my life.	He gives his life for his sheep. Difference between the good shepherd and the mercenary.

He suffers to bring the lost sheep back to the fold. It is through suffering that he earns his Father's love. He suffers voluntarily (Jn. 10,11-18).

I have come to bring fire upon earth.	He has come to bring the fire of love which makes us love suffering (Lk. 12,49-50).
I have a baptism with which I must be baptized.	
Jesus weeps over Jerusalem. (Lk. 13,31-35).	
Whoever does not renounce everything he has...	Poverty [first] characteristic of the true disciple (Lk. 14,33).
Jesus weeps over Lazarus	He suffers in his soul on seeing Lazarus dead (Jn. 11, 34-36)
Jesus announces his passion to his apostles.	Jesus speaks of his sufferings to his apostles and it was a mystery to them (Lk. 18,31-34).
What Jesus' answer to his two apostles who ask for the first places.	What Jesus answers the mother of Zebedee's sons who was asking that her sons be placed on his right and left:

Can you suffer? second characteristic of the disciple. The two characteristic of the true disciples: poverty, suffering[10] (and charity). They will know that you are my

---

[10] Ms XII 684 - The crucifix, Calvary, it is the second state in which Our Lord shows himself to us as model. The cross is everywhere; the sign of suffering exists everywhere: thus did our Lord show himself to us. What is the meaning of a crucifix if not the suffering of Christ?

disciples. It is not a question of place or honor, it is a question of suffering. Can you drink my [chalice]? be baptized...(Mk. 10,35-41).

He came to serve.	He suffers in serving and giving his life; he came to serve and give his life (Mk. 10,45).
To bear fruit, we must suffer. (Jn. 12,24)	
He who loves his soul will lose it, he who hates his soul will save it.	We must hate our soul, our life (Jn. 12,25).
His soul is troubled at the sight of sufferings.	He came to suffer and die (Jn. 12,27,28).
On the way to Jerusalem, he was walking before them. (Lk. 19,28).	
And when I am raised up, I shall draw all things to me.	It is by suffering that we draw all things to us. (Jn. 12,32-33)

481
I have desired with great desire to eat [this passover with you].	He desires with great desire to give himself to them (Lk, 22,14-16).
How his heart must have suffered on seeing Judas.	He suffers in his soul on seeing Judas, his disciple who will betray him (Mt.26,21-25).

St. Peter to whom he announces his denial. The disciples go away from Jesus because of the word difficult to understand: durus est hic sermo; and will you also go? (Jn. 13,37; 6,67).

This is my blood which will be shed for you.	He gives his blood for the forgiveness of sins (Mt. 26,27-28).
And now the hand that is to betray me. (Lk. 22,21-22).	
Jesus foretells Peter's denial.	Third characteristic of the true disciple: love, charity, Sign. (Jn. 13,35-38).

I am holy so that they also may be holy.	He immolates himself to sanctify others in truth (Jn. 17,17-19).
He feels fear, sadness, desolation.	He suffer in his soul at the sight of the sins that men will commit. His soul is sad unto death (Mt. 26,37-38).
Sweat of blood.	He suffers to the point of sweating blood at the sight of the crimes of the world (Lk. 22,44).
Jesus betrayed by Judas (Lk.22,47).	
Jesus bound and led away like a criminal.	It is I: he does not cringe before suffering (Jn. 18,4; 18,12).
Jesus struck before Caiaphas (Jn. 18,22).	
Blows, insults and humiliations in Caiaphas' house (Lk. 22,63-65).	
Peter's denial (Lk. 22,55-62).	
Judas' despair and death (Mt. 27,3-10).	
Jesus scorned by Herod and sent back to Pilate (Lk. 23,8-11).	
Jesus compared to Barrabas and scourged (Mt. 27,15-21; Jn. 19,1).	
Crowning with thorns (Jn. 19,2-3).	
Jesus presented to the people and given to be crucified (Jn. 19,4-16).	
Jesus carries his cross (Jn. 19,16).	
Jesus given gall to drink (Mt. 27,34).	

482

Jesus crucified (Lk. 23,33).

He put himself on the level of evil doers (Mk. 15,28).

Jesus is blasphemed (Mt. 27,39-43).

Jesus is given vinegar to drink (Mt.27).

Jesus' thirst (Jn. 19,28).

Jesus gives up his spirit (Jn. 19,30).

> The cross, sign of suffering, is shown everywhere.
> Redemption was achieved only by the cross.

How Jesus bore in himself and on himself this mark of suffering[11].

483 **He offers himself generously to his Father, to suffer**

He accepts with submission everything that his Father's justice demands.

For this, he forcefully fights against the feelings of nature.

Father, deliver me from this hour; yet that is why I came (Jn. 12,27).

He speaks calmly of his passion and death.

He desires it ardently.

He goes to meet his enemies and announces himself for what he is, makes himself known to them and does not fear to say that it is he.

---

[11] Ms XII 681 - No mark of the bourgeois, well-being, comfort, ease. Work.

He speaks to them with dignity, without fear.

He treats them kindly.

He lets himself be taken and led everywhere, without resistance.

He speaks to his judges with dignity, without deviation or weaknes. Truth. He suffers patiently.

He listens patiently to all the accusations brought against him.

He defends himself by keeping silence[12].

He suffers everything with the greatest patience.

Scorn, insults, humiliations, bad treatment.

He forgives with goodness.

He obeys in everything with the greatest perfection.

He suffers everything with love.

He forgets himself in his suffering to think only of others.

---

[12] It is interesting to see in the manuscript itself, how Father Chevrier worked his commentary. The corrections that he makes are for simplicity, sobriety. He first noted an exclamation: How he keeps silent! Then he crossed it off and explains: Instead of defending himself, he keeps a profound silence. This also is crossed off and he writes: He defends himself by keeping silence. There is no doubt that this last phrase is more simple and forceful than the preceding ones.

He seeks no consolation.

He dies as a martyr to obedience and love.

He is always shown nailed to his cross.

There is no greater love than to give one's life for somebody.

We must hate our own life (Lk.14,26).

Need of suffering for every Christian and epecially for the priest.

Did Christ not have to suffer and enter into his glory? (Lk. 24,26).

485 After the example of Jesus, we must suffer.

We must suffer to obtain God's grace.

We must suffer scorn, insults and scourgings from the neighbor, without saying anything.

We must suffer the thievery of the neighbor.

We must endure and even bear the sins of the world,
its pride,
its greed,
its jealousy,
its wickedness,
its hatred,
its anger,
its laziness.

Suffering in the privation of the things of the earth:

He was hungry, thirsty, homeless.

Suffering in voluntary penance:

Fastings, prayers, vigils.

Suffering imposed by God his Father.

Suffering is in the world since the sin of Adam.

Take the sins of others.

Take the sorrows and miseries of others.

Suffering is the characteristic of the true apostle of Jesus Christ[13].	Acts of the Apostles, 9,8-16. It is the characteristic of the apostle.
St. Paul notes that God treats his true apostles as the least of men.	Opposition between protestant ministers, Jews[14], and the true apostles of Jesus Christ. To be a spectacle to the world through sufferings.

486

Difference between the true ministers and the false ones. We, true ministers are weak and you are strong; you are honored and we are scorned. Suffering of the apostle. How he suffers (1 Cor. 4,9-13).

---

[13] Ms XII 680 - There are sufferings that come from poverty, others from charity, others from God, others from ourselves, from the efforts that we make to accomplish our duty. Suffering in the sorrow that we endure to save a soul. It is the great sign of true love. Effects of suffering. Nothing attracts more than suffering. Suffering is an attraction that converts the most hardened souls, attracts the most hardened hearts. It is the seal of great souls. Wherever there is suffering there is gener-osity, devotedness, sacrifice, love and, consequently, grace, merit and reward from the Master for whom we suffer. He suffered in his body and in his soul; he suffered from his apostles, the Jews, his Father.

[14] This unexpected attact on protestant ministers and Jews is strange. We don't see the reason for it here. At any rate, if Father Chevrier knew and respected some protestant minister, it is very probable that he had no personal relations with protestant ministers or Jews. He simply echoes a bad apologetic which was current at the time: to prove the truth of Catholicism by denigrating the non Catholics.

487

St. Paul would rather suffer by working with his hands to earn his living than put the least obstacle to the Gospel.	St. Paul bore the trait of the poverty of the disciple of Jesus Christ. Poverty gives freedom. To suffer to win souls for Jesus Christ (1 Cor. 9,11-26).
I chastize my body and reduce it to servitude.	He does voluntary penance to assure his salvation (1 Cor. 9,27).
St. Paul does not seek what is advantageous to him but what is useful to others.	He renounces all personal advantage to be useful to others (1 Cor. 10,33).
The salvation of others is accomplished by our sufferings.	Excessive evils, even to being condemned to death (2 Cor. 1,3-9).
We carry this treasure in earthen vessels, always bearing in our body the death of Jesus Christ, so that the life of Jesus Christ may appear in our body. Death is at work in us and life in you.	Suffering and death in us produce life and and salvation in you (2 Cor. 4,7-11).
The exterior man is destroyed in us but the interior man is renewed. (2 Cor. 4,13-18).	
We must make ourselves commendable by great patience in evils. (2 Cor. 6,3-11).	
He looks on his sufferings as the true sign of the priest.	Suffering is the mark that he invokes to claim his title of apostle (2 Cor. 11,21-23).
St. Paul boasts of his weakness (2 Cor. 12,9-11).	
Sufferings that he imposes upon himself for his faithful; he is very careful not to be a burden to them.	Characteristic of suffering and poverty, through charity for souls. Sign of my apostolate (2 Cor. 12,12-15).

He is in chains when he writes to the Ephesians (Eph. 4,1-2).

He wants to glorify Jesus Christ in his body through life and death (Phil. 1,20-21).

St. Paul rejoices on seeing his blood shed for the salvation of the faithful.	For the faith of his faithful (Phil. 2,17).
We must seek Jesus Christ's interests and not ours.	We must seek the interests of Jesus Christ to the detriment of ours (Phil. 2,21).
St. Paul wants to know Jesus Christ and become conformed to his death.	He wants to participate in the sufferings of Jesus Christ and be like him (Phil. 3, 10).
We must not behave as enemies of the cross (Phil. 3,18-19).	
St. Paul rejoices in sufferings because he accomplishes in his flesh what is lacking in the sufferings of Jesus Christ.	He rejoices that he accomplishes in his flesh what is lacking in the sufferings of Jesus Christ, by suffering for his body which is the Church (Col. 1,24).
St. Paul reminds the Thessalo nians of the labors and fatigues he has endured.	He wished [to make himself small among them]. He worked with his hands to be a burden to no one (1 Thes. 2, 1-12).

St. Paul reminds the Thessalonians of how he lived among them (2 Thes. 3,7-12)

St. Paul, apostle of the nations. That is what draws down upon him the evils he suffers. (2 Tim. 11-12).

St. Paul endures everything for love of the elect.	so that they may have salvation (2 Tim. 2,8-13).
St. Paul tells Timothy that he must know his life, his doctrine, his persecutions (2 Tim. 3,10-12).	
Watch, endure work constantly; I am like a victim; the time of my death is approaching.	He is a victim designated for the sacrifice (2 Tim. 4, 5-8).
489 The victim has to be rational, capable of suffering. The blood of oxen.	Offering of Jesus to his Father: here I am (Heb. 10, 4-9).
I boast in nothing else but the cross of Jesus Christ. Why I bear the stigmata in my body.	Characteristic of suffering. St. Paul bears the stigmata imprinted upon his body (Gal. 6,14-17).
He is as crucified. Those who belong to Jesus Christ have crucified their flesh. (Gal. 5,24).	
If we have died with Jesus Christ, we shall live.	Reward if we have died (Rom. 6,8).
Every day we are given to death for you. We are as sheep destined for the slaughter (Rom. 8, 36).	
Those who wish to live in righteousness will be persecuted. (2 Tim. 3,12)	Ibant gaudentes apostoli a conspectu concilii quoniam digni habiti sunt pro nomine Jesu contumeliam pati[15].

Quotidie morior per vestram gloriam[16]. Hoc fac et vives[17].
The one who does these things can truly say: my life is Jesus Christ (Phil. 1,21). Si hoec scitis, beati eritis, si feceritis ea[18].

---

[15] The apostles left the Sanhedrin joyful that they had been deemed worthy of suffering for the name of Jesus (Acts 5,41).

[16] Every day, I die for your glory (1 Cor. 15,31). Translation of the Latin text.

[17] Do this and you shall live (Lk. 10,28).

[18] Knowing this, blessed will you be if you do it (Jn. 13,17).

11. Follow me in my death[1]   491

---

[1] Ms XII 699.

Under this title of "Follow me in my death" we find only a very brief, hardly developed study on the Passion.
This study begins with Jesus' prayer which, in St. John, immediately precedes the account of the passion[2]*. In fact, this prayer is like an anticipated liturgical expression of the mystery which was accomplished in the death of Christ.*
In another manuscript that was not destined for The True Disciple, *we find an interesting commentary. Father Chevrier comments the title of* Savior *attributed to Jesus. He describes Christ's attitude during the Passion noting his* submission, ardor, courage, silence, dignity, meekness, humility, goodness, love, the perfection *of his obedience and in all this, he writes this phrase:* with what power he dies[3].
To follow Jesus Christ in his death is to participate in the work by which, by virtue of his divine omnipotence, he saved the world.

---

[2] Jn. 17.
[3] Ms VIII 253-256.

I have glorified you on earth   495

I have accomplished the work that you have given me and now I have manifested [your name].... (Jn.17,4-6).

Those that you have given me, I have kept and not one has perished (Jn. 17,12)

How Jesus behaves when they come to take him:

   I am he (Jn. 18,4-5)
   He does not want the apostles to fight for him (Jn. 18,11).
   He heals Malchus (Lk. 22,51).
   And the chalice that I must drink.....(Jn. 18,11).
   He is silent before the high priest Caiaphas (Mk. 14,60-61).
   He allows himself to be bound and led away (Jn. 18,12).

(Notebook: manner in which he suffers)[4]

The fight leads to death.

Hatred and jealousy, having reached the ultimate degree, demand death.

---

[4] This note refers certainly to one of the studies on the Passion, cf. for example, Ms VI 434-435 where we find the phrase: With what power he suffers (P. 443).

12. You will follow me in my glory[1]

---

[1] Ms XII 689-699.

The last title is different from the preceding ones. It is no longer an invitation: 499
follow me, *but a promise:* you will follow me in my glory.
From the promises that the Lord had made to them, the princes of the apostles, Peter and Paul, drew the courage to accomplish the work that had been given them[2]. *Those promises are also addressed to us and since Jesus Christ wished to make them to us, we owe him to listen to them, receive them to find courage, strength and joy.*

---

[2] P. 452.

Promises that Jesus Christ made to 501
his disciples.

The one who confesses me before men,
I will confess him before my Father in
heaven.

He who follows me does not walk in
darkness, but he will have the light
of life[3].

Qui mihi ministrat me sequatur et ubi
ego sum illic sit et minister meus[4].

Si quis mihi ministraverit honorificabit
eum Pater meus qui est in caelis[5].

Volo Pater ut ubi ego sum,
illic sit et minister meus[6].

Beatus vir qui suffert tentationem 502
quoniam eum probatus fuerit accipiet
coronam vitae quam repomisit Deus
deligentibus se (Jas. 1,12)[7].

Quicumque hanc regulam secuti fuerunt
pax super illos et misericordia (Gal. 6,16)[8].

Jesus' prayer after the meal.

You are my friends if you follow my commandment.
I no longer call you servants, because the servant does not know what his master does,

---

[3] The first five sentences are the antiphons for Lauds of the common of martyrs.

[4] If anyone serves me, let him follow me, and where I am, there shall my servant be also (Jn. 2,26).

[5] If anyone serves me, my Father who is in heaven will honor him (Jn. 12,26).

[6] Father, I wish that where I am, my servant may be also (Jn. 17,24).

[7] Happy the man who bears trials! once his valor is recognized, he will receive the crown of life that the Lord promised to those who love him.

[8] To all those who will follow this rule, peace and mercy.

But I have called you friends because I have told you everything that I heard from my father (Jn. 15,14-15).

Words to St. Peter:

St. Peter said to Jesus:
Behold that we have left everything and followed you.
What will be our reward?

Jesus answered:
In truth, I tell you that you who have followed me, when the time of regeneration comes, the Son of man will be seated on the throne of glory, you will be seated on twelve thrones and you will judge the twelve tribes of Israel.

And whoever will have left house, or brothers or sisters, or his father or mother, or his wife and children for me and for the Gospel, will receive the hundredfold of houses, brothers, sisters, mothers, children, lands, with persecutions in this life, and eternal life in the next (Mt. 19,27-29).

St. Paul's confidence before dying.

Bonum certamen certavi
cursum consummavi, fidem servavi[9].

Henceforth there is laid up for me the crown of righteousness which the Lord, the just judge will award to me. (2 Tim. 4,7-8).

---

[9] I have fought the good fight, I have finished the race, I have kept the faith.

ANNEXES 505

506   *As announced in the general introduction, the documents that follow are useful and almost indispensable for a better understanding of Father Chevrier's thought. In particular, they have the advantage of giving a more summarized, more terse expression of that thought.*
They are annexed to The True Disciple *to explain it, not complete it. They do not give Father Chevrier's whole thought. On topics of such importance, and on others, Father Chevrier explained himself at length in other writings, in particular, in the preparation of catechisms, and in commentaries on the mysteries of the Rosary.*

ANNEX I - Ms XI 543-550.

This manuscript opens and closes with the word disciple. The end is even a bit odd; the word disciple is detached from the rest of the text and includes a paragraph like a signature. That is why we have highlighted it by writing it in capital letters.

The most remarkable passage is perhaps the one that describes the sovereign liberty with which the Spirit of God communicates himself to us. The Spirit blows where he wills; Father Chevrier experienced it[1].

Nothing deals with the Mass as such, and nothing on the Blessed Virgin by herself.

---

[1] P. 459.

		what he is
	to know	
duties		what he says
	to love	
	to follow	

Disciple

Obstacles to becoming a disciple.   I saw that you did not have the love of God in you... if another comes [in his own name, you receive him]... [you] do not seek the glory that comes from [God alone] (Jn.5:42,44).
The kingdom of heaven is like a hidden treasure....he sells everything to buy it (Mt. 13,44).
My words are spirit and life (Jn. 6,63).
We must ask God for the understanding of his word and doctrine.
Jesus rebukes Peter who does not want him to suffer (Mt. 16,23), you do not understand what is from God, but from men.
Qui potest capere capiat[2].
Qui habet aures audiendi audiat[3].
His apostles do not understand the mystery of suffering when Jesus speaks of it (Lk. 18,34).
My doctrine is not from me but from the one who sent me.

They will know if my doctrine comes from me.   If any man's will is to do his will, he shall know whether the teaching is from God or whether I am speaking on my own authority (Jn.7,16-17).

If you persevere in my doctrine, you will truly be my disciples and you will know the truth and the truth will make you free. (Jn. 8,31-32).
The one who is from God listens to the word of God (Jn. 8,47).
I speak to you and you do not believe me; but you do not believe me because you are not of my sheep; my sheep hear my voice, I know them and they follow me (Jn. 10,25).

---

[2] Let he who can understand, understand (Mt. 13,43).
[3] If anyone has ears to hear, let him hear (Mk. 4,23).

I speak to you and you do not believe me; but you do not believe me because you are not of my sheep; my sheep hear my voice, I know them and they follow me (Jn. 10,25).
Non omnes, not everyone understands this word. But those to whom it has been given to understand (Mt. 19,11).

Promise to the disciple.	If anyone serves me, let him follow me, and where I am, there will my servant be.

If anyone serves me, my Father will honor him (Jn. 12,26).

Servant no greater.	The servant is not greater than his master, nor the apostle greater than the one who sent him (Jn. 13,16).
Blessed if you know.	If you know these things, blessed shall you be, as long as you put them into practice (Jn. 13,17).
To love Jesus Christ.	If anyone loves me, he will keep my word and my Father will love him and we will come to him and dwell in him.

The one who does not love me...(Jn. 14,23).
It is to my Father's glory that you become my disciples and that you bear much fruit (Jn. 15,8).

The disciple of Jesus Christ is a man who is filled with his Master's spirit, who thinks like his Master, who acts like his Master, who follows him everywhere and in everything.
But in practice, few receive, understand or admit this spirit of God. Only those who belong to God, who listen to his word, to whom he has given to receive it.
No one goes to the Son except through the Father.

Therefore it is a great grace to receive this spirit that the world cannot receive. If we are of the world, if we think like the world - ideas of the world - we cannot receive it; we must be stripped of ourselves to receive and understand it.
This spirit is poured in the Holy Gospel. That is where it is planted like flowers that we must gather one by one to take as many as possible.

511 Our Lord had this spirit totally; we can only have it partially, but at least let us try to take as much as possible to be animated by it as much as possible and glorify Jesus Christ and his Father.

This spirit is little known, little tasted, little understood, even by those who should possess and understand him: the habits, customs, ideas that we have, the reasonings that we do, exterior examples, draw the people and even priests, to live according to the spirit of the world and not according to the spirit of God.

In such a way that, if we want to act according to the spirit of God, we must struggle greatly against the ideas, customs, manners of others; and that is why the saints, who had the spirit of God, had to suffer so much, even on the part of their brothers.

But we must not stop there; we must trust in Jesus Christ and his word. That is the unshakable and solid foundation on which we can rest assured: Jesus Christ and the Church.

Based on these two foundations, we can only walk in confidence, in spite of the annoyances, combats, struggles and persecutions.

O my God, give me your spirit: that is the prayer that we must make constantly and always, at every moment; the spirit of God, that is everything! If we are animated by it, we have everything, we possess all the riches of heaven and earth.

But we must ask for it with the real intention of receiving it, with the will to do everything possible, with the will to make every sacrifice possible and required to have it and receive it; otherwise we will not be able to receive it and God will not be able to give it.

The spirit of God is neither in a positive rule, nor in formalities; not in exterior practices or clothes, nor in regulations; it is in us when it is given to us.

We hear this sound but we do not know where it comes from nor where it goes, it blows where it wills. It comes when we least expect it. When we seek it we do not find it; when we do not seek it we find it; it is independent of our will, the moment, the time, the hour; it comes when it wants, it is up to us to receive it when it comes. It has full liberty of action, it is independent of us, but it communicates itself to us when we think the least about it; it is not in reasonings, nor in study nor in theories nor in rules; but it is the divine fire that is always at work, which rises irregularly, it shows itself and disappears, like the flame in the wood; we must take it and rejoice when it shows itself... and conserve it every time that it communicates itself to us.

St. Paul knows only Jesus Christ and him crucified (1 Cor. 2,2).

Nobody knows what is in God except the spirit of God (1 Cor. 2,11).

Animal man does not conceive of the things of God, they appear as folly to him, but the spiritual man judges everything (1 Cor. 2,14).

Degrees to become disciples of Jesus Christ: carnal - child - food (1 Cor. 3,1).

Who will separate us from the love of Jesus Christ? Nothing (Rom. 8,35).

Let no one deceive himself, if anyone appears wise according to the world, let him become foolish in order to become wise. For the wisdom of this world is folly before God (1 Cor. 3,19).

We are foolish because of Jesus Christ (1 Cor. 4,10.).

If anyone does not love Our Lord Jesus Christ, let him be cursed (1 Cor. 16,22).

Good odor [of Jesus Christ].	We are the good odor of Jesus Christ (2 Cor. 2,15).
live according to the spirit and not according to the letter.	The letter kills but the spirit vivifies (2 Cor. 3,6).
freedom.	Where the spirit of the Lord is, there is freedom (2 Cor. 3,17).
love must make us live through Jesus Christ.	The love of Jesus Christ urges us, considering that if one died for all, we are all dead and we must live for the one who has died (2 Cor.

5,14).If I still wished to please men, I would not be the servant of Jesus Christ (Gal. 1,10). Paul's fidelity to his vocation, to God's call on him...(Gal2,8).
Knowledge of Jesus Christ: height and depth... of this great mystery (Eph. 3,18).
Jesus Christ, that is my life (Phil. 1,21).
His love for Jesus: coarctor e duobus[4] (Phil. 1,23).
Everyone seeks his own interests and we seek those of Jesus Christ my Savior, for love of whom...(Phil. 3,8).
We are already living in heaven, from which we expect...(Phil 3,20).
He became used to everything, to misery and to abundance (Phil. 4,12).

513 Therefore, walk in the ways of Jesus Christ our.... rooted and built on him as on your foundation (Col. 2,7).
Jesus our model: be holy in your conduct, like the one who has called you is holy (1 Pet. 1,5).
Jesus has left us an example so that we may walk in his steps (1 Pet. 2,21).
The one who claims to dwell in Jesus Christ must walk like Jesus Christ himself walked (1 Jn. 2,6).

Take up one's cross.

is to accept sufferings that come from: poverty,
renunciation of creatures,
renunciation of oneself.
is to accept persecutions that a disciple of Jesus must expect.
whoever does not want to carry his cross and follow me cannot be

DISCIPLE

---

[4] I feel caught in this dilemma (to go and be with Christ... to stay in the flesh... for your good).

ANNEX II - Ms XII 25-26.

We have already seen the essential place that the study of the Gospel holds in Father Chevrier's thought.

We must first read and re-read the Holy Gospel, be penetrated by it, study it, know it by heart, study each word, each action, to grasp the meaning and have it pass in our thoughts and actions.
It is in daily prayer that we must make this study and make Jesus Christ pass in our lives[1].

This assiduous prayer, this meditation must be nourished with the knowledge of Jesus Christ that is not vague but precise. That is why we must be attentive to the details of the Gospel. Not get fixed on a detail to draw a whole development from it; this would be to make the Gospel say what we want it to say. Not choose the details that justify preconceived ideas; that would be to submit the Gospel to our own thought, when we should do the contrary.
Father Chevrier suggests taking from the Gospel everything that relates to a question and he likes to make a complete chart to have the whole before his eyes. That is what he seeks when he makes a summary of the examples, of the teachings of Jesus Christ, St. Paul.
As for the meditation that should assimilate this work, it can be very simple. Father Chevrier never thought that meditation should be compelled to reasoning on every detail drawn from the Gospel; on the contrary, the advice that he gives for meditation takes the way of simplicity.
This spiritual use of the Gospel is not opposed to a proper exegetic study, that is clear in principle. Yet, in practice, that creates difficulties.
Those difficulties are inevitable for theology students. When they discover the value of modern exegesis, they are a bit dazzled and have a tendency to think that, with this, they will be able to penetrate the Gospel in depth. Yet, sooner or later, we must come back to the more fundamental questions. Is the Gospel made to allow me to meet Jesus Christ or only to hear of him? Is it to transform my life or only to give me some ideas that I will use as I please? We know what faith's answer is and we are obliged to have recourse to the grace of the Spirit who alone can put the Gospel at our disposal to make us know, love, follow Jesus Christ.

---

[1] P. 199.

Father Chevrier compares the study of the Gospel to the discovery of a house. A psalm that uses the same comparison expresses very well what this study of the Gospel is.

> *Walk about Zion, go round about her,*
> *Number her towers,*
> *Consider well her ramparts,*
> *go through her Citadels;*
>
> *that you may tell the next generation,*
> *that this is our God,*
> *our God for ever and ever,*
> *He will be our guide for ever*[2].

---

[2] Ps. 48, 13-15.

[To know the Gospel]

In our Lord's life we find Wisdom and light. It is in these little details that we find our rule and conduct and perfection and a sure teaching according to God, since it is God himself who shows it to us.
What is the use of the Gospel, if not for study?
To know the Gospel well, we must enter into every fact, every action; it is there that we will find wisdom.
When we go down a street and see a nice house, we look at it and say: that is a nice house; we only see the exterior, we are not aware of what is inside, what there is of decoration, beauty, comfort, etc. We go by, we look, we say: that's nice, and that's it: we do not use it... But if we enter it and visit each story, each room, we may admire the order, the interior beauty, the perfect order.
It is the same with the Gospel. Many look at it and say: its nice and have not entered into it to examine the interior beauties and cannot use it, enjoy it and use the things they find therein.
To know a house we must enter it and use the rooms that make it up. To know the Gospel we must enter into it, see the details and put in practice the things that we find there; and we need only enter a little, to study its details to understand immediately how beautiful, great, perfect this house is. It is truly Wisdom's house.
In the study of our Lord, we find true light; we find our rule of life ready made, all prepared, already chewed; only, we have to look for it and find it. When we go into an open field, we see all sorts of plants; if you need a violet you have to look for it, if you need a borage you have to look for it; if you need rare leaves, you have to look for them.
Look in the Gospel and you will find all the plants and flowers that we need to give us life and maintain it in us.

518 ANNEX III - Ms X 653-61

These thoughts on poverty *deal with the poverty of the* priest. *We may refer to the particular introductions on* Renunciation of the goods of the earth[1] *and on* Follow me in my poverty[2]. *Two Latin phrase give emphasis to these pages, like a kind of refrain:* nos vero orationi and praedicationi instantes erimus[3]. *It is the words of the apostles at the time of the institution of the diaconate: As for us, we will remain assiduous in prayer and in the service of the word*[4].
Virtus de illo exibat[5]. *A strength came out of him, says the Gospel of St. Luke, concerning Jesus*[6].
These words give us the meaning of the priest's poverty according to Father Chevrier. This poverty is based on the conviction that only the Word of God is efficacious to do the work of God.

---

[1] P. 241.
[2] P. 355.
[3] Acts 6,4.
[4] Cf. P. 465, note 7; pp. 468-469.
[5] Lk. 6,19.
[6] Cf. pp. 466-467.

Thoughts on Poverty - The priest, man stripped of everything.

It is in poverty that the priest finds his strength; his power and freedom. What can anyone do against a poor, detached priest. Today more than ever, we must be poor to fight against the world, against terrestrial pleasures, luxury and well-being which are growing prodigiously everywhere.

The priest must not follow the world, he must go before it to be its master, to stop it and lead it.

If the priest does like everybody, how will he be able to instruct them and lead them?

Today, well-being and luxury lose people; it is up to us to act differently and give men examples opposed to theirs.

The priest is the ornament and the glory of God's house; he must be its wealth and glory; what are all the exterior ornaments without the priest?

Let us not put our spirit and our time in accessories, leaving aside the principal.

What is the use of so many candles and lights if the priest is not the true light of the faithful?

What is the use of that wealth of ornaments and exterior lustre if the priest is not clothed with charity and humility?

God's wealth, God's grandeur is in the holiness of the priest and not in the exterior ornaments or wealth of our temples.

Let us not confuse the principal with the accessory. Unfortunately, that is what we do today; we think only of decorating churches, building beautiful temples, beautiful houses, giving them a beautiful exterior and we do not see that this is displeasing to God and makes us neglect the true and only useful necessary. Let us not be concerned with building and embellishing; let us leave that to the lay people. The time used for this is wasted time. The contacts that this necessitates and the troubles that it causes take us away from the principal occupation which is the salvation of the neighbor and our sanctification; often also there are disputes, court cases, difficulty in payment; we spend our lives asking for money and boring people. *Nos vero orationi et praedicationi erimus*[7]. *Martha, Martha porro unum est necessarium*[8].

Build nothing, do not seek to embellish your house: That is the rule that I take with the grace of God, leaving all that to the lay people and the people charged with this, when it is absolutely necessary and never undertake more that we can pay for. It is better to have only a board and a tile to cover ourselves than to put ourselves in

---

[7] We will remain assiduous in prayer and preaching the word (Acts, 6.4). The exact Latin text: nos vero orationi et ministerio verbi instantes erimus.

[8] Martha, Martha, only one thing is necessary (Lk. 10,41).

trouble, and on seeing us suffer and lack everything, the faithful will only be the more edified by the good example that will come out of it.
Jesus Christ, our model, had neither house nor exterior trappings; he used what he had, where he was and we do not see that he had anything built. He himself was the wealth and beauty of the faithful.
A holy, poor priest is all the wealth.
A poor, holy priest, in a wooden church is more agreable to God, useful to the faithful than an ordinary priest in a golden church. What converts the sinner is not exterior wealth; on the contrary, that only serves to excite their curiosity and jealousy.
It is not usually before the gold and silver statues that miracles and pilgrimages occur, but before the humble, poor statues disdained by the honors of the world.
What excites curiosity does not lead to piety, yet the principal aim that we should have in everything is piety, faith, love of our Lord. That is why we must be poor everywhere, even in our discourses, sermons, so that luxury and curiosity and a certain complacency may not replace faith and piety.
When we do not have other but lodgings and we are sent elsewhere and are obliged to move, like the poor, that is when we have true poverty. Why would the soldiers of Jesus Christ not practice poverty like the emperor's soldiers. They carry everything with them, move at the first order, sleep on a board. What right do we have to be better lodged, better fed, than the poor of the earth?

521 Poverty maintains us in humility, meekness, trust, prayer, in relation with God and men. It suffices that our feet touch the ground; we need not put our hands and head.
The priest is the most beautiful candle in the church.
The priest is the most beautiful lustre, the most beautiful chandelier in the church.
It is a great mistake to think that we attract by this exterior brilliance; that only excites curiosity. But produce grace by exterior means: that is a mistake. A poor and holy priest will convert more people by his example than all the lustre in the world, than all the candles in the world, than all the exterior beauty that is badly displayed in vain to attract people. Jesus Christ, poor and denuded, attracted more to himself by his poverty than all the gold in the world, *virtus de illo exibat*[9], which we cannot say of any exterior thing.
It is easier to have candles, lustre, coffers, drapes and all those trappings than to have holiness; an ounce of holiness is worth more than all the brilliance in the world.
We must not tire the faithful with useless requests; if we preach and practice poverty and, on the side, are continuously asking for things, objects, etc., we tire them, bore them and repel them; let us leave the offerings free so that they may have nothing to say.
It is better to have one cent offered freely than a thousand francs given reluctantly.

---

[9] A strength came out of him (Lk. 6,19).

If we are really poor, they will respect us more and give more; let us not tire the faithful with our importunate and repeated demands. The truly poor suffers and asks only for what is necessary, which God does not refuse.

A poor and holy priest in a wooden church converts more sinners than an ordinary priest in a gold and marble church decorated with all sorts of exterior beauty.

It is a proof of our poverty of virtue and holiness when we are obliged to borrow the brilliance and beauty of exterior things to attract people to us.

Our Lord Jesus Christ said: When I am lifted up, I will draw all things to me. The poor cross covered with blood drew the world. Poverty and suffering will attract more than all the splendor and exterior beauty of the world.

Is it not shameful to have to borrow from exterior things that brilliance, that pomp that we should have within ourselves? Is it not a proof of our poverty, of our indigence when, to draw people, we have to go to such exterior expense? Is it not to scorn the faithful and consider them as children when we attract them with baubles, games and other things, as is done in the fairs, market places or shows; they said of Jesus Christ: *virtus de illo exibat*[10].

Not that we must condemn exterior worship, since the Church requires it and we are composed of body and soul and that exterior things should lead us to God. But let us not be led by that passion that exists nowadays and let us not take the accessory for the principal.

Simplicity and poverty: that is what is appropriate for us in particular and that we should embrace.

We must beware of using natural means to obtain money; they do not come from God but are invented to excite the cupidity of people; such as lotteries, concerts, evenings, amusements; nothing is more opposed to true charity. It is no longer an alms but it is curiosity, cupidity and more sins are committed in using these means than acts of charity.

Let us not go look for money in the world, by spending our time in parlors, visits to the great; we have to lose time, tell lies, receive praise or give praise to people; lose our time, scandalize perhaps and tire people who do not always receive us with pleasure. Remember that when we ask for money from the people of the world, we are not doing them a favor. Go only when they say so, ask you, and briefly.

Let us be truly poor and come close to the poor as much as possible. We are more in our right and state when we beg at the door of a church or in the street than in making useless and painful visits. In begging at the door of a church or in the street we do not tire anybody and each one is free to give what they wish. All those people who run after money, seek money do not do God's work, and a priest especially must not waste time in something so harmful to himself and others.

What right do we have to be better lodged, better dressed, better fed than the poor of the world?

---

[10] Cf. p. 466, note 9.

Is it not shameful to see priests become rich, buy lands, houses with the Church's money, and priests who, in the world would have been poor workmen, would hardly have eked out a living in the world, priests who owe to the Church the alms of being priest and who become rich?
Do we become priests to be rich?
How unfortunate for the Church!
Those who do not have a patrimony must not acquire one.

523   In our day, the passion to build seems to invade every priest. Especially those who are at the head of religious establishments or churches: they all want to enlarge their church, the rectory, their boarding school. So, what happens? They have to leave the spiritual work, the work of souls to take care of the material work, stones, walls, pulpits, altars... and they are obliged to leave the catechism, prayer, confession, the work of souls.

The apostles had said: *nos vero orationi et praedicationi instantes erimus*[11]: We must leave those exterior things and be concerned only with the things of God: that is the principal thing for the priest.

How much time lost for God, for souls, for our own sanctification!

They are constantly obliged to run to the Prefect, the Mayor, the Emperor, Mr. Somebody, Mrs. Somebody. Is that God's work? No, it is human work. *Seek the kingdom of God and all the rest will be given you.*

Was the Curé of Ars concerned with building? Did he go seeking money, running to one and the other? And yet, what priest had more money than he? They brought it to him from all the corners of the earth.

The reason is that it is easier to run from one to the other than to be holy.

Do you want to have money, beautiful churches, beautiful ornaments? *become holy, be poor.*

In a church, as in our room, we must avoid having things that excite curiosity and destroy attention to God. In ornaments and other things... the thought of God must emerge and not the thought of art or good taste. Spiritus est Deus et eos qui adorant eum in spiritu et veritate oportet adorare[12].

It is also against the spirit of poverty to hold lotteries, give concerts, have meetings to make money under whatever pretext. It is not true charity and they are too natural mean for a priest.

The poor man finds his glory in the regulation of his life and in fear of God, others are honored for their great wealth[13].

It is also against the spirit of poverty and humility to impose ourselves on people, to believe that people owe us anything, that those who do not give to us are remiss in

---

[11] Cf. p. 465, note 7.

[12] God is spirit and those who adore him must do so in spirit and in truth (Jn. 4,24).

[13] Probably a free translation of Scripture, see for example Ecc. 10,30.

their duty. It is ridiculous to demand alms, gifts of them. Do they owe us anything? What right do we have?

It is also against the spirit of poverty and of the Gospel to encumber ourselves with a thousand temporal concerns, to be merchants or integrate ourselves in the affairs of the world, even under the pretext of good works, such as, for example, making the children work, directing workshops.

The work of the priest must be totally spiritual.

Nos vero orationi et praedicationi instantes erimus[14].

Those works necessarily oblige us to have relations of negotiation with the world, markets, buying and selling, and by the very fact create a thousand concerns and a thousand troubles.

Never put ourselves at the head of such houses.

We must remember that voluntary and sought for poverty is not equal to the effective poverty of the poor of the world, mothers of families, unemployed workers, the poor without food and lodging... and that a voluntarily poor religious will never suffer as much as the poor of the world.

That is why St. Francis, who truly loved poverty, envied the lot of the poor and worked to become like them.

---

[14] Cf. 465, note 7.

525 ANNEX IV - Ms X 150-156.

In January, 1879, a few months before his death, Father Chevrier asked the Archbishop of Lyons to accept his resignation as superior of the Prado and name Francois Duret, who was then 26 years old and ordained 18 months[1], as the new superior.
A few notes that we have show that he had been thinking about it for some time and that he was still perplexed.
 Nomination of a superior.
 Necessity.
 Difficulties: young and unable to chose well themselves.
 Nomination: it would be better to have him named by the authorities.
 How: general meeting, older priests, two thirds of the votes.

A little further, concerning the qualities that he would like in the new superior, we read:
The most the spirit of the work: catechism, poverty, disciple[2].
This last enumeration is important for it summarizes all Father Chevrier's concepts on the apostle and poverty.
He is a catechist, that is, he dedicates himself totally to making Jesus Christ known with simplicity.
He is poor, that is, poverty is the principal sign that accompanies his preaching of the Gospel.
He is a disciple, that is, his ministry and his life find their source in his union to Jesus Christ.
We have already shown what idea of the Mission and in particular the mission of the priest, underlies The True Disciple[3].
526 *Concerning the mission of the superior, we find here the same doctrine: the superior does not replace someone who is absent, he does not succeed to someone who is*

---

[1] Cf. P. 9.
[2] Ms X 145.
[3] Cf. P. 182.

gone; he represents an Invisible one who manifests himself through him. Therefore, the obligation for the superior, as for every apostle, to say nothing and do nothing of himself, *but to* say everything and do everything through Jesus Christ or with Jesus Christ and in union with Jesus Christ[4].
The reference to the conclusion of the Eucharistic Prayer in the Roman liturgy is evident. Through him, with him and in him....
The indications that Father Chevrier then gives are interesting. He insists on the fact that the superior must not leave his specific function, the governent, to others. This insistence is explained by the situation in which Father Duret was to find himself. Young superior, he has three confrères of the same age and a few who are older. Among the latter, some had not approved Father Chevrier, far from it; others did not have the judgement, the firmness necessary to govern properly. Thus he had to warn Father Duret against indiscreet incursions.
Certain expressions, like general surveillance, *have a displeasing resonnance today. It suffices to read Father Chevrier's explanations to understand the meaning properly*[5].
We do not have the copy of that text, the manuscript is lost.

---

[4] P. 472.
[5] P. 474.

527	*To my brother Francois Duret*
Superior of the Providence of the Prado

Warning. You must remember that there is only one Master and Superior in heaven and on earth, who is Jesus Christ to whom God gave all power and all authority in the world. That, consequently, any superior is only the representative of Jesus Christ and that he must act and speak only in union with Jesus Christ. And that if Our Lord says of himself that he says and does nothing of himself, all the more reason for a superior on earth not to say and do anything of himself but he must say and do everything through Jesus Christ, or with Jesus Christ and in union with Jesus Christ and be so united to Jesus Christ, the only and true Master in order to be able to say in truth: it is not I who speak or command, it is Jesus Christ who speaks and commands in me.

This is the first truth with which you must be imbued to become a good superior.

Qualities of a good superior. *Calm*: Always posses one's soul, in all circumstances, good or bad. Never show anger, impatience, weakness, irritation, and for this, moderate your interior feelings.

Serious. Put aside everything that is childish, have the seriousness of age in spite of your youth.

Reflect. Say and do nothing without having reflected on it at length before God who alone is able to enlighten us.

528	*Prudent*. Understand and foresee the implications of our words and actions so as not to say or do anything that might be detrimental to ourselves or others.

Discreet. Be reserved in our words, never reveal the secrets of others, speak of everything with reserve and moderation.

Capable. Of instructing on the things of God and the things concerning the Work, and for that, be able to study in depth what relates to these things.
To rebuke faults, and for this, to know the different faults that are harmful to souls and the Work: see the faults, know them, grasp them.
To deal with all that concerns the interior or the order of the house, persons, individuals. He must be the councilor and father of all. Outside, with business people, obligations, buyers, sellers, notaries...

Meek. To possess souls. Blessed are the meek, they shall possess the earth. Avoid all brusqueness, wickedness, bitterness.

Patient. Be able to bear many things because no one is perfect. Be able to wait, endure many things, as long as the faults do not harm the community; when they harm the general good...

Charitable. With everybody. Love everybody in God and for God, having no preference or partiality for anyone, but loving everybody in God and for God.

Conciliatory. Always seeking to put peace among everyone, avoiding divisions, schisms, separations, seeking to unite everybody in the same bond of love and charity.

Firm. Once something good and useful for the Work or an individual has been decided, maintain it so that the duty may be accomplished. We must not only say and command, we must also see that what we command is done, otherwise it turns to nothing.

Persevering. Undertake, begin nothing before having weighed, reflected well; but once something is begun, pursue it to the end; it is the only way of achieving something solid and lasting. To begin and not pursue is a sign of weakness and misunderstood zeal and this so frequent fault makes us lose our authority. It is better to do little and finish it than to begin many things and finish nothing; and do things one after the other.

Role of the superior.   *Preside.* It is the superior's duty to be first in everything; that is what his title expresses and that is why... sign of authority given to him. He must remember that he must be first in virtue and humiliate himself.

Admit and dismiss. He is the one to receive subjects in the house. Nobody can enter or leave, be received in or dismised from the house without his approbation.

Relations with the Bishop or Superiors. It is up to him to report to the Bishop or his delegate from time to time on the state of the Work, its progess, its failings.

Govern. The government of the house is his exclusively. He it is who has received God's grace for that and no one can or should do anything or change anything or undertake anything without his authorization. Everything must be done by you, head of the house. Give judgement. Receive strangers, benefactors, visits.

Duties

Give good example. He must be the model and example for everybody by his regularity and his whole exterior. Our Lord did not say anything else to his disciples: "Sequere me"[6], showing by his words that they had nothing else to do but to follow him.

Instruct. He must be filled with the spirit of God to be able to communicate to everybody, at every moment, what is necessary for his instruction and progress.

Rebuke. That is a great duty. It does not suffice to say, he must rebuke, pull out the weeds, advise people of their fault, make them know and understand them and help them to pull them out.

Great duty: it is because we do not rebuke enough that the householder's field is invaded by evil. We must constantly root out evil as we notice it.

Action. We must also make people do, make them execute what we have commanded and ordered. That is where courage, firmness and perseverance are really needed; to have others do what we have judged to be good.

Before God. The charge of superior comes from God; it is he who will ask for an account of our stewardship.

Responsible before men. If something inconvenient or bad occurs in a community, it is to the superior that people complain and it is he who must justify the conduct of his subject.

General surveillance. Therefore, he must watch over the whole community, the keeping of the rule, the accomplishment of charges, exercises, have an eye on everything, be aware of everything that is going on, be alert to see, hear, without people being aware of it.

Particular. That is, watch every individual, be aware of each one, what he is, what he does, his behavior, his character, know everybody.

Councilor. Must be all things to everyone. Each one must have recourse to him as to his light. He is the friend and father of everyone in this world. His room must be open to everyone without distinction. He is the father and friend of everyone.

---

[6] Follow me.

Difficult task. Woe to the one who wants to be superior, who seeks to be superior. He takes upon himself a great burden that he will not be able to carry without God's grace. A good superior is the salvation of souls, the glory of God, the Church; as a bad superior is the ruin of souls, the distruction of communities, the shame of his house.

Charges and responsibilities.

Means to fulfill worthily this great responsibility.

Prayer. He must pray more than the others because he has more responsibility than the others, he needs more graces for himself and for others. He must pray at every moment to remain up to his task.

Union with our Lord Jesus Christ. To be one with him so that he may speak in you, act in you and that you may say like St. Paul: I live, now not I, but Jesus Christ speaks, commands in me.

Love of God. Do every thing for God, in view of God, his glory. Seek only the glory of God. Do you love me? Do you love me? said Jesus to Peter before entrusting him with the government of the Church. In fact, to govern others we must love God. Suffer.

souls: In the orders that we may give, seek only the salvation of souls, we must not seek what is pleasing to them, what is agreeable, we must seek their spiritual good. That is why, at times we may appear cruel in demanding thing that annoy them and yet are necessary for the glory of God and their spiritual good.

Jesus Christ's words to his apostles.

Many of the first [will be last]. I did not come to serve...

Haec Meditare[7]. St. Paul to Titus.

Director[8].

531

    Direct. Spiritual, not temporal director.
    Prayers.
    Meditation. Notebook. Spiritual reading.
    Catechism.

---

[7] Meditate these things (1 Tim. 4,15).

[8] Here should have begun a list of the various charges done by the people in the house of the Prado. It was never drawn up.

Cards.
Spiritual correspondence.
Replace the superior in spiritual thing, meetings.
Give permissions in the absence of the superior.
Give the order, assign Masses, preaching to the sisters.

ANNEX V

Father Chevrier had been given a small house in Saint-Fons, in the suburbs of Lyons.
The house, which has been preserved, was then in the middle of fields, on the plateau that overlooks the Rhone valley, the Clochettes Plateau. It was set up as a retreat house and in the room on the ground floor where there was a manger for animals, Father Chevrier had the idea of transferring to the walls a tableau that he had drawn up on paper a long time before. Thus, it became the habit at the Prado to refer to it as the Tableau of Saint-Fons[1].
The arrangement of the walls invited Father Chevrier to modify the order that he had put on paper. Thus, the tableau became a veritable tryptic: the mystery of the Eucharist is in the center with the door that opens into the little chapel while the panel of the crib and that of the cross converge on the central panel.
This panel was not invented by Father Chevrier. Others before him have had the idea of summarizing the evangelical ideal in the light of three main aspects of the mystery of Christ:
the Incarnation, characterized by Jesus, the child in the crib,
the Redemption, characterized by Jesus on the cross,
the Life of Christ resurrected in the Church, characterized by the Eucharist[2].

"*Such, in fact, is the order of the divine plan: Wisdom takes on a humanity, immolates it and gives it as food: Incarnation, Redemption, Church! Such is the divine logic of the mysteries, such are the stages of the divine achievements, the Church being the end of all things. We must find this logic and this order everywhere. Consequently, that is what must mark the stages of holiness.*"[3]
If the idea of this tableau in three parts is not the invention of Father Chevrier, the commentary that he gives is very much his and especially the triple affirmation:

---

[1] Cf. Introduction, P. 29.
[2] Six, P. 181.
[3] Marie-Eugène de l'Enfant Jesus, "Je veux voir Dieu", Ed. du Carmel, 1956, p. 666.

the priest is a man stripped of everything,
the priest is a man crucified,
the priest is a man eaten.

The last of these phrases has had its day. Please note that it is necessarily preceded by the other two without which it does not make sense because it does not mean that the priest must have an activity that eats him up but that his whole ministry must be vivifying; that is why he must become a good bread. Besides, the reference to the Eucharistic mystery suffices to dissipate all equivocation.
The title of the tableau: Sacerdos alter Christus, *the priest is another Christ, is not proper to Father Chevrier; he certainly took it from the Capuchin, Father Laurent d'Aoste, his contemporary*[4]*. Where did the Capuchin get this formula? From the Fathers of the Church, he says. Yet, he is very careful not to name any, for a just reason, no doubt.*
The formula in itself is rather recent; it probably does not go farther than the XIX century, though the idea is older.
Today, theologians are often very reserved with this formula. They fear that people will forget that "Christian" also means "other Christ". In forgetting this, we could end up with an erroneous concept of the priest.
As we have already said, all Father Chevrier's doctrine on the priest refers to this word of Christ: As the Father has sent me, I also send you[5]*, and it is in this sense that he understands the formula "another Christ".*
Vatican II confirmed that, by the sacrament of Holy Orders, the priest is specially configured to Christ, to act in dependence on Christ[6]*. It also confirmed that the priest must conform his life to that of Christ*[7]*. Each one is free to use this formula or not, but it seems totally acceptable if we want to express the priestly tradition in line with the Fathers of the Church.*
"Such therefore is the way, in fact, that the priesthood was transmitted from one successor of the apostles to the next, the way of imitation. Of course, at the same time the Spirit was communicated by the imposition of hands and consequently, the priestly power were also communicated. That was essential. But besides that, there was also the constant, and no less fundamental, concern of copying, because it was the practical means wanted by God, of retaining the Model and assuring the reproduction. There is no code in all this, no theory on the priesthood, no

---

[4] Cf. Six 154-155 and note 66.
[5] Jn. 20,21; cf.169.
[6] P.O. 2, 3; 12, 1.
[7] P.O. 14, 1.

instruction manuel, nor even the embryo of a treatise; immediate recognition, on seeing and hearing a priest, the replica of the True Priest. [8]

Moreover, let us add that Father Chevrier did not intend to reserve to priests the ideal expressed by the Tableau of Saint-Fons. He himself made an adaptation for the brothers and sisters of the Prado by simply deleting the mention of the powers of the priest.

---

[8] G. Jouassard: Pour une étude du sacerdoce au temps des Pères, in "la Tradition sacerdotal", pp. 111-112, Ed. Mappus, 1959.

SACERDOS ALTER CHRISTUS [1]

| by his powers | by his examples |
| | model |

EXEMPLUM DEDI VOBIS	UT QUEMADMODUM EGO FECI	ITA ET VOS FACIATIS [2]
(child Jesus)	(cross) [3]	(host)
poverty		
POOR AND HUMBLE	**DEATH TO SELF**	**CHARITY**
in		
lodging — spirit	death to — immolated in	give — give life
clothing — heart	his body — solitude	his body — his faith
food — vis-a-vis	his spirit — prayer	spirit — doctrine
goods — God	will — penance	goods — prayers
work — men	reputation — work	time — words
ministry — oneself	family — suffering	health — powers
	world — death	life — examples
the priest is a man stripped of everything	the priest is a crucified man	the priest is a man eaten
the more we are poor the more we glorify - love	the more we die the more we give life	become good bread
God and are useful to the neighbor		

---

[1] *Photograph manuscript text reproduced elsewhere.*

[2] *I have given you an example so that, as I have done, so also you may do (Jn. 13,15).*

[3] *Here there are three pictures; a child Jesus in the crib, a cross and a host (cf. outside text).*

INDEX [2]

Abraham (See Scripture).

Action : to act ; it must always accompany words, in one way or another : 72, 76, 101, 103, 105, 198, 224, 251-253, 272, 385,388, 393, 399, 400, 402, 430, 431, 441, 451, 458, 469, 508, 509, 514, (see also : example, works, practice, rebuke).

Adam (See Scripture).

Affection : the sentiments of the heart are placed in true charity : 152, 153, 158, 177, 180-181, 234, 259, 330, 430, 435, 446 - (See also : heart).

Alms : to give alms, to ask alms, beg : the only acceptable alms is that which comes from an authentic charity ; it requires great interior freedom from the one who gives as well as from the one who receives : 219, 290, 299, 300-304, 306-317, 385, 413, 461, 522, 523.

Angels : according to Scripture, we have recourse to the angels to affirm Christ's supremacy over all creatures, those that are perceptible as well as those who are not : 62, 69, 70, 93, 100.

Apostles : apostolate, apostolic, frequent reference to the twelve, the first "true disciples of Jésus Christ" ; other times, the word is applied to today's apostles : 72, 73, 76, 82, 98, 102, 118, 135, 178, 183, 188, 189, 192, 217, 218, 222, 232, 270, 287, 297, 300, 304, 306, 307, 311, 318, 322, 339, 341, 342, 350, 351, 360, 361, 362, 372, 373, 374, 377, 388, 389, 393, 394, 396, 399, 400, 401, 409, 422, 441, 443, 444, 446, 447, 450, 458, 460, 461, 464, 465, 470, 471, 472, 479, 486, 487, 488, 489, 495, 530 ... see also : 45-46, 103, 120, 198, 222, 226, 321, 339, 447, 512 - 222 - (See also : Counsels, apostolic life, mission, union with God, Jésus Christ, vocation, zeal.

Attachment : 46, 109, 117, 143 - (See also : love).

---

[2] The numbers are those of the french edition given in the margins of this edition.

Authority : especially, the authority proper to the priest : 95, 123, 156, 219, 255, 296, 315, 376, 443, 447, 471, 527, 528, (See also : superior).

Baptism : 267, 306, 389, 444, 447. - (See also : sacrament).

Beauty, beautiful, nice : 108, 115, 118, 119, 124, 126, 189, 212, 295, 296, 298, 299, 322, 323, 351, 516, 519, 520, 521, 523. -

Begging : See alms

Believe : See faith.

Bishop : 218, 256, 292, 311, 312, 313, 314, 529 -(See also : priest).

Body : almost always designates the physical and physiological aspects of human life. : **169-204**, 219, 239, 267, 305, 330, 428, 444, 486, 487, 522, 583.

Bourgeois : the one who is well-off and does not worry about evangelical poverty : 188, 319, 321, 330, 412, 413, 414, 483 - (See also : poverty).

Bread : 104, 183, 190, 310, 319, 448, 535.

Breviary : 120, 193, 363, 501 - (See also : Prayer)

Call : See vocation

Calm : See Peace

Calvary : See Cross

Catechism : all forms of simple instruction addressed either to children or adults : 192, 299, 307, 333, 354, **437-452**, 523, 531.

Celestial and Terrestrial: in heaven and on earth ; from above and from below; the words are often used simultaneously, sometimes alone; in general, celestial referes to God, savior of the world and terrestrial referes to the worle in need of salvation : 60, 69, 72, 89, 90, 94, 96, 108, 114, 124, 146, 149, 151, 153, 166, 175, 183, 197, 256, 267, 269, 288, 302, 304, 342, 457, 458, 511, 519, 520, 527.

Center : title of Jesus Christ : **104-105**, 181, 231, 233, 234.

III

Charity : always in the strong sense of a love for others poured in our heart by the Holy Spirit : 120, 150, 158, 186, 190, 198, 202, 203, 219, 223, 229, 230, 232, 233, 240, 241, 259, 268, 270, 272, 289, 290, 292, 293, 296, 299, 300, 301, 302, 303, 309, 313, 315, 318, 321, 342, 343, 344, 349, 352, 353, 354, 363, 398, 399, 401, **415-435**, 452, 462, 464, 481, 486, 487, 488, 519, 522, 523, 528, 535.

Chastity, purity, impurity : 175, 182, 185, 230, 350, 457, 458, 464.

Church : the word is often used in the too juridical and too restricted sense that it had at that time ; sometimes it designates only the hierarchy : 82, 100, 120, 218, 222, 226, 233, 234, 252, 256, 257, 311, 315, 316, 319, 353, 363, 410, 427, 434, 449, 451, 511, 522, 530 - Buildings : 194, 223, **297-298**, 307, 310, 315, 451, 519, 520, 521, 523.

Clothes, dress : 219, 231, **293-294**, 386, 399, 407, 409, 423, 432, 533.

Combat, struggle : sometimes it means the struggle against oneself, but most often it refers to the struggle against others to remain faithful to Christ : 119, 127, 133, 153, 216, 229, 267, 341, 344, **453-464**, 478, 503, 511, 519 (See also : rebuke, persecutions).

Community : in common, the apostolic, evangelical community is a spiritual family that has precedence over the natural family : 139, 158, 186, 229-233, 252, 257, 270, 274, 289, 361, 362, 528, 539.

Compassion : a very important aspect of affectivity in the service of apotolic charity : 241, 419, 433 - (See also : charity, heart, unhappiness).

Conditions : to be realistic, we must weith and assume the necessary conditions for what we want : **129-503**, 133-137, 139, 159, 229, 275, 285, 320, 325, 329, 335, 339, 414, 446, 448, 463, 464.

Confession : 272, 523.

Confirmation : 267 (See also : Sacraments)

Conform to Jesus Christ : 225, 227, 413, 488 - (See also : imitation).

Conversion, Convert : the proclamation of the Gospel necessarily entails a call to conversion : 114, 137, 223, 232, 307, 446, 478, 521 - (See also : penance).

Corruption : See evil

Creator : Title of Jésus Christ : 102.

Creatures : most often it refers only to human creatures and not to creation as a whole : 143, 153, 177, 239, 240, 241, 270, 293, 318, 330, 331, 332, 342, 513.

Crib : Bethlehem, stable, etc. The crib is the characteristic symbol of the mystery of the Incarnation ; the birth of the Son of God made man was achieved in poverty : 70, 101, 104, 223, 225, 228, 290, 296, 298, 341, 342, 396, 400, 407, 412, 469, 477, 532-533.

Crime : in the Latin sense which means all sin : See sin).

Cross : the Cross of Jesus, Calvary, the Passion, the cross in our life, crucified, etc : 91, 104, 120, 133, 137, 157, 195, 223, 225, 228, 255, 256, 296, 298, 307, 323, **325-334**, 341, 342, 352, 360, 362, 394, 396, 400, 401, 444, 445, 447, 449, 451, 463, 465, 470, 471, 472, **473-489, 491-495**, 512, 513, 521, 532-533.

Crucifix : the image of Jesus on the Cross is the symbol of the central place of the Paschal mystery in God's plan : 174, 291, 294, 334, 480, 484.

Curé of Ars, St John Mary Vianney : 189, 192, 223, 523.

David (See Scripture).

Death : ours : 184, 187, 196, 341, 363, 389, 393, 394, 407, 445, 471, 472, 487, 488, 489, 491-495, 533.

Demon, devil, Satan : See evil.

Devotedness : 121, 137, 272, 288, 308, 313, 343, 402, 486 - (See also : charity).

Disciple : almost without exception, the word designates man's attitude toward God, Jesus Christ, those sent by Jesus Christ : 45-46, 81, 99, 113, 120, 121, 126, 129, 133, 134, 145, 148, 151, 152, 182, 183, 223, 228, 239, 255, 296, 329, 330, 331, 332, 339, 342, 344, 359, 372, 373, 386, 389, 427, 434, 441, 442, 444, 460, 471, 478, 479, 480, 481, 486, 501, **507-513**, 529.

Elijah : (See Scripture)

End : title of Jesus Christ : 105.

Energy : 127, 230 - (See also strength).

Envoy (See send)

Eternity, eternal (See : heaven).

Eucharist : 184, 360, 362, 459, 532-533 - (See also : Last Supper, Sacrament, Tabernacle).

Evangelical Counsels, evangelical virtues, evangelical life, apostolic life : 121, 229, 289, 311, 363 - (See also : disciple, perfection, religious).

Eve (See Scripture).

Evil, corruption, demon, Satan, devil : 71, 95, 190, 191, 203, 213, 218, 230, 233, 241, 341, 376, 419, 423, 429, 433, 434, 458, 469, 487, 529 - (See also : Sin).

Example : this word is always used in the strong sense of a behavior which renders testimony to truth : 95, 101, 124, 136, 178, 225, 231, 273, 291, 304, 315, 322, 339, 341, 342, 349, 351, 363, 373, 392, 407, 411, 412, 413, 433, 444, 446, 448, 465, 478, 485, 511, 513, 519, 520, 529, 533.

Exterior and Interior : two corresponding ideas, important to understand well Father Chevrier's thought : interior is the divine action in man and man's consent to this action ; exterior is man's whole exterior behavior, the visible result of his action : 61, 73, 96, 101, 103, 185, 197, 199, 241, 298, 334, 342, 360, - Exterior 174, 198, 211, 272, 273, 293, 296, 299, 307, 321, 339, 349, 461, 463, 511, 519, 520, 521, 529 ; - Interior 119, 133, 152, 258, 285, 386, 413, 533 -

Faith, believe : 71-72, 108, 114, 136, 137, 152, 182, 183, 196, 198, 221, 230, 241, 253, 258, 271, 307, 309, 315, 342, 428, 429, 435, 442, 445, 449, 450, 457, 459, 462, 503, 510, 520, 535.

Family : 134, 139-158, 165, 231, 241, 289, 302, 363, 422 - (See also : Community).

Fast, fasting : 219, 268, 341, 344, 345-354, 359, 362, 372, 385, 392, 400, 460, 461, 463, 478, 485.

Fault (See : Sin).

Firmness : 274, 341, 443, 447, 449, 528, 529 - (See also : Strength)

Follow Jesus Christ : 45-46, 100, 103, 116, 120, 121, 133, 134, 165, 178, 222, 229, 251, 287, 335-503, 509, 510, 513, 529.

Food (See : nourishment)
Forgiveness of those who have offended us : 230, 303, 424 - (See also : charity).

Foundation : fundamental, to do something solid, durable and efficacious, we must base ourselves on what is fundamental ; in an analogous sense, the words principal and principle are used : 222, 228, 283, 343, 444, 445, 449, 451, 511, 513 ; - 102-103 - (See also : principle, principal).

Free of charge : 311-317, 409, 411, 443, 445, 447 - (See also : alms).

Freedom (See : Liberty)

Fundamental (See : Foundation).

Generosity, generous, a characteristic of true love, of the true disciple : 116, 126, 203, 308, 318, 320, 330, 331, 342, 343, 483, 486 - (See also : love).

Glory, glorious, glorify : glory of God, of Jésus Christ : 120, 153, 173, 191, 194, 197, 198, 202, 257, 260, 273, 299, 303, 321, 332, 339, 344, 414, 458, 463, 487, 495, 510, 530, 533 ; - our glory : 270, 298, 315, 330, 332, 333, 344, 388, 395, 397, 398, 400, 401, 402, 411, 442, 445, 446, 461, 484, 489, 497-503, 509, 519, 523.

Goods of the earth : 134, 218, 239, 275-323, 403, 413, 422, 428, 432, 433, 519, 523, 535 -

Grace : The word is used with various meaning ; often, in the singular, it means supernatural participation in divine life, sanctifying grace, in theological language ; in the plural, it means rather the gifts, exterior helps to our person : 114, 118, 119, 120, 121, 136, 212, 221, 222, 230, 268, 293, 333, 486, 510, 520, 521, - 196, 272, 273, 309, 349, 351, 354, 363, 365, 375, 391, 400, 431, 485, 529, 530 - (See also : Spirit, Sacrament, Life).

Gratitude : 183, 184, 203, 204, 241, 413.

Happiness, happy : 114, 147, 157, 191, 203, 270, 315, 316, 387, 402, 410, 414, 444, 458, 469, 478, 489, 502, 510, 528, (See also : Joy.

Head : title of Jesus Christ : 429.

Heal : Father Chevrier notes that, in the Gospel, the proclamation of the Gospel is linked to the healing operated by Jesus and the apostles : 222, 299, 304, 307, 309, 339, 371, 393, 409, 433, 441, 447, 460, 462, 469, 495.

Health, sickness : 181, 186, 187, 193, 203, 204, 221, 354, 448, 535.

Heart : affective live in general in relationships with God and men ; except in scripture quotation where it should be taken in the biblical sense : 117, 124, 135, 223, 235-243, 251, 252, 259, 267, 270, 302, 316, 371, 426, 432, 451, 458, 462, 479, 481, 486 - (spirit and heart, see : exterior and interior ; see also : affection, compassion).

Heaven, eternal, eternity, the word heaven is most often used to designate eternal life : 59, 81, 89, 95, 98, 99, 105, 157, 167, 184, 191, 229, 241, 332, 339, 341, 353, 386, 410, 462, 503, 512 -

Host (See sacrifice)

Housing (See lodging).

Humility, humble: 183, 184, 198, 202, 204, 218, 228, 230, 233, 252, 268, 271, 272, 293, 304, 306, 308, 309, 310, 319, 332, 342, 344, 363, 364, 371, 375, **381-402**, 408, 409, 412, 413, 414, 464, 519, 521, 523, 528 - (See also : pride, reputation).

Idleness : (See laziness).

Imitation, imitate, imitator : it is a matter of imitating Jesus Christ, of being conformed to him : 116, 120, 156, 341, 344, 402, 431 - (See also : conform).

Instruct : 45, 89, 95, 96, 183, 222, 299, 304, 306, 307, 339, 360, 375, 423, 478, 519, 529 - (See also : teach, preaching, rebuke).

Isaiah (See Scripture).

Jews : there are many references to the Jews because it was to them that Jesus was speaking, most of the time : 71, 93, 98, 102, 124, 137, 213, 372, 408, 458, 459, 462, 464, 469, 470, 471, 472, 486 - (See also : Pharisees).

Job (See Scripture).

John the Baptist : 70, 71, 93, 185, 224, 294, 296, 349, 350, 392, 400, 410, 463, 478.

Joseph : 70, 118, 391, 459, 469, 478.

Joy, joyful, rejoice : 122, 323, 332, 333, 377, 431, 447, 471, 488, 489, 511 - (See also : happiness, unhappiness, misery, sadness).

Justice : Jesus Christ, our Justice : **92**.

King : Title of Jesus Christ : **93-95**.

Know Jesus Christ : 46, 108, 113, 114, 115, 212, 216, 230, 253, 451, 509, 512.

Lamb of God : 71, 92, 422, 478.

Last supper : 231, 481, 502 - (See also : Eucharist).

Law : 351, 400, 462, 477 - (See also : obedience, will).

Laziness, idleness : 124, 190, 195, 228, 268, 300, 485 - (See also : rest, work).

Liberty, freedom : 153, 165, 179, 185, 270, 309, 310, 315, 322, 402, 445, 486, 509, 511, 512, 519, 521, 522 - (See also : slave, renunciation).

Life : 220, 223, 225, 228, 239, 267, 274, 297, 432, 433, 442, 445, 448, 449, 487, 489, 501, 509, 512, 533 ; 60, **106**, 117-118, 165, 342 - (See also : grace, counsels, evangelical life).

Light, shine, brilliance : oftenused image : 52, 89-91, 106, 108, 114, 119, 135, 136, 137, 156, 184, 215, 217, 225, 227, 251, 292, 342, 432, 444, 445, 457, 469, 501, 516, 519, 530.

Lodging, housing : 218, 231, **290-292**, 306, 443, 520, 522, 535.

Love : to love, most of the time it refers to the love that comes from God and goes to God ; when it refers to the supernatural love of others, it is the word charity that crops most often : 258, 267, 322, 332, 342, 351, 422, 430, 431, 432, 434, 450, 451, 481, 484, 486, 509, 510, 512, - : 93, 108, 198, 228, 407, 409, 421, 479 ; - : 60, **109-127**, 145, 151, 221, 223, 233, 239, 253, 271, 292, 299, 300, 308, 364, 413, 461, 512, 520, 530, 535 -

Man : most often in the plural : 51, 60, 61, 89, 91, 95, 98, 102, 121, 146, 184, 217, 220, 228, 229, 294, 308, 330, 344, 350, 371, 378, 386, 387, 390, 399, 401, 434, 445, 448, 462, 469, 478, 509, 512, 520, 529, 535.

Martyr : martyrdom : 95, 268, 428, 484, 501.

Mary, mother of Jesus : 69, 118, 148, 149, 363, 390, 441, 459, 469, 477.

Mass : 120, 234, 290, 315, 316, 363, 449, 451, 531, - (See also : Eucharist).

Master : Refers especially to the title of Jesus Christ : 45, 79, 95-99, 107, 108, 116, 122, 125-126, 127, 134, 137, 153, 156, 158, 183, 188, 227, 233, 256, 286, 293, 296, 306, 323, 331, 332, 341, 343, 349, 374, 387, 388, 396, 410, 443, 444, 451, 471, 486, 510, 527.

Meditation : mental, meditative, silent prayer : 194, 226, 363, 531 - (See also : prayer).

Meekness : Very important trait for one who participates in the work of salvation ; essential apostolic virtue that respects each one's journey : 120, 198, 202, 233, 268, 300, 303, 342, 344, 363, 367-379, 420, 424, 428, 431, 434, 435, 446, 447, 463, 472, 520, 528 - (See also : patience).

Ministry, minister : 154, 155, 304, 311, 392, 446, 486 - (See also : priest).

Miracles : 76, 77-82, 393, 400, 428, 459, 462, 469, 470, 520.

Mission, missionary : 147, 150, 191, 304, 307, 318, 342, 349, 389, 433, 444, 447, 448, 451, 458, 470 - (See also : apostle, envoy).

Model : title of Jesus Christ : 91, 100-101, 116, 256, 342, 480, 513, 520.

Mortification : 182, 185, 187, 188, 194, 229, 268, 428.

Moses : See Cripture.

Nature : Sometime meaning creation in general ; more often meaning our human nature and usually to underline its aspect of weakness : 72, 76, 90, 102, 196, 215, 229, 330, 333, 363, 365, 377, 390, 483.

Nazareth : 96, 147, 224, 290, 339, 391, 400, 441, 450, 459, 470.

Necessary, necessity : two complementary meanings that define evangelical poverty : to be satisfied with the necessary in created goods to attach ourselves all the more to the only necssary, the kingdom of God : 113, 133, 156, 178, 181, 182, 185, 186, 189, 203, 274, 283, 288, **290-299**, 350, 353, 354, 410, 411, 413, 446, 448, 458, 517, 520, 521, 530.

Neighbor, that is, the others : 174, 196, 198, 202, 223, 228, 241, 268, 272, 273, 301, 333, 339, 351, 352, 353, 365, 373, 423, 433, 434, 446, 485, 520, 533.

Nourishment, food, in the natural sense, it is often in relation with spiritual nourishment : faith, the word of God, the will of God, the Eucharist, etc. : 182-190, **292-293**, 407, 409, 432, 485, 522, 533.

Obedience : **245-261**, 306, 341, 349, 391, 407, 409, 431, 484 - (See also : Law, rule, regulation, superior, will).

Passions : Human : generally in the bad sense when they designate our inordinate natural tendencies : 124,, 126, 241, 251-252, 268, 462.

Peace, calm : 114, 145, 230, 260, 270, 272, 299, 300, 303, 306, 376, 431, 457, 458, 470, 483, 502, 528.

Penance : In relation with conversion but the word refers more to what we call practices of penance, ascetic efforts so that conversion may bear fruit : 119, 124, 137, 180, 229, 268, 272, 274, 350, 354, 428, 435, 444, 485, 533 - (For the sacrament of penance see : confession, see also : conversion).

Perfection, perfect : Sometimes means holiness and sometimes the practice of the evangelical counsels : 120-121, 123, 133, 222, 252, 259, 311, 301, 330, 341, 343, 410, 425, 430, 434, 484, 516, 528 - (See also : counsels, saint).

Persecution : does not necessarily signify something tragic like the bloody persecutions, it may mean contradictions : 147, 229, 230, 330, 322, 341, 344, 350, 387, 434, 444, 445, 447, **465-472**, 477, 489, 503, 511, 513.

Peter Apostle : 76, 78, 81, 98, 118, 127, 147, 153, 226, 227, 300, 316, 374, 394, 427, 434, 442, 471, 479, 481, 502.

Pharisees : 99, 156, 219, 231, 297, 372, 373, 377, 386, 387, 395, 424, 442, 443, 459, 460, 461, 462, 469, 470, 471 - (See also : Jews).

XI

Poor : designates above all the world of worker ; those whose subsistence depends entirely on daily work : 126, 155, 187, 189, 191, 218, 268, 287, 288, 289, 304, 333, 353, 395, 400, 401, 402, 407, 420, 424, 441, 520, 522, 523, 524 - (See also : workers).

Poverty : to be poor, truely poor, etc. : 120, 122, 124, 136-137, 182, 188, 189, 229, 230, 233, 240, 268, 275, 323, 330, 331, 341, 342, 343, 344, 354, 363, 391, 402, **403- 414**, 428, 435, 443, 444, 446, 447, 464, 477, 478, 480, 486, 487, 513, **518-524**, 535 - (See also : goods of the earth, Bourgeois, providence, worry, greed, prodigal).

Practice : put into practice, practice, often used to mean action ; a pratical man is a man of actions ; sometimes, but rarely, practice of piety : 45-46, 108, 124, 126, 134, 135, 151, 229, 253, 285, 315, 363, 378, 402, 410, 461, 510, 516, 521 - (See also : action).

Prayer : 101, 119, 180, 181, 182, 184, 193, 196, 219, 220, 227, 229, 231, 234, 268, 299, 300, 304, 307, 318, 319, 333, 341, 344, 349, 350, 354, **355-365**, 385, 387, 394, 400, 425, 426, 434, 446, 447, 449, 452, 461, 463, 478, 485, 511, 520, 523, 524, 530, 531, 533 ; - 108, 122, 227, 272, 323 - (See also : Breviary, meditation, retreat, silence).

Preaching : 120, 191, 223, 304, 344, 349, 362, 363, 409, **437-452**, 520 - (See also : cathechism)

Pride : 124, 218, 232, 270, 298, 311, 399, 429, 457, 458, 460, 463, 464, 485 - (See also : Humility, reputation).

Priest : Minister of Jesus Christ ; the term "priest" is very rarely applied to Christ himself : 101, 113, 115, 120, 147, 150, 152, 154, 157, 158, 178, 180, 191, 193, 194, 198, 218, 228, 229, 242, 257, 286, 290, 291, 297, 299, 301, 304, 305, 309, 311, 314, 315, 316, 317, 319, 322, 330, 331, 350, 412, 444, 448, 449, 450, 460, 484, 487, 511, 519-524, 533.

Principle, Principal: 102, 211, 223, 241, 260, 298, 339, 344, 378, 430, 443, 519, 523 - (See also : foundation, fundamental).

Prodigal : 203, 240, 414 - (See also : Goods of the earth).

Promises : Jsus Christ made promises to those whom he called to follow him : 120, 137, 157, 261, 320, 322, 410, 414, 471, 501, 510.

Prophetes (See : Scripture)

Providence (See : God)

Providences : Charitable organizations that often deviated from their end and against which Father Chevrier often warned : 223, 304, 305.

Prudence : 124, 230, 434, 464, 528 - (See also : wisdom)

Psalms (See : Scripture)

Reason, to reason, reasoning; often taken in the bad sense meaning a rationalist attitude of an intelligence that does not want to open to something bigger than itself : 61, 123-124, 125, 126, 189, 215, 256, 430, 451, 462, 511 - (See also : Spirit).

Rebuke : instruct, reprove, put into action : the three aspects of evangelical pedagogy according to Father Chevrier ; to rebuke is to point out what is not right : 222, 298, 424, 446, 449, 458, 464, 478, 528, 529 - (See also : Combat).

Redemption : Title of Jesus Christ : **92-93**.

Regulation (See : rule).

Relaxation (See : rest).

Religion : Sometimes means the church in the modern and traditional sense ; other times it means Christian life, life of faith, etc. : 151, 198, 218, 268, 303, 307, 315, 360, 450, 451, 460-461, 463, 464 - (See also : Church).

Religious : Sometimes designates all those who practice the evangelical live and at other time those who live the juridically determined religious state : 121, 137, 179, 181, 194, 198, 219, 228, 242, 286, 297, 303, 330, 334, 462, 524 - (See also : evangelical counsels).

Renunciation, renounce : 133, 134, **139-334**, 342, 513 - (See also : Freedom, liberty).

Reputation : 230, 533 - (See also : Humility, pride).

Rest, relaxation, liesure, walk, stroll, promenade, sleep, vacation, trip : 156, 158, 192-194.

Resurrection, title of Jesus Christ : 106, 114, 196, 343, 401, 451, 469, 470 - : (See also : Glory).

Retreat : 204, 353, 359, 362, 364 - (See also : Prayer, silence).

Riches, wealth : 136, 157, 187, 189, 218, 226, 511, 519 - (See also : Goods).

Root : title of Jésus Christ : 104.

Rule, regulation, the word is often in the deep and living sense ; the true rule, the way, is Jésus Christ : 194 , 219, 221, 226, 233, 273, 283, 285, 332, 413, 433, 460, 502, 511, 516, 523, 529 - (See also : Obedience, will).

Sacrament : 92, 152, 204, 313, 315, 451 - (See also : baptism, confession, confirmation, Eucharist).

Sacrifice, host : very often in the sense of privations that we impose upon ourselves ; but the idea of offerring to God is never absent : 116, 121, 137, 252, 254, 259, 288, 339, 343, 352, 373, 378, 414, 430, 448, 460, 486, 488, 489, 511 - : (See also : Cross).

Sadness, sad : 228, 240, 285, 377, 450, 481 - (See also : Joy).

Saint, holiness, sanctification : 91, 92, 121, 176, 220, 230, 257, 260, 315, 317, 322, 431, 481, 513, 519, 520, 521, 523, ; - 95, 124, 126, 155, 175, 185, 189, 196, 226, 227, 228, 268, 288, 294, 296, 299, 321, 333, 343, 353, 362, 401, 410, 432, 511 - : (See also : perfection, Curé of Ars, Francis of Assisi, John the Baptist, Mary).

Salvation, save : 153, 191, 198, 241, 242, 257, 260, 273, 286, 329, 330, 339, 352, 478, 486, 487, 488, 520, 530.

Savior : title of Jesus Christ : 98, 304, 343.

Scandal : 120, 145, 155, 178, 179, 180, 185, 189, 190, 192, 198, 204, 258, 343, 372, 441, 446, 458, 459, 469, 522.

Science, knowledge : 61, 91, 95, 113, 123, 218 ; - 430, 461, 464 ; - 217, 226, 228, 229, 320, 398, 401, 428, 430 -

Scripture : We do not note the innumerable uses of the word GOSPEL or the mention of St Paul's Epistles ; we only note the use of the word Scripture which shows a concern to refer to the Bible as much as possible, and the main references to the Old Testament : Scripture : 90, 143, 173, 450, 459, 461, 462, 463, - Abraham : 62, 74, 143, 195, 399, 401, 462, - Adam : 62, 166, 212, 267, 353, 485, - David : 93, 178, 372, 399, 401, - Elijah :70, 77, 479, ; Eve : 178, Isaiah : 96, 224, 441, 463, Job : 178 ; - Moses : 62, 71, 350, 386, 459, 463, 478, 479 ; Prophets : 62, 93, 147, 371, 441, 459, 461, 470 ; - Psalms : 93, 363, 457 - (See also : study).

Send, envoy : 147, 150, 191, 304, 306, 318, 322, 342, 349, 389, 409, 433, 442, 444, 447, 448, 451, 457, 459, 470 - 394 - : (See also : Mission).

Servant, serve : 147, 154, 156, 272, 306, 317, 318, 341, 387, 388, 389, 396, 400, 402, 423, 431, 445, 501, 510, 512 ; - 96, 371, 395, 401, 480.

Shine : (See : Light).

Sick : As in the Gospel, the sick hold an important place in The True Disciple (See also : Heal, health).

Sickness : (See : health).

Silence : : 202, 228, 232, 234, 341, 362, 472, 483 - (See also : prayer, reteat)

Simplicity, simple : an important characteristic of poverty and evangelical live in general, as an inteior attitude as well as in outward behavior : 123, 126, 175, 186, 187, 189, 218, 321, 354, 442, 447, 448, 450, 462, 470, 522 - (See also : Necessary).

Sin, fault, crime : 81, 89, 92, 93, 120, 136, 166, 175-195, 257, 267, 269, 273, 293, 316, 377, 444, 451, 457, 461, 470, 478, 481, 485, 522 - (See also : Evil).

Sinners : 184, 297, 316, 363, 387, 392, 395, 400, 401, 402, 420, 421, 424, 434, 446, 460, 520, 521.

Slave : 173, 196, 252 - (See also : Liberty).

Sleep (See : rest)

Sobriety, gluttony : 182, 189, 228, 268, 315 - (See also : fasting, nourishment).

Soul : sometimes as distinct from the body ; most often, especially in the plural, (salvation of souls), means the human person that God wants to save in Jesus Christ : 105, 121, 183, 188, 194, 196, 198, 202, 203, 221, 223, 300, 303, 308, 317, 318, 419, 432, 479, 480, 520, ; 94, 106, 120, 151, 152, 153, 154, 158, 182, 191, 198,

218, 221, 228, 257, 260, 268, 270, 271, 286, 296, 307, 309, 316, 332, 351, 445, 448, 458, 486, 523, 528, 530 ; - 429.

Spirit : An important and very rich notion : **205-234** ; Holy Spirit : 69, 70, 71, 118, 151, 187, 303, 316, 349, 362, 363, 389, 392, 430, 444, 445, 447 ; Spirit of God, of Jesus Christ, of the Lord, sometimes it is a question of the Spirit of man animated by the Holy Spirit : 96, 146, 147, 308, 375, 376, 445, 457, 460, 461, 464, 482, **510-512**, 529 ; Spirit in the good sense, is the mentality of the true disciple who has a taste to live according to the Gospel, to do God's work : 174, 175, 257, 267, 288, 293, 295, 298, 300, 302, 303, 304, 306, 310, 317, 319, 321, 342, 353, 354, 361, 362, 365, 371, 460, 509, 512, 523 ; Spirit of man, often in the bad sense to mean the mentality that is natural to man and in which we cannot trust : 173, 189, 196, 211, 239, 251, 252, 259, 269, 288, 330, 398, 458, 459, 460, 461, 462, 464, 470, 519, 533 - (See also : reason, wisdom, spiritual, exterior and interior).

Spiritual : this adjective must always be understood in relation with the Holy Spirit and not as opposed to the corporal and temporal : 61, 89, 90, 93, 95, 103, 105, 120, 146, 150, 151, 179, 190, 191, 256, 302, 304, 305, 307, 309, 311, 315, 322, 339, 354, 412, 431, 512, 523, 524, 530, 531 - (See also : Spirit).

Spouse : title of Jesus Christ : 372.

Strength, strengthen : the evangelical man must show strength : 230, 260, 270, 271, 283, 319, 322, 361, 362, 444, 464, 519, 521, 522 - (See also : Firmness, vigor).

Struggle, see : Combat.

Study, intellectual work in general : 113, 220, 442, 448, 452, 511, 528 ; study Jesus Christ, the Gospel : 119, 225, 227, 234, 256, 257, 285, 510, **514-517** - (See also : Scripture, science).

Submission : 202, 204, 232, 319, 483 - (See also : obedience).

Suffering, suffer : to know how to suffer is a characteristic of the true disciple : 194, 196, 203, 204, 222, 230, 233, 255, 256, 268, 291, 295, 300, 307, 308, 320, 321, 344, 353, 389, 407, 408, 411, 412, 423, 428, 429, 435, **473-489**, 509, 513, 520, 521, 524, 530, 533 - (See also : cross, sacrifice).

Superior : the one who holds authority : 150, 219, 226, 232, 233, 233, 234, 240, 242, 272, 273, 289, 306, 311, **525-531**.

Tabernacle : 104, 228 - (See also : Eucharist).

Teach : 45, 89, 95, 96, 183, 222, 299, 304, 306, 307, 339, 360, 375, 423, 478, 519, 529 - (See also : instrust, preaching).

Temporal matters : 134, 304-306, 522, 524 - (See also : Goods of the earth).

Temptation : our temptations : 180, 183, 189, 191, 193, 242, 286, 316, 361, 362, Christ's temptations in the desert : 320, 359, 392.

Time : 155, 174, 178, 190, 191, 192, 232, 255, 287, 293, 399, 303, 304, 305, 308, 330, 352, 451, 520, 522, 523, 533.

Transfiguration of Jesus Christ : 394, 400, 479.

Treasure : it is almost always an allusion to the parable of the hidden treasure (Mt. 13: 44-46) ; we can even say that this word may be a title of Jesus Christ : 114, 117, 229, 240, 302.

Trinity : (See : God)

Truth, true, truly : it is not only a logical truth but a real one, as we speak of real pearl, real teeth as opposed to a false pearl, false teeth : 61, 90, 91, 92, 93-98, 183, 187, 211, 216, 218, 222, 230, 231, 239, 253, 260, 269, 272, 288, 295, 298, 301, 304, 310, 334, 339, 342, 361, 362, 372, 410, 413, 429, 435, 445, 449, 451, 457, 458, 469, 479, 481, 483, 486, 487, 489, 509, 519, 520, 522, 523, 527 ; true disciple : 121, 126, 129, 134, 149, 152, 154, 158, 182, 228, 239, 255, 274, 299, 329, 339, 342, 343, 427, 434, 480, 481.

Unhappiness, unhappy, woe : 145, 153, 191, 240, 271, 272, 301, 317, 319, 320, 371, 419, 421, 433, 434, 445, 522, 530 - (See also : Joy).

Union : to God and Jesus Christ ; it is the essential situation of the envoy, the apostle, as Jesus Christ himself was one with the one who sent him : 101, 228, 231, 254, 257, 422, 463, 527, 530 - (See also : unity).

Unity : in a community : 151, 231, 259, 271, 283, 299, 308, 422, 528 - (See also : community, union).

Vianney (See : Curé of Ars).

Vigor : 196, 316, 319 - (See also : Strength).

Virtue : An interior dynamism which makes us act according to the Gospel : 101, 196, 202, 219, 268, 272, 296, 298, 303, 363, 376, 458, 521, 528 - (See also : Counsels).

Vocation : 120, 121, 154, 182, 311, 320, 512 - (See also : apostle).

Way of the Cross : 227, 364, 449, 450.

Will : God's will and ours : **245-261**, 267, 330, 339, 351, 451, 462, 478, 509, 511, 533 - (See also : Strength, obedience).

Wisdom : that of Jesus Christ who is our Wisdom or the terrestrial wisdom which is opposed to that of Jesus Christ : 62, **89-91**, 95, 101, 107, 113, 114, 115, 120, 146, 156, 292, 303, 307, 315, 322, 445, 457, 461, 464, 516 ; - 389, 397, 401, 512.

Word of God : 72-73, 91, 96, 108, 113, 114, 122, 124, 151, 154, 286, 342, 458, 464, 509 - ("Verbe" : 51-52, 59-63, 69, 72-73, 89, 95, 102, 106, 108, 113, 123, 342, 390, 391, 457.

Work : we must work ; the apostolate, the priest's ministry, evangelization is work ; we must work like the poor, etc. : 46, 173, 182, 184, 185, 187, 189, 190-194, 196, 212, 220, 231, 234, 268, 274, 296, 299, 300, 301, 304, 305, 306, 309, 310, 316, 318, 319, 321, 322, 330, 350, 391, 407, 408, 410, 411, 412, 413, 445, 452, 458, 463, 486, 488, 524, 533 - (See also : laziness, rest, time).

Workers : - (See also : the poor).

Works : often used in the plural to mean apostolic undertakings, charitable institutions : 137, 151, 166, 175, 183, 191, 222, 232, 270, 273, 283, 305, 310, 314, 319, 320, 321, 342, 386, 395, 401, 427, 431, 446, 458, 459, 462, 463, 469, 495, 523, 524, 528 ; Works of God always means, more or less, God's designs, the salvation of the world through Jesus Christ : 148, 307-312, 320, 397, 522, 523.

World : 115, 116, 121, 126, 134, 136-137, **139-158**, 175, 183, 188, 191, 198, 217, 227, 228, 229, 240, 257, 268, 271, 287, 291, 293, 295, 296, 298, 299, 302, 304, 306, 307-308, 309, 320, 322, 330, 332, 333, 339, 349, 352, 371, 375, 386, 397, 400, 409, 420, 423, 425, 429, 434, 441, 444, 445, 451, **453-464**, 469, 471, 478, 485, 510, 519, 521, 522, 523, 528, 530, 535.

Worry : 240, 271, 299, 309, 413 - (See also : poverty, providence).

Zeal : 120, 190, 268, 316, 421, 429, 528 - (See also : generosity, devotedness).

XVIII

TABLE OF CONTENTS

Letter from His Eminence Cardinal Garrone 3
General Introduction 5
Opening 43

First Part - KNOWLEDGE OF JESUS CHRIST

I. THE TRINITY 45
    Introduction 47
    Preliminary notions on the existence of the three Divine Persons 49

II. What is Jesus Christ 51
    Introduction 53

III. Divinity of Jesus Christ 59
    Introduction 61

IV. Titles of Jesus Christ 75
    Introduction 77

    1. Our Wisdom 79
    2. Our Justice 81
    3. Our Sanctification 81
    4. Our Redemption 82
    5. Our King 82
    6. Our Master 84
    7. Our Head 87
    8. Our Model 88
    9. Principle and Creator of all things 89
    10. Foundation of all things 89
    11. The Root that gives life 90
    12. The Center 91
    13. The End 91
    14. The Resurrection and the Life 92

    Summary of the Titles of Our Lord Jesus Christ 92

V. Attachment to Jesus Christ 95
    Introduction 97
    To know Jesus Christ is everything 99
    To what does he call us 105

Second Part - THE FIVE CONDITIONS TO FULFILL TO BECOME A TRUE DISCIPLE OF JESUS CHRIST

Introduction 113

First Condition - Renounce one's Family and the World 121
   Introduction 123
   Doctrine of Our Lord Jesus Christ on renunciation of family and world . . 127
   Conclusion of this chapter 137

Second Condition - Renounce Oneself 139
   Introduction 141
   Doctrine of Our Lord Jesus Christ on renunciation of oneself 145

   1. Renounce one's body 147
      Introduction 149

   2. Renounce one's spirit 179
      Introduction 181
      Doctrine of Our Lord Jesus Christ on renunciation of one's spirit . . 185
      Faults of the spirit 186
      Where the good spirit is found 190
      The Spirit of God is in Jesus Christ 196
      How to acquire the Spirit of God 199
      Those who have the Spirit of God 199
      The Spirit of God is neccessary in community 203
      Summary 204
      Practices 205

   3. Renounce one's heart 207
      Introduction 209

   4. Renounce one's will 215
      Introduction 217
      To whom should we obey 223
      How should we obey 225
      Excellence of obedience 226
      Conclusion of renunciation of oneself 229

Third condition - Renounce the goods of the earth 241
   Introduction 243

1. Renounce the goods of the earth in spirit and in heart 251
2. Be satisfied with what is necessary 255
3. Give to whoever asks 264
4. Not become involved in temporal matters 267
5. Ask nothing of anybody 269
6. Do not worry about the future 279
7. Count on God alone 281

Fourth condition - Carry one's cross 285
    Introduction 287

Fifth Condition - Follow Jesus Christ 293
    Introduction 295

    1. Follow me in my Fasting 303
        Introduction 305

    2. Follow me in my Prayer 311
        Introduction 313

    3. Follow me in my Meekness 321
        Introduction 323

    4. Follow me in my Humility 333
        Introduction 335

    5. Follow me in my Poverty 355
        Introduction 357

    6. Follow me in my Charity 369
        Introduction 371

    7. Follow me in my Preaching 389
        Introduction 391

    8. Follow me in my Combats 405
        Introduction 407

    9. Follow me in my Persecutions 417
        Introduction 419

10. Follow me in my Sufferings 425
    Introduction 427

11. Follow me in my death 441
    Introduction 443

12. You will follow me in my Glory 447
    Introduction 449

ANNEXES 453
Introduction 454

Introduction to Annex I 455
Annex I - Disciple - 457

Introduction to Annex II 461
Annex II - Knowledge of the Gospel - 463

Introduction to Annex III 464
Annex III - Thoughts on Poverty 465

Introduction to Annex IV 470
Annex IV - Letter to Father Duret - 472

Introduction to the Tableau of St-Fons 477
Annex V - Tableau of St-Fons - 480

INDEX 481

TABLE OF CONTENTS . . . .